Italian and Italian American Studies

Series Editor
Stanislao G. Pugliese
Hofstra University
Hempstead, NY, USA

This series brings the latest scholarship in Italian and Italian American history, literature, cinema, and cultural studies to a large audience of specialists, general readers, and students. Featuring works on modern Italy (Renaissance to the present) and Italian American culture and society by established scholars as well as new voices, it has been a longstanding force in shaping the evolving fields of Italian and Italian American Studies by re-emphasizing their connection to one another.

Editorial Board
Rebecca West, University of Chicago
Josephine Gattuso Hendin, New York University
Fred Gardaphé, Queens College, CUNY
Phillip V. Cannistraro†, Queens College and the Graduate School, CUNY
Alessandro Portelli, Università di Roma "La Sapienza"
William J. Connell, Seton Hall University

More information about this series at
http://www.palgrave.com/gp/series/14835

Bastian Matteo Scianna

The Italian War on the Eastern Front, 1941–1943

Operations, Myths and Memories

Bastian Matteo Scianna
University of Potsdam
Potsdam, Brandenburg, Germany

Italian and Italian American Studies
ISBN 978-3-030-26523-6   ISBN 978-3-030-26524-3 (eBook)
https://doi.org/10.1007/978-3-030-26524-3

© The Editor(s) (if applicable) and The Author(s), under exclusive license to Springer Nature Switzerland AG 2019
This work is subject to copyright. All rights are solely and exclusively licensed by the Publisher, whether the whole or part of the material is concerned, specifically the rights of translation, reprinting, reuse of illustrations, recitation, broadcasting, reproduction on microfilms or in any other physical way, and transmission or information storage and retrieval, electronic adaptation, computer software, or by similar or dissimilar methodology now known or hereafter developed.
The use of general descriptive names, registered names, trademarks, service marks, etc. in this publication does not imply, even in the absence of a specific statement, that such names are exempt from the relevant protective laws and regulations and therefore free for general use.
The publisher, the authors and the editors are safe to assume that the advice and information in this book are believed to be true and accurate at the date of publication. Neither the publisher nor the authors or the editors give a warranty, expressed or implied, with respect to the material contained herein or for any errors or omissions that may have been made. The publisher remains neutral with regard to jurisdictional claims in published maps and institutional affiliations.

Cover illustration: History and Art Collection/Alamy Stock Photo

This Palgrave Macmillan imprint is published by the registered company Springer Nature Switzerland AG
The registered company address is: Gewerbestrasse 11, 6330 Cham, Switzerland

For my dear father Salvatore Scianna (1956–2019). Ci mancherai!

Acknowledgements

The most joyful part of finishing a book is being able to thank individuals who supported its creation. An earlier version of the following was accepted as Ph.D. dissertation in the Faculty of Philosophy (Department of History) at the University of Potsdam and awarded with 'summa cum laude' on 19 October 2017. First among those playing mother and father was (and remains) my supervisor, Professor Sönke Neitzel, who sustained this project from its very beginnings in London. Moving to Potsdam was not only an exciting step in itself, but more so a period of many new beginnings. Thus I am grateful for the endless support in any way imaginable. Likewise, Professor Simon Ball, my second supervisor, continued his help and assistance from across the channel. John Gooch became an important conversation partner and fatherly figure whose help was in many ways much appreciated—grazie di cuore!

The Konrad-Adenauer-Stiftung kindly provided me with a scholarship for the first two years of this project, which allowed me to focus on its progress and visit numerous archives and libraries, where I was helped by friendly staff in Rome, London, Freiburg and Berlin to whom I wish to extend my gratitude.

During my research I benefitted from the work of many scholars to which I owe great debt: Thomas Schlemmer, Giorgio Scotoni, Maria Teresa Giusti, James Burgwyn, MacGregor Knox, James Sullivan, David Glantz, Lucio Ceva, Davide Conti, Paolo Fonzi, Amedeo Osti Guerrazzi, Federico Ciavattone, Peter Lieb, Oliver Janz, Hans Woller, Felix Römer and Pier Paolo Battistelli—to name but a few. My students in London and Potsdam also proved an invaluable source of ideas and criticism. I wish to thank Peter Schuld and Julius Becker, in particular, for their assistance.

Many friends helped distract me, reviewed my arguments or provided fresh thoughts: Gabriel Suprise, Jarrad Willis, Kester Keating, Tobias Patrick Benjamin von Karg, Takuma Melber, Olaf Kauz, Nils Lange, Lukas Schmelter, Carlo Dürbeck, Fabian Heide, Tobias Süß, Ingmar Zielke, Sebastian Michael Müller, Stefan Scheller, Fabian von Heimburg, Martin Haberland, Marius Mazziotti, Alexander Wilhelmi, Tino Pawlowski, Ernst Kronreif, Jens Gerber, Michael Dornkasch, Marius Schäfer, Björn Grötzner, Alexis Wegerich, Pete Millwood, Alan Sked, Josh Clement, Sarah-Katharina Kayss, Oliver Stein, Christian Hellwig, Marcel Werner, Christian E. Rieck, Phillip Hartberger, Marcel Berni, Hans-Peter Kriemann, Thorsten Loch, and Cedric Bierganns.

In London, I wish to thank with gratitude Henrietta and Giles for their kindness and our many discussions (and the 'bunker'). In Rome, Niccolò Serri, Vicchi and Toni De Marchi always made me feel home. I also wish to thank David Broder as well as Franco and Thomas for the countless good memories.

I was warmly welcomed at Palgrave Macmillan. Megan Laddusaw and Christine Pardue have been an enormous help in the final stage of this project. I also wish to thank the two anonymous reviewers for their helpful feedback.

Most importantly, I would not have been able to write this book without the support from my family. I wish to thank Tetyana Dragoliub for the colourful anecdotes on Ukrainian and Russian history, and the equally enriching culinary diversions. Olga Dragoliub shared the good and challenging moments of this project, always pushing me to be more self-critical. Her greatest assest, patience, played out favourably with my Russian skills, which she helped improve. May our Ukrainian-Italian love stand for a brighter chapter in the history of these two countries. Nothing would have been possible without my parents: from my mother's cherishing of my early interest in books to the unlimited support during my days as a student. The most bitter aspect of this book is that my father will not be able to see it in its final form after following this project with such keen interest and spending many hours discussing its content. It shall thus be dedicated to him—with endless love and gratitude.

Contents

1	Introduction	1
2	Historiography: Past Problems and Recent Trends	19
3	The Italian Army Before the Second World War (1861–1940)	39
4	The *guerra fascista*—10 June 1940–25 July 1943	65
5	The Italian Operations on the Eastern Front (1941)	87
6	The Italian Operations on the Eastern Front (1942)	119
7	The Battle on the Don, 11 December 1942–31 December 1943	151
8	The Italian Combat Performance: 'Chicken Led by Donkeys'?	189
9	Narratives About Victimhood: Evil Germans, Good Italian Occupiers and Evil Soviets?	229
10	Shaping the Myths: Memoirs, the Army and the *Alpini*	267

11 Contested Memories During the Cold War	293
12 Conclusion	329
Bibliography	337
Index	363

Abbreviations and Glossary

A Note on Spelling

English names have been used for locations in Russia or Africa. Soviet Union and Russia will be used interchangeably, even though there was no 'Russia' in this period. Various armies will be capitalized (First Army, but also Romanian Army), Army Corps will be used with Roman numerals (e.g. XXXV Corps). Italian infantry divisions will be referred to by their honorifics for the sake of legibility: e.g. *Ravenna* for the 3rd *Ravenna* Infantry Division; battalions will also be referenced with Roman numbers (for example IV/72, i.e. the fourth battalion of the 72th Infantry Regiment). Since it is often important to know if an author is a military figure, their rank (at the time of writing) has been included in brackets (e.g. [Gen.] *author's name*).

Glossary

Alpino (pl. *Alpini*)—Italian Alpine troops (mountain infantry with regional recruitment)
Anti-tank gun (AT gun)
Anti-aircraft gun (AA gun)
Archivio Centrale dello Stato (ACS)—Italian Central State Archives (Rome)
Archivio dell'Ufficio Storico dello Stato Maggiore del Esercito (AUSSME)—The Archives of the Italian Army General Staff's Historical Office (Rome)

Ardito (pl. *Arditi*)—Assault shock troops in the First World War
Armata Italiana in Russia (ARMIR)—Italian Army in Russia, or Eighth Army
Bersagliere (pl. *Bersaglieri*)—Light Infantry
Bundesarchiv Militärarchiv (BA-MA)—German Military Archives
Busta (b.)—Folder
Cartella (c.)—File
Camicia Nera (pl. *Camicie Nere*, CC.NN.)—Blackshirt(s)
Carabiniere (pl. *Carabinieri*, CC.RR.)—Italian military police
Carristi—Armoured troops
Chief of Staff—Chief
Corpo di Spedizione Italiano in Russia (CSIR)—Italian Expeditionary Corps in Russia
Diario Storico del Comando Supremo (DS CS)—The *Comando Supremo*'s War Diary
Deutsches Verbindungskommando (DVK)—German Liaison Command
Documenti Diplomatici Italiani (DDI)—Italian Diplomatic Documents
Frame (microfilm)—f.
Frames (microfilm)—fs.
Folio (stamped archival material)—fol.
Folios (stamped archival material)—fos.
Folgore—Italian paratroopers
Infanterie-Division (ID)—Infantry Division (German)
Intendanza—Rear command
IWM—Imperial War Museum (Collections)
Kriegstagebuch (KTB)—War Diary
Luftwaffe—German Air Force
Medaglia d'Oro al Valor Militare (MOVM)—Gold Medal for Military Valour
Milizia Volontaria per la Sicurezza Nazionale (MVSN)—National Security Volunteer Militia
No date—n.d.
Panzer-Division (PD)—Armoured Division (German)
Oberkommando des Heeres (OKH)—Germany Army High Command
Oberkommando der Wehrmacht (OKW)—German Armed Forces High Command
Ostheer—German Army in the East
Regio Esercito—Royal Italian Army

Repubblica Sociale Italiana (RSI)—Italian Social Republic. The new Fascist rump state under Mussolini in German-occupied northern Italy 1943–1945 (also informally known as the Republic of Salò)
General Officer Commanding (GOC)
Servizio Informazioni Militare (SIM)—Italian Military Intelligence
Stato Maggiore Generale (Comando Supremo)—Italian Armed Forces High Command and General Staff
Stato Maggiore Regia Aeronautica (Superaereo)—Italian Air Force High Command and General Staff
Stato Maggiore Regio Esercito (SME or Superesercito)—Italian Army High Command and General Staff
Stato Maggiore Regia Marina (Supermarina)—Italian Navy High Command and General Staff
Ufficio Storico dello Stato Maggiore del Esercito (USSME)—Italian Army Historical Office
TNA—The British National Archives, Kew
Wehrmacht—German Armed Forces

Italian ranks with English and German equivalent

Italian rank	Blackshirts	English	German
Maresciallo d'Italia	Caporale d'Onore	Field Marshal	Generalfeldmarschall
Generale d'Armata	/	General	Generaloberst
Generale designato d'Armata	/	/	/
Generale di Corpo d'Armata	Comandante generale	Lieutenant-General	General
Generale di Divisione	Luogotenente generale	Major General	Generalleutnant
Generale di Brigata	Console generale	Brigadier	Generalmajor
Colonello comandante	/	/	/
Colonello	Console	Colonel	Oberst
Tenente Colonello	Primo Seniore	Lieutenant- Colonel	Oberstleutnant
Maggiore	Seniore	Major	Major
Primo Capitano	/	/	/
Capitano	Centurione	Captain	Hauptmann
Primo Tenente	Capo manipolo	Lieutenant	Oberleutnant
Tenente	Sotto capo manipolo	2nd Lieutenant	Leutnant

List of Figures

Fig. 3.1	Italian infantry division scheme, from Greene, *Mare Nostrum*, 9	56
Fig. 3.2	Italian *Alpini* division scheme, from Greene, *Mare Nostrum*, 16	57
Fig. 3.3	Military units—identification, from Greene, *Mare Nostrum*, 2	58
Fig. 5.1	Organisational scheme of a *celere* type division, here the 1st '*Eugenio di Savoia*' *Celere* division in 1940, from Greene, *Mare Nostrum*, 54	92
Fig. 5.2	The theatre of operations. The order of battle shows the situation on 1 December 1942. The Italian Eighth Army is marked as '8 A (I)', from Glantz, *From the Don*, 11	101
Fig. 7.1	Settlements and heights over 200 metres around the Mamon bridgehead, from Glantz, *From the Don*, 26	158
Fig. 7.2	Situation on 16 December 1942, from Glantz, *From the Don*, 43	162
Fig. 7.3	Evening situation, 16 December 1942, from Glantz, *From the Don*, 43	167
Fig. 7.4	Evening situation, 17 December 1942, from Glantz, *From the Don*, 48	170
Fig. 7.5	Evening situation, 18 December 1942, from Glantz, *From the Don*, 50	172
Fig. 7.6	Evening situation, 19 December 1942, from Glantz, *From the Don*, 54	173

Fig. 7.7   Evening Situation, 21 December 1942, from Glantz,
           From the Don, 55   177
Fig. 7.8   Evening situation, 30 December 1942, Glantz,
           From the Don, 70   178

CHAPTER 1

Introduction

'Cowards', 'clowns', 'useless soldiers', and 'treacherous allies'—the Second World War has bequeathed many stereotypes and enduring myths about the Italians. Mussolini's regime had a central role as Nazi Germany's closest diplomatic ally, and its fortunes during the war also influenced the Axis's overall position. Yet, as the noted historian MacGregor Knox observed: "despite a fifty years' undergrowth of memoirs and popular accounts, Fascist Italy at war remains poorly understood."[1] This holds particularly true for one key piece in the puzzle: the Italian Army (*Regio Esercito*). Most myths are linked to the armed forces and the campaigns that it fought. But while the operations in North Africa have attracted notable attention, another vital theatre for the Italian Army, the Eastern Front, has thus far been almost completely neglected. This happened notwithstanding the fact that over one-third of Italian combat losses between 1940 and 1943 were suffered on Russian soil and five times more soldiers (229,000) fought on the Don in 1942–1943 than at the battle of El Alamein—the coinciding turning point in the North African desert. Collective memory in Italy has focused on the winter retreat (*la ritirata dal Don*) and largely portrayed the Italian soldiers as victims. This has meant that the previous operations have been seen as prelude to the inevitable catastrophe of a supposedly inept

---

[1] MacGregor Knox, *Hitler's Italian Allies: Royal Armed Forces, Fascist Regime, and the War of 1940–43* (Cambridge: Cambridge University Press, 2003), 195.

© The Author(s) 2019
B. M. Scianna, *The Italian War on the Eastern Front, 1941–1943*, Italian and Italian American Studies,
https://doi.org/10.1007/978-3-030-26524-3_1

military machine. In principle, three topoi emerged from the campaign in Russia, each with diverging interpretations that often depended on political views. First was the question of military performance, second, the Italian soldiers as victims (of their poor materiel and bad leadership, their government, their German ally and the Soviets) and third, whether the Italians had been *brava gente* (decent people) or ruthless Fascist occupiers. The Italian involvement in the war against the Soviet Union is, then, an important element of understanding the country's general role during the Second World War and the contested memories after 1945.

While cultural histories on collective memory analyse a constructed reality and public narratives, they often show little interest in the actual operations or in the armed forces as organisation. And yet events are never commemorated without myths and different layers of memories. Thus, reality—in a hermeneutic sense of *what really happened*—and the myths fashioned about an event often (or rather always) diverge, and notably influence the narrative and memory. The new school of military history as a study of mentality, cultural and everyday history has widened the hitherto narrow field, but has left operational aspects neglected. At the same time, operational military histories often did not investigate the memory of battles and campaigns or remained restricted to a single nation. A truly modern military history has to include several methodological strands, taking political, operational and cultural aspects into proper account without excluding the actual fighting.[2] This first step, analysing the military and its operations, is fundamental to drawing wider assessments of Italy's role in the Second World War. Yet, particularly the operational history of the Italian Army has been under-researched.

The myths about Italian military incompetence are closely linked to the difficulties of assessing military effectiveness. In the Second World War, one benchmark was arguably the ability to wage combined arms manoeuvre warfare (with infantry, artillery, armour and aircraft) on the divisional

---

[2] Sönke Neitzel, "Militärgeschichte ohne Krieg? Eine Standortbestimmung der deutschen Militärgeschichtsschreibung über das Zeitalter der Weltkriege," in *Geschichte der Politik. Alte und Neue Wege. Beiheft 44 der HZ*, eds. Hans-Christof Kraus and Thomas Nicklas (Munich: Oldenbourg, 2007), 287–308; Stig Förster, *The Battlefield: Towards a Modern History of War* (London: GHI, 2008); John A. Lynn, "The Embattled Future of Academic Military History," *The Journal of Military History* 61, no. 4 (1997): 777–89.

and corps levels. This included the capability to command, control, supply and maintain these forces in the field. Military effectiveness has further to be subdivided into the political, strategic, operational and tactical levels, and has been defined as "process by which armed forces convert resources into fighting power. A fully effective military is one that derives maximum combat power from the resources physically and politically available. Effectiveness thus incorporates some notion of efficiency."[3] In his seminal work, Martin van Creveld had additionally highlighted the importance of combat motivation and morale for an army's 'fighting power'.[4] On the other hand, the contributions from political science to this field have been vast—and are unfortunately often neglected by historians. Stephen Biddle has argued that modern material and sound finances alone are not sufficient for an army to be effective. His 'modern system' theory of force employment emphasised doctrine, tactical education for combined arms cooperation and the importance of force exposure reduction over sheer numbers and technology.[5] Other scholars have hinted at the importance of national cultures in explaining the military as an organisation and in understanding combat outcomes.[6]

Added to this, military effectiveness has to be considered as a relative benchmark: that is, one to be seen in comparison to other armies and taking proper account of situational and structural factors, such as weather or materiel (lest we forget the enemy). The metrics for measuring effectiveness are both difficult to establish and hotly disputed.[7] Defeat is certainly an indicator, but no one would claim that German defeat in two world wars means that her army was ineffective. Cohen and Gooch have pointed to the complexity of military failure, and shifted the analytical

---

[3] For detail on this, see Allan R. Millet, Williamson Murray, and Kenneth H. Watman, "The Effectiveness of Military Organizations," in *Military Effectiveness. Vol. 1. The First World War*, eds. Allan R. Millett and Williamson Murray (Cambridge: Cambridge University Press, 2010), 1–30, quoted on 2.

[4] Martin van Creveld, *Kampfkraft. Militärische Organisation und Leistung 1939–1945* (Freiburg: Rombach, 1989), 4.

[5] Stephen Biddle, *Military Power: Explaining Victory and Defeat in Modern Battle* (Princeton: Princeton University Press, 2004), 2–5.

[6] Stephen P. Rosen, "Military Effectiveness: Why Society Matters," *International Security* 9, no. 4 (1995): 5–31.

[7] The capture-kill ratio or the awarding of medals have been proposed as measures, but this has also been countered; see Roman Töppel, "Das Ritterkreuz des Eisernen Kreuzes und der Kampfwert militärischer Verbände," *Zeitschrift für Heereskunde* 12 (2012): 180–90.

focus from seeing individual commanders as sole culprits to organisational flaws.[8] They also criticised often-unsubstantiated theories about collective incompetence, institutional failure and uncritical military minds caught in their rigid doctrinal thinking.[9] They thus argued against understanding institutions as a static concept and preferred to analyse armed forces as organisations, i.e. how they work in practice.[10]

Any serious examination of a given army must analyse its planning for war, organisational culture, battlefield performance and learning processes. Indeed, poor civilian-military relations, restrictions on training, hyper-centralisation, duplication in command chains and lack of international contacts will hamper hypothetical capabilities and may take decades to be overcome.[11] Therefore, military adaptability was and remains a key virtue for armies: even if cynics argue that the military always prepares for the last war, we also know that predictions are always difficult. Unpredictability and peacetime dividends add to the problem of military readiness,[12] which increases the need to instil armed forces with capability for critical self-assessment in peacetime and to stimulate a culture of change and adaptation with realistic training to prepare for the fog of war.[13] According to John Nagl, "military organisations often demonstrate remarkable resistance to doctrinal change as a result of their organisational cultures. Organisational learning, when it does occur, tends to happen only in the wake of a particularly unpleasant or unproductive event."[14] Outside threats and defeat on the battlefield clearly are such unpleasant events,[15] which still require a framework for effective

---

[8] Eliot A. Cohen and John Gooch, *Military Misfortunes: The Anatomy of Failure in War* (New York: Free Press, 1990), 3.

[9] Ibid., 10–16.

[10] Ibid., 15.

[11] Wade P. Hinkle et al., *Why Nations Differ in Military Skill* (Alexandria: Institute for Defence Analyses, 1999), ES–2f.

[12] Richard K. Betts, *Military Readiness: Concepts, Choices, Consequences* (Washington: Brookings, 1995).

[13] Barry Watts and Williamson Murray, "Military Innovation in Peacetime," in *Military Innovation in the Interwar Period*, eds. Williamson Murray and Allan R. Millett (Cambridge: Cambridge University Press, 1996), 369–415.

[14] John A. Nagl, *Learning to Eat Soup with a Knife: Counterinsurgency Lessons from Malaya and Vietnam* (London: Praeger, 2002), 8.

[15] Williamson Murray, *Military Adaptation in War* (Cambridge: Cambridge University Press, 2011), 6.

reorganisation. Yet, other outside influences, e.g. within alliances, can have positive effects by channelling innovation to less developed armed forces. Thus, an army's combat performance depends as much on pre-war training as on time, context, enemy, materiel, strategic goals and policies and the nature of operations.

The second wider theme of this study is memory, which includes aspects of how myths[16] and narratives are formed and contested. The main issues will be the interrelation between discourses and how some narratives prevailed and influenced memories, and the deviation of an organisational memory (e.g. the military's) from public discourses and the dominant collective memory. In the following, memory will be understood as contested and dynamic process of remembering and interpreting the past in order to provide identity. Memory will be seen as an active 'recollection' and search for meaning, e.g. in public political discourses to evoke images and narratives of the past for the present—or else to mute certain aspects.[17]

In order to explain why even military defeats are glorified, one needs to understand the political significance of myths about redemption and resurgence. Political myths have always held a central place for nation-building purposes, including in the Italian case.[18] Likewise, war has always played an important role for founding myths and memories of nations.[19] All these battle myths revolve around several recurring topoi: the few against the many (David versus Goliath), volunteerism, youth, elitism, hostile terrain, heroic sacrifice, refusal to surrender in hopeless situations and the association of a stronghold with a sacred home soil. These myths are often based on false official statements that set the tone for the 'glorious defeat' narrative and can be altered to suit a desired

---

[16] Or legends. The word 'myth' will not be used in a religious or strict mythical sense. In Italian, the *mito* is more akin to a mix between myth, legend, and tale in the English language.

[17] Paul Ricoeur, *Memory, History, Forgetting* (Chicago: Chicago University Press, 2004); Aleida Assmann and Linda Shortt, eds. *Memory and Political Change* (New York: Palgrave Macmillan, 2012); Jan-Werner Müller, "Introduction," in *Memory and Power in Post-War Europe*, ed. Jan-Werner Müller (Cambridge: Cambridge University Press, 2002), 1–35.

[18] Silvana Patriarca, *Italianità. La costruzione del carattere nazionale* (Bari: Laterza, 2010); Ernesto Galli della Loggia, *L'identità italiana* (Bologna: Il Mulino, 1998).

[19] Gerd Krumeich, "Schlachtenmythen in der Geschichte," in *Schlachtenmythen: Ereignis – Erzählung – Erinnerung*, eds. Gerd Krumeich and Susanne Brandt (Cologne: Böhlau, 2003), 1–18.

memory—e.g. that of a 'last stand' against all odds.[20] Myths about defeat have often been willingly falsified by politics: military disaster could thereby be transformed into a political argument, for example to damn a corrupt social system and an undesired war, or the military could point to a lack of popular support and blame defeat on a 'stab in the back'. In Italy, the lost battles of Custoza (1866), Adwa (1896) and Caporetto (1917) were deeply engrained in national identity—and a recent study of defeats in Italian history put the retreat in Russia 1942–1943 at the end of this 'tradition'.[21] Therefore, military myths were often linked to narratives of rebirth and renewal, e.g. the Italian *Resistenza*.[22] Yet, while these myths are usually described as "homogenizing" and forming at least an "illusion of community"[23] through good communication, they are as much exclusive as they are inclusive; the battlefield victory of one group means defeat for another. Civil wars—such as that which ravaged Italy between 1943 and 1945—pose particular problems. In fact, defeat and recovery creates a particular kind of collective memory. Wolfgang Schivelbusch has created a "heroic defeat" paradigm to analyse how different nations coped with lost wars.[24] Indeed, victory is by no means a precondition for a battle becoming a mythical *lieu de mémoire* or positively connotated reference point for armed forces (think of the Spartans' stand at the Thermophylae, or the Alamo). Where civilian societies see disgrace and futile bloodletting, the military might see heroic conduct upholding its values of obedience and sacrifice. Yet, even excellent volumes on the impact of defeats have habitually focused on society but omitted the memory of the main participating organisation: the military.[25]

---

[20] Bryan Perrett, *Last Stand! Famous Battles Against the Odds* (London: Cassell, 1991), 7–10.

[21] On the importance of these events, see Marco Patricelli, *L'Italia delle sconfitte: Da Custoza alla ritirata di Russia* (Bari: Laterza, 2016).

[22] George Schöpflin, "The Functions of Myth and a Taxonomy of Myths," in *Myths and Nationhood*, eds. Geoffrey Hosking and George Schöpflin (New York: Routledge, 1997), 19–35, here 32–33.

[23] Schöpflin, "Functions," 23.

[24] Wolfgang Schivelbusch, *The Culture of Defeat: On National Trauma, Mourning, and Recovery* (London: Granta, 2003), 1–35.

[25] An exception, which did not include Italy, was Peter Dennis and Jeffrey Grey, eds., *Victory or Defeat: Armies in the Aftermath of Conflict* (Newport: Big Sky, 2010).

On the other hand, even such 'recollections' of the past can remain confined to a specific social group. Just as nations are formed around founding myths and 'invented traditions' that repetitively use symbols and rituals to instil norms and values by implying continuity with the past,[26] so, too, are organisations. Yet the many theories on discourses and memories have focused on society at large rather than the armed forces.[27] As an independent institution, the armed forces have a distinct memory, which interacts with and is influenced by society's memories, but it is not identical to it or static. Every organisation has a set of values and refers back to positively connoted events in its own past. The military, too, creates such positive points of reference for its identity: from individual battles and role models to 'timeless' military values, such as obedience, honour, sacrifice and duty.[28] Official and semi-official military publications, as well as memoirs by former generals have always been important references for the 'military sphere.'[29] It would be rather surprising and, indeed, run counter to the logic of organisational self-protection, if the military did not try to write a *fable convenue* for itself. Another difference is that the military's (organisational) memory may diverge considerably from the war experience and memory of individual soldiers. A soldier may have been disturbed by terrible experiences and subsequently attempt to narrate the 'good memories' and suppress less rosy ones, thus constructing different realities and narratives.[30]

---

[26] Eric Hobsbawm, "Introduction: Inventing Traditions," in *The Invention of Tradition*, eds. Eric Hobsbawm and Terence Ranger (Cambridge: Cambridge University Press, 1984), 1–14.

[27] For example, Norman Fairclough, *Discourse and Social Change* (Cambridge: Polity, 1993); John R. Searle, *The Construction of Social Reality* (New York: Free Press, 1995).

[28] Williamson Murray and Richard Hart Sinnreich, eds., *The Past as Prologue: The Importance of History to the Military Profession* (Cambridge: Cambridge University Press, 2006). Research has stressed the dynamic interrelation between identity, stereotypes, group norms, values, attitudes, and actual behaviour; see Volker Franke, *Preparing for Peace: Military Identity, Value Orientations, and Professional Military Education* (Westport: Praeger, 1999), 26ff.

[29] I will use the term 'military sphere' to include veterans, families, those close to the military and active soldiers.

[30] Aleida Assmann, "Re-framing Memory: Between Individual and Collective Forms of Constructing the Past," in *Performing the Past*, eds. Jay Winter, Karin Tilmans, and Frank Van Vree (Amsterdam: Amsterdam University Press, 2010), 35–50.

Besides looking at operational performance and deconstructing certain myths and memories, another point is worth noting. While myths are mainly positively connotated for a nation's memory, their negative counter-part is the stereotype. There are many domestic and foreign stereotypes about Italians.[31] One dominant theme is the view of Italians as unmilitary people.[32] But as much as this stereotype has influenced Italian society's view of her armed forces after 1945, by no means does it stop at the country's borders. The Eastern Front—and especially Stalingrad—became an important part of Germany's postwar memory.[33] As with other theatres, the German generals' narrative and the Italian victim-cliché have overshadowed serious analysis of Italy's participation. Why has this been the case?

A Distorted Outside View Defined by Propaganda and Stereotypes

Our view on the Italian Army is distorted by Anglophone and German discourses and scholarship, memoir literature (whether domestic or foreign), anecdotal evidence and propaganda. The Abyssinian War (1935–1936) effectively started the *guerra fascista* and was a disaster for French and British foreign policy. During the dispute, cartoonists started to depict the Italians and Mussolini in a clownish and unsoldierly way—especially in *The Beano*.[34] This propaganda offensive was continued during the Spanish Civil War.[35] During the Second World War, propaganda movies, such as *Desert Victory* (1943), *Tunisian Victory* (1944) or *Five Graves to Cairo* (1943) set the tone for many postwar narratives.[36]

---

[31] Loredana Sciolla, *Italiani: Stereotipi di casa nostra* (Bologna: Il Mulino, 1997).

[32] Christie Davies, "Itali Sunt Imbelles," *Journal of Strategic Studies* 5, no. 2 (1982): 266–69; Virgilio Ilari, "Il valore militare degli italiani" (Conference paper presented at the Istituto di Studi Militari Marittimi, 2002).

[33] Christina Morina, *Legacies of Stalingrad: Remembering the Eastern Front in Germany Since 1945* (Cambridge: Cambridge University Press, 2011).

[34] Philip Willan, "Benito and the Beano," *The Guardian*, 28 Nov. 2002.

[35] Sweet has described depictions of the Italian involvement in Spain as still based on Republican propaganda, John J. T. Sweet, *Iron Arm: The Mechanization of Mussolini's Army, 1920–1940* (Westport: Greenwood, 1980), xvii.

[36] See e.g. the depiction of Italian soldiers in *The Best of Enemies* (1961). Still, the movie was the fourth most popular in 1961, attracting 1,076,211 viewers, Pietro Cavallo, *Viva l'Italia. Storia, Cinema e identità nazionale (1932–1962)* (Naples: Liguori, 2009), 406.

Similarly, while British posters portrayed the Japanese as animal-like beasts and the Germans as cruel Huns, "only the Italians were painted in sympathetic colours. Comic, unmilitary and rarely threatening, Italians were simply a variation on the pre-war 'funny foreigner' stereotype. [...] Even adventure fiction refused to take the Italian armed forces seriously."[37] The same held true for American propaganda. Not only Italian soldiers, but also civilians were depicted as hapless victims of Fascism and "infantile, emotional and largely apolitical people whose character was marked by cowardice and unpredictable violence."[38] After the war many Italians gratefully endorsed this narrative of victimhood. Additionally, the events of 8 September 1943 and the following two years had a strong impact on both discourse and memory in Italy and abroad. The change of alliances, the collapse of the Italian state and the armed forces, and the subsequent civil war posed many embarrassing questions and influenced judgements on the period before 1943, which was mainly seen through the lens of this year.[39] In Germany, Joseph Goebbels unleashed a massive propaganda campaign against the Badoglio government in the south,[40] and Italy was depicted—much like in 1914–1915—as an untrustworthy turncoat.[41] Mussolini's rump state in northern Italy also

[37] Michael Paris, *Warrior Nation: Images of War in British Popular Culture, 1850–2000* (London: Reaktion, 2000), 217.

[38] Andrew Buchanan, "'Good Morning, Pupil!' American Representations of Italianness and the Occupation of Italy, 1943–1945," *Journal of Contemporary History* 43, no. 2 (2008): 217–40. See also Filippo Focardi, *Il cattivo tedesco e il bravo italiano: la rimozione delle colpe della seconda guerra mondiale* (Bari: Laterza, 2013), 3ff.; Ilaria Favretto and Oliviero Bergamini, "'Temperamentally Unwarlike': The Image of Italy in the Allies' War Propaganda," in *War and the Media Reportage and Propaganda 1900–2003*, eds. Mark Connelly and David Welch (London: Tauris, 2005), 112–26.

[39] Elena Agarossi, *A Nation Collapses: The Italian Surrender of September 1943* (Cambridge: Cambridge University Press, 2000); Claudio Dellavalle, ed., *8 settembre 1943. Storia e memoria* (Milan: FrancoAngeli, 1989); Ernesto Galli della Loggia, *La morte della Patria* (Bari: Laterza, 2003); Mario Isnenghi, *La tragedia necessaria: Da Caporetto all'otto settembre* (Bologna: Il Mulino, 1999).

[40] Aristotle A. Kallis, *Nazi Propaganda and the Second World War* (London: Palgrave Macmillan, 2005), 159ff.

[41] Italy had remained neutral at the outbreak of the First World War, which left a bitter memory in Germany, see Gian Enrico Rusconi, *Deutschland-Italien/Italien-Deutschland. Geschichte einer schwierigen Beziehung von Bismarck zu Berlusconi* (Paderborn: Schöningh, 2006), 100ff., 170ff., 190ff.; more broadly on German stereotypes, Klaus Bergdolt, *Kriminell, korrupt, katholisch? Italiener im deutschen Vorurteil* (Stuttgart: Franz Steiner Verlag, 2018). In fact, this narrative of treason has left a mark on the image of the

used propaganda to discredit the military elites who remained loyal to the King and now fought against Fascism. However, the new allies were also problematic. While the Italian Army in the south strove to be perceived as an equal *co-belligerent*, the British in particular treated them with scorn. As the Chief of the General Staff, General Paolo Berardi, later remarked in his memoirs: "also formally, we were delegated by the English to the humiliating level of an army from their colonies."[42] Yet, the impact of 8 September on the Italian Army's domestic and international prestige has rarely been studied.[43] The Army's postwar narrative about the 'war of liberation' became one of purification and redemption through combat: it sought to secure its role in the country's memory, which strongly centered on the *Resistenza*.[44] This campaign, however, hardly attracted attention outside military circles—let alone outside Italy:

Italians and the Army in particular. When the former assistant military attaché in Rome, Friedrich-Karl von Plehwe, argued in 1967 that the deployment of German forces across the Brenner had been the real treason, his message was warmly received, and the book was eagerly translated (in 1970); the Italian general staff printed a special edition in 1978, which became required reading for all army officers, [Lt. Col.] Friedrich-Karl von Plehwe, *Blick durch viele Fenster. Erinnerungen 1919–1978* (Berlin: Frieling, 1998), 287. The book in question is [Lt. Col.] Friedrich-Karl von Plehwe, *Schicksalsstunden in Rom* (Berlin: Propyläen, 1967; Italian ed. *Il patto d'acciaio* by Longanesi). Plehwe became a noted diplomat after the war.

[42][Gen.] Paolo Berardi, *Memorie di un capo di stato maggiore dell'Esercito (1943–1945)* (Bologna: ODCU, 1954), 127. This cooperation and the Italian performance have been subject to very little serious study; for now, see Mario De Prospo, "Reconstructing the Army of a Collapsed Nation: The Kingdom of the South of Italy (September 1943–March 1944)," *Journal of Modern Italian Studies* 18, no. 1 (2013): 1–16; Richard Carrier, "The Regio Esercito in Co-Belligerency, October 1943–April 1945," in *Italy and the Second World War: Alternative Perspectives*, eds. Emanuele Sica and Richard Carrier (Leiden: Brill, 2018), 95–125.

[43]More detailed in Filippo Stefani, "L'8 settembre e le forze armate italiane," in *L'Italia in guerra. Il quarto anno – 1943*, eds. Romain H. Rainero and Antonello Biagini (Gaeta: Stabilimento Grafico Militare, 1994), 155–60.

[44]This remains a history to be written. For now, see [Gen.] Oreste Bovio, *L'Ufficio Storico dell'Esercito* (Rome: USSME, 1987), 93ff.; Carlo Vallauri, *Soldati. Le forze armate italiane dall'armistizio alla Liberazione* (Turin: UTET, 2003); Nicola Labanca, ed., *I Gruppi di combattimento. Studi, fonti, memorie (1944–1945)* (Rome: Carocci, 2005).

the *Resistenza* myth was too strong, and internationally the memory of Anzio and Cassino were too dominant.[45]

After the Second World War, the Allied cooperation with German military elites had a decisive impact on our perception of the military operations. In the period up till 1961, around 300 former Wehrmacht officers authored over 2500 reports.[46] Their aim was to write the war from a German perspective. As Field Marshal Georg von Küchler expressed in a circular to all collaborating German officers: "We describe *German* deeds from a German viewpoint and thereby build a memorial to our soldiers."[47] They blamed Hitler for operational errors and attempted to establish a narrative of a purely professional, apolitical and chivalrous 'clean Wehrmacht.'[48] While some scholars have laid bare these myths, the depictions of the Italians in these reports have endured: militarily useless partners, culprits for defeat, or at best a troublesome addendum. The same narratives were found in the influential memoirs of German senior commanders that further demoted the allies (including the Romanians and Hungarians).[49] Not only did the public readership buy into their narrative, but for decades scholars heavily relied on these memoirs.[50] Thus, the British and American desire to extol the beaten enemy (and gloss over their own shortcomings); the Wehrmacht generals' yearning for recognition and self-exculpation, Basil H. Liddell Hart's

---

[45] Furthermore, the Italian campaign always ranked second to the Normandy operations for the British and Americans, and thus received less attention.

[46] James A. Wood, "Captive Historians, Captive Audience: The German Military History Program, 1945–1961," *The Journal of Military History* 69, no. 1 (2005): 123–47; Esther-Julia Howell, *Von den Besiegten lernen? Die kriegsgeschichtliche Kooperation der U.S. Armee und der ehemaligen Wehrmachtselite, 1945–1961* (Berlin: De Gruyter, 2016).

[47] Quoted in Bernd Wegner, "Erschriebene Siege. Franz Halder, die 'Historical Division' und die Rekonstruktion des Zweiten Weltkrieges im Geiste des deutschen Generalstabes," in *Politischer Wandel, organisierte Gewalt und nationale Sicherheit*, eds. Ernst Willi Hansen, Gerhard Schreiber, and Bernd Wegner (Munich: Oldenbourg, 1995), 287–302, here 294.

[48] Wegner, "Erschriebene Siege," 291–92.

[49] Rolf Düsterberg, *Soldat und Kriegserlebnis. Deutsche militärische Erinnerungsliteratur (1945–1961) zum Zweiten Weltkrieg* (Tübingen: Niemeyer, 2000), 11. See also Grant T. Harward, "First Among Un-Equals: Challenging German Sterotypes of the Romanian Army During the Second World War," *The Journal of Slavic Military Studies* 24, no. 3 (2011): 439–80.

[50] Wegner, "Erschriebene Siege," 299. Captured German war records also heavily influenced scholarship—providing mainly the German point of view on operations.

cooperation with them,[51] the tales about Rommel,[52] the British myths about their own allegedly highly successful war[53]; and Churchill's influential *The History of the Second World War*[54]; were all poisonous to the Italian reputation.[55]

Hence, it is fair to say that our views on the 'Italian side of the hill' are still to considerable degree distorted by German generals' writing and their sympathetic British and American audiences. At the same time, the Italians remained very vigilant about how their armed forces were judged abroad and positive evaluations were readily cited.[56] In a sense, if one joins these dots, one could relate Antonio Gramsci's concept of 'cultural hegemony' to the interpretation of the Italian war effort. This hegemony was created both by a certain authority over discourses at home and abroad, and language: the dominant English narratives were also communicated through movies and novels, and everyday culture left its

---

[51] Alaric Searle, "A Very Special Relationship: Basil Liddell Hart, *Wehrmacht* Generals and the Debate on West German Rearmament, 1945–1953," *War in History* 5, no. 3 (1998): 327–57.

[52] Patrick Major, "'Our Friend Rommel': The *Wehrmacht* as 'Worthy Enemy' in Postwar British Popular Culture," *German History* 26, no. 4 (2008), 530–45. For Italian views on Rommel, see Bastian Matteo Scianna, "Rommel Almighty? Italian Assessments of the 'Desert Fox' During and After the Second World War," *The Journal of Military History* 82, no. 1 (2018): 125–46.

[53] Brian Bond, *Britain's Two World Wars Against Germany: Myth, Memory and the Distortions of Hindsight* (Cambridge: Cambridge University Press, 2014), 8ff.

[54] On Churchill's instrumentalisation of his memoirs, see David Reynolds, *In Command of History: Churchill Fighting and Writing the Second World War* (New York: Random House, 2005). While he panned the Italian war record, his depiction of a bogeyman Mussolini who misled the Italian people suited the overall narrative; thus the Italian reactions to his works were passive to friendly, see Emanuela Scarpellini, "Winston Churchill e la memoria della seconda guerra mondiale in Italia," in *La seconda guerra mondiale e la sua memoria*, eds. Piero Craveri and Gaetano Quagliariello (Soveria Mannelli: Rubbettino, 2006), 223–33.

[55] Another result was the rather negative depiction of the Italians in British service histories that served as background for many scholars, James J. Sadkovich, "Italian Service Histories and Fascist Italy's War Effort," in *The Writing of Official Military History*, ed. Robin Higham (Westport: Greenwood, 1999), 91–125, here 106ff.

[56] Pietro Pallotta, *L'esercito italiano nella seconda guerra mondiale attraverso i guidizi dei comandanti avversari e alleati* (Rome: Tip. Madonna delle Grazie, 1955); Giuseppe Mayda and Nicola Tranfaglia, eds., *Come ci hanno visti* (Rome: Della Volpe, 1965), and also the review article, Piero Pieri, "Jugements sur l'armée italienne et responsabilités," *Revue d'histoire de la Deuxième Guerre Mondiale* 26, no. 7 (1957): 112–14.

mark on Italian public perceptions of the war, in some ways also through "imported memories."[57] Accordingly, it should not be surprising that historical events were profoundly contested and used in political quarrels after the Second World War.

Aims of This Study

One important factor in the longevity of such myths is the poor state of scholarship. While the general level of studies on the Italian Army still lags decades behind those on the Wehrmacht, the research on its actions on the Eastern Front is still in its infancy, as mainly the North African theatre and the Balkans have been more closely scrutinised. Thus, choosing the Eastern Front as a case study has several benefits for an analysis of the *Regio Esercito*. Additionally, this study will not only demystify wartime myths and postwar memories, but also analyse how they were formed. The debates about a 'correct interpretation' of the campaign after 1945 has never been studied. Delving into memory studies can help us much better contextualise the legacies of 1940–1943 and also shed light on Italy's domestic tensions during the Cold War, which derived in large part from the Fascist period and troubled wartime memories after 1943. This study cannot offer an all-encompassing analysis of the armed forces' role in Fascist society, Mussolini's foreign policy and strategic aims, or a detailed breakdown of military operations on all fronts. The following will focus exclusively on the Italian Army. While the navy (*Regia Marina*) and airforce (*Regia Aeronautica*) would deserve analyses of their own, this would far exceed the scope of this study.[58] Several key questions therefore run through the following chapters: What was the *Regio Esercito*'s performance on the Eastern Front like? How was it

---

[57] Daniele Pipitone, "Imported Memories: The Italian Audience and the Reception of American Movies About the Second World War," *Journal of Modern Italian Studies* 21, no. 4 (2016): 627–48. See also Ronald Smelser and Edward J. Davies II, *The Myth of the Eastern Front: The Nazi-Soviet War in American Popular Culture* (Cambridge: Cambridge University Press, 2008).

[58] English readers may refer to Jack Greene and Alessandro Massignani, *The Naval War in the Mediterranean 1940–1943* (London: Chatham, 1998); for the airforce Brian R. Sullivan, "The Downfall of the Regia Aeronautica, 1933–1943," in *Why Air Forces Fail: The Anatomy of Defeat*, eds. Robin Higham and Stephen J. Harris (Lexington: University Press of Kentucky, 2006), 135–76. See also Giorgio Rochat, *Le guerre italiane, 1935–1943. Dall'impero d'Etiopia alla disfatta* (Turin: Einaudi, 2008), 206–35, 335ff.

viewed by their German allies at the time? Which myths were forged (by whom) about the operations at the time and subsequently? How were these myths, memories and narratives about the Eastern Front created, perpetuated and debated after the war?

The study will proceed as follows: first, it will describe the primary sources used and the difficulties accessing the Italian archives. Then, it will review the literature on different aspects of the Italian Army, the Eastern Front, and memory. The third chapter will outline the developments of the *Regio Esercito* before the Second World War, looking at its materiel, doctrines and soldiers. The fourth chapter offers a comparative view on other campaigns' prior to June 1941—their operations and memories—in order to contextualise the Eastern Front case study. The following chapters will provide a detailed analysis of the Italian operations on the Eastern Front between August 1941 and March 1943. This will be the first primary-source based account of the campaign, which is vital for the following step: examining the myths on the Italian performance and the narratives of victimhood. These myths and narratives will be subject to scrutiny based on hitherto-neglected documents and German judgements, guided by the following questions: Were the Italian inept at learning the hard lessons of fighting the Red Army? Were the Italian divisions on the Don useless allies? How about their officers? In short, were the Italians really 'chickens led by donkeys' as conventional wisdom so often suggests? This will include a treatment of recently raised issues concerning war crimes: Had Italian soldiers murdered and plundered their way through the Soviet plains like their Axis comrades? Was there an Italian *Vernichtungskrieg* (war of extermination)?

The tenth chapter will analyse the memoir literature and the Army's narratives. Hereafter, the last chapter will examine contested memories by looking at postwar debates surrounding the Italian operations on the Eastern Front. The onset of the Cold War and the tense domestic situation established an intrinsic connection between historical interpretations and current affairs. Individuals, the press and even courts became vital elements in this contested space about victims and perpetrators: Palmiro Togliatti (1893–1964) readily jumped into the ring for his Communist Party (*Partito Comunista d'Italia*, PCI) against Marshal Giovanni Messe (1883–1968), who remained a vital role model and spokesperson for the Army even after his retirement in 1947. The earlier chapters on operations will thus serve as groundwork for understanding these debates and challenges in the onset of the Cold War. By analysing the disputes surrounding the Italian peace settlement, the unexpected return of prisoners from Soviet captivity in 1945, the constitutional referendum on 2 June 1946, and the parliamentary elections on 18 April 1948, this part will show how interconnected and hotly debated the myths and memories of the *campagna di Russia* remained in postwar Italy.

This study will demonstrate that while the narrative of the 'tragic retreat from the Don' may have suited society at large—and indeed, groups who tried to discredit the senior leadership—the nuances that mattered so much to the military are often overlooked. Retreat and defeat could not form an acceptable narrative for the Italian Army, yet nothing was set in stone, and the different narratives were even more debated than, for instance, those on the North African campaign, due to the political situation of the Cold War. As this book will show, the defenders of the Army's effectiveness and chivalrous behaviour were in many cases closer to the truth than the accusers.

A Note on Sources

Any analysis has to start with the obstacle-strewn access to the Italian Army's archives (*Archivio dell'Ufficio Storico dello Stato Maggiore dell'Esercito*, AUSSME).[59] In addition to restrictive policies, many unit diaries for the vital periods before and during decisive encounters on the Eastern Front in 1942–1943 were lost.[60] The Central State Archives (*Archivio Centrale dello Stato*, ACS) in Rome keep many documents related to military operations. The private papers of Filippo Diamanti,

---

[59] Silvia Trani and Pier Paolo Battistelli, "The Italian Military Records of the Second World War," *War in History* 17, no. 3 (2010): 333–51.

[60] Trani and Battistelli, "Italian Military Records," 344; Robin Higham, ed., *Official Military Historical Offices and Sources*, Vol. 1 (Westport: Greenwood, 2000), 197; US National Archives and Records Service, *Guide to Records of the Italian Armed Forces*, 3 Vols. (Washington: The National Archives, 1967). The USSME has published some files in their official depictions, and some of the documents captured by the Red Army (that are now held near Moscow) were printed in Giorgio Scotoni and Sergej I. Filonenko, eds., *Retroscena della disfatta italiana in Russia nei documenti inediti dell'8ª Armata*, 2 Vols. (Trento: Panorama, 2008). Antonello Biagini and Fernando Frattolillo edited the *Diario Storico del Comando Supremo* (hereafter DS CS) with an appendix of documents. It contains daily routine matters, but also minutes of high-level meetings and telephone calls with Mussolini, as well as incoming messages, orders to the war ministry etc. The authors also published the verbatim transcripts of the Chief of Staff's meetings, see ibid., *Verbali delle riunioni tenute dal capo di S.M. generale*, 4 Vols. (Rome: USSME, 1982–1985).

commander of a Blackshirt formation on the Eastern Front, have hitherto been neglected. The ACS holds another treasure. The Wehrmacht captured many Italian documents after September 1943, which the Americans in turn seized at the end of the war. They were microfilmed in the 1960s and preserved in the US National Archives and Record Administration (NARA) in Washington, while the original files and microfilm copies were returned to the ACS in 1967.[61] Scholars have estimated that these 508 rolls contain around ten per cent of Italian military documents from the Second World War.[62] These microfilms are therefore no small feat, and they are readily accessible. Still, scholars have hardly used them—especially in regards to the Eastern Front.

Another option is to explore foreign collections. Both the German military archive in Freiburg (*Bundesarchiv Militärarchiv*, BA-MA) and the British National Archives in London (TNA) provide much easier access, and these documents offer outside views and critical evaluations of Italian files. The very nature of the Fascist regime meant that after-action reports were often too positive and Italian operational documents have to be treated with caution. Military attaché and military intelligence reports have rarely been consulted to look at the qualities and shortcomings of the *Regio Esercito*. The reports of Enno von Rintelen (1891–1971)—the German military attaché in Rome (1936–1943) and during the war also liaison officer at the *Comando Supremo*[63]—constitute an excellent source. Deakin deemed him the best-informed and most-balanced observer of the Italian Army.[64] But while Rintelen's memoirs are widely cited,[65]

---

[61] Howard McGaw Smyth, *Secrets of the Fascist Era* (Carbondale: Southern Illinois University Press, 1975).

[62] Trani and Battistelli, "Italian Military Records," 341. The Americans photographed the documents selectively; thus around sixty per cent of the total captured documents are available on microfilm, Smyth, *Secrets*, 156–57.

[63] His new role was entitled "German General at the Italian Army's High Command." He reported directly to the OKW. His appointment was based on a mutual agreement (20 September 1940), which made General Luigi Efisio Marras liaison officer to the OKW in addition to his attaché role, BA-MA, ZA 1/2028 [Maj. Gen.] Burkhart Müller-Hillebrand, The Coordination of the Military Effort of Germany and Her Allies during World War II, n.d., fos.115, 268.

[64] Plehwe, *Blick*, 270.

[65] [Gen.] Enno von Rintelen, *Mussolini als Bundesgenosse. Erinnerungen des deutschen Militärattachés in Rom, 1936–1943* (Stuttgart: Wunderlich, 1951; Italian translation in 1952).

his papers in Freiburg are rarely consulted.[66] Similarly, German liaison officers to Italian units are an invaluable source.[67] One might expect that the Germans always slurred the Italian performance, but the reality is different. A further advantage is the time these documents were written: before 8 September 1943, which make them less blemished by prejudice or hindsight than e.g. memoirs. The British National Archives hold valuable captured Italian documents (especially the GFM 36 series), British diplomatic correspondence and espionage reports on postwar debates, as well as the recently found secret bugging reports of Italian officers in British captivity.[68] Additionally, the available Russian memoirs and academic literature have been consulted to offer a view from the 'opposite trenches'. Thus both external and unblemished internal views (on the Italians) will be analysed and contrasted with Italian documents.

The second overriding theme of this study—contested memory—posed rather less difficulties regarding sources. As well as Marshal Giovanni Messe's private papers in the AUSSME, newspapers, memoirs, and secondary literature, the following also draws on an often-neglected source: military journals. These magazines are an excellent source as they contain the writing of soldiers *for* soldiers, i.e. a semi-public discourse. If one adds in the writings of the USSME one can trace the efforts of the most powerful organs of the Italian Army to publicly (and semi-publicly) influence the narrative and memory. The difficulties of access to Italian war records are not only off-putting for scholars,[69] it also leads to other lamentable results: a heavy reliance on memoirs, even for factual claims.

---

[66] Unfortunately, Rintelen was badly wounded in an air crash on 24 November 1942 and was not in office until 19 April 1943, i.e. during the crucial period in Russia, BA-MA, N433/7, Rintelen to Warlimont, 26 Feb. 1950, fol.15. However, his assistant, army attaché Friedrich-Karl von Plehwe, frequently visited him in the Roman (Luftwaffe) hospital and kept him informed, Plehwe, *Blick*, 285.

[67] The military archive in Freiburg holds copies of Italian documents that German liaison staffs received.

[68] Sönke Neitzel and Harald Welzer, *Soldaten: On Fighting, Killing, and Dying. The Secret Second World War Tapes of German POWs* (London: Simon & Schuster, 2011). The conversations of captured Italian senior officers have been analysed by Amedeo Osti Guerrazzi, *Noi non sappiamo odiare. L'esercito italiano tra fascismo e democrazia* (Turin: UTET, 2010).

[69] The latest document disclosures date from the 1950s.

Given the events of 8 September 1943 and many generals' attempts to distance themselves from Fascism or to place blame on the footsteps of dead or discredited comrades, this is rather problematic.[70] The following chapter will therefore provide an overview on the existing literature.

[70]The published diaries of Galeazzo Ciano, Giuseppe Bottai, Filippo Anfuso, or by Marshal Ugo Cavallero should be treated with caution; MacGregor Knox, *Mussolini Unleashed, 1939–1941: Politics and Strategy in Fascist Italy's Last War* (Cambridge: Cambridge University Press, 1982), 291–92.

CHAPTER 2

Historiography: Past Problems and Recent Trends

The writing of military history in Italy has long remained confined to soldiers and official accounts. After 1945, the official histories often provided in-depth accounts, and while they were often rather uncritical, they remain indispensable for operational studies.[1] Moreover, Sadkovich has described the Italian service histories as more objective and self-critical than, for example, the British and German ones.[2] Still, the USSME volumes have often been disregarded outside of Italy. A lamentable fact for which the USSME is also responsible: the first translated volume (on El Alamein) was published as late as 2007. Higham saw France and Italy in a similar disadvantageous position, as both "have largely been confined to telling their story in a language that few others read. The Italian case is made harder by the fact that in late 1943 they switched sides, fighting with their old opponents against their former allies—not a situation to inspire respect."[3] While the Italian historical office was writing operational studies, civilian historians hardly touched such issues (also due to troublesome access to archives). Even when they did so, the results were

---

[1] For an overview related to the Second World War, see Bovio, *L'Ufficio*, 81–99. The operational accounts often included a second volume, which supplemented the first one with (pre-selected) documents.
[2] Sadkovich, "Italian Service Histories."
[3] Robin Higham, "Introduction," in *The Writing of Official Military History*, ed. Robin Higham (Westport: Greenwood, 1999), vii–xii, here x.

© The Author(s) 2019
B. M. Scianna, *The Italian War on the Eastern Front, 1941–1943*, Italian and Italian American Studies, https://doi.org/10.1007/978-3-030-26524-3_2

rather mixed. Giorgio Rochat, usually regarded as Italy's leading military historian, barely consulted foreign scholarship, nor did he include footnotes to primary sources in any of his books on the Second World War. Angelo Del Boca recently suffered his academic *Caporetto* in an interview when he admitted to having produced biased accounts (to the military's disadvantage) over decades.[4] Journalists have also influenced the narrative and Italian perceptions of the Second World War, and important stimuli also came from abroad. For example, it fell to a German scholar— Thomas Schlemmer—to initiate a debate about Italian war crimes and occupational practices on the Eastern Front.[5] The following overview will only cover the most important scholarly contributions: it will first contrast the main opposing views with regard to Italian military effectiveness, before then analysing the state of research on the senior leadership, individual commanders, key units, the Italian involvement in the war against the Soviet Union, cooperation with the Germans, and finally the memory on the Second World War, especially in the 'military sphere'.

GENERAL OVERVIEWS ON THE ITALIAN ARMY 1940–1943

The last decades have improved our understanding of life under the Fascist regime and at the front,[6] the fate of Italian prisoners,[7] and the Italian involvement in the Holocaust,[8] and studies on imperial designs and

[4] A. Carioti, "Etiopia, l'esercito corregge gli storici," *Corriere della Sera*, 6 Jan. 2011.

[5] Thomas Schlemmer, *Die Italiener an der Ostfront 1942/43. Dokumente zu Mussolinis Krieg gegen die Sowjetunion* (Munich: Oldenbourg, 2005). The extended Italian edition bore the title: *Invasori, non vittime* (Invaders, not victims).

[6] Richard J. B. Bosworth, *Mussolini's Italy: Life Under the Dictatorship, 1915–1945* (London: Penguin, 2006); Christopher Duggan, *Fascist Voices: An Intimate History of Mussolini's Italy* (Oxford: Oxford University Press, 2013); Mario Avagliano and Marco Palmieri, *Vincere e vinceremo! Gli italiani al fronte, 1940–1943* (Bologna: Il Mulino, 2014); Pietro Cavallo, *Italiani in guerra. Sentimenti e immagini dal 1940 al 1943* (Bologna: Il Mulino, 1997).

[7] See for example Gabriele Hammermann, *Zwangsarbeit für den "Verbündeten": Die Arbeits- und Lebensbedingungen der italienischen Militärinternierten in Deutschland 1943– 1945* (Tübingen: Niemeyer, 2002); Flavio Giovanni Conti, *I prigionieri di guerra italiani* (Bologna: Il Mulino, 1986); Bob Moore and Kent Fedorowich, *The British Empire and Its Italian Prisoners of War, 1940–1947* (New York: Palgrave Macmillan, 2002).

[8] Jonathan Steinberg, *All or Nothing? The Axis and the Holocaust 1941–1943* (London: Routledge, 1991); Davide Rodogno, *Fascism's European Empire: Italian Occupation During the Second World War* (Cambridge: Cambridge University Press, 2006), 356ff.

occupation policies on the Balkans and in Africa have shattered the myth of the Italians as allegedly good-hearted people (*brava gente*) who never committed any crimes.[9] In fact, the most fruitful research has focused on exposing the *brava gente* myth and occupational policies. Yet, one should not neglect analysing the Army as organisation and its primary task: fighting conventional operations. A vital contribution to the functioning of the Army were the works by Pier Paolo Battistelli, Piero Crociani and Filippo Cappellano for Osprey, who also accentuated the Italian ability to fight decently within the constraints of their available material.[10] The same holds true for Jack Greene's invaluable *Handbook on the Italian Army*.[11] Yet, most scholars have focused on Mussolini and the strategic level. There are some classic edited volumes and overviews, which are indeed helpful, but the authors did not consult primary sources and only mention the Eastern Front in passing.[12]

---

[9] David Bidussa, *Il mito del bravo italiano* (Milan: Il Saggiatore, 1994); Angelo Del Boca, *Italiani, Brava Gente?* (Vicenza: Neri Pozza, 2005); Elena Agarossi and Maria Teresa Giusti, *Una guerra a parte. I militari italiani nei Balcani 1940–1945* (Bologna: Il Mulino, 2011); Amedeo Osti Guerrazzi, *The Italian Army in Slovenia: Strategies of Antipartisan Repression, 1941–1943* (New York: Palgrave Macmillan, 2013). On the legacy of these crimes see Michele Battini, *The Missing Italian Nuremberg: Cultural Amnesia and Postwar Politics* (New York: Palgrave Macmillan, 2007); Davide Conti, *Criminali di guerra. Accuse, processi e impunità nel secondo dopoguerra* (Rome: Odradek, 2011); Filippo Focardi and Lutz Klinkhammer, "The Question of Fascist Italy's War Crimes: The Construction of a Self-Acquitting Myth (1943–1948)," *Journal of Modern Italian Studies* 9, no. 3 (2004): 330–48; Alberto Stramaccioni, *Crimini gi guerra. Storia e memoria del caso italiano* (Bari: Laterza, 2016).

[10] Filippo Cappellano and Pier Paolo Battistelli, *Italian Light Tanks 1919–1945* (Botley: Osprey, 2012); Ibid., *Italian Medium Tanks 1919–1945* (Botley: Osprey, 2012); Piero Crociani and Pier Paolo Battistelli, *Italian Soldier in North Africa 1941–1943* (Botley: Osprey, 2013). The same holds true for Battistelli's (unpublished) thesis, Pier Paolo Battistelli, "La 'guerra dell'Asse'. Condotta bellica e collaborazione militare Italo-Tedesca, 1939–1943" (PhD diss., University of Padua, 2000).

[11] Printed in Jack Greene, *Mare Nostrum: The War in the Mediterranean* (Watsonville: Typesetting, 1990).

[12] Giorgio Rochat and Giulio Massobrio, *Breve storia dell'Esercito italiano dal 1861 al 1943* (Turin: Einaudi, 1978); Lucio Ceva, *Le Forze armate* (Turin: UTET, 1981), 283–364; [Gen.] Oreste Bovio, *In alto la bandiera. Storia del Regio Esercito* (Foggia: Bastogi, 1999); Massimo De Leonardis, *L'Italia e il suo Esercito. Una storia di soldati dal Risorgimento ad oggi* (Rome: Rai, 2005). See also the multivolume *L'Italia in Guerra* edited by Romain H. Rainero and Antonello Biagini.

Knox's *Hitler's Italian Allies* marks the starting point for any serious analysis of the Italian Army.[13] Knox went beyond accepting bad materiel as the chief reason for the defeat and delved deeper into Italian military culture. In short, Knox saw the armed forces as a deficient organisation whose officers were poorly trained and unable to adapt to modern warfare.[14] He focused strongly on the campaigns in 1940–1941 arguing that the period where Italy fought alone marked "the best evidence of the armed forces' capabilities," while he admitted that thereafter, the *guerra subalterna* threw "some light on the armed forces' ability—or inability—to learn from the German and British examples."[15] Knox correctly stressed Italy's new role as a junior partner at a strategic level. Nonetheless, the Italians did operate independent armies (the Eighth in Russia) and army corps in North Africa, thus we should not stop an analysis in 1941, like we continue analysing the British Army beyond Dunkirk and after the country became the American junior partner.

One limitation of Knox's overall oeuvre is the omission of a detailed look at the operations on the Eastern Front—a problem other scholars have noted as well.[16] Still, many authors have followed Knox's arguments,[17] if sometimes only in parts. It is fair to argue that flaws in organisation, training and materiel influenced the Army's performance during the war. However, this should not be turned into an uncritical one-sided picture, where officers are depicted merely as corrupt, overly theoretical, badly trained and in any case the least talented men of society; which led Petracarro conclude that the "Italian higher command

---

[13] Knox, *Hitler's Italian Allies*. His *Mussolini Unleashed* focused even less on military operations and rather more on Italy's entry into the war and the initial campaigns. His contribution to the *Military Effectiveness* series presented similar arguments; see MacGregor Knox, "The Italian Armed Forces, 1940–3," in *Military Effectiveness, Vol. 3: The Second World War*, eds. Allan R. Millett and Williamson Murray (Cambridge: Cambridge University Press, 2010), 136–79.

[14] Knox, *Hitler's Italian Allies*, 165, 170ff.

[15] Knox, "Italian Armed Forces," 137.

[16] Schlemmer, *Italiener*, 5.

[17] Osti Guerrazzi, *Italian Army*, 4ff.; Rochat, *Le guerre*, 295; H. James Burgwyn, *Mussolini Warlord, Failed Dreams of Empire 1940–1943* (New York: Enigma, 2012), 311ff.; Brian R. Sullivan, "The Italian Soldier in Combat, June 1940–September 1943: Myths, Realities and Explanations," in *Time to Kill: The Soldier's Experience of War in the West*, eds. Paul Addison and Angus Calder (London: Pimlico, 1997), 177–205.

had no idea of how to conduct a modern war of mobility."[18] Yet, even Petracarro cited poor materiel as the chief factor hampering combat performance, and argued that the "distinct characteristics of particular units, improved morale, better leadership, better training, close liaison with the German and favourable terrain" had helped overcome deficiencies in North Africa.[19] The explanations for low Italian military effectiveness have often revolved around factors, such as small unit cohesion, esprit de corps, training, officer-to-man relations, intellectual preparation, ideology and spiritual support.[20] Relating Italian battlefield performance in the 1940s back to "at least the Renaissance period" and to a loose sense of popular loyalty to the state and the armed forces is not only a precarious explanation,[21] but also runs counter to research on combat motivation and behaviour of men in battle.[22] Yes, Italian recruits were drawn from several regions for their basic training and certainly there were cultural differences; but the question remains as to whether this affected their performance in December 1942 (after having served together for months or even years), or if faulty officer education prior to 1914 (a time during which most generals of the Second World War were educated) influenced decisions and performance in 1940 after twenty years of service in peacetime and in the field. Indeed, the most recent research on other armies in the Second World War has shown how fighting together outbalanced pre-war training and structural deficits.[23]

There is also another school of thought. Knox has been heavily attacked by Sadkovich for seizing "every opportunity to criticize

---

[18] Domenico Petracarro, "The Italian Army in Africa 1940–1943: An Attempt at Historical Perspective," *War & Society* 9, no. 2 (1991): 103–27, here 108.

[19] Petracarro, "Italian Army," 105, 114.

[20] Stanislav Andreski, "Causes of the Low Morale of the Italian Armed Forces in the Two World Wars," *Journal of Strategic Studies* 5, no. 2 (1982): 248–56; John Gooch, "Italian Military Competence," *Journal of Strategic Studies* 5, no. 2 (1982): 257–65; Alexander Lopasic, "Italian Military Performance in the Second World War: Some Considerations," *Journal of Strategic Studies* 5, no. 2 (1982): 270–75.

[21] See Davies, "Itali Sunt Imbelles."

[22] The classic account on the importance of small unit cohesion and situational factors on the front is Creveld, *Kampfkraft*, 54, 116, 124. Also Richard Holmes, *Acts of War: The Behaviour of Men in Battle* (London: Cassell, 2004).

[23] See e.g. Tarak Barkawi, *Soldiers of Empire: Indian and British Armies of World War II* (Cambridge: Cambridge University Press, 2017).

[the Italian Army], even when there was little reason to do so."[24] Sadkovich identified a mixture of wartime propaganda and post-war neglect as the cause of feeble knowledge about Italy's war effort and the persistence of ill-informed stereotypes.[25] In fact, Higham held that Sadkovich's claims "should make the reader think again about the nature of truth, objectivity, and the importance of revisionism."[26] Yet, Sadkovich, Sullivan and other scholars' work on Italian military effectiveness has largely centred on the North African theatre.[27] Ceva, Sadkovich, Greene and Massignani have argued that the Italian performance was belittled because of an exaggeration of Rommel's deeds, but better than commonly accepted[28]; an argument with which Knox himself concurred (in part).[29] More recently, Carrier has provided archival evidence of learning and adapting processes in the North African desert. He argued that the Italian forces became more efficient thanks to additional training, German assistance and the combat experience they gained.[30] This demonstrated that while the debates on Italian military effectiveness have been fruitful in revealing cultural and deep-rooted explanations for battlefield performance, they should never substitute for detailed archival research and in fact there still are tremendous gaps in the analysis of subjects such as the key decision-makers.

[24] James J. Sadkovich, "Anglo-American Bias and the Italo-Greek War of 1940–1941," *The Journal of Military History* 58, no. 4 (1994), 617–42, here 628.

[25] James J. Sadkovich, "Understanding Defeat: Reappraising Italy's Role in World War II," *Journal of Contemporary History* 24, no. 1 (1989): 27–61.

[26] Higham, "Introduction," x.

[27] The most detailed account is [Gen.] Mario Montanari, *Le operazioni in Africa Settentrionale*. 4 vols. (Rome: USSME, 1993–2000). A rare case where the memory and narratives of a campaign were analysed is Lucio Ceva, *Africa Settentrionale 1940–1943. Negli studi e nella letteratura* (Rome: Bonacci, 1982).

[28] Lucio Ceva, "The North African Campaign 1940–43: A Reconsideration," *Journal of Strategic Studies* 13, no. 1 (1990): 84–104; Jack Greene and Alessandro Massignani, *Rommel's North Africa Campaign* (Conshohocken: Combined Books, 1999); James J. Sadkovich, "Of Myths and Men: Rommel and the Italians in North Africa, 1940–1942," *The International History Review* 13, no. 2 (1991): 284–313; Sadkovich, "Understanding Defeat," 38ff.

[29] Knox, *Hitler's Italian Allies*, 154.

[30] Richard Carrier, "Some Reflections on the Fighting Power of the Italian Army in North Africa, 1940–1943," *War in History* 22, no. 4 (2015): 503–28.

There have been several studies on Mussolini as 'warlord' and his problematic relations with Hitler.[31] Yet, the *Comando Supremo* is poorly researched.[32] Lucio Ceva analysed Cavallero's actions in 1941–1942 on the basis of his diaries, describing his role in the ambiguous relationship between the military's upper echelons and Mussolini.[33] Likewise, the officer corps' education, structure and dynamics, are scantily researched.[34] The two best-known Italian officers—Pietro Badoglio (1871–1956) and Rodolfo Graziani (1882–1955)—have been subject to several studies.[35] However, both played almost no role in operations between 1941 and 1943. On the other hand, both marshals are important to understanding the Army's troubled memory. Graziani's military record was blemished by defeat in North Africa (and rather less so by his war crimes); he was put on trial after 1945 for his role as head of the Salò Republic's army, but still became a rallying point for neo-Fascists. Badoglio was dismissed in December 1940 and also remained absent from the centre of power until 25 July 1943. On the political left, Badoglio became the embodiment of a corrupt Fascist official and turncoat, while he was also criticised for his behaviour on *8 settembre*. This image of a cold and cruel general was linked to his role in the Caporetto

---

[31] See for example Richard J.B. Bosworth, *Mussolini* (London: Arnold, 2002); Hans Woller, *Mussolini. Der erste Faschist* (Munich: Beck, 2016); Denis Mack Smith, *Mussolini as a Military Leader* (Reading: Reading University Press, 1974); Burgwyn, *Mussolini*; Christian Goeschel, *Mussolini and Hitler: The Forging of the Fascist Alliance* (New Haven: Yale University Press, 2018).

[32] The only study on the general staff stands far below modern academic standards and is more an anecdotical work on various individuals; Carlo De Biase, *L'Aquila d'oro. Storia dello Stato Maggiore Italiano (1861–1945)* (Milan: Borghese, 1970).

[33] An abridged version was published in 1948. The AUSSME retained some parts, which it declassified for Ceva's study and the following new edition edited by Giuseppe Burcciante in 1984, see Ugo Cavallero, *Diario 1940-1943* (Rome: Ciarrapico, 1984) [hereafter cited as Cavallero Diary, date of entry]; Lucio Ceva, *La condotta italiana della guerra. Cavallero e il Comando Supremo 1941/1942* (Milan: Feltrinelli, 1975).

[34] For now, see Gian Luca Balestra, *La formazione degli ufficiali nell'accademia militare di Modena (1895–1939)* (Rome: USSME, 2000); Rochat, *Le guerre*, 174ff.

[35] Most detailed is Romano Canosa, *Graziani: Il Maresciallo d'Italia dalla Guerra d'Etiopia alla Repubblica di Salò* (Milan: Mondadori, 2005). Badoglio's memoirs were the only account by a senior officer to be translated into English, see [Marhsal] Pietro Badoglio, *Italy in the Second World War* (London: Oxford University Press, 1948). He certainly deserves a thorough biography. Dated, but still useful is Piero Pieri and Giorgio Rochat, *Pietro Badoglio* (Turin: UTET, 1974).

disaster during the First World War and the botched attack on Greece in 1940. Thus, his pronounced royalism and dislike for the Germans gave him a majority appeal, but did not necessarily transform him into a role model. Other key commanders have received even less attention[36]; only Giovanni Messe stands out. Schlemmer has shed more light on his career and his closeness to the Fascist regime,[37] yet there is no full-scale academic biography.[38] Schlemmer also pointed out that Messe had possibly fought the "battle over the memory" more successfully than the battles during the Second World War[39]; thereby hinting at Messe's vital role in establishing the Army's narrative. The vast output of Italian generals' memoirs—that still dominate much of the footnote landscape—has never been analysed.

The scholarship is similarly lamentable with regard to crucial units of the *Regio Esercito*, which have received—in contrast to the regular

---

[36] A much needed first start of small biographies has now been published; see Giovanni Cecini, *I generali di Mussolini* (Rome: Newton Compton, 2016). I would like to thank Pier Paolo Battistelli for drawing my attention to this. Ambrosio and Roatta are looked at more closely in the respective chapters in Osti Guerrazzi, *Italian Army*. On Marras see [Gen.] Sergio Pelagalli, *Efisio Marras. Addetto militare a Berlino 1936–1943* (Rome: USSME, 1994); also Luigi Emilio Longo, *L'attività degli addetti militari italiani all'estero fra le due guerre mondiali (1919–1939)* (Rome: USSME, 1999), 263ff. One positive development in this regard (albeit for the navy) is Fabio De Ninno, *Fascisti sul mare. La marina e gli ammiragli di Mussolini* (Bari: Laterza, 2017).

[37] Thomas Schlemmer, "Giovanni Messe. Ein italienischer General zwischen Koalitions- und Befreiungskrieg," in *Von Feldherren und Gefreiten. Zur biographischen Dimension des Zweiten Weltkriegs*, ed. Christian Hartmann (Munich: Oldenbourg, 2008), 33–44. See also the remarks on Messe's anti-communism and royalism in Osti Guerrazzi, *Noi non sappiamo odiare*.

[38] Despite shortcomings, the most helpful is Luigi Argentieri, *Messe. Soggetto di un'altra storia* (Bergam: Burgo, 1997); most recently various letters to his wife have been published (pre-selected by his son) with an introduction by Maria Teresa Giusti, see ibid., "Giovanni Messe. L'Uomo e il soldato," in *Lettere alla moglie. Dai fronti Greco-Albanese, Russo, Tunisino e dalla prigionia 1940–1944*, ed. Giovanni Messe (Milan: Mursia, 2018), 11–67.

More caution is advised in using Luigi Emilio Longo, *Giovanni Messe. L'ultimo Maresciallo d'Italia* (Rome: USSME, 2006); rather hagiographical is Italo Garzia, Carmelo Pasimeni, and Domenico Urgesi, eds., *Il Maresciallo d'Italia Giovanni Messe. Guerra, forze armate e politca nell'Italia del Novecento. Atti del convegno di studi (Mesagne 27–28 ottobre 2000)* (Mesagne: Congedo, 2003).

[39] Schlemmer, "Messe," 44.

infantry—much praise and are frequently referred to as 'elite'.[40] These include the *Bersaglieri*,[41] the *Alpini*, the *Folgore* paratroopers[42] and the armoured corps.[43] The artillery and individual divisions have not been researched with academic rigour,[44] and the existing scholarship is even weaker on the Blackshirt units.[45] The (short) span of the operations of the *Alpini* on the Eastern Front has led to a flood of memoir literature that still dominates how we view the campaign. And yet there is surprisingly little serious academic research on the *Alpini*.[46] Oliva wrote a journalistic overview,[47] Hamilton based her account merely on memoir literature,[48] while Mondini has offered a superb analysis of the *Alpini* myth.[49] Yet, these studies never scrutinised the *Alpini*'s narrative that came from the Eastern Front.

[40] The concept of elite units is problematic in itself. How do we measure elite status? Did the *Alpini* and *Bersaglieri* receive more training and better men, or more supply and better material?

[41] For now see Fermo Roggiani, *Bersaglieri d'Italia. Dal ponte di Goito a Beirut* (Milan: Cavallotti, 1983).

[42] Marco Di Giovanni, *I paracadutisti italiani: Volontari, miti e memoria della seconda guerra mondiale* (Gorizia: Ed. Goriziana, 1991); Paolo Morisi, *The Italian Folgore Parachute Division: Operations in North Africa 1940–1943* (Solihull: Helion 2016).

[43] The most helpful in English is Ian W. Walker, *Iron Hulls, Iron Hearts. Mussolin's Elite Armoured Divisions in North Africa* (Ramsbury: Crowood, 2012); Sweet, *Iron Arm*.

[44] Nonetheless helpful are Vittorio Luoni, *La "Pasubio" sul fronte russo* (Rome: Ateneo & Bizzarri, 1977); Giulio De Giorgi, *Con la divisione Ravenna: tutte le sue vicende sino al rientro dalla Russia 1939–1943* (Milan: Longanesi, 1973).

[45] The so-called Blackshirts of the Voluntary Militia for National Security (*Milizia volontaria per la sicurezza nazionale*, MVSN) were the military wing of the National Fascist Party (*Partito Nazionale Fascista*, PNF). A good English introduction is Piero Crociani and Pier Paolo Battistelli, *Italian Blackshirt, 1935–45* (Botley: Osprey, 2010).

[46] General Emilio Faldella's three volume semi-official history of the *Alpini* has to be treated with caution, but is still valuable for operational aspects, [Gen.] Emilio Faldella, *Storia delle truppe alpine. Vol. 3* (Milan: Cavallotti, 1972). See also Aldo Rasero, *Alpini della Julia. Storia della divisione miracolo* (Milan: Mursia, 1972); Aldo Rasero, *Tridentina avanti! Storia di una divisione alpina* (Milan: Mursia, 1982); Aldo Rasero, *L'eroica "Cuneense". Storia della divisione alpina martire* (Milan: Mursia, 1985).

[47] Gianni Oliva, *Storia degli Alpini. Dal 1872 a oggi* (Milan: Mondadori, 2001).

[48] Hope Hamilton, *Sacrifice on the Steppe: The Italian Alpine Corps in the Stalingrad Campaign, 1942–1943* (Havertown: Casemate, 2011).

[49] Marco Mondini, *Alpini. Parole e immagini di un mito guerriero* (Bari: Laterza, 2008). For the early myth creation see also Claudia De Marco, *Il mito degli Alpini. Vol. 1* (Udine: Gaspari, 2004).

The Italians on the Eastern Front

Indeed, the research on the Eastern Front leaves much to be desired. Besides the early flood of memoir literature, official histories[50] and journalistic accounts,[51] a conference in 1979 improved the scholarly treatment of the Eastern Front.[52] Yet, these small sketches were not linked to the ongoing debates on Italian military efficiency and often had an overview character.[53] In the 1980s, two German scholars based their work on the ARMIR on primary sources (from German archives). They focused mainly on operational aspects and coalition warfare. Förster presented the negative German view on the Eighth Army,[54] while Schreiber corrected the image of militarily inept allies.[55] Italian scholars have also used German sources to depict the *Alpini*'s retreat and to add in more shades of grey on the alleged uselessness of the ARMIR.[56]

Schlemmer wrote the first monograph on the Italians on the Eastern Front that went beyond operational matters.[57] His studies are fundamentally

---

[50] USSME, *Le operazioni del C.S.I.R. e dell'ARMIR dal Giugno 1941 all'Ottobre 1942* (Rome: USSME, 1947); Costantino De Franceschi et al., *I servizi logistici delle Unità Italiane al fronte russo (1941–1943)* (Rome: USSME, 1975); USSME, *Le operazioni delle Unità Italiane al fronte russo (1941–1943)* (Rome: USSME, 2000). This volume was first published in 1977 and subsequently updated in 1993 and in 2000. The cited page numbers are from the 2000 edition.

[51] E.g. the two-volume Aldo Valori, *La campagna di Russia. CSIR-ARMIR: 1941–1943* (Rome: Grafica nazionale editrice, 1951); Arrigo Petacco, *L'armata scomparsa. L'avventura degli italiani in Russia* (Milan: Mondadori, 1998).

[52] The result was an edited volume, see Enzo Collotti, ed., *Gli italiani sul fronte russo* (Bari: De Donato, 1982). Note also the contributions by Rinaldo Cruccu and Lucio Ceva in this volume.

[53] Aldo Gianbartolomei, "La campagna in Russia del CSIR e dei suoi veterani nell'ARMIR," in *L'Italia in guerra. Il terzo anno – 1942*, eds. Romain H. Rainero and Antonello Biagini (Gaeta: Stabilimento Grafico Militare, 1993), 273–96; Mario Gariboldi, "L'Italia in Russia: L'ARMIR," in *L'Italia in guerra. Il terzo anno – 1942*, eds. Romain H. Rainero and Antonello Biagini (Gaeta: Stabilimento Grafico Militare, 1993), 297–307.

[54] Jürgen Förster, "Il ruolo dell'8ª armata italiana dal punto di vista tedesco," in *Gli italiani sul fronte russo*, ed. Enzo Collotti (Bari: De Donato, 1982), 229–59.

[55] Gerhard Schreiber, "Italiens Teilnahme am Krieg gegen die Sowjetunion. Motive, Fakten und Folgen," in *Stalingrad. Ereignis – Wirkung – Symbol*, ed. Jürgen Förster (Munich: Piper, 1993), 250–92.

[56] Alessandro Massignani, *Alpini e tedeschi sul Don* (Novale di Valdagno: Rossato, 1991).

[57] Before him, Gentile had hinted at many research deficits in the research on Italian occupation policies; see Carlo Gentile, "Alle spalle dell'ARMIR: documenti sulla repressione antipartigiana al fronte russo," *Il Presente e la Storia* 53 (1998): 159–81.

important, as he is (arguably) the only scholar who has used German and Italian sources to discredit myths about the *campagna di Russia*. Schlemmer himself was initially interested, in the context of the debate on the Wehrmacht's involvement in the war of extermination, in the extent to which the Italian Army had participated in war crimes. In his brief literature review, he hinted at many problems linked to the *campagna di Russia*: notably the dominance of memoir literature and eyewitnesses defending their own narratives, which prevented an objective look at real events.[58] Schlemmer criticised the limited value of the official histories beyond operational matters, but also disapproved of the somewhat biased tendency in Enzo Collotti's edited volume and the almost complete neglect of the Eastern Front in Knox's works.[59] His subsequent essays further investigated the ARMIR's occupation policies[60] and relations with Soviet civilians and POWs.[61] Schlemmer stressed the Italians' awareness of the criminal character of the war in the East and their role as aggressors and not as victims. His results showed the difficulties in providing precise accounts of what actually happened. Schlemmer's only real operational study focused on the German 318th Infantry Regiment's retreat from the Don in winter 1942–1943—including its interplay with the Italians.[62]

[58] Schlemmer, *Italiener*, 4.

[59] Ibid., 5.

[60] Thomas Schlemmer, "Die comandi tappa der 8. Italienischen Armee und die deutsche Besatzungsherrschaft im Süden der Sowjetunion. Momentaufnahmen aus dem Spätjahr 1942," *Quellen und Forschungen aus italienischen Archiven* 88 (2008): 512–46.

[61] Thomas Schlemmer, "'Gefühlsmässige Verwandtschaft'? Zivilisten, Kriegsgefangene und das königlich-italienische Heer im Krieg gegen die Sowjetunion 1941 bis 1943," in *Die "Achse" im Krieg. Politik, Ideologie und Kriegführung 1939–1945*, eds. Lutz Klinkhammer, Amedeo Osti Guerrazzi, and Thomas Schlemmer (Paderborn: Schöningh, 2010), 368–97. A summary essay of Italy's political and military role in 1941 has recently been published in English, see Thomas Schlemmer, "Italy," in *Joining Hitler's Crusade: European Nations and the Invasion of the Soviet Union, 1941*, ed. David Stahel (Cambridge: Cambridge University Press, 2017), 134–57.

[62] Thomas Schlemmer, "'Tedeschi a piedi'. Der Rückzug deutscher und italienischer Truppen am Don im Winter 1942–1943 am Beispiel des Grenadierregiments 318," in *Annali dell'Istituto storico italo-germanico in Trento XXXII 2006* (Bologna: Il Mulino, 2007), 127–49. Some operational aspects were included in his "Das königlich-italienische Heer im Vernichtungskrieg gegen die Sowjetunion. Kriegführung und Besatzungspraxis einer vergessenen Armee 1941–1943," in *Faschismus in Italien und Deutschland. Studien zu Transfer und Vergleich*, eds. Armin Nolzen and Sven Reichardt (Göttingen: Wallstein, 2005), 148–75.

Schlemmer has attracted some criticism from Italian scholars: for example from Giorgio Scotoni, who has devoted a monograph to the *Alpini*'s occupation on the Don,[63] and more recently, Maria Teresa Giusti, who had written a groundbreaking study on Italian prisoners in Soviet hands,[64] which was followed by an overview on the war on the Eastern Front.[65] Both authors countered Schlemmer's arguments—or rather his tendency to liken Italian actions to a war of extermination. They have highlighted vital nuances between German and Italian occupational policies, even while avoiding backsliding to the *brava gente* myth. Indeed, the focus on occupation and war crimes led to the aforementioned problems—primarily a lack of well-founded studies on what actually happened and a tendency to swing the pendulum from *brava gente* to 'criminal *gente*'.

Other scholars have offered a history 'from below' through analysing soldiers' letters[66] and looking at the experience of war.[67] Giannuli has used reports of the Fascist secret police (the OVRA) to depict the Italian public's reactions to the happenings on the Eastern Front in general.[68] And two recent conference volumes analysed several aspects ranging from operations, to occupation, naval operations, logistics and memory.[69]

---

[63] Giorgio Scotoni, *Il nemico fidato. La guerra di sterminio in URSS e l'occupazione alpina sull'Alto Don* (Trento: Panorama, 2013).

[64] Maria Teresa Giusti, *I prigionieri italiani in Russia* (Bologna: Il Mulino, 2003; updated and slightly revised in 2014).

[65] Maria Teresa Giusti, *La campagna di Russia, 1941–1943* (Bologna: Il Mulino, 2016).

[66] Gustavo Corni, "Briefe von der Ostfront. Ein Vergleich deutscher und italienischer Quellen," in *Die "Achse" im Krieg. Politik, Ideologie und Kriegführung 1939–1945*, eds. Lutz Klinkhammer, Amedeo Osti Guerrazzi, and Thomas Schlemmer (Paderborn: Schöningh, 2010), 398–432; Nicolas G. Virtue, "'We Istrians Do Very Well in Russia': Istrian Combatants, Fascist Propaganda, and Brutalization on the Eastern Front," in *Italy and the Second World War. Alternative Perspectives*, eds. Emanuele Sica and Richard Carrier (Leiden: Brill, 2018), 266–98.

[67] Amedeo Osti Guerrazzi and Thomas Schlemmer, "I soldati italiani nella campagna di Russia. Propaganda, esperienza, memoria," in *Annali dell'Istituto storico italo-germanico in Trento XXXIII 2007* (Bologna: Il Mulino, 2008), 385–417.

[68] Aldo Gianuli, *Le spie del Duce (1939–1943). Lettere e documenti segreti sulla campagna di Russia* (Sesto San Giovanni: Mimesis, 2018).

[69] Antonello Biagini and Antonio Zarcone, eds., *La campagna di Russia. Nel 70° anniversario dell'inizio dell'intervento dello CSIR* (Rome: Nuova Cultura, 2013); Olga Dubrovina, ed., *Battaglie in Russia. Il Don e Stalingrado 75 anni dopo* (Milan: Ed. Unicopli, 2018).

Burgwyn included some remarks in his general overview[70] and his essay on the Eastern Front touched on important subjects, such as occupation, ideology and coalition warfare.[71] Burgwyn also emphasised evident differences between Italian and German behaviour on the Eastern Front.[72] An excellent master's dissertation consulted the microfilm reels in Washington to investigate the 'brutalisation' of the Italian Army.[73] The author included Bartov's ideas on the Wehrmacht, which influenced also Giusti's study.[74] However, one should consider that recent scholarship has challenged many of Bartov's theses and one must not neglect the major influence of situational aspects.[75] Trigg and Buttar have both written helpful overviews of the wider operations on the Don for the general reader, but did not consult Italian archival material.[76]

Russian scholars have never devoted much attention to the Italian involvement on the Eastern Front.[77] Their focus has always been either the Red Army itself or the Wehrmacht as its main enemy. Yet, some studies on the Italian involvement do exist and will be included in the following—as will Russian studies on the Red Army's operations and memoirs by Soviet commanders. Scotoni has edited a volume, which offers a collection of Soviet points of view on the military operations.[78] Based on several assessments in the memoir literature and official histories, Scotoni

---

[70] Burgwyn, *Mussolini*, 113–27, 201–24.

[71] H. James Burgwyn, "The Legacy of Italy's Participation in the German War against the Soviet Union: 1941–1943," *Mondo Contemporaneo* 2 (2011): 161–81.

[72] Burgwyn, "The Legacy," 180.

[73] Nicolas G. Virtue, "Fascist Italy and the Barbarisation of the Eastern Front, 1941–43" (MA diss., University of Calgary, 2007).

[74] Omer Bartov, *Hitler's Army. Soldiers, Nazis, and War in the Third Reich* (Oxford: Oxford University Press, 1992) and his *The Eastern Front, 1941–1945. German Troops and the Barbarisation of Warfare* (London: Routledge, 2001).

[75] Neitzel and Welzer, *Soldaten*, 321ff. See also the most recent contribution by David Stahel, "The Wehrmacht and National Socialist Military Thinking," *War in History* 23, no. 3 (2017): 336–61.

[76] Jonathan Trigg, *Death on the Don: The Destruction of Germany's Allies on the Eastern Front, 1941–1944* (New York: History Press, 2013); Prit Buttar, *On a Knife's Edge: The Ukraine, November 1942–March 1943* (Oxford: Osprey, 2018).

[77] Vancetti G. Safronov, *Italyanski voiska na sovetsko-germanskom fronte 1941–1943* (Moscow: Nauka, 1990), 5ff.

[78] Giorgio Scotoni, *L'Armata Rossa e la disfatta italiana (1942–43)* (Trento: Panorama, 2007).

has shown the Italians' stubborn resistance and lively counter-attacks on the Don, which forced the Soviets to employ their armour sooner than they had anticipated.[79] Filatov published a general overview of the Italian conduct on the Eastern Front in 1969 (translated into Italian in 1979)[80] and Safronov followed suit with a more detailed depiction, also by using Russian sources.[81] Yet neither of these authors consulted Italian primary documents.

Even though the war on the Eastern Front has been thoroughly researched (for the German side), there are still many gaps in the study of coalition warfare—this, notwithstanding the fact that non-German soldiers contributed up to one-third of Axis forces against the Soviet Union (in total around 700,000 non-German soldiers took part in operations in 1941).[82] Additionally, most studies on coalition warfare have focused on the early period of the Second World War, the strategic level, relied largely on German views, or did not include the Eastern Front.[83] A German-Italian conference resulted in a valuable edited volume that looked at several levels of the 'Axis at war'.[84] Massignani's piece presented the creation

[79] Scotoni, *L'Armata Rossa*, 29, 313.

[80] Georgy S. Filatov, *La campagna orientale di Mussolini* (Milan: Mursia, 1979).

[81] Safronov, *Italyanski voiska*.

[82] Rolf-Dieter Müller, *An der Seite der Wehrmacht. Hitlers ausländische Helfer beim 'Kreuzzug gegen den Bolschewismus' 1941–1945* (Berlin: Ch. Links, 2007), 243ff; David Stahel, ed., *Joining Hitler's Crusade. European Nations and the Invasion of the Soviet Union, 1941* (Cambridge: Cambridge University Press, 2017). Still valuable is Peter Gosztony, *Hitlers Fremde Heere. Das Schicksal der nichtdeutschen Armeen im Ostfeldzug* (Düsseldorf: Econ, 1976).

[83] Still helpful are Renzo De Felice, *Mussolini l'alleato, 1940–1945. I. L'Italia in guerra 1940–1943. Tomo 1 – Dalla guerra 'breve' alla guerra lunga* (Turin: Einaudi, 1990); Renzo De Felice, *Mussolini l'alleato, 1940–1945. I. L'Italia in guerra 1940–1943. Tomo 2 – Crisi e agonia del regime* (Turin: Einaudi, 1990); Brian R. Sullivan, "The Path Marked Out by History: The German-Italian Alliance, 1939–1943," in *Hitler and His Allies in World War II*, ed., Jonathan R. Adelman (London: Routledge, 2007), 116–51; Richard L. DiNardo, *Germany and the Axis Powers: From Coalition to Collapse* (Lawrence: University Press of Kansas, 2005); Malte König, *Kooperation als Machtkampf. Das faschistische Achsenbündnis Berlin-Rom im Krieg 1940/41* (Cologne: SH-Verlag, 2007); Jürgen Förster, *Stalingrad. Risse im Bündnis 1942/43* (Freiburg: Rombach, 1975); Gerhard Schreiber, "Problemi generali dell'alleanza italo-tedesca 1933–1941," in *Gli italiani sul fronte russo*, ed. Enzo Collotti (Bari: De Donato, 1982), 63–117.

[84] Lutz Klinkhammer, Amedeo Osti Guerrazzi, and Thomas Schlemmer, eds., *Die "Achse" im Krieg. Politik, Ideologie und Kriegführung 1939–1945* (Paderborn: Schöningh, 2010).

of stereotypes after 1943, and argued that cooperation on the operational and tactical level had been surprisingly efficient before this point.[85] On the other hand, Italian perspectives on the Germans as allies are rare, but show a similar level of criticism.[86] Indeed, coalition warfare is never easy and is full of reciprocal stereotypes, competition and backhand slandering of one's ally. The British-French-American coalition too was full of such episodes that should make us think again whether the relatively smooth cooperation at the strategic level also held true with regard to operational and tactical matters. As a remark from the German Naval Attaché in Rome from August 1942 shows, these layers ought not be blurred into one: "the senior military leaders and the simple soldiers generally got along quite well, whereas the cases of friction mainly occurred between mid-level officers who had to implement the agreements in practice."[87] Future scholars will have to look at this level in particular.

Memory

There are also historiographical problems with regard to memory. In the Italian case, the main focuses have been the legacy of Mussolini's regime and the role of the *Resistenza* as a civil religion and rallying ground of anti-Fascism.[88] While this *Resistenza* myth was durable, the memory was never static.[89] In one way or another, the experience of war played a vital role in

---

[85] Alessandro Massignani, "Die italienischen Streitkräfte und der Krieg der 'Achse'," in *Die "Achse" im Krieg. Politik, Ideologie und Kriegführung 1939–1945*, eds. Lutz Klinkhammer, Amedeo Osti Guerrazzi, and Thomas Schlemmer (Paderborn: Schöningh, 2010), 122–46.

[86] James J. Sadkovich, "German Military Incompetence Through Italian Eyes," *War in History* 1, no. 1 (1994): 39–62; Scianna, "Rommel Almighty."

[87] BA-MA, RM 11/61, Löwisch to Naval High Command, 6 Aug. 1942, fol.2.

[88] See foremost Santo Peli, *La Resistenza in Italia. Storia e critica* (Turin: Einaudi, 2004). The best overviews in English are provided by Philip Cooke, *The Legacy of the Italian Resistance* (New York: Palgrave Macmillan, 2011). See also Pietro Craveri and Gaetano Quagliariello, eds., *La seconda guerra mondiale e la sua memoria* (Soveria Mannelli: Rubbettino, 2006); Filippo Focardi, *La guerra della memoria: la Resistenza nel dibattito politico italiano dal 1945 a oggi* (Bari: Laterza, 2005); Focardi, *Il cattivo tedesco*; Gianni Oliva, *L'alibi della Resistenza, ovvero come abbiamo vinto la seconda guerra mondiale* (Milan: Mondadori, 2003).

[89] Lutz Klinkhammer, "Kriegserinnerung in Italien im Wechsel der Generationen. Ein Wandel der Perspektive?" in *Erinnerungskulturen. Deutschland, Italien und Japan seit 1945*, eds. Christoph Cornelißen, Lutz Klinkhammer, and Wolfgang Schwentker (Frankfurt: Fischer, 2003), 333–43.

the founding myth of the First Republic.[90] The end of the Cold War spurred debates about Italy's 'civil religion' along with revisionist attempts to downplay the character of Mussolini's regime, bitter truths about the de facto civil war,[91] and other fundamental questions about the Fascist *ventennio* for the course of Italian history.[92] Indeed, if one investigates academic writings on Italian collective memory, it is apparent how the recollections of some memories have overshadowed other periods and social groups. Put simply, the memory of 1940–1943 was reduced to purely military matters and mainly produced by the military sphere, while the collective memory (and scholarship) focused rather more on political events and the anti-fascist fight between 1943 and 1945.[93] In fact this selective and 'divided memory' has been recognised,[94] but the fault lines were usually drawn between different political forces. In the one corner were the supporters of the *Resistenza*, and on the other those who fought with Mussolini in the so-called *Italian Social Republic* (RSI, also referred to as the Republic of Salò) who often formed the new (extreme) Right in post-war Italy.[95] A necessary next step would be to explore the Army's commemoration of the conflict and how these myths were cemented and narratives 'negotiated'.

Dividing lines in terms of different institutions have barely been analysed; thus we know little about the Army after 1945. This is unsurprising, as in the Italian collective memory the armed forces were widely connected to defeat and then to the shameful *8 settembre*; 1940–1943

[90] Leonardo Paggi, *Il popolo dei morti. La repubblica italiana nata dalla guerra (1940–1946)* (Bologna: Il Mulino, 2009); Gustavo Corni, "Von der nordafrikanischen Wüste bis zum Don: Der Zweite Weltkrieg in der öffentlichen Erinnerung Italiens nach 1945," in *Krieg. Erinnerung. Geschichtswissenschaft*, eds. Siegfried Mattl et al. (Vienna: Böhlau, 2009), 87–110.

[91] The groundbreaking work of Claudio Pavone, *Una guerra civile* (1991) is now available in English, *A Civil War: A History of the Italian Resistance* (London: Verso, 2013).

[92] Richard J. B. Bosworth, "A Country Split in Two? Contemporary Italy and Its Usable and Unusable Pasts," *History Compass* 4, no. 6 (2006), 1089–1101; Isnenghi, *La tragedia necessaria*.

[93] Giorgio Rochat, "La guerra di Grecia," in *I luoghi della memoria. Vol. 3: Strutture ed eventi dell'Italia unita*, ed. Mario Isnenghi (Bari: Laterza, 1997), 346–64, here 348.

[94] John Foot, *Italy's Divided Memory* (New York: Palgrave Macmillan, 2009); Mario Isnenghi, *Le guerre degli italiani. Parole, immagini, ricordi 1848–1945* (Bologna: Il Mulino, 1989; reprinted 2005).

[95] Davide Conti, *Gli uomini di Mussolini* (Turin: Einaudi, 2017); Giuseppe Parlato, *Fascisti senza Mussolini. Le origini del neofascismo in Italia, 1943–1948* (Bologna: Il Mulino, 2006); Francesco Germinario, *L'altra memoria. L'Estrema destra, Salò e la Resistenza* (Turin: Bollatti, 1999).

could thus have few positive connotations.[96] Even before Fascism and 8 September 1943, the defeats at Custoza (1866), Adwa (1896) and Caporetto (1917) hardly improved the prestige of the Italian military and had a lasting legacy.[97] After 1945, the victories and victors of the First World War were—despite (or maybe because of) Fascist rambling during the *ventennio*—sidelined outside the military sphere after 1945; instead, the *Risorgimento* of the nineteenth century became the desired link to the second period of 'national awakening' after 1943. However, the Italian Armed Forces after 1945 are even less examined—including their memory and dealings with the legacies of the Second World War.[98] Only a handful of studies looked at how society and individuals commemorated the war and the fallen (soldiers),[99] the memory of internment,[100] or the role of veterans in postwar Italy.[101]

The master narrative of the Italian Army was to blame Mussolini for plunging the country (and army) into an 'unwanted war' with inadequate materiel. However, mainstream politics was, despite the focus on the anti-fascist struggle after 8 September 1943, more influential in the contested memory of the period between 1940 and 1943 than some authors would have us believe. At the same time it is true that 'epic

---

[96] See Mario Isnenghi's multi-volume *I luoghi della memoria*; Giovanni Belardelli et al., eds., *Miti e storia dell'Italia unita* (Bologna: Il Mulino, 1999).

[97] John Gooch, *The Italian Army and the First World War* (Cambridge: Cambridge University Press, 2014), 16, 28. Garibaldi might be the only political-military figure (of a peculiar kind) that developed a strong cult of remembrance outside military circles; see Lucy Riall, *Garibaldi. Invention of a Hero* (New Haven: Yale University Press, 2007).

[98] Virgilio Ilari, *Storia militare della prima repubblica 1943–1993* (Ancona: Nuove Ricerche, 1994); Leopoldo Nuti, *L'Esercito italiano nel secondo dopoguerra 1945–1950* (Rome: USSME, 1989); Agostino Bistarelli, "Le forze armate nella Repubblica: memoria e interpretazioni della transizione," in *Violenza, tragedia e memoria della Repubblica sociale italiana*, ed. Sergio Bugiardini (Rome: Carocci, 2006), 291–307.

[99] Gustavo Corni, *Raccontare la guerra. La memoria organizzata* (Milan: Mondadori, 2012); Guri Schwarz, *Tu mi devi seppellir. Riti funebri e culto nazionale alle origini della Repubblica* (Turin: UTET, 2010).

[100] Giorgio Rochat, "La prigionia di guerra," in *I luoghi della memoria. Vol. 3: Strutture ed eventi dell'Italia unita*, ed. Mario Isnenghi (Bari: Laterza, 1997), 381–402.

[101] Agostino Bistarelli, *La storia del ritorno. I reduci italiani del secondo dopoguerra* (Turin: Bollati Boringhieri, 2007); Claudio Pavone, "Appunti sul problema dei reduci," in *L'altro dopoguerra. Roma e il sud, 1943–1945*, ed. Nicola Gallerano (Milan: FrancoAngeli, 1985), 89–106; Marco Mondini and Guri Schwarz, *Dalla guerra alla pace. Retoriche e pratiche della smobilitazione nell'Italia del Novecento* (Verona: Cierre, 2007).

depictions' of some operations and units were always retained within the military: the *Folgore* paratroopers, the navy's frogmen, the *Aeronautica*'s torpedo bombers, and the *Alpini* in Russia.[102] Particularly the *Alpini* memory was extended well beyond the military sphere. The operations on the Eastern Front—chiefly the retreat from the Don—became part of the almost holy Italian topoi of the Second World War, but hardly any study exists on how this myth and memory was formed. Schlemmer has explained how the experience and memory were full of contradictions and how the victim narrative had been laid over actual events.[103] Osti Guerrazzi and Schlemmer scrutinised the formation of the misbalanced memory and victim perspective. They considered the *campagna di Russia* was used as part of an attempt to free 'official Italy' from the accusation of treason, to raise one's own profile, to rebuild trust in public organs, and to lay the blame for crimes on the Germans.[104] Yet, their analysis did not include the military's perspective and was mainly focused on war crimes rather than combat efficiency. Rochat's analysis of the memoir literature deriving from the Eastern Front itself leaves many questions open.[105] Indeed, it was very telling for the influence of the memoir literature that in a large-scale scholarly project on Italian *lieux de mémoire*, the *Alpini*-veteran Nuto Revelli, whose prior works had been anything but scholarly or objective,[106] wrote the section on the Eastern Front.[107]

This review of the existing literature shows the many remaining desirabilities and unanswered questions: Has the *Resistenza* myth—in its public form—been a welcome narrative for the post-1943 Italian Army? Did the Army (and 'official Italy') silently accept that it had become a

[102] Rochat, "La guerra di Grecia," 349.

[103] Thomas Schlemmer, "Zwischen Erfahrung und Erinnerung. Die Soldaten des italienischen Heeres im Krieg gegen die Sowjetunion," *Quellen und Forschungen aus italienischen Archiven und Bibliotheken* 85 (2005), 425–66. The article can be seen as an early version of Osti Guerrazzi and Schlemmer, "I soldati italiani."

[104] Osti Guerrazzi and Schlemmer, "I soldati italiani," 414–17.

[105] Giorgio Rochat, "Memorialistica e storiografia sulla campagna italiana di Russia 1941-1943," in *Gli italiani sul fronte russo*, ed. Enzo Collotti (Bari: De Donato, 1982), 465–82; also Giorgio Rochat, *L'Esercito italiano in pace e in guerra* (Milan: Rara, 1991), 305–19.

[106] Schlemmer, *Italiener*, 4.

[107] Nuto Revelli, "La ritirata di Russia," in *I luoghi della memoria. Vol. 3: Strutture ed eventi dell'Italia unita*, ed. Mario Isnenghi (Bari: Laterza, 1997), 365–80.

laughing stock abroad? Not only will an investigation of these questions contribute to a more academic assessment of the Italian military, but it will also hint at 'silenced pasts' and improve our knowledge of Italy's collective and distinct institutional memories. In fact, the 'Fascist War' of 1940–1943 is fundamental to understand the ensuing civil war and the Cold War fault lines. In order to understand the Italian Army, the mindset of its officers and its historical framework, it is necessary to begin with a short introduction by looking at the *Risorgimento*, the colonial endeavours, and the First World War.[108] Not least because most senior officers in the Second World War had been junior or even mid-level officers between 1911 and 1918 and gained their formative experiences in these years.[109]

---

[108] The best overview on this period remains John Gooch, *Army, State and Society in Italy, 1870–1915* (London: Macmillan, 1989). See also Lorenzo Benadusi, *Ufficiale e gentiluomo. Virtù civili e valori militari in Italia, 1896–1918* (Milan: Feltrinelli, 2015).

[109] Rochat, *L'Esercito italiano*, 113–30.

CHAPTER 3

The Italian Army Before the Second World War (1861–1940)

The First World War, the Colonies and the Army Under Fascism

The *Risorgimento* led to the (late) creation of an Italian nation state and a unified Army (1861). Yet, strong regional peculiarities and the lack of any successful military campaign burdened the armed profession, which never gained a prestigious role in society. Faced with the concept of a nation in arms that had attracted popularity after Garibaldi's endeavours and the French experiences in 1870–1871, the Italian Army was prefixed with the word 'Royal' in February 1879 to underscore its loyalty to the King.[1] Military service served as a tool to bridge regional differences, as it mixed men from at least two different regions and trained them in yet another—a process which did not necessarily advance small unit cohesion. However, it shows the Army's political role from its very beginning: not only was it meant to 'create Italians', but regional recruitment also gave the military commands a better hold over the population. The widening gap with civil society was apparent during the campaigns to suppress the so-called *brigantaggio* (mainly in southern Italy). At the high point in the 1880s, up to 100,000 soldiers had to be employed for this domestic counter-insurgency campaign. At the same time, the *Regio Esercito* suffered a number of setbacks in colonial undertakings in

[1] De Leonardis, *L'Italia*, 9.

© The Author(s) 2019
B. M. Scianna, *The Italian War on the Eastern Front, 1941–1943*, Italian and Italian American Studies, https://doi.org/10.1007/978-3-030-26524-3_3

Africa. The battles of Dogali (1887), Amba Alagi (1895), and finally at Adwa (1896) were humiliating defeats for an aspiring European power in the age of imperialism.[2] In 1911, Italian leaders decided to embark on another adventure: the conquest of the Ottoman provinces in today's Libya. The war became relatively popular in Italy, but while the Ottomans accepted defeat in 1912, the invasion unleashed a resistance movement that was combatted with ruthlessness and accompanied by many Italian war crimes until 1932.

Meanwhile a storm was gathering in Europe. When war broke out in 1914, Italy declared her neutrality, as there was no *casus foederis* with the German Empire and Austria-Hungary, who attacked the Entente and not vice versa. In a decision that was met with accusations of egoism and treason, Italy placed its bets on the Entente and entered the war in May 1915. In the following three years, the Italians suffered heavy casualties under the aegis of General Luigi Cadorna (1850–1928), who became a symbol for inept leadership, and the frontlines were locked in an indecisive stalemate against Austrian-Hungarian (and later German) forces.[3] Yet, even after its worst year in 1917, culminating in the Caporetto disaster, the Italian Army managed to reorganise itself on the Piave river—before British and French help arrived. General Armando Diaz (1861–1928) initiated reforms and led the Army to victory in the battle of Vittorio Veneto in October 1918 (with allied help).[4] Victory came at a high price however. The death toll amounted to around 650,000 men—almost three times the casualty figure between 1940 and 1943 (230,000).[5] Additionally, the Paris Peace Conference turned into a disaster. It discredited the Italian politicians and led to the legend of the 'mutilated victory'. Irregular units and renegade officers under Gabriele D'Annunzio seized Fiume (today's Rijeka) and demobilisation of the Army was not the only concern. Instead of celebrating the victories of the Piave and Vittorio Veneto, the investigation into the responsibilities

---

[2] More soldiers died at Adwa on 1 March 1896 than in all three campaigns of the *Risorgimento*. On the importance of the colonial wars, see e.g. Giuseppe Maria Finaldi, *Italian National Identity in the Scramble for Africa: Italy's African Wars in the Era of Nation Building, 1870–1900* (Bern: Peter Lang, 2009).

[3] For general operations, see foremost Gooch, *Italian Army*.

[4] Ibid., 226–301.

[5] Rochat, *Le guerre*, 442.

behind the Caporetto disaster was a humiliation for the men in *grigio-verde* (the grey-green Italian field uniform).[6]

Moreover, the Army was involved in the domestic uproar of the time and became notably politicised between 1919 and 1922. Military elites flirted with the continuation of a stronger military rule, based on the recent war experiences.[7] Therefore, the military, by and large, welcomed the Fascist seizure of power in October 1922. Mussolini guaranteed its position in the state and offered a return to stable conditions after the traumatic experiences of the civil-war like domestic situation, the Fiume imbroglio, and the drastic demobilisation.[8] The military establishment thus secured its place in the new regime and did not intervene to stop the foundation of Mussolini's dictatorship on 3 January 1925.[9] In turn, it retained much of its autonomy, continued its staunch monarchist tradition,[10] but also shared Mussolini's expansionist goals.[11] Indeed, the Italians constantly waged war in their colonies. In Libya, the brutal 're-conquista' started even before the advent of Fascism and continued until 1932.[12] The following three years were the only time when Italian soldiers were at peace until the Second World War. In October 1935, Mussolini effectively started the *guerra fascista* with his invasion of Ethiopia (at the time mainly called Abyssinia). While the regular operations ended in May 1936, hostilities never ceased completely and the counter-insurgency campaign continued until the start of the Second

---

[6] Marco Mondini, "La festa mancata. I militari e la memoria della Grande Guerra, 1918–1923," *Contemporanea* 7, no. 4 (2004): 555–78; Gooch, *Italian Army*, 302ff.; Benadusi, *Ufficiale e gentiluomo*, 311–27.

[7] Marco Mondini, "Between Subversion and Coup d'État: Military Power and Politics After the Great War (1919–1922)," *Journal of Modern Italian Studies* 11, no. 4 (2006): 445–64; Giorgio Rochat, *L'Esercito italiano da Vittorio Veneto a Mussolini, 1919–1925* (Bari: Laterza, 2006; first ed. 1967).

[8] Rochat, *Le guerre*, 145ff.

[9] Ibid., 183.

[10] Ibid., 147–49.

[11] John Gooch, *Mussolini and His Generals: The Armed Forces and Fascist Foreign Policy, 1922–1940* (Cambridge: Cambridge University Press, 2007), 188ff.; Robert Mallett, *Mussolini and the Origins of the Second World War, 1933–1940* (Basingstoke: Palgrave, 2003), 5, 9.

[12] John Gooch, "Re-conquest and Suppression: Fascist Italy's Pacification of Libya and Ethiopia, 1922–39," *Journal of Strategic Studies* 28, no. 6 (2005): 1005–32; Federica Saini Fasanotti, *Libia 1922–1931. Le operazioni militari italiane* (Rome: USSME, 2012).

World War.[13] Yet contrary to the oft-held assumption that Italy barely managed to achieve victory in the regular campaign, contemporary military observers were rather positive in their assessment of the Italian efforts.[14]

Shortly afterwards Mussolini plunged up to 80,000 soldiers—chiefly poorly trained Blackshirts—into the Spanish Civil War.[15] As mentioned-above, the Italian efforts in Spain have repeatedly cast in a bad light, drawing to a large amount on propaganda. The British military attaché noted these biased depictions, stating that "reports of the actual conduct of the Italian troops have generally been so coloured by political prejudice on one side or the other that is has been extremely difficult to arrive at the truth."[16] Once Franco's victory became likely, most of the Italian forces returned home, and Mussolini immediately started the next chapter of his aggressive foreign policy by annexing Albania in April 1939. All these interventions had damaging consequences: they emptied ammunition stocks, diminished time for reform and training, and swallowed large parts of the military budget, which could not be used for new material or increased pay to attract bright junior officers.[17] But the campaigns did not come and go without effect. The British military attaché in Rome described the invasion of Albania as "an example of the great progress made by the Italian Army in military organisation

---

[13] Nicola Labanca, *La guerra d'Etiopia, 1935–1941* (Bologna: Il Mulino, 2015); Federica Saini Fasanotti, *Etiopia 1936–1940. Le operazioni di polizia coloniale nelle fonti dell'Esercito italiano* (Rome: USSME, 2010).

[14] Bastian Matteo Scianna, "A Prelude to Total War? The Abyssinian War (1935–36) in the Eyes of Foreign Military Observers," *The International Journal of Military History and Historiography* 38, no. 1 (2018): 5–33.

[15] John F. Coverdale, *Italian Intervention in the Spanish Civil War* (Princeton: Princeton University Press, 1975); Brian R. Sullivan, "Fascist Italy's Military Involvement in the Spanish Civil War," *The Journal of Military History* 59, no. 4 (1995): 697–727; Rochat, *Le guerre*, 98ff. On the memory, see Gabriele Ranzato, "La guerra di Spagna," in *I luoghi della memoria. Strutture ed eventi*, ed. Mario Isnenghi (Bari: Laterza, 1997), 331–44.

[16] TNA, WO 106/6086, Col. R.O. Stone—Annual Report 1937, 5 Jan. 1938, fos.26–27. According to Corum the Italian airforce had "a competent officer corps and proved in Spain that it could learn lessons and adapt doctrine", quoted in James S. Corum, "The Spanish Civil War: Lessons Learned and Not Learned by the Great Powers," *The Journal of Military History* 62, no. 2 (1998): 313–34, here 333.

[17] Rochat, *Le guerre*, 127ff.; Brian R. Sullivan, "The Italian Armed Forces, 1918–40," in *Military Effectiveness: Vol. 2: The Interwar Period*, eds. Allan R. Millett and Williamson Murray (Cambridge: Cambridge University Press, 1988), 169–217.

on a large scale. Although the opposition was negligible, it was no mean feat to transport a force of about 30,000 men, disembark it in Albania at three separate ports and occupy all the strategic points in the country in so short a time. The General Staff has undoubtedly learned valuable lessons from experience in Abyssinia and Spain."[18] In order to provide a better impression how Italy entered the Second World War, the following section will provide a brief assessment of the Army's readiness for war in 1940, its material, doctrine and 'human resources'.

READINESS FOR WAR: 8 MILLION BAYONETS OR 8 MILLION MYTHS?

There are four vital assumptions about the Italian Army on the eve of the world war that are essential to understanding its performance, its inadequacies, and memories of the subsequent campaigns: (1) The insufficient industrial base; (2) Antiquated and scarce material and equipment; (3) Inadequate doctrine; and (4) Incapable officers and poorly trained NCOs and ranks. The following will briefly address these fields and hint at the need for further research and comparisons to other armies, which may alter our view on these assumptions. In a way, all these issues reflect uncritical ideas of a 'superhuman Wehrmacht' that allegedly possessed the best weapons, doctrines and officers. Indeed, recent scholarship has corrected many flawed assumptions about the operational art and strategic genius in the German Army,[19] including the much propagandised fighting power of the Waffen-SS.[20] According to Marco Sigg, the practical application of the famous 'mission command' (*Auftragstaktik*) was different to what the myth implies: command and control was much stricter and more centralised, the possibility for initiative depended heavily on the superior officers, ideas how to use this freedom varied greatly, and independent actions in fact often went against the higher

---

[18] TNA, WO 106/6086, Col. Brocas Burrows—The Italian Army, 4 May 1939, fol.3.

[19] Gerhard P. Groß, *Mythos und Wirklichkeit. Geschichte des operativen Denkens im deutschen Heer von Moltke d.Ä. bis Heusinger* (Paderborn: Schöningh, 2012), 200ff.; Geoffrey P. Megargee, *Inside Hitler's High Command* (Lawrence: University Press of Kansas, 2000), xiv.

[20] Jochen Lehnhardt, *Die Waffen-SS: Geburt einer Legende. Himmlers Krieger in der NS-Propaganda* (Paderborn: Schöningh, 2017).

command's intentions and undermined unity of action, i.e. they were not necessarily *Auftragstaktik*, but simply disregard for orders.[21]

THE ECONOMY: INSUFFICIENT INDUSTRIAL BASE

The basis to waging war lies in a strong economy. The Second World War was characterised by a technological race, in which material quality mattered as much as quantity.[22] Of all major Western powers, Italy's economic foundations were the weakest, and her population was the least educated, most agricultural, and poorest. Consequently, Italian society produced a shortage of technical expertise, which resulted in problems e.g. to find an adequate number of engineers and mechanics.[23] Many large companies had become state-owned during the crises of the 1930s and held a strong position *vis-à-vis* the Fascist authorities through their monopolies, which opened way to inefficiency and expensive products.[24] Neither did the country possess vital raw materials. Her coal and steel output was meagre and once the war started she had to rely largely on shipments (and lectures)[25] from Germany, which defined her war economy and had painful political consequences.[26] In the 1920s, the Italians had cut costs by relying on wartime surplus material that meshed with doctrine and was then still up-to-date.[27] Yet, as shown above, many resources had been squandered by the wars in Spain and Abyssinia, which led to demands for a break of several years in which to replenish

---

[21] Marco Sigg, *Der Unterführer als Feldherr im Taschenformat. Theorie und Praxis der Auftragstaktik im deutschen Heer 1869 bis 1945* (Paderborn: Schöningh, 2014), 173ff.

[22] For different interpretations as to the war-winning effect of the 'simple' Soviet T-34 and the land war on the Eastern Front, in contrast to the Allied activities in the West, see Phillips Payson O'Brien, *How the War Was Won: Air-Sea Power and Allied Victory in World War II* (Cambridge: Cambridge University Press, 2015). For an opposite view, see Richard Overy, *Russia's War* (New York: Penguin, 1998), 323ff.; Alexander Hill, *The Red Army and the Second World War* (Cambridge: Cambridge University Press, 2016), 4.

[23] Knox, *Hitler's Italian Allies*, 30.

[24] Ibid., 40ff. A Ministry for War Production was only created in February 1943.

[25] ACS, T-821/9/IT 24/322-338, Verbale colloquio Cavallero e Keitel (sera), 25 Aug. 1941, fs.331–32. See Keitel's comments on restructuring the Italian war economy along German lines; and Cavallero's reply.

[26] Angela Raspin, *The Italian War Economy, 1940–1943* (New York: Garland, 1986).

[27] Rochat, *Le guerre*, 188.

stocks.[28] The military's forecasts in 1939 also noted a limited capability to produce new material up until 1941, which would severely hamper ongoing operations of the—incomplete—formations.[29]

Indeed, Italy's entry into the war in June 1940 and the parallel start of rearmament programs meant modern equipment only became available in greater amounts in 1942, by which time it was often out-dated, whereas combat operations consumed large quantities of ammunition and raw materials. In particular, vehicles, tanks, warships and merchantmen and ammunition remained the Italian Achilles heel. Mussolini's regime produced only around 60,000 transport vehicles, 17,000 artillery guns of varying calibre (around 3000 of which the 47/32 anti-tank guns), and 4152 tanks and armoured cars (only 535 with 75 mm or 90 mm calibres)—substantially less than any other major belligerent.[30] In mid-1941, ammunition production already lagged behind monthly needs.[31] The armaments and ammunition supply stagnated or declined after 1941, and total production in key areas between 1940 and 1943 shows the scarce level of raw materials and the lamentable circumstances under which Italian soldiers had to fight, which Knox has described as "the single most decisive influence on Italy's fate."[32] Moreover, priority was often attached to long-term investments, heavy industry, and attempts to achieve autarchy from raw material imports instead of more immediate needs, i.e. sustaining and augmenting battlefield performance.[33] On the other hand, even restrictions were not always successful: industry never really switched to wartime production and food regulation remained incomplete until September 1941.[34] While peacetime civilian fuel consumption had been around 150,000 tons per

---

[28] Ibid., 127ff. Military expenditure as percentage of GDP lay around ten per cent before 1940 and did not rise above twenty during the conflict—not least due to failures in taxation policies, Knox, *Hitler's Italian Allies*, 26, 39–40.

[29] See the tables in [Gen.] Mario Montanari, *L'Esercito italiano allla vigilia della 2a guerra mondiale* (Rome: USSME, 1982), 293–96.

[30] Knox, *Hitler's Italian Allies*, 48–49; Ceva, *Le Forze armate*, 343ff.

[31] ACS, T-821/9/IT 24/322-338, Verbale colloquio Cavallero e Keitel (sera), 25 Aug. 1941, 336ff.

[32] Knox, *Hitler's Italian Allies*, 49.

[33] Ibid., 36.

[34] Vera Zamagni, "Italy: How to Lose the War and Win the Peace," in *The Economics of World War II*, ed. Mark Harrison (Cambridge: Cambridge University Press, 2000), 177–223, here 180; Knox, *Hitler's Italian Allies*, 34.

month, and could be restricted to 40,000 tons (of which a large part was used for war production), the Italian Navy only received half of its monthly requirements (100,000 tons) in 1941—which meant that supply to overseas theatres was problematic.[35] In sum, the level of industrial output, speed of technological development, quality of material and quantity of available resources "did not allow the country to fight the war decently, let alone win it."[36] In short, the Army would have to make do with the material that existed.

Bad Material in Low Quantities?

The standard infantry rifle was the Mannlicher-Carcano Model 91. Built-in 1891, it had already been used in the First World War, but has been labelled "not inferior to the standard weapon of the German infantry."[37] The Beretta 9 mm Modello 38[38] was a formidable light submachine gun. However, it was costly and difficult to manufacture; it thus only reached the hands of few selected units. Heavy machine guns (the 8 mm Fiat-Revelli 35 and the Breda 37) were available in small numbers, very weighty and had a lower firing frequency than comparable guns in other armies. Still, both heavy machine guns were "much better" than the standard light machine gun (the 6.5 mm Breda 30), which was inclined to jam and complicated to operate.[39] Other infantry support weapons were the troublesome and overcomplicated light mortar (45 mm Brixia Model 35) that fired a 480-gram round up to 500 metres with only 70 gram explosives,[40] while the heavy 81 mm mortar was an excellent weapon, delivering grenades (up to 18 per minute, including smoke bombs or flares) of three to six kilograms over a distance of one

---

[35] ACS, T-821/9/IT 24/322-338, Verbale colloquio Cavallero e Keitel (sera), 25 Aug. 1941, 330ff.

[36] Zamagni, "Italy," 177.

[37] Osti Guerrazzi, *Italian Army*, 7. The effectiveness of the *fucile 91* (and its different variants) has been debated at length; for a rather negative view on its feasibility, see e.g. Montanari, *L'Esercito*, 231.

[38] The standard infantry version during the Second World War was the MAB 38A (*Moschetto Automatico Beretta*) an update of the original 1938 model.

[39] Crociani and Battistelli, *Italian Soldier*, 31–32; Montanari, *L'Esercito*, 232–33.

[40] In contrast, the French and British had a more powerful 60 mm light mortar.

kilometre.[41] The basic Italian hand grenades (OTO, Breda, and SRCM) were often unreliable and had little explosive power.[42]

The main fighting power of infantry divisions in the Second World War came from their support weapons: machine guns, but also the often-neglected mortars and artillery.[43] The Italian Army had initiated a modernisation of its First World War artillery in 1929. However, delays, scarce resources and insufficient finances impeded the program. A new attempt in 1938 came too late and material shortages led to the cancellation of another, even more ambitious scheme in 1940.[44] The qualitative and quantitative disadvantage grew larger as the war progressed. One can broadly divide the Italian artillery park into three categories: the light pieces operating as support weapons within infantry regiments, the divisional artillery and the heavy guns at the free disposal of corps and armies—anti-aircraft guns were assigned on all levels.[45] The Italian designation typically used two numbers: the first indicated the calibre in millimetres and the second the barrel length, expressed as a multiple of the bore diameter.[46]

Italian corps (and armies) had their own heavy field artillery unit, which usually consisted of several battalions with pieces over 105 mm.[47] Their main task was counter-battery, long-range preparatory and interdiction fire. The 105/32 gun had an effective range of 14 kilometres, which was fairly short and exposed it to counter-battery fire.[48] The modern 149/19 howitzer (14 km range) was supposed to substitute the

[41] Crociani and Battistelli, *Italian Soldier*, 32.

[42] Ibid., 32. The 200-gram variants were mainly used for attacks and the more potent (500-gram) version for defensive actions, Montanari, *L'Esercito*, 230.

[43] Most detailed in Gordon L. Rottman, *World War II Infantry Fire Support Tactics* (Botley: Osprey, 2016).

[44] The first had envisaged building 3500 new pieces, the second 4600, Enrico Finazzer and Ralph A. Riccio, *Italian Artillery of WWII* (Sandomierz: Stratus, 2015), 6.

[45] For a detailed list of all guns with in-depth information, see Greene, *Mare Nostrum*, 59.

[46] "For example, taking the 47/32 gun, the number 47 indicates that the calibre is 47 millimetres (mm), which, multiplied by 32, results in a barrel length of 1,504 millimetres", Finazzer and Riccio, *Italian Artillery*, 7. The model type numbers intended the year of construction, yet, for simplicity's sake, they will largely be cut out here.

[47] On corps level between three and eight battalions.

[48] Longo, *Messe*, 119.

149/12 (9 km range) and the 105/28 (10 km range) in 1940–1941.[49] Still, the 105/28 proved effective against enemy armour, and together with the 149/13 it continued to form the backbone of the corps artillery.[50] The Italians produced excellent large calibre pieces, but they came very late and in small numbers, which gave them a notable deficiency in heavy artillery and resulted in frequent fire dominance for the enemy.[51] An Italian divisional artillery regiment comprised three battalions (*gruppi*) of 75 mm field guns and 100 mm howitzers—many of which were outdated models. The 75/27 had first seen action in the Italo-Ottoman War (1911–1912), but remained the backbone of Italian divisional artillery. The Czech-built 75/13 (mountain) howitzer and the 100/22 continued to serve throughout the Second World War.[52] Large stocks of 75 mm ammunition had spurred the development of new guns with this calibre in the 1930s. The Fiat Ansaldo 75/32 mod.37, and the Ansaldo 75/18 (mod.34 and mod.35) howitzers were fine pieces (despite these latters' short range), but were never produced in required numbers: by September 1942, only 230 of the 75/18 were in service and only 36 of the 75/32 were sent to Russia.[53] This was particularly lamentable, as the 75/32 had proved very effective against enemy armour thanks to its high muzzle velocity.

The most direct support for the infantry came from the light pieces within the infantry regiments: mainly the 47 mm Ansaldo-Böhler 32 L (hereafter 47/32)[54] anti-tank gun, the light 65/17 (mountain) gun and the 100/17 howitzer. The 65/17 and the 100/17 still dated from the First World War. Yet, the 65/17 was modernised and its large calibre and the (scarcely available) hollow charge ammunition "provided anti-tank performance superior to the newer 47/32 gun."[55] Thus, it was employed both as infantry support and as an anti-tank gun. According to Crociani and Battistelli the "anti-tank weapons were the Italian soldiers' reel Achilles heel," especially as the 47/32 was already outdated

---

[49] Montanari, *L'Esercito*, 22, 241–42.
[50] Finazzer and Riccio, *Italian Artillery*, 82–83, 89ff.
[51] Ibid., 44–53.
[52] Ibid., 59–71.
[53] More detailed in ibid., 23–31.
[54] The Austrian Böhler company licensed the gun to the Italians in 1935.
[55] Finazzer and Riccio, *Italian Artillery*, 58.

by 1940.[56] When it was introduced in the 1930s, the 47/32 was an advanced model: very accurate, small, light, easy to transport and able to penetrate most of the armour of existing tank models.[57] But developments during the war nullified these characteristics. Still, the 47/32 remained the main AT gun throughout the war. It was employed within infantry regiments (a battery of eight pieces, manned with artillery personnel) and one battery was assigned to each artillery regiment, which was later increased when the Italians created anti-tank battalions of 24 guns each. Industrial shortages restricted production to 170 units per month, which only sufficed to replace combat losses.[58] It had a muzzle speed of 630 m/s for a 1.5 kg armour-piercing (AP) shell, and a speed of 250 m/s for the 2.5 kg high-explosive (HE) shell.[59] Thus, Knox has set the effective range of the 47/32 against most British tanks (with 40 mm armour) at 400 m[60]—which meant the (comparatively slower) Italian medium tanks and self-propelled assault guns furnished with a 47/32 gun had to get painfully close to their enemy. To make matters worse, the 78.2 kg 47/32 had been designed for mountain warfare and thus for mule transport, making it unsuitable for towing; this was later amended, but until that point, soldiers either had to pull it or transport it on the few available lorries.[61]

The Italians readily noted their deficiency in AT weapons, but attempts to furnish anti-tank rifles, such as the Swiss 20 mm Solothurn and the Polish 7.92 mm model 35 (supplied by the Germans), could not remedy this fundamental problem, and nor could mines, flamethrowers or improvised devices.[62] Moreover, the development of a 90 mm anti-tank and anti-aircraft gun—similar to the infamous German

[56] Crociani and Battistelli, *Italian Soldier*, 32. Finazzer and Riccio argued the gun was "almost useless" in AT roles since mid-1941, particularly as hollow charge ammunition was always short in supply, Finazzer and Riccio, *Italian Artillery*, 22.

[57] Ibid., 19. The 47/32 could be easily concealed, but the lack of a protective shield also dangerously exposed the crew (of five) to small arms fire.

[58] Knox, *Hitler's Italian Allies*, 48.

[59] Cappellano and Battistelli, *Light Tanks*, 24.

[60] Knox, *Hitler's Italian Allies*, 153.

[61] Crociani and Battistelli, *Italian Soldier*, 32. On the general problems of moving artillery, see Montanari, *L'Esercito*, 247–48.

[62] Filippo Cappellano and Nicola Pignato, *Andare contro i carri armati: L'evoluzione della difesa controcarro nell'Esercito italiano dal 1918 al 1945* (Udine: Gaspari, 2007), 141ff.

88 mm—came too late and only in small numbers. Indeed, it did rather hint at another deficiency: a suitable anti-aircraft gun. The 20/65 Breda mod.35 and mod.39, and the less widespread Scotti 20/77, light anti-aircraft guns were employed in low-altitude defence roles, but also against light armour and reconnaissance vehicles.[63] One battery (eight pieces) Breda 20/65 was assigned to the divisional artillery regiments and also mounted on trucks in infantry support roles (in North Africa). Yet, the 20/65 was outdated by 1940 and lacked firepower—and the 20/77 performed even worse. The Germans occasionally supplied some of their 88 mm anti-aircraft to the Italians, of which they made good use against ground targets.[64] The different variants of the 75/46 were potent pieces with modern fire control, high fire rate, good elevation and high muzzle velocity that could also be used for ground combat. Yet, by January 1943 only 92 had been produced—of which 54 were lost in Russia and by May 1943 more than 98 more in North Africa.[65] The most powerful AA gun, the mighty 90/53 was only introduced in small numbers in late 1942.[66]

Not only was the general level of motorisation in the *Regio Esercito* low at the start of hostilities, it could also not be improved during the war.[67] Most of the heavy artillery had been machine-towed since the First World War.[68] Still, the large calibre guns were hard to transport, as only the few artillery tractors could move them efficiently. The field guns of the divisional artillery never underwent full motorisation and remained dependent on animal traction. These problems with mobility were emblematic. In 1940, the annual production amounted to merely 42,000 trucks and 19,500 other vehicles.[69] On the eve of the war, the available vehicles per division had to be reduced: only 19,127 of the envisaged 44,150 trucks existed (for the whole Army)—thus, when they were divided among the 71 divisions, each (theoretically) had 269 trucks

[63] Finazzer and Riccio, *Italian Artillery*, 8–15.

[64] It is also cited as 88/55 in Italian documents, ibid., 106–8.

[65] Ibid., 33.

[66] The 90/53 was "in several respects a better gun than the 88" according to ibid., 36–37.

[67] Montanari, *L'Esercito*, 251, 307–8.

[68] Detailed in Finazzer and Riccio, *Italian Artillery*, 137–58.

[69] James J. Sadkovich, "The Italo-Greek War in Context: Italian Priorities and Axis Diplomacy," *Journal of Contemporary History* 28, no. 3 (1993): 439–64, here 457.

in November 1939, and at best 400 by May 1940.[70] Even by including civilian requisitions (around 8000 vehicles), the divisions were far from being fully motorised.[71] Additionally, the Italians entered the war without an armoured reconnaissance vehicle, which severely troubled scouting and liaison between units. The newly developed *Autoblindo 40* (AB 40) reached Africa in October 1941 and until May 1942 only 93 AB 40 (and AB 41) had been supplied.[72] Until then, light tanks had to carry out combat reconnaissance.

As a latecomer in tank development during the First World War, the Italians continued to produce licence-built French tanks in the immediate aftermath of the conflict. The tanks corps, established in October 1927, closely followed British developments and doctrine, which placed an emphasis on light tanks in infantry-support roles.[73] The first Italian-built tank entered service in 1933: the three-ton *Carro Veloce* 33 (Fast Tank, CV 33, or L/3).[74] Its manoeuvrability hinted at the Italians' preparations for war in their mountainous border regions, and it was intended for reconnaissance and infantry-support duties. The two-man crew of the L3 s were armed with two machine-guns (8 mm Fiat 35 or 8 mm Breda 38) or a flamethrower,[75] which hardly gave them enough firing power in tank against tank encounters. The tank showed many deficiencies in the Abyssinian War and during the Spanish Civil War and in 1941, the Italians developed the L 6/40, which was based on the CV 33 casemate, and equipped with the 20/65 anti-aircraft gun and one 8 mm Breda 38 machine gun. In sum, its low weight and insufficient armour did not mark it a notable improvement, and its bad cross-country capabilities made it less suitable for reconnaissance duties than the

---

[70] Montanari, *L'Esercito*, 308. The *Comando Supremo* was optimistic to reach 28,397 vehicles by May 1940—for the entire Army.

[71] An official count in June 1939 listed 61,495 vehicles in the civilian sphere. Only 24,680 were deemed suitable, but even within this pool around 150 different models existed; and as only vehicles that were less than seven years old and had sufficient spare parts could be used, the available number dropped to 12,986, Montanari, *L'Esercito*, 317.

[72] Carrier, "Some Reflections," 515.

[73] On the development of Italian armour doctrine and platforms, see Lucio Ceva and Andrea Curami, *La meccanizzazione dell'Esercito italiano dalle origini al 1943*, 2 vols. (Rome: USSME, 1989); Sweet, *Iron Arm*, 51ff.

[74] Italian tank denomination followed category (L for light, M for medium, P for *pesante*, i.e. heavy), weight in tons, and production year.

[75] On the different models, see Cappellano and Battistelli, *Light Tanks*, 6, 16ff.

AB 40 and AB 41.[76] In May 1941, another variant entered service: the L 40 assault gun (L 40 *Semovente*). It was armed with the 47/32 AT gun and saw service on the Eastern Front.[77] Yet, the Spanish Civil War had not fuelled the development of a (in fact badly needed) medium tank, as the Italians deployed their own light tanks—like the Germans—to lure enemy armour into action and then combat it with the superior firepower of their 47/32 and 65/17 guns, which "led to an overestimation of the CV 35 capabilities, either in reconnaissance or infantry support role, while its inadequacy in tank-versus-tank combat was, if not ignored, at least temporarily set aside."[78] The lack of a powerful medium tank substantially impeded Italian combat performance: the M 13/40 and the M 14/41 came too late, had not enough firepower or armour; and were—like the more powerful assault guns—not employed in Russia.[79] Besides the platforms themselves, command and control equipment was insufficient: the few radios often worked poorly, battlefield supply and maintenance suffered from low motorisation, while uniform shortage was another negative aspect.[80]

A concluding assessment on the Italian Army's principal material shows two things: first, it was deficient in numbers, but not necessarily in quality. However, industry failed to produce sufficient replacements (and ammunition) for combat losses and, more importantly, could not keep pace with the constant technological progress—particularly regarding tanks and anti-tank guns. Most of the new material arrived in low quantities and too late. Thus, assessments of Italian combat capabilities must bear in mind these handicaps.

[76] Ibid., 22ff.

[77] Ibid., 24ff.; Finazzer and Riccio, *Italian Artillery*, 114–17.

[78] Cappellano and Battistelli, *Light Tanks*, 30.

[79] On their development and deployment, see Cappellano and Battistelli, *Medium Tanks*; Walker, *Iron Hulls*; Sweet, *Iron Arm*.

[80] Montanari, *L'Esercito*, 318.

The Structure of an Italian Infantry Division

After the First World War, Marshal Diaz had maintained the four-regiment division until the Cavallero-Badoglio reforms in 1926, which followed a general European trend of reducing regiments to three.[81] Another reorganisation in 1934 largely confirmed this structure and enabled Italy to equip thirty peacetime divisions with old, but still valuable material.[82] General Alberto Pariani—Undersecretary at the War Ministry and the Army's Chief of Staff since October 1936—initiated transformations based on the experiences of the Abyssinian War. He developed the concept of the *guerra di rapido corso* (lightning war) and the binary division (*divisione binarie*)—reducing the infantry regiments per division from three to two.[83] The binary division has attracted plenty of criticism—mainly for its reduced firepower.[84] One should not forget, however, that the lighter structure owed its existence to the likely war scenarios, i.e. combat in the mountainous border regions to France and Yugoslavia. The reduction of the infantry regiments was no bad thing, per se—postwar developments towards brigade strength confirmed this trend. But rather more problematic was the inadequate supply of more powerful infantry support weapons and (armoured) vehicles.[85] Yet, while the reform increased the overall number of divisions by 20-51 it created shortages of experienced staffs able to direct and to supply them in the field.

In 1940, an infantry division consisted—simply put—of two infantry regiments with three battalions each, one divisional artillery regiment (*reggimento d'artiglieria divisionale*) with two or three groups, and one sapper battalion—encompassing 12,000 men (449 officers and 614 NCOs), 108 trucks, 71 motorcycles, thirteen cars, six transport vehicles and 3424 pack

---

[81] Detailed in Filippo Stefani, *La storia della dottrina e degli ordinamenti dell'Esercito italiano. Vol. 2: Tomo 1* (Rome: USSME, 1985), 49–109.

[82] Rochat, *Le guerre*, 184–85. So, too, did personnel shortages hamper these plans.

[83] Montanari, *L'Esercito*, 9ff.

[84] For example, Petracarro, "Italian Army," 101–2; Cappellano and Pignato, *Andare contro*, 68. More balanced is Ferruccio Botti and Virgilio Ilari, *Il pensiero militare italiano dal primo al secondo dopoguerra, 1919–1949* (Rome: USSME, 1985), 215ff., 227–30.

[85] Pariani had realised the risk of reducing the divisions' combat power, but expected a period of peace, which would provide time for reforms and procurement of new material, Montanari, *L'Esercito*, 13.

animals.[86] In theory, a division comprised eighty 45 mm mortars, eighteen 81 mm mortars,[87] 270 light and 80 heavy machine guns, eight 20 mm anti-aircraft guns, eight 47/32 anti-tank guns, eight 65/17 and the artillery regiment added another three battalions (*gruppi*) of artillery pieces, usually twenty-four 75/27 and twelve 100/17 light howitzers (later also 105/28).[88] A Blackshirt Legion (a lightly armed force of around 1300 men),[89] cavalry or *Bersaglieri* regiments were often used to supplement the infantry divisions. Yet, this was another vain attempt to pour in men to make up for a lack of firepower. The Italians had six different types of divisions, most of which were altered as the war progressed.[90] Thus citing 1940 numbers alone gives an inadequate impression. The *Celere* type division, for example, had (on paper) 539 trucks and 418 cars.[91] Italian infantry divisions had lower motorisation and firepower in comparison to their Soviet, British and German counterparts, where the quantity and quality of machine guns, artillery,[92] and trucks increased as the war progressed (relative to the Italians).[93] Yet, peacetime strength and theoretical numbers must

[86] Sadkovich, "Italo-Greek War," 457.

[87] The heavy mortars were initially allocated in an own battalion, instead of spreading them widely on platoon and company level, Botti and Ilari, *Il pensiero*, 228.

[88] The numbers found in secondary literature vary and (in any case) only show a theoretical strength. For example, the Italians increased the artillery pieces—extending the assignment of 47/32 anti-tank guns down to (infantry) battalion level in 1942, Cappellano and Pignato, *Andare contro*, 170.

[89] One Legion consisted of 52 officers, 76 NCOs, 1130 men, 206 horses, six cars, two motorcycles, thirteen bicycles, eighteen 45 mm mortars, 48 light machine guns, and twelve heavy machine guns, Greene, *Mare Nostrum*, 10.

[90] The infantry divisions (*divisione fanteria* or Df.) were subdivided in regular and in mountain infantry divisions, then there were the fast divisions with cavalry elements (*divisione celere* or D.cl.), the motorised divisions (*divisione autotrasportabile* or D.at.), the *Alpini* mountain divisions (*divisione alpina* or D.al.), the security divisions (Df. ccc.), and the infantry divisions adopted for North Africa (*divisione A.S.* and *divisione A.S. 42*), Longo, Messe, 118–19. The formations in North Africa, for example, received additional vehicles and artillery groups, Morisi, *Folgore*, 189; Knox, *Hitler's Italian Allies*, 125.

[91] Greene, *Mare Nostrum*, 54.

[92] So, too, did the defensive and offensive firepower of German infantry divisions largely rely on their artillery, Stahel, *Operation Barbarossa*, 119.

[93] Even though the theoretical levels of Soviet strength were far from the reality, and the divisions' reorganisation in July 1941 reduced the number of trucks by 64 per cent, David M. Glantz and Jonathan M. House, *When Titans Clashed: How the Red Army Stopped Hitler* (Lawrence: University Press of Kansas, 2015), 39–41, 77–78. Likewise, the 1939 strength levels for a German infantry division demonstrate the danger of citing early numbers: the

always be treated with caution: for instance, a badly mauled German infantry division may have a different de facto strength and training standards decreased during the war (Figs. 3.1, 3.2, and 3.3).[94]

Antiquated Doctrines?

The following remarks on Italian doctrine cannot encompass all debates or every field. Unfortunately, the studies by Ferruccio Botti and Virgilio Ilari,[95] Filippo Stefani,[96] Filippo Cappellano and Nicola Pignato[97] on the development of theory and doctrine (and these two fields must not be confused) are not available in English. Hence, Italian doctrine is often overlooked or discarded off-hand as antiquated trench-warfare thinking. Based on her analysis of military journals, Brogini Künzi has claimed that initially (i.e. the 1920s) only limited lessons were drawn from the First World War and only few self-critical studies emerged.[98] However, she and others have also delineated the 1930s as a period marked by widespread debates about modernisation, rationalisation, mechanisation and professionalisation.[99] Indeed, the development of armour doctrine—commonly accepted as benchmark for innovation in the interwar period—can illustrate this argument further.[100] French, British and German theoretical

---

divisions' four regiments possessed 178 cars, 155 trucks, and 242 motorcycles, Christian Hartmann, *Wehrmacht im Ostkrieg. Front und militärisches Hinterland 1941/42* (Munich: Oldenbourg, 2009), 32. DiNardo put the average number of horses in a German division at 4000, and the Wehrmacht actually invaded the Soviet Union with more horses than (unarmoured) vehicles (up to 700,000 against 600,000), Richard L. DiNardo, *Mechanized Juggernaut or Military Anachronism? Horses and the German Army of World War II* (Westport: Greenwood, 1991), 25, 40.

[94] Hartmann, *Wehrmacht*, 29–80.
[95] Botti and Ilari, *Il pensiero*.
[96] Stefani, *Storia della dottrina, II:I*.
[97] Cappellano and Pignato, *Andare contro*.
[98] Giulia Brogini Künzi, "Die Herrschaft der Gedanken. Italienische Militärzeitschriften und das Bild des Krieges," in *An der Schwelle zum totalen Krieg. Die militärische Debatte über den Krieg der Zukunft 1919–1939*, eds. Stig Förster, Bernhard R. Kroener, and Bernd Wegner (Paderborn: Schöningh, 2002), 37–111, here esp. 42, 45; Botti and Ilari, *Il pensiero*, 35ff.
[99] Brogini Künzi, "Herrschaft der Gedanken," 66, 74; Botti and Ilari, *Il pensiero*, 163ff.
[100] James J. Sadkovich, "Some Considerations Regarding Italian Armored Doctrine Prior to June 1940," *Global War Studies* 9, no. 1 (2012): 40–74.

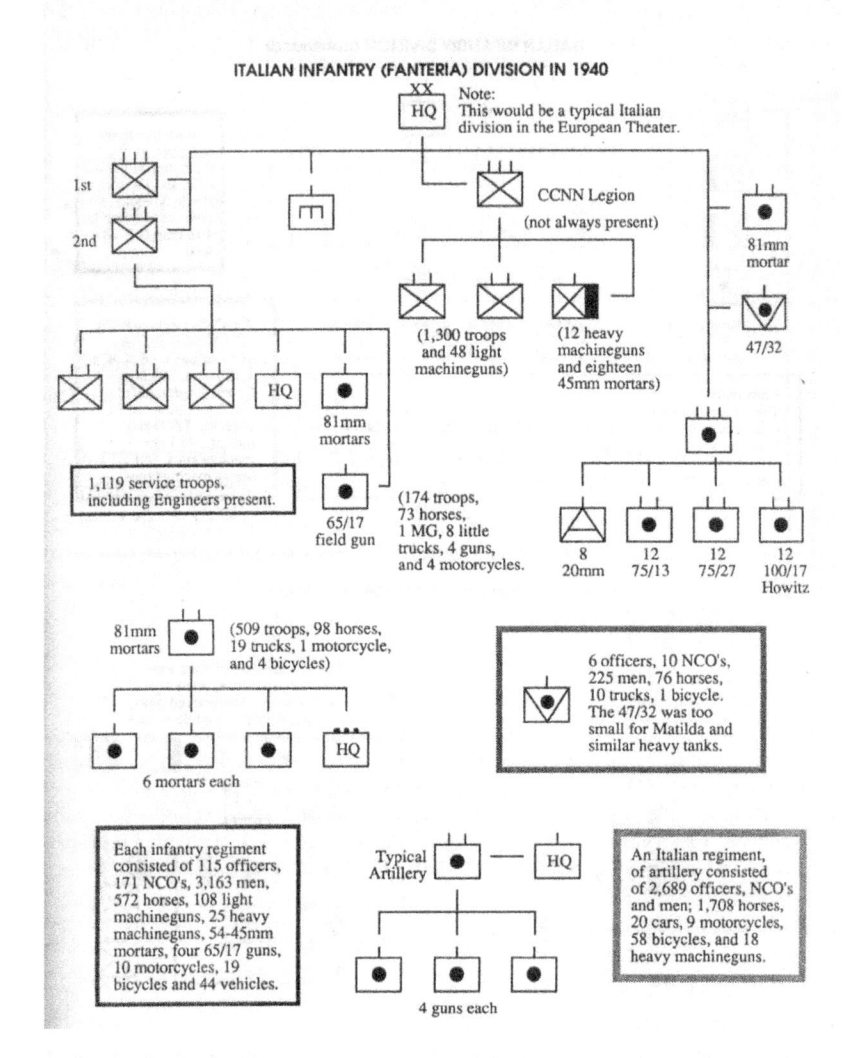

Fig. 3.1 Italian infantry division scheme, from Greene, *Mare Nostrum*, 9

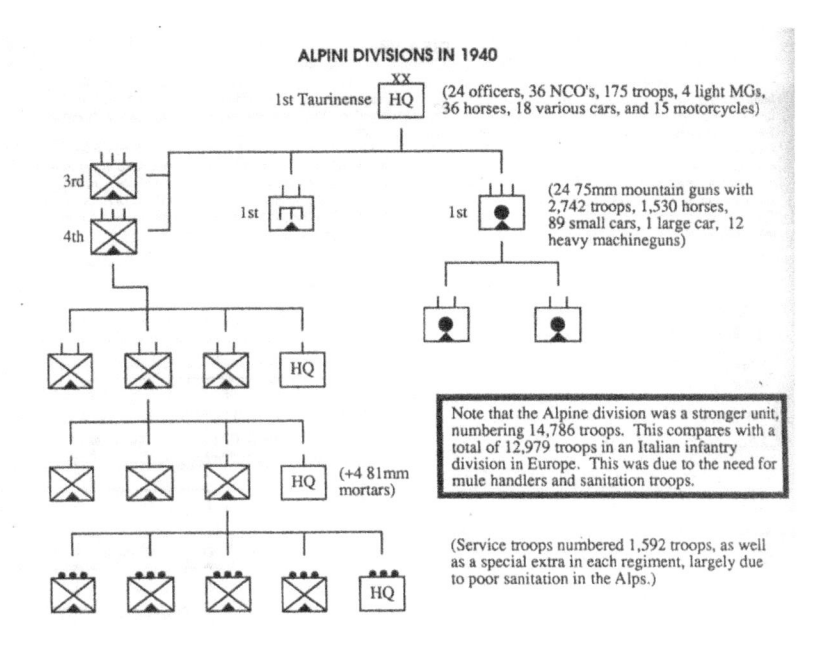

3 THE ITALIAN ARMY BEFORE THE SECOND WORLD WAR (1861–1940)   57

Fig. 3.2 Italian *Alpini* division scheme, from Greene, *Mare Nostrum*, 16

debates were closely followed and discussed in Italian journals, while writings by Ottavio Zoppi and Sebastiano Visconti Prasca also emphasised the need for armoured surprise assaults in cooperation with air power.[101] On the other hand, French concepts of strategic defences along natural borders were also present in Italian thought. Rather naturally, one could argue, bearing in mind Italy's geographic location, possible enemies, poor resource base and limited means for acquiring new weapons.[102]

Clearly, there were different strands and groups within the military: traditionalists probably dominated the *Regio Esercito* as in other countries, but in the late 1930s one can also identify willingness for change. Montanari identified three key moments for the development of Italian doctrine after 1918: first, updates in artillery and infantry doctrine in

---

[101] Gooch, "Clausewitz Disregarded," 318; Sweet, *Iron Arm*.

[102] Particularly Ettore Bastico, later Marshal during the war, was a proponent of this 'French school' of thought, see Botti and Ilari, *Il pensiero*, 165.

MILITARY UNITS — IDENTIFICATION

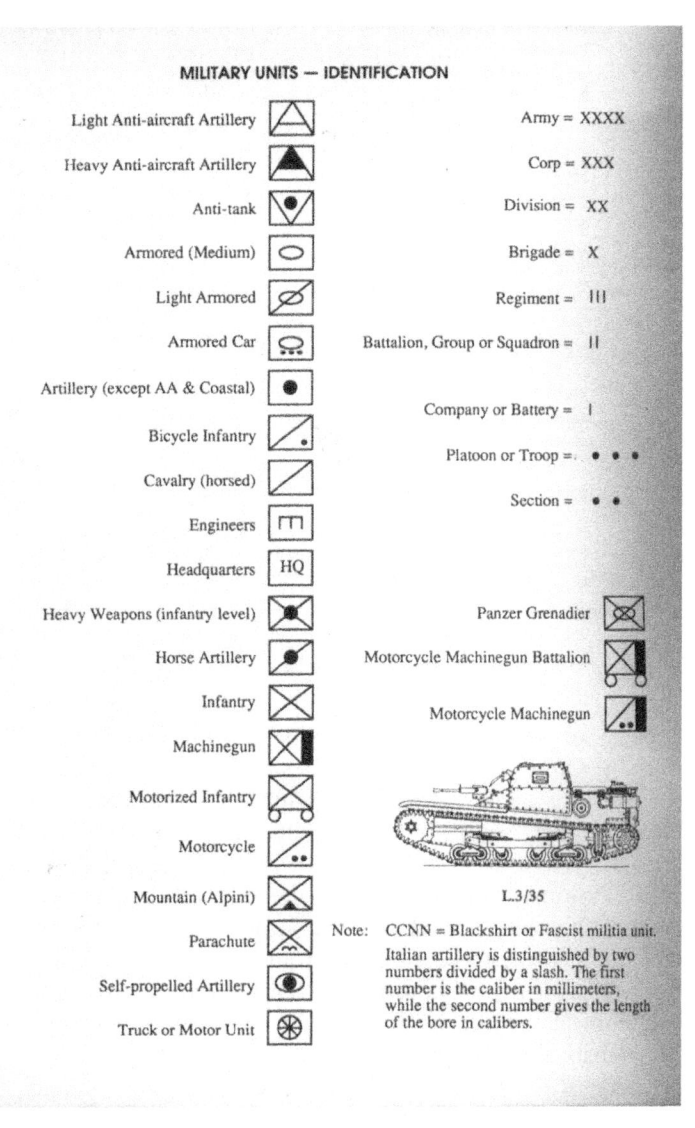

Light Anti-aircraft Artillery	△	Army =	XXXX
Heavy Anti-aircraft Artillery	▲	Corp =	XXX
Anti-tank	▽	Division =	XX
Armored (Medium)	○	Brigade =	X
Light Armored	⌀	Regiment =	III
Armored Car	⌒	Battalion, Group or Squadron =	II
Artillery (except AA & Coastal)	●	Company or Battery =	I
Bicycle Infantry	◪	Platoon or Troop =	● ● ●
Cavalry (horsed)	◨	Section =	● ●
Engineers	⊓		
Headquarters	HQ		
Heavy Weapons (infantry level)	⊠	Panzer Grenadier	⊠
Horse Artillery	●	Motorcycle Machinegun Battalion	⊠
Infantry	⊠	Motorcycle Machinegun	⊠
Machinegun	⊠		
Motorized Infantry	⊠		
Motorcycle	⊡		
Mountain (Alpini)	⊠	L.3/35	
Parachute	⊠		
Self-propelled Artillery	⊙		
Truck or Motor Unit	⊕		

Note: CCNN = Blackshirt or Fascist militia unit. Italian artillery is distinguished by two numbers divided by a slash. The first number is the caliber in millimeters, while the second number gives the length of the bore in calibers.

Fig. 3.3 Military units—identification, from Greene, *Mare Nostrum*, 2

1928, second, the reforms under Federico Baistrocchi (1871–1947)[103] concerning the mobility and operations of motorised units (the *guerra di movimento*) in 1935–1936, and thirdly, Alberto Pariani's (1876–1955)[104] *guerra di rapido corso* (lightning war) in 1938.[105] Baistrocchi was a fundamental force for change: he stipulated unity of effort and the integrated thinking of different branches to cooperate effectively in modern manoeuvre warfare (including airpower).[106] Yet, this did not mean rigid norms, but basic concepts and harmonised leadership principles (initiative and responsibility) that commanders would apply according to circumstances.[107] Pariani formulated his visions in several manuals, which placed greater emphasis on manoeuvre at corps level than on the (downsized) divisions.[108] Both offensive and defensive actions were intended to be mobile to exploit successes or counter enemy attacks. Thus, seizing and maintaining the initiative were cornerstones in Pariani's thinking. This preordained a close cooperation between armour, artillery and motorised infantry.[109] Consequently, the Italians envisaged a close cooperation (and protection of one's infantry) in a very close main defence perimeter.[110]

Obviously, the effectiveness of these theoretical changes has to be scrutinised, yet, one has to acknowledge the Italian participation in modern doctrinal developments and emphases on guidelines instead of rigid norms: the Army was clearly capable of—at least—imagining the war of the future.[111] The failure to produce an important military theorist

[103] Cecini, *I generali*, 188–200.

[104] Ibid., 201–13.

[105] Montanari, *L'Esercito*, 252.

[106] Ibid., 256–57.

[107] Ibid., 256. The two principal manuals for corps and divisional employment—*Direttive per l'impiego delle grandi unità* (or D.I.G.U., 1935) and *Direttive per il combattimento della divisione* (or N.C.D., 1936)—and other directives are discussed in Montanari, *L'Esercito*, 255–67; Stefani, *Storia della dottrina*, II:I.

[108] Montanari, *L'Esercito*, 269ff.

[109] Botti and Ilari, *Il pensiero*, 203ff.

[110] The perimeter was intended to be two to three kilometres deep with a main combat line (including active and passive defence systems and the infantry regiments' artillery) of one kilometre depth, Montanari, *L'Esercito*, 270.

[111] For this argument, see also Sweet, *Iron Arm*, 189. Moreover, general staff's studies before the war analysed the armour doctrines of all major European powers and derived conclusions for the Italian armoured corps, see the lengthy memoranda from 1938 and 1939 in ACS, T-821/384/IT 4996.

(besides Giulio Douhet) is often raised as argument to support the idea of 'Italian backwardness'. But according to Gooch "Italy fared no better without Clausewitz than many countries which fell under his influence" and was as enlightened (or as ignorant) as other armies about the true nature of modern war in 1939.[112] Likewise, the Wehrmacht (not to speak of other armies) did not have a coherent 'Blitzkrieg concept', either, but instead based its designs on traditional German operational thought: a swift and mobile encirclement of the enemy.[113] In conclusion, the problem was not so much that the Italian Army did not think about the future of war, but that its officers (reserve officers) and soldiers were never extensively schooled in novel doctrines. Time did not permit the reforms to take full effect, inter-service rivalries (a common problem) remained, and the material to apply these theories was not available.[114] In order to understand the mediocre results when doctrine met the test of battle, one has to look at the officer corps' structure, the level of military training and the quality of the manpower—especially the largely unqualified reserves.

Officers and Men

In June 1940, the Italians had 1,600,000 men under arms (of which around 550,000 overseas). The Army could muster 19,500 permanent career officers (*Servizio permanente effettivo*, or *in s.p.e.*), 37,000 *ufficiali di complemento* (complementary, or rather, reserve officers), 17,200 *sottufficiali in carriera continuativo* (career NCOs), and 24,000 auxiliary NCOs (*sottufficiali in corso di ferma, trattenuti o richiamati*).[115] Evidently, an army with fewer non-commissioned officers (NCOs) than officers should raise red flags. Indeed, it had severe consequences: on average, one or two career officers were available per battalion and the

---

[112] Gooch, "Clausewitz Disregarded," 322.

[113] Karl-Heinz Frieser, *Blitzkrieg-Legende: Der Westfeldzug 1940* (Munich: Oldenbourg, 1995), 7ff.; Groß, *Mythos*, 197, 202, 216. The disregard for flank protection can be seen as break with Schlieffen's thinking, ibid., 204.

[114] Montanari, *L'Esercito*, 277; Botti and Ilari, *Il pensiero*, 219, 229, 249ff.

[115] Rochat, *L'Esercito italiano*, 267ff.; Montanari, *L'Esercito*, 220. The General Staff officer corps comprised 48 colonels and 178 lieutenant-colonels, while the number of officers serving in staff functions was not regulated in detail, ibid., 210.

same number of NCOs for each company.[116] The limited availability of long-serving NCOs hampered both the training and the effectiveness in combat. Additionally, the Italian Army suffered from a rapid expansion of its forces, so that basic training had essentially been cut to six months to train the rising number of recruits.[117]

Despite its support for Fascist Italy's wars, the officer corps remained primarily bound to the King and always maintained a notable autonomy.[118] Of course this varied in degree and was also used as alibi after the war—yet, its distance from the regime and its ideology appear especially pronounced in comparison to Germany.[119] Some of the key problems of the officer corps, such as its size and training methods, went back to pre-Fascist times.[120] The failed reform in 1925—one that sought drastically to reduce the active-duty officer corps—spelled doom for improved selection, training and advancement of a new generation of officers.[121] The *Regio Esercito*'s expansion in the 1930s only worsened this trend. On the eve of the war, only 30,000 of 79,900 reserve junior officers who underwent training between 1935 and 1939 were considered fit for mobilisation.[122] These men—who could be in their mid-fifties—were the future platoon and company leaders on the battlefield. Additionally, Mussolini's designs to accommodate senior officers reduced the proportion of

---

[116] Ibid., 221.

[117] Brian R. Sullivan, "The Primacy of Politics: Civil-Military Relations and Italian Junior Officers, 1918–1940," in *Forging the Sword: Selecting, Educating, and Training Cadets and Junior Officers in the Modern World*, ed. Elliott V. Converse III (Chicago: Imprint, 1998), 65–81, here 71.

[118] Lucio Ceva, "Fascismo e militari di professione," in *Ufficiali e società. Interpretazioni e modelli*, eds. Giuseppe Caforio and Piero Del Negro (Milan: FrancoAngeli, 1988), 379–436.

[119] MacGregor Knox, "'Totality' and Disintegration. State, Party, and Armed Forces in National Socialist Germany and Fascist Italy," in *Die "Achse" im Krieg. Politik, Ideologie und Kriegführung 1939–1945*, eds. Lutz Klinkhammer, Amedeo Osti Guerrazzi, and Thomas Schlemmer (Paderborn: Schöningh, 2010), 80–107.

[120] Ceva, "Fascismo," 406.

[121] Sullivan, "Primacy," 67ff. However, Montanari has argued with regard to promotions that a large majority of lieutenants became captains, fifty per cent of captains made it to major, two thirds of the majors reached the lieutenant-colonel rank, and one third of those became colonels. Twenty per cent of the colonels became generals, Montanari, *L'Esercito*, 216. This means that of 100 lieutenants, around thirteen became colonels and three generals—numbers that are, however, comparable to the Wehrmacht. I wish to thank Thorsten Loch for this information.

[122] Sullivan, "Primacy," 76.

lieutenants in the regular officer corps from 50.4 to 31.1 per cent, which meant that reserve officers would have to fill many command positions in case of war.[123] Once the war started, the active career officers became a minority and the *ufficiali di complemento*—who were poorly selected, had little field practice, and often also had bad theoretical education—severely influenced the Italian performance.[124]

According to Knox, the Italian officers (and the Army in general) had enjoyed rigid and insufficient training, was marked by a cult of obedience, and showed little to no initiative.[125] While there is much truth in these assertions of theory-focused education and an inflexible outlook, other authors have emphasised the good quality of officer education—despite the accent on theory, and lack of concise training[126]—and considered it as equal to British and French schooling.[127] However, few works have looked at officer training in detail, including efforts to focus on practical exercises before the war, the failed attempts to instil the Army with ideology through *cultura militare* courses, and how units prepared for operations once the Second World War had begun.[128] The British military attaché in Rome remarked in 1936 that "certain changes were effected in the syllabus of the course at the Staff College with a view to making the instruction more practical and reducing the time spent on purely theoretical study. It is believed that this institution now compares favourably with any other similar establishment in Europe as regards the quality of the instruction and the type of officer turned out."[129] Yet, German officers appear to have been more critical. It has been argued that the Wehrmacht's mainly negative view of the Italian Army was defined at the

[123] Ibid., 71–73.

[124] Giorgio Rochat, "Qualche dato sugli ufficiali di complemento dell'Esercito nel 1940," *Ricerche storiche* 18, no. 3 (1993): 607–35; Sullivan, "Primacy," 74–75. Yet, the quality of the *ufficiali di complemento* also differed, not least depending on their age and the training they had received, Montanari, *L'Esercito*, 221–23. Still, it was mainly career officers who had gathered experiences in Spain and in Ethiopia.

[125] Knox, *Hitler's Italian Allies*, 51ff.

[126] Montanari, *L'Esercito*, 221, 224.

[127] Sullivan, "Primacy," 73.

[128] Botti and Ilari, *Il pensiero*, 330ff.

[129] TNA, WO 106/6086, Col. R.O. Stone—Annual Report 1936, 30 Dec. 1936, 'Training'.

3 THE ITALIAN ARMY BEFORE THE SECOND WORLD WAR (1861–1940)   63

top and was based "to a large extent"[130] on the ad hoc impressions that the Minister for War, Werner von Blomberg, had spread after a visit in June 1937.[131] Blomberg's low esteem of Mussolini, Italy in general, and the peculiar character of the trip itself further increased his opposition against a military alliance with Rome.[132] In 1970, Hans Meier-Welcker, who had attended the Italian war academy in 1938–1939 and served as a staff officer in the Wehrmacht during the war, described his oft-negative impression of schematic teaching.[133] Yet his original reports from 1938 to 1939, especially the early ones,[134] also included more positive remarks about the war academy in Turin, which, however, became more critical the longer he stayed there and the more he visited various units.[135]

However, even if Italian officers spent less time on field exercises in academies and were burdened with administration, one could ask how much this mattered in late 1942. The commander of a division or regiment had most likely attended the military academy before the First World War and not only collected experience in the interwar period, but also after June 1940. Furthermore, Italian officers realised these problems and often tried to overcome them. For example, General Gervasio Bitossi, commander of the *Littorio* armoured division, noted deficiencies in training and the existing materiel, and criticised the discrepancies between the rhetoric of mechanisation and the bleak reality.[136] Likewise, much has been made of cultural explanations for low efficiency—i.e. a lack of trust in the state, and of cooperation extending family bonds, as well as the military's generally low social prestige.[137] Yet these arguments should be reconsidered when one is concerned with units that fought

[130] Hans Meier-Welcker, "Zur deutsch-italienischen Militärpolitik und Beurteilung der italienischen Wehrmacht vor dem Zweiten Weltkrieg," *Militärgeschichtliche Mitteilungen* 7, no. 1 (1970): 59–94, here 65.

[131] Kristin A. Schäfer, *Werner von Blomberg. Hitlers erster Feldmarschall* (Paderborn: Schöningh, 2006), 166.

[132] Ibid., 166–67.

[133] Meier-Welcker, "Militärpolitik," 71ff.

[134] BA-MA, N 241/15, Meier-Welcker, 1. Bericht, 18 Nov. 1938, fol.17.

[135] See his various reports in BA-MA, N 241/15. The French officers who attended the academy were apparently even more critical, see e.g. BA-MA, N 241/15, Meier-Welcker, 2. Bericht, 16 Jan. 1939, fol.25.

[136] Nicola Pignato and Antonio Rosati, "Gervasio Bitossi: Primo Comandante della cavalleria carrista," in *Studi Storico-Militari 2004* (Rome: USSME, 2007), 5–95, here 31ff.

[137] Knox, *Hitler's Italian Allies*, 28ff.

together for several months or even years. Many scholars have pointed to the distance between officers and men, which clearly did not improve unit cohesion.[138] While there are many remarks in German sources on this fact, they also noted the decrease of this gap after prolonged frontline deployment—which was, after all, the rule for Italian units due to restrictive leave (that led to other problems, however). Indeed, especially in elite units—like the armoured divisions, the *Alpini*, and the paratroopers—officer to men relations were described as close. Additionally, officers' distance from the men does not imply any incompetence on their part; neither did it prevent the Soviets—arguably the worst in mistreating their men—from winning the war.[139]

In conclusion, while Mussolini boasted the readiness of 'eight million bayonets', the reality was much bleaker: the constant operations since October 1935 had put a great strain on the Italian Army and its material, which the underdeveloped armament industry could not satisfactorily improve. In total, only 21 of 71 divisions were considered complete by 1 November 1939.[140] The Italian industrial base was only capable of supplying twenty frontline divisions,[141] which necessitated relying on infantry divisions that consumed far less supplies and material than motorised or armoured formations. Financial restrictions and resource scarcity further impeded material and ammunition production. The failure to catch up and improve wartime production was arguably a greater problem than the disadvantageous position in 1939–1940. Besides the inefficient and chaotic structure of the armed forces' high command,[142] there was a shortage of trained officers and NCOs, which would greatly undermine effectiveness in the coming battles.[143] However, the Italian military elite was not ignorant of modern warfare; rather, it was acutely aware of its own shortcomings, and attempted to overcome them— yet did also not oppose Mussolini's decision to go to war more strongly.

---

[138] Sullivan, "Primacy," 78; Petracarro, "Italian Army," 109–10.

[139] Italian military justice was notably less severe than between 1915 and 1918, and desertions fewer, Knox, *Hitler's Italian Allies*, 31, 34. It would be interesting to link this aspect to the question of ideological indoctrination and the level of 'Fascist' thinking in the Army.

[140] Montanari, *L'Esercito*, 310. Yet, the readiness level only slighty improved (even on paper) until May 1940, ibid., 27–28.

[141] Knox, *Hitler's Italian Allies*, 48.

[142] Montanari, *L'Esercito*, 319–55; Rochat, *Le guerre*, 244ff.

[143] Greene and Massignani, *North Africa*, 13–15.

CHAPTER 4

The *guerra fascista*—10 June 1940–25 July 1943

In order to understand the importance of the Eastern Front, it is necessary also to consider Italian experiences until summer 1941. Even though they all deserve closer study, these operations cannot be analysed in detail. This chapter therefore briefly assesses the operations, as well as the resulting memories and legacies from these campaigns:

1. The operations against France (10–25 June 1940)
2. The conquest of British Somaliland (August 1940) and the subsequent loss of Italian East Africa in 1941
3. The invasion of Greece (28 October 1940–2 April 1941) and the subsequent occupation of the Balkans
4. The disastrous rout in North Africa (December 1940–February 1941), the arrival of German help and changing fortunes in 1941, the improvement of Italian performance up till the battle of El Alamein in October 1942 and in Tunisia in 1943.

The campaigns from autumn 1940 to spring 1941 marked an irreversible blow to the Army's prestige. They also drove disregard for the later developments that improved Italian combat performance. Indeed, many scholarly studies have ended their analysis in spring 1941. According to Sullivan, "in the spring and summer of 1942 the Italian Army was at the peak of its Second World War effectiveness in regard to training, equipment, morale and tactical-operational leadership."[1] Hence, he advocated subdividing an analysis into three phases: first, a period of defeat lasting from autumn 1940 until spring 1941, second, a phase of improvement until summer 1943, and, thirdly, the defence of Sicily and the events of the 8 September.[2]

When Hitler invaded Poland on 1 September 1939 and Britain and France 'rushed' to its defence, Italy at first declared her 'non-belligerence'. Yet, despite the 'unreadiness' for war (notwithstanding preparations since March 1940), the reservations among the general staff, and the tacit agreement with Hitler to avoid a major conflict before 1943, Mussolini plunged the country into a grand-scale European war on 10 June 1940.[3] By summer 1943, around 3.5 million men had been called to arms—of which a majority never served outside the Italian peninsula. Italian fatalities during the *guerra fascista* (1940–1943) amounted to 230,000—notably less than the 650,000 casualties between 1915 and 1918.[4] In regular operations, the Italians suffered their highest casualties against Greece and during the retreat in Russia in winter 1942–1943.[5] The Italians' costs in terms of human life were fairly small in comparison to German or Soviet fatalities, but similar to the British, American, French, Hungarian and Romanian casualty figures.[6]

THE ATTACK ON FRANCE (JUNE 1940)

When Germany launched its offensive in the West on 10 May 1940, daily public processions in Rome were beating the interventionist drum. The quick French collapse made an intervention even more appealing, but the population was by no means enthusiastically supportive of such an

---

[1] Sullivan, "Italian Soldier," 195.

[2] Ibid., 187–88.

[3] On the period of non-belligerence, see Knox, *Mussolini Unleashed*, 69ff.; Montanari, *L'Esercito*, 81ff., 135ff. On Mussolini's decisions, Bosworth, *Mussolini*, 358.

[4] Rochat, *Le guerre*, 442. On casualty numbers, see ibid., 440ff.

[5] Detailed in Zamagni, "Italy", 213.

[6] In total, 2.7 million of 5.3 million German military fatalities were suffered on the Eastern Front; the Soviets mourned 6,885,100 combat dead and had a further 4,559,000 missing or taken prisoner out of 29,574,900 mobilised men, Overy, *Russia's War*, 288. The Hungarians lost up to 360,000 soldiers, the Romanians up to 380,000, Müller, *An der Seite*, 53, 79. France lost around 210,000 and Britain 338,000 men.

endeavour, which had been decided in secret in spring 1940.[7] The military cautioned against an offensive in the Alps and many officers felt little enthusiasm to fight a former ally, but Mussolini insisted and declared war on 10 June. The French stalled the offensive with relative ease in a terrain that greatly favoured the defender.[8] The Italian attack was perceived by the French (and world opinion) as stab in the back of an already beaten enemy.[9] Therefore, the Italian military had little interest in remembering this short and unsuccessful campaign. The subsequent occupation period—marked by a notable Italian restraint—descended into oblivion,[10] and the surrender of the Fourth Army to the Germans after 8 September 1943 was already perceived as humiliation by Italian generals in British captivity.[11]

Despite the French defeat, the Italians were no closer to becoming the masters of the Mediterranean: Britain was clinging on to Gibraltar, Malta, and Suez—the very 'prison bars' that Mussolini desired to break. The strategic situation further deteriorated after the successful British raid on the Italian naval base at Taranto on the night of 11–12 November 1940 and the Battle at Cape Matapan on 28 March 1941. Both operations were fatal blows for the Navy, which became even more hesitant to conduct large-scale operations.[12] In the air, the Italians attempted to improve their position. Badoglio told Efisio Marras, the military attaché in Berlin, to hand the Germans a request for hundreds (sic!) of *Stukas* and fighter aircraft.[13] Unsurprisingly, at the height

[7] Paul Corner, *The Fascist Party and Popular Opinion in Mussolini's Italy* (Oxford: Oxford University Press, 2012), 259–67.

[8] On the operations see Rochat, *Le guerre*, 246–51; Emanuele Sica, "June 1940: The Italian Army and the Battle of the Alps," *Canadian Journal of History* 47, no. 2 (2016): 355–78.

[9] The French had sued (the Germans) for peace on 17 June—seven days after Italy's entry into the war. Yet, Mussolini urged continued operations while the armistice talks were taking place.

[10] Emanuele Sica, *Mussolini's Army in the French Riviera: Italy's Occupation of France* (Chicago: University of Illinois Press, 2015).

[11] TNA, WO 208/4187, S.R.I.G. no.283, Conversation between Marshal Messe, and generals Orlando and Berardi, 11 Sept. 1943. The Italian officers agreed that the attack on France had been ill-conceived and the senior command had cut a bad figure, TNA, WO 208/4185, S.R.I.G. no.110, Conversation of several senior officers, 30 June 1943.

[12] Rochat, *Le guerre*, 289–93.

[13] DS CS, II: I, 19 Sept. 1940.

of the 'Battle of Britain' nothing came of this. Nonetheless, parts of the *Aeronautica* were sent to aid the Germans in the fight against the British. Yet, they were of little use and the larger share of the Italian Air Force was employed in the Mediterranean. In sum, the *Regia Marina* and the *Aeronautica* stayed on the defensive against British forces in the Mediterranean, but both remained vital to supplying the Italo-German forces operating in North Africa.

THE LOSS OF ITALIAN EAST AFRICA

The Italians had united their possessions in the Horn of Africa in 1936 and the forces under the Duke of Aosta appeared strong on paper, but suffered from a bad strategic position, inferiority in the air, poorly trained troops, low reserves and antiquated material.[14] In August 1940, the successful attack on British Somaliland—if a small campaign with only secondary gains—proved important for Italian prestige.[15] "Italian jubilation knew no bounds and British public opinion suffered a severe shock when the news of the Italian victory reached Europe. Mussolini trumpeted his victory to the world."[16] It is thus necessary to relate the British propaganda, triumphalism and public denigrations of the Italians in December 1940 and March 1941, to the Somaliland campaign—as well as to other British setbacks in 1940. After their defeat in August, the British rallied more forces and managed to secure decisive victories on the Eritrean front, overcoming the fierce Italian resistance at Keren in March, before conquering Addis Ababa in May 1941. This practically ended the campaign in East Africa as only a few isolated Italian strongholds continued to hold out until November 1941. After the war, the Army glorified these desperate battles as gestures of heroism against the

---

[14] A good assessment is Sadkovich, "Understanding Defeat," 38–39. For a detailed account, see [Gen.] Alberto Rovighi, *Le operazione in Africa Orientale (giugno 1940–novembre 1941), Vol. 1* (Rome: USSME, 1988); from the British perspective, see now Andrew Stewart, *The First Victory: The Second World War and the East Africa Campaign* (New Haven: Yale University Press, 2016).

[15] Rovighi, *Le operazione*, 101–25; Stewart, *First Victory*, 71ff.

[16] [Col.] Arthur J. Barker, *Eritrea 1941* (London: Faber and Faber, 1966), 59.

odds; the battle of Keren in particular became a symbol of Italian tenacity and Amedeo Guillet was turned into a guerrilla hero.[17]

SETTING THE BALKANS AFLAME: ALBANIA, GREECE AND JUGOSLAVIA

The invasion of Albania in 1939 and its formal annexation in April 1940, together with the attack on Greece on 28 October 1940, indicated Mussolini's will to pursue an independent 'parallel war' and to strengthen his position on the Balkans and in the Mediterranean.[18] His actions set the Balkans aflame, and started a period of occupation, civil wars and troubled memories. The attack on Greece also revealed deficiencies in terms of setting strategic targets within the reach of Italy's limited financial and material assets.[19] While the so-called 'war faction' around Foreign Minister Ciano anticipated a quick Greek surrender, the *Comando Supremo* (initially) strongly counselled against an offensive. The military attaché in Athens and the head of Italian military intelligence (SIM), had both visited the Albanian front in early 1940 and cautioned of the perils in store.[20] All these warnings notwithstanding, Mussolini went ahead. The motives for Mussolini's decision to hasten the invasion have been extensively debated,[21] but it is important to flag the dictator's expectation (or rather fears) of an early end to hostilities.[22] Consequently, force (re-)mobilisation and logistical preparations were hurried, and the problem of limited port facilities dismissed as secondary in a presumably short campaign.[23]

[17] Bastian Matteo Scianna, "Forging an Italian Hero? The Late Commemoration of Amedeo Guillet (1909–2010)," *European Review of History: Revue européenne d'histoire* 26, no. 3 (2019): 369–85.

[18] Burgwyn, *Mussolini*, 54ff.

[19] Sadkovich, "Italo-Greek War."

[20] Cesare Amé, *Guerra segreta in Italia, 1940–1943* (Milan: Bietti, 2011; first ed. 1954), 43ff.

[21] Knox, *Mussolini Unleashed*, 134ff., 189ff.

[22] Woller, *Mussolini*, 206–12. Yet, the Italian military attaché in Berlin, Efisio Marras, had already signalled on 17 August 1940 that the realistic window for a German invasion of Britain—which in his eyes could end the war—would close by October 15th, DS CS, I:I, 17 Aug. 1940. Thus, the argument about the need for a quick victory before an early close to the war is not wholly convincing—or else shows how Mussolini ignored vital advice.

[23] BA-MA, N64/9, Senger Report, 22 June 1942, fol.15.

The war unfolded in three periods: the ill-conceived onslaught in October, followed by Greek counter-offensives from November to January, and a period of defensive action until the renewed Italian (and then German) attacks in March and April 1941.[24] The "small and tough" Greek Army was well trained for mountain warfare,[25] despite relying largely on reserves, suffering from obsolete equipment, and shortages in spare parts, ammunition and communications equipment.[26] By mid-November, the Greeks had reinforced their troops to 232,000 men.[27] They outnumbered their enemy and the following counter-attack pushed the Italians back, but the Greeks "bled white"[28] trying to push them out of Albania into the sea. The Italians held out despite severe supply problems caused by insufficient port facilities and motor transport,[29] bad weather and appalling infrastructure.[30] Yet, the weather also affected the Greek offensive, and British observers argued it was "difficult to say exactly how far the recent slow progress of the Greeks is due to lack of supplies, and how far to Italian resistance."[31]

After this reverse, the widely respected Badoglio was singled out as scapegoat[32] and handed Mussolini his resignation on 26 November

[24] Discussed in more detail in Knox, *Mussolini Unleashed*, 189ff.; [Gen.] Mario Montanari, *La campagna di Grecia. Vol. 1* (Rome: USSME, 1980); Rochat, *Le guerre*, 259–85.

[25] Robin Higham, *Diary of a Disaster: British Aid to Greece 1940–1941* (Lexington: Kentucky University Press, 1986), 41.

[26] Ibid., 3, 82. Their lower motorisation levels had little impact in the particular terrain of this theatre—rather, what most influenced their operations was the constant loss of pack animals.

[27] The Greeks thus came very close to the number forecasted by the Italian General Staff, compare DS CS, II:I, 26 Sept. 1940.

[28] Sadkovich, "Anglo-American Bias," 620.

[29] The Germans noted these two features as major obstacles for the operations, BA-MA, RH 2/2936, Rintelen to Tippelskirch, 27 Nov. 1940, fos.204–6.

[30] Sadkovich, "Anglo-American Bias," 633.

[31] TNA, WO 106/3123, M.I. Contribution to C.I.G.S., 22 Dec. 1940. Yet, the British had noted stubborn and tenacious Italian defensive actions already in early December— but also cases where whole Italian units (up to battalion-size) had been captured, TNA, WO 106/3123, Heywood Mission to War Office, 6 Dec. 1940 and ibid., British Military Mission Greece to C.in.C. Middle East, 5 Dec. 1940.

[32] Dyed in the wool Fascists like Roberto Farinacci saw Badoglio as embodiment of the royalist spirit in the Army and called for his resignation to instill a more ideological spirit, see TNA, GFM 36/170, Farinacci to Mussolini, 9 Nov. 1940. The large majority of the

1940. This led to the appointment of Ugo Cavallero (1880–1943)[33]: first as commander in Greece and then as new Chief of the Armed Forces General Staff on 8 December 1940. The majority of the officer corps—where Cavallero was unpopular,[34] as he was deemed a Fascist yes-man or incompetent "scoundrel" (Messe)[35]—did not welcome these developments in the *Comando Supremo* and the Fascist party's accusations against the Army.[36] While the fronts quite literally froze to an indecisive stalemate over winter, Hitler declared his willingness to intervene in January 1941. Mussolini's appeal for German help ended illusions of a *guerra parallela* and Italy subsequently became more dependent and subordinated to Hitler's plans in what has been called the 'subaltern war' (*guerra subalterna*).[37]

In order to regain prestige, Mussolini decided to augment troop levels and to launch an offensive of his own before the Germans could strike on the northern front. The Italian General Staff (again) advised caution, but to no avail.[38] According to a German report one year later, their partner's offensive on 9 March 1941 turned out to be a "complete failure [...and the] best Italian divisions suffered unnecessary losses, wasted ammunition, and disrupted the planned joint operations."[39] In more immediate assessments, the Germans acknowledged

---

officer corps supported Badoglio and saw his removal as unjust, Pieri and Rochat, *Badoglio*, 757ff.

[33] Cavallero was seen rather as an organiser (having been Under Secretary in the War Ministry between 1925 and 1928) than as an operational genius, Cecini, *I generali*, 113–27.

[34] Frederick W. Deakin, *The Brutal Friendship: Mussolini, Hitler and the Fall of Italian Fascism* (New York: Harper & Row, 1962), 118.

[35] TNA, WO 208/4185, S.R.I.G. no.9, 17 May 1943. Initially, Messe spoke rather benevolent about Cavallero, but their relation soured in 1942, see Messe, *Lettere*, 109, 148, 153.

[36] Knox, "'Totality' and Disintegration," 104; Galeazzo Ciano, *Diaries 1939–1943* (Garden City: Doubleday, 1946), 6 Dec. 1940 [Hereafter cited as Ciano Diaries, date].

[37] Elisabeth Wiskemann, *The Rome-Berlin Axis* (London: Oxford University Press, 1949), 247–48; König, *Kooperation*, 49ff.; Knox, *Mussolini Unleashed*, 231ff.

[38] BA-MA, RM 11/60, Italienische Offensive Albanien, 25 Mar. 1941, fol.294. See also the documents in ACS, T-821/127/IT A1147.

[39] BA-MA, RH 2/1666, German Report, 8 Jan. 1942, fos.4–5. On operations, see Montanari, *La campagna di Grecia*, 585ff., 667ff., 709ff.; Burgwyn, *Mussolini*, 75ff.

the highly unfavourable conditions and argued that it had been impossible to compensate for this with several hours of artillery preparations and "courageously attacking infantry."[40] Thus, during the April offensive the Eleventh Army could not support the German onslaught, but had to "restrict itself to follow the Greeks face-on as they mounted an orderly retreat."[41] However, it is misleading to argue that the Germans had 'saved' the Italians, who in March 1941 were far from collapse.[42]

When the operations ended with the Greek capitulation on 23 April 1941, the Italians had suffered 13,755 fatalities, 25,067 missing (of which most died on the battlefield), 50,874 wounded, 52,108 sick, and 12,368 frostbite injuries, making for a realistic estimated death toll of around 30,000; meanwhile Greek casualties amounted to 13,408 killed, 42,485 wounded and 4253 missing.[43] Thus more Italian soldiers perished in this campaign than in the North African sands.[44] But while the operations were far from textbook examples for a successful offensive and undermined Rome's position in the Axis, it was not the nail in the coffin of Italy's war effort and nor did it result in an irreversible decline of morale among soldiers and citizens. In fact, the downward swing in winter 1940–1941 was offset by an increased optimism over the following spring and summer.[45] If anything, the winter reverse estranged the military elites from the Fascist party leadership[46] while the soldiers—particularly the infantry—were publicly lauded as heroes who had stoically dealt with the hardships faced.[47]

Outside of Italy (and Greece), the campaign has largely been forgotten, or else is interpreted as a German-British affair or example of Italian

[40] BA-MA, RM 11/60, Italienische Offensive Albanien, 25 Mar. 1941, fol.293. Rintelen had warned already in February that an offensive was doomed to fail.

[41] BA-MA, RH 2/1666, German Report, 8 Jan. 1942, fol.5.

[42] Sadkovich, "Anglo-American Bias," 637.

[43] Montanari, *La campagna di Grecia*, 943.

[44] Zamagni, "Italy," 213.

[45] Avagliano and Palmieri, *Vincere*, 23; James J. Sadkovich, "Italian Morale During the Italo-Greek War of 1940–1941," *War & Society* 12, no. 1 (1994): 97–121.

[46] BA-MA, RM 11/60, Löwisch Memorandum, 14 Dec. 1940, fol.203. In a private outburst, Mussolini allegedly deemed the Italians of 1915 of better value and was furious about his military elites, Ciano Diaries, 23 Dec. 1940, also ibid., 16 Jan. 1941.

[47] [Lt.] Remo Fratoni, "Saggio sull'eroismo," *Rivista di Fanteria* 8, no. 2 (1941): 72–77.

ineptitude.[48] The narrative about little Greece embodying David and beating a self-proclaimed Goliath became an enduring one—not least because of Greek and Allied propaganda about their stoic resistance. In Italy, there was a widespread agreement that little glory could be derived from the campaign, but interpretations nonetheless differed. In society and the anti-Fascist camp, the early narrative about the Greek imbroglio was linked to the rottenness of the corrupt Fascist regime and the *campagna di Grecia* was seen as the beginning of its end. Other reminiscences also entered into play: the narrative of poor infantrymen sent to the slaughterhouse by inept generals could easily be likened to Cadorna's leadership in the First World War. Yet, it never gained a truly important place in the collective memory: one indicator was the low output of memoirs (fifteen) and its minimal representation in media.[49] The military, on the other hand, immediately rallied to defend the Italian soldiers' sacrifices and blamed Mussolini and the 'political' generals.

The spring campaign in 1941 led to the subsequent occupation of Croatia, Herzegovina and Slovenia by the Second Army, of Montenegro by the XIV Corps, of Albania and Kosovo by the Ninth Army, and of Greece by the Eleventh, which brought the total Italian forces in the theatre between 1941 and 1943 to over half a million men.[50] As mentioned above, the practices and crimes of the Italian occupation are now well documented and are not of concern here.[51] However, a brief look at the occupation period is vital to understand why the Balkans never became significant for the Italian Army's memory and only selectively so for society at large. The occupation can be split into two parts: first, the period until 8 September 1943, and, second, the time after that, in which the Italians also clashed with the Wehrmacht. Neither period witnessed large-scale operations where any military 'glory' could be

---

[48] Sadkovich, "Anglo-American Bias," 626–27. It was also linked to the myth that the German operations on the Balkans had delayed and thereby 'derailed' Barbarossa.

[49] Giorgio Rochat, "La guerra di Grecia," in *I luoghi della memoria. Vol. 3: Strutture ed eventi dell'Italia unita*, ed. Mario Isnenghi (Bari: Laterza, 1997), 346–64, here 351ff.; Lucio Ceva, "Testimonianze sulla guerra di Grecia," *Risorgimento* 31, no. 1 (1979): 103–6.

[50] Numbers in Davide Rodogno, "Italian Soldiers in the Balkans: The Experience of the Occupation," *Journal of Southern Europe and the Balkans* 6, no. 2 (2006): 125–44, here 127–28.

[51] See e.g. Conti, *L'occupazione italiana*; Agarossi and Giusti, *Una guerra*.

won and bugged conversations in captivity show that Italian generals had been rather bored by their 'inglorious' duties.[52] After the war, the Italians were showcased as benign occupiers—a narrative helped by the possibility of depicting themselves as victims after the German actions surrounding 8 September. The struggle against the Wehrmacht—most prominently on the islands of Corfu and Cephalonia[53]—was used to gloss over earlier Italian atrocities. But while this myth gained relevance in the public sphere in the 2000s (and concentrated primarily on victimhood), the military did commemorate Cephalonia immediately after the war and always placed an emphasis on their active resistance against the Germans—thereby branding this, too, as a kind of beginning of the *Resistenza*.[54] Indeed, the behaviour of the soldiers based overseas was contrasted to the inglorious (de facto non-existent) defence of Rome on 8 September 1943.

Additionally, cooperation with partisans—including Communist formations—constituted a troubled legacy, as did the tens of thousands Italians who remained prisoners of Yugoslav and Greek authorities.[55] Both countries also demanded the extradition and punishment of Italian war criminals, which Rome tried to prevent at all costs.[56] Domestic politics played a great role in this diplomatic contest. The Italian Communist press was very supportive of the new Tito government and tried to persecute—what they deemed to be—the same old Fascist generals that were fighting in the Western camp after the *8 settembre*.[57] On the other hand, 'official Italy' and the military opposed such demands. Marshal Giovanni Messe defended the accused and sent letters to the Prime and Foreign Minister (as Chief of Staff, on 17 February 1945).[58] The *Ufficio*

---

[52] TNA, WO 208/4185, S.R.I.G. no.18, Conversation generals Orlando and Berardi, 19 May 1943.

[53] The events and the myth have been studied most thoroughly by Elena Agarossi, *Cefalonia. La resistenza, l'eccidio, il mito* (Bologna: Il Mulino, 2016).

[54] See the articles in the *Rivista Militare* on Corfu, [Lt. Col.] Alfredo D'Agata, "Diario della resistenza italiana a Corfù (8–26 settembre 1943)," *Rivista Militare* 1, no. 6 (1945): 648-58, and the second part in *Rivista Militare* 1, no. 7 (1945): 775-86; "Cefalonia. Giuseppe Moscardelli," *Rivista Militare* 1, no. 7 (1945): 822-26.

[55] Agarossi and Giusti, *Una guerra*, 238-46.

[56] Ibid., 371-445.

[57] Ibid., 428.

[58] Ibid., 612-13.

informazioni of the Italian General Staff (together with the Foreign Ministry) also collected evidence on Greek atrocities against Italian soldiers.[59] In the end, generals like Taddeo Orlando and Carlo Geloso (who had circulated the infamous C3 order as head of the Eleventh Army) continued their careers and Mario Roatta (GOC of the Second Army) was instead tried for his actions surrounding the 8 September in Rome and crimes against Italian citizens.

The botched initial campaign and inglorious occupation demonstrate why the Italian military had little interest in commemorating this theatre. This should not, however, automatically be considered merely as a measure to cover up crimes during the occupation—after all, ruthless actions against partisans were not perceived as criminal, in military eyes. Other campaigns were simply more relevant to the Italian Army and more suitable for forging a positive narrative about the Second World War.

THE NORTH AFRICAN THEATRE

The war in North Africa is usually cast as a gentlemanly affair between the British and the Germans. The Italian contribution is often forgotten or belittled,[60] but it played a significant role for the domestic audience and for the military sphere after the war. Yet, if there was a campaign with a lasting impact on the stereotype of Italians as unmilitary creatures, it was the British offensive in the Western Desert in December 1940: Operation Compass. The loss of over 130,000 men (most of them prisoners) led Anthony Eden to quip that "never had so much been surrendered by so many to so few."[61] What had gone wrong?

The Italian Fifth Army was protecting Libya (*de jure* Italian soil since 1937) against a possible French intervention coming from Tunisia, while the Tenth Army faced the small British peacetime garrison in Egypt. Badoglio had wanted to allocate the bulk of mobile forces, men, and material to the Tenth Army to prevent force dispersion,[62] but Mussolini prevented this, as he still kept an eye on (and feared an attack from) French-occupied Tunisia. In July, Mussolini ordered Graziani to march

---

[59] Ibid., 436. Reconciliation with Albania was even more difficult and diplomatic relations were only reinstalled in 1949, see ibid., 439–45.
[60] Detailed in Sadkovich, "Of Myths and Men."
[61] Cited in Knox, *Mussolini Unleashed*, 256.
[62] DS CS, II:I, 9 Sept. 1940.

into Egypt. Yet, the Marshal did all he could to forestall the attack[63]: he and his generals repeatedly warned of a "rapid and total disaster" in case of an unprepared attack with rambling masses of second-rate, footbound infantry divisions and the dangers of a counter-attack.[64] His predecessor, Marshal Italo Balbo (1896–1940) had conveyed a picture of precarious Italian preparedness to Major Heinz Heggenreiner, the German assistant military attaché.[65] On the other hand, the Italian staffs in Rome were more optimistic.[66] It would therefore be wrong to lay the responsibility for the following catastrophe on Mussolini's footsteps alone. Yet, the blame placed on the military has to be more specific: the generals on the spot were aware of the risks, while the authorities in Rome tended to disregard their warnings.

Graziani possessed 3500 vehicles to support the Tenth Army's 100,000 soldiers. Sadkovich has rightly asked how Graziani was meant to "manoeuver more" with such means, as Knox has demanded.[67] Moreover, the Italians had no reconnaissance vehicle, and would thus have been 'manoeuvring more' in the dark, for want of accurate operational intelligence and possibility of coordinating units.[68] Extended lines of communications, vast distances, poor infrastructure and other logistical problems further limited offensive actions. Consequently, Graziani signalled that while a German armoured division would be welcome, it was impossible to secure its supply.[69]

---

[63] Canosa, *Graziani*, 240ff. Giovanni Messe was rumoured as a candidate to replace him, Ciano Diaries, 12 Oct. 1940.

[64] Ibid., 8 and 20 Aug. and 2 Oct. 1940. Even his arch-enemy Badoglio was sceptical about the prospects and favoured delay, ibid., 7 Sept. and 2 Oct. 1940. See also DS CS, II: I, 7 Sept. 1940.

[65] Heggenreiner took verbatim notes and cabled them to Rintelen. Quoted in his post-war report in BA-MA, ZA 1/1560, Heggenreiner – Italo-German Cooperation, fol.18. He linked this to his prior experience in Spain, where he had been liaison officer at the headquarters of the Italian Expeditionary Corps for almost two years. However, there are documents indicating Balbo's growing optimism about possible offensives on the Suez Canal, Montanari, *L'Esercito*, 57–58, 69, 73; and there is a blueprint for wide-ranging operations in ACS, T-821/482/IT 6424.

[66] ACS, T-821/109/IT 1012/341-349, SME Ufficio Situazione – Studio sulle possibilità di una nostra offensiva contro l'Egitto, 30 June 1940.

[67] Sadkovich, "Italo-Greek War," 458.

[68] The *AB 40* and *AB 41* only reached North Africa in October 1941.

[69] DS CS, II:I, 26 Sept. 1940.

Between 13 and 16 September 1940, the Italians advanced (largely unopposed) into Egypt with two-thirds of their forces. After 80 kilometres, they stopped at Sidi Barani, where they erected new defensive positions. The British counter-attack on 9 December 1940 resulted in the Italian loss of Sidi Barani (9–11 December), Bardia (3–5 January) and Tobruk (22 January) and the subsequent abandonment of the entire Cyrenaica, which culminated in the battle of Beda Fomm, south of Benghazi (5–6 February). The British captured 130,000 men (largely from surrendering garrisons, such as Bardia with 45,000 men and Tobruk with 30,000) at the cost of 2000 killed and wounded. The Italians had second-rate footbound divisions and nothing to match British tanks and air power.[70] Their armour was almost non-existent, as the L/3 tankettes were useless, and the M/11 and M/13 were not only inferior, but also deployed too late.[71] It should be emphasised that the British were struggling with their own problems and were brilliantly led, and the fall of Italian garrisons stands in contrast to Commonwealth forces who later clung onto their fortresses. Still, what happened to the Italians in the Cyrenaica in December 1940 would later repeat itself as the 'pendulum of war' (Barr) swung back and forth.

The disastrous results of Operation Compass were nevertheless a fatal blow to Italian prestige and Mussolini's boastful propaganda after the Somaliland campaign backfired: now the British were thrilled to claim victory after their many dark hours in 1940. Rochat has described it as the "worst Italian defeat, because it was the most mediatised one: the pictures of endless prisoner columns, ragged as all prisoners of war look, were screened across the globe and consolidated the stereotype about the Italian 'who does not fight'."[72] Moreover, Mussolini had to plead for German help and was confronted with a first ebbing of war enthusiasm.[73] Politically, Italy thus entered the phase of the 'subaltern war' (*guerra subalterna*) and the setbacks affected German views on their military capabilities. In June 1941 Goebbels caricatured the Italians as the "most hated people in the whole of Europe" and seconded Hitler's

---

[70] Rochat, *Le guerre*, 294ff.; Burgwyn, *Mussolini*, 63–67.

[71] The *Comando Supremo* took until 18 December 1940 to decide sending all available M/13 tanks to Tripoli, see Mussolini to Graziani, in DS CS, II:I, 18 Dec. 1940.

[72] Rochat, *Le guerre*, 297.

[73] Avagliano and Palmieri, *Vincere*, 219–34.

belief that they had become a laughing stock.[74] This shift to the *guerra subalterna* brought some benefits: the Italians were forced to cooperate with the Germans, received assistance, and started an internal lessons-learned process. As noted above, one should not stop analysing the Italian Army after its fortunes reached their lowest ebb in spring 1941. Indeed, some scholars have demonstrated a constant improvement of Italian combat performance in North Africa—with German help, but also by own lessons-learned procedures—over the course of 1941 up till the battles of El Alamein, and the stubborn defence of Tunisia in 1943.[75] Also German documents show the improvement of Italian capabilities.[76]

The importance of the North African campaign for Italian postwar society and its Army has never been studied thoroughly.[77] For one, the operations were always linked to imperial nostalgia and hopes of regaining the lost colonies. Yet, improved combat performance also secured the North African theatre a vital place in the Army's memory after the war. The *Folgore* paratroopers in particular forged a myth of a 'glorious defeat', but so, too, did the *Bersaglieri* and the armoured corps, by placing great emphasis on their operations in the desert.[78] The gentleman's war narrative eased a transfer to the civilian memory; the fact that Germany and Britain became alliance partners in NATO also made this legacy less contested.

[74] Bosworth, *Mussolini*, 379.

[75] See Carrier, "Reflections;" Ceva, "North African War;" Rochat, *Le guerre*, 335–59; Burgwyn, *Mussolini*, 156. And, of course, Sadkovich's (sometimes one-sided) writings: foremost Sadkovich, "Of Myths and Men."

[76] BA-MA, RH 2/1666, German Report, 8 Jan. 1942, fol.6. Likewise, German POWs confirmed to the British that "during the last phase of the Tunisian campaign fought better than they had done before", TNA, WO 208/4547, Italian Morale, 14 June 1943. On Tunisia see also Knox, *Hitler's Italian Allies*, 154.

[77] Ceva's study of the memoir literature deriving from the North African war included some remarks pointing in this direction, Ceva, *Africa settentrionale*. See also Focardi, *Il cattivo tedesco*, 99ff.

[78] Marco Di Giovanni, "El Alamein: l'epica della sconfitta," in *Gli Italiani in guerra. Conflitti, identità, memorie dal Risorgimento ai nostri giorni. Vol. 4: Tomo 2*, eds. Mario Isnenghi and Giulia Albanese (Turin: UTET, 2008), 203–9.

A Learning Organisation?

Before turning to the Eastern Front it is intriguing to pursue the aspect of organisational learning a little further. According to conventional wisdom, the Italians undervalued the Wehrmacht's use of aerial and armoured means.[79] Knox, too, has identified the Italian Army's alleged inability to learn from its own—let alone foreign—experiences as one of its fundamental defects.[80] But a closer look at primary sources reveals a more nuanced picture. There are several Italian reports on the German operations in 1939–1940, which were widely circulated throughout the *Regio Esercito*. Italy was still a 'non-belligerent', but her military attachés observed the operations closely.[81] The reports were distributed to the *Comando Supremo* and military intelligence (the SIM), but also to lower commands—who directly asked for such *relazioni*.[82] During the campaign against Poland, the interim attaché in Berlin, Mario Roatta (1887–1968),[83] visited the front on 16 September. He stressed the Wehrmacht's approach to find weak spots and merely bypass strong resistance with armoured and motorised divisions who would then independently push forward with loosely defined objectives—supported by the Luftwaffe.[84] Roatta clearly realised the Wehrmacht's new approach, but also cited the Polish forward deployment as the chief reason for their swift defeat. He was little impressed by the German senior command, chaos in the rear, and remained curious how the Wehrmacht would perform against more equal opposition.[85] Also in subsequent reports, Roatta described the wide-ranging armoured thrusts that encircled Polish forces, the importance of communications, and the grim chances of defending static defence lines in modern war.[86] On 15 October, he

---

[79] Cappellano and Pignato, *Andare contro*, 91; Botti and Ilari, *Il pensiero*, 209–11.

[80] Knox, "'Totality' and Disintegration," 83.

[81] Despite some travel restrictions and the brevity of the campaigns. For example, Marras only visited the French theatre once, Pelagalli, *Marras*, 98.

[82] See e.g. ACS, T-821/109/IT 1003/116, Bastico to General Staff, 16 Sept. 1939.

[83] He replaced Marras in July 1939, but was called up to become the Army's Deputy Chief of Staff in November, after which Marras returned to Berlin.

[84] ACS, T-821/109/IT 1003/30-55, Roatta – Relazione visita fronte polacco, 16 Sept. 1939, fs.36, 41–42, 44, 50–52.

[85] Ibid., f.47.

[86] ACS, T-821/113/IT 1021a/47-58, Roatta – Operazioni Polonia, 8 Oct. 1939, fs.52–54, 57.

summarised some of his observations; stressing the importance of employing tanks cooperatively together with infantry and artillery for wide-ranging missions.[87] This ended, in Roatta's view, the possibility of piecemeal tank deployment that so many German officers had favoured.

Captain Marco Perogo, member of the military staff at the Berlin embassy, visited the areas around Lodz and Warsaw between 9 and 12 October. He noted the Luftwaffe's crucial role during the recent operations and appeared to be stunned by the "complete destruction" of Warsaw,[88] but showed little sympathy when he spoke of up to 30,000 civilian deaths.[89] His and other reports demonstrate the Italian knowledge of German crimes. Roatta reported partisan activities and harsh reprisals, including the shooting of civilians,[90] and Perogo observed the separation of POWs based on racial hierarchies, forced labour and expropriations of Jews.[91] An intelligence report after the campaign portrayed the criminal German occupation in detail.[92] Only minor objections were raised—mainly with a view to Polish resistance that might be spurred by these actions.

Lt. Col. Giuseppe Roero di Cortanze, the military attaché in Warsaw since 1937, provided a different interpretation of these operations. According to Roero, antiquated and romantic ideas about war, an underestimation of the enemy, the erroneous distribution of forces, as well as late mobilisation and tardy counter-actions had caused an unexpectedly quick collapse of the Poles.[93] He also emphasised that as much as they had lost the campaign, the Wehrmacht won it by employing modern operational concepts and armour in combination with airpower.

[87] ACS, T-821/383/IT 4988/898-906, Roatta – Campagna Tedesco-polacca, 15 Oct. 1939, f.904.

[88] ACS, T-821/383/IT 4988/941-952, Cpt. Marco Perogo – Relazione sul viaggio effetuato in Polonia, 15 Oct. 1939, fs.945–46, 949.

[89] As for Polish atrocities against Germans, he noted that such cases had occurred, but deemed this a limited phenomenon, see ibid., f.952.

[90] ACS, T-821/109/IT 1003/30-55, Roatta – Relazione visita fronte polacco, 16 Sept. 1939, fs.47–50, 53.

[91] ACS, T-821/383/IT 4988/941-952, Cpt. Marco Perogo – Relazione viaggio Polonia, 15 Oct. 1939, f.948.

[92] ACS, T-821/383/IT 4988/907-933, SIM, Notiziario Mensile Stati Esteri, N.7, Appendice Seconda, L'occupazione della Polonia, 15 Dec. 1939.

[93] ACS, T-821/383/IT 4988/886-896, Lt. Col. G. Roero di Costanze – Relazione campagna polacco-tedesca, 25 Sept. 1939, fs.887–91.

Nevertheless, Roero believed these developments would not change the basic character of war. He expected trench warfare and mass employment of artillery and infantry to remain the decisive factors—a miscalculation that other scholars have attributed to him writing so shortly after the campaign.[94] Is his report further proof of Italian backwardness? A closer look reveals that Roero was as much of a romantic officer as he described the Poles. A cavalryman himself, he had been aide to the King during the First World War and subsequently served mainly in diplomatic functions. In short, he was not necessarily a battle-hardened commander, nor did his views carry any prominence. In fact, the original document shows heavy markings and the reader's strong disagreements with his assertions.[95] Thus, one should be careful in singling out this document as proof of an Italian misapprehension of modern war.

In contrast, Roatta clearly grasped the Polish campaign's significance and his views were more influential—all the more so, as he left Berlin in November 1939 to become Deputy Chief of Staff of the Army. His reports had been directed to the Chief of the Armed Forces General Staff and the head of the SIM, but also beyond their desks. The remarks on German tank deployment, for example, were circulated to the General Staff's *Ufficio Operazioni* (Operations Section) and *Ufficio Addestramento* (Training Section), and to divisional and corps level in order to provide cutting-edge knowledge on cooperation between armour and aviation.[96] Likewise, a Luftwaffe assessment on the Polish campaign was widely circulated within the *Aeronautica*.[97] Also based on these reports, Graziani concluded that the *Esercito* did not have the tanks and equipment, which had made the recent German successes possible.[98] Thus, he advised a continued defensive stance on the French border and

---

[94] Longo, *L'attività*, 477–78.

[95] Probably by General Giacomo Carboni, head of the SIM, ACS, T-821/383/IT 4988/886-896, Lt. Col. G. Roero di Costanze – Relazione campagna polacco-tedesca, 25 Sept. 1939, f.896.

[96] ACS, T-821/109/IT 1003/113, SME to Army Crops Command *Celere* and *Autotrasportabile*, 23 Sept. 1939.

[97] ACS, T-821/113/IT 1021a/18, Sorice – Rilievi dello S.M. tedesco sulla campagna di Polonia, 5 Mar. 1940.

[98] ACS, T-821/109/IT 1003/89-98, Graziani to Mussolini, 25 May 1940, fs.90–91.

to prevent a conflict with Yugoslavia, thereby gaining more time to refill stocks and prepare the Army for war.[99]

The Italians continued to observe German operations during the campaign against France and the Low Countries. According to Marras, the mass deployment of armour had been the chief reason for German success, which was a far superior to the French Army's piecemeal deployment of tanks as an infantry support weapon,[100] and he stressed the importance of motorised infantry and ground-air cooperation.[101] One could again argue that these were merely theoretical assessments and no one in Rome indulged his cables, let alone transferred knowledge down the military ladder. Yet, the detailed lessons of the campaign in France and the Low Countries were readily summarised by the General Staff's *Ufficio Addestramento* and sent (signed by Roatta) to each army and corps command, troops in Albania, Libya, and all heads of branches.[102] In July 1940, Badoglio—then Chief of the General Staff—had allegedly commented on the reports on German armoured doctrine with a mere "we will study this after the war."[103] Still, the Information Section passed the study to the Operations Section—and the Training Section's subsequent circulars actually hint at good cooperation and a willingness to learn within the General Staff, despite an apparent opposition at the very top. It should not surprise us that after the Italian defeats in winter 1940–1941 and the ousting of Badoglio, many of these memoranda served as blueprint for new training procedures and doctrines. Thus, these reports must be understood in a wider context.

These documents stand in contrast to claims that Roatta understood the new development, but "did not feel the need to distribute his knowledge at home."[104] In fact, Roatta became a key figure: he

[99] Ibid., fs.97–98.

[100] ACS, T-821/130/IT A1167/503-509, Marras – Dati e insegnamenti, 23 July 1940, f.506.

[101] ACS, T-821/130/IT A1167/515-524, Marras – Altre notizie e considerazioni, 26 May 1940, f.524. The employment of combat engineers also aroused notable interest, ACS, T-821/130/IT A1167/486-487, Gen. S. Degiani – Genieri d'assalto, 15 July 1940; and ACS, T-821/130/IT A1167/510-514, Marras – Alcune notizie, 24 July 1940.

[102] ACS, T-821/130/IT A1168/895-897, Roatta – Notizie sui procedimenti tattici, 10 July 1940.

[103] ACS, T-821/130/IT A1168/898, Head of Information Section to Operations Section, 21 July 1940.

[104] Cecini, *I generali*, 248.

replaced Graziani as the Army's Chief of Staff when the latter was sent to Libya.[105] Both the German and the Italian operations against France (and Poland beforehand) influenced the updated training directives in June and July 1940,[106] and another study on all recent campaigns drew sensible lessons, which further demonstrated a keen awareness of modern warfare.[107] This trend to spread and to review information was continued throughout the year: Italian records contain memoranda on British and Soviet armoured doctrine,[108] and also army journals discussed the recent developments in detail.[109]

In late 1940, the recruitment of additional troops was hotly debated.[110] Roatta made clear that simply rallying more men would not do the job. In a long memorandum to Badoglio, Roatta described the present situation. The material situation had not improved: anti-tank guns, artillery, tanks, armoured cars and trucks were badly needed. But Roatta maintained that increased moral and additional training had improved effectiveness.[111] Was he lying or over-optimistic? Roatta was a very ambiguous figure, but his report is also full of direct criticism. He insisted that the forces on the mainland would not be of great help, given their shortcomings in materiel and resources, and warned it was unreasonable to assume one could sustain operations on the current fronts in Albania and Libya indefinitely.[112] What caused him headaches, however, was not the men but the quality of the junior officers and NCOs.[113] Still, he demanded patience for a thorough reorganisation and new deliveries of equipment to arrive.

[105] He formally took over the position on 25 March 1941, but had filled it de facto already before, ibid., 251.
[106] ACS, T-821/130/IT A1167/488-489, Graziani – Addestramento dei reparti, 31 July 1940.
[107] ACS, T-821/494/IT 2046/943-989, Comando Corpo d'armata Celere – Studio sulle recenti campagne, Sept. 1940, particularly fs.988–89.
[108] ACS, T-821/113/IT 1021a/7-12, Dati sulla Divisione Cr. Britannica e sulla Brigata Cr. Russa, 19 Dec. 1940.
[109] "Note sull'impiego della divisione corazzata germanica nelle campagne di Polonia e di Francia," *Rivista di Fanteria* 7, no. 10 (1940): 425–37.
[110] Rochat, *Le guerre*, 311ff.
[111] ACS, T-821/127/IT A1144/665-669, Roatta to Badoglio – Situazione dell'Esercito metropolitano, 19 Nov. 1940, here f.665.
[112] Ibid., f.668.
[113] Ibid., f.669.

Knox has cited the Roatta circular of 15 March 1941 to show how badly led the Italian operations in 1940 had been, but moreover argued that these minor diagnoses never translated into an "organisational revolution."[114] Knox is clearly right in pointing to these shortcomings and the difficulty in assessing the effects of Roatta's demands for reform. However, he underrated the lessons-learned procedures that were going on at the same time. The frankness with which Roatta listed the reasons for the recent defeats has to be set—and can only be understood—within the wider background of on-going lessons-learned approaches. Roatta had already declared in December 1940 that formal education had only secondary importance and recruit training in the coming year should be oriented towards real combat.[115] His demands for more initiative among commanders and more realistic training embraced officers, NCOs, and the rank-and-file.[116] As a sort of culmination of all improvement efforts, Roatta issued another circular on training, operations, and doctrines to all divisional commanders in July 1941—now officially as the Army's Chief of Staff. It repeated the same arguments about the importance of realistic challenging training, more initiative, well-planned attacks with artillery and armour, rapid exploitation of successes, flexible defence, a close protection of the infantry by the (divisional) artillery and anti-tank units (particularly against tanks), improved liaison with the air force and also a closeness of the officers to the frontline.[117] This report hints at many deficiencies in the Italian Army and German observers raised similar opinions.[118] However, it also shows the senior commands' attempts to confront them and even highly critical outside views, such as a memorandum by retired General Luigi Bongiovanni in March 1941, were

[114] Knox, "Italian Armed Forces," 165, 170; Petracarro, "Italian Army," 109.

[115] ACS, T-821/130/IT A1168/880-881, Roatta – Addestramento nuovo contingente di leva, 31 Dec. 1940. The Training Section had also issued guidelines to use the winter period for additional exercises of all troops based on the mainland, ACS, T-821/130/IT A1168/884-885, Col. Testi – Addestramento invernale, 30 Oct. 1940.

[116] ACS, T-821/130/IT A1168/870-872, Roatta – Lacune rilevate, 15 Mar. 1941.

[117] ACS, T-821/354/IT 4507/589-601, Roatta – Addestramento e operazioni, 28 July 1941.

[118] BA-MA, N64/9, Senger Report, 22 June 1942, fol.23. General Senger emphasised the Italian soldiers' bravery and saw the reasons for the setbacks in 1940–1941 in other fields: poor general staff education with too much theory and too little hands-on experience, insufficient resources and war material, overestimation of one's capabilities and underestimation of the enemy.

not just recognised, but proposed to be circulated and incorporated in on-going transformations.[119] Even if one argues—contrary to this author's opinion as laid out above—that the Italian Army had been asleep and disregarded modern war before 1940, the internal learning process evidently shows that they had at least woken up and faced realities after the botched operations against the French, the Greeks and in North Africa.

Other armies underwent similar adaptation processes after their first campaigns.[120] Many scholars have shown that the reality of the initial German campaigns differed from Hitler's propagandised depiction. The Wehrmacht had shown operational and tactical deficiencies in the war against Poland,[121] and its lessons-learned approach after the campaign has been called an exemplary "case study in professionalism."[122] We should, therefore, understand the Italians' attempts at reform as corresponding to a general impetus operating within armies at war: battlefield lessons and new weapons constantly force them to adapt, while training 'on the job' creates new dynamics. Further studies are needed to investigate in detail how the 'lessons-learned' were incorporated into training methods and operations, but Carrier's work has shown the way in this regard. The campaign against the Soviet Union offers a much-neglected case for studying not only an Italian occupation regime, but also independently executed operations on corps and army level.

---

[119] See the introductory summary to Bongiovanni's study, ACS, T-821/249/IT 2298/378-382, Esposto al Duce del generale Luigi Bongiovanni, 1 Apr. 1941, here f.382. The study remarked basic strategic flaws, scarcity of officers, insufficient structure of the high command, hasty creation and state of unreadiness of many divisions, ACS, T-821/249/IT 2298/383-442, Gen. Bongiovanni – Vincere la guerra, 15 Mar. 1941.

[120] Bond, *Britain's Two World Wars*, 144ff.; for Soviet improvement after the Finland disaster, see Hill, *Red Army*, 169ff.

[121] Frieser, *Blitzkrieg-Legende*, 33ff.; Groß, *Mythos*, 209.

[122] Williamson Murray, "The German Response to Victory in Poland: A Case Study in Professionalism," *Armed Forces and Society* 7, no. 2 (1981): 285–98; Groß, *Mythos*, 210ff.

CHAPTER 5

The Italian Operations on the Eastern Front (1941)

Italian soldiers had fought on Russian soil as part of the *Grande Armée* in 1812, in the Crimean War, and during the chaotic years of the Russian Civil War. Despite the relatively good relations between Rome and Moscow after 1922, which deteriorated after 1936, Mussolini decided to support Hitler's invasion in 1941. He had not been involved in the operational planning for Operation Barbarossa but was aware of German intentions from May 1941.[1] He wanted to take part for political, ideological and economic reasons, but the Germans were hesitant to agree to a further dispersion of Italian forces. However, this did offer a chance to keep the feuding Romanians and Hungarians separated.[2] After the political decision was communicated to the *Regio Esercito* on 30 May 1941, Cavallero convinced Mussolini to send one fully independent corps instead of three separate divisions.[3] The restriction to one corps

[1] Still, the Italian envoy in Moscow only heard the news of the Italian declaration of war in the radio, DDI, IX:VII, doc.302, Rosso to Ciano, 23 June 1941. For an in-depth pre-history of the campaign see Giusti, *La campagna*, 47ff.; Burgwyn, *Mussolini*, 113–18; De Felice, *Mussolini, 1:1*, 390ff.; Lucio Ceva, "La campagna di Russia nel quadro strategico della guerra fascista," in *Gli italiani sul fronte russo*, ed. Enzo Collotti (Bari: De Donato, 1982), 163–93.

[2] Detailed in Giusti, *La campagna*, 50ff.; Müller, *An der Seite*, 83.

[3] Mussolini's original idea had been to send one armoured, one motorised, and one infantry division; which would have made a unified employment even more difficult, USSME, *Le operazioni*, 71–73.

© The Author(s) 2019
B. M. Scianna, *The Italian War on the Eastern Front, 1941–1943*, Italian and Italian American Studies,
https://doi.org/10.1007/978-3-030-26524-3_5

owed not least to German reservations about sufficient motorisation and the possibility of furnishing supplies (especially fuel).[4] The *Corpo di Spedizione Italiano in Russia* (Italian Expeditionary Corps in Russia, or CSIR) was formed of three divisions and the corps command—in total 62,000 men, 5500 vehicles,[5] 4600 pack animals, 220 artillery pieces and 92 anti-tank guns.[6] The CSIR received additional engineer units (especially from the pontoon corps), a small aerial section of 83 aircraft for reconnaissance and close air support (and on Messe's demand additional transport planes),[7] and an *Intendanza* (logistical service) for rear and

---

[4] Keitel proposed that the Italians should rather send their trucks and vehicles to North Africa. Cavallero, however, claimed that a less motorised (second) corps could be deployed in early September, ACS, T-821/9/IT 24/322-338, Verbale colloquio Cavallero e Keitel (sera), 25 Aug. 1941, here fs.323–24.

[5] Of which 4600 were spread on nine *autoreparti* that were allocated across the CSIR based on need. While this gave more flexibility, it could not overcome general problems with motorisation. It is necessary to deduct at least ten per cent from the total vehicle numbers as they routinely broke down, had accidents, or underwent maintenance. Indeed, between the second half of August and mid-October 1941, the CSIR had received 167 tons of spare parts by train and aircraft, see TNA, GFM 36/170, Comando Supremo – Automezzi e parti di ricambio per il CSIR, 13 Oct. 1941. Thus, the total numbers should not be confused with de facto operable figures. Also in the German case a twenty per cent maintenance rate is taken for granted, which was further complicated by the countless different types of vehicles, see Stahel, *Operation Barbarossa*, 129ff. DiNardo even argued that of around 500,000 'German' vehicles at the beginning of Barbarossa only 75,000 were serviceable in mid-November 1941, DiNardo, *Mechanized Juggernaut*, 50. The *Celere* reported in November that a majority of its vehicles was worn out and undergoing repair, ACS, T-821/20/IT 98/1001-1007, Marazzani – Impiego della divisione in Ukraina, Nov. 1941, f.1005. Also civilian vehicles proved of little added value, as their standard two-wheel drive was unsuitable for the terrible roads in Russia; likewise captured Soviet vehicles were quickly short of repair parts.

[6] USSME, *Le operazioni*, 537; Müller, *An der Seite*, 84.

[7] ACS, T-821/255/IT 3036/911-917, Relazione sull'attività dell'Aviazione del CSIR fino al 15 novembre 1941, 24 Nov. 1941; Giusti, "Messe," 37. Cavallero had emphasised the need for reconnaissance capabilities, Cavallero Diary, 11 Aug. 1941. The assignment of airpower directly to ground force command had been a lesson from operations in 1939–1940, Botti and Ilari, *Il pensiero*, 214. Yet, the CSIR's air arm engaged merely in nine close-air support operations and fourteen air-to-air fights with 23 aerial victories and three own lost aircraft; further, 7431 persons were transported, 800 wounded evacuated, and 711 tons of material supplied, ACS, T-821/255/IT 3036/924-925. On the *Aeronautica* in the Russian campaign see Giusti, *La campagna*, 88–89.

supply duties under corps command.[8] As Schlemmer has noted, "from the outset, only elite troops and units with the highest possible mobility" were considered for the Eastern Front, which were scare at the time.[9]

The 9th Infantry Division *Pasubio* (79th and 80th infantry regiments, 8th Artillery Regiment)[10] and the 52nd Infantry Division *Torino* (81st and 82nd infantry regiments, 52nd Artillery Regiment) were 'motor-transportable' (*divisione autotrasportabile*, or D.at.)—which primarily meant their artillery was motorised and that the troops had extensively trained motor transport. Yet, the reality was often bleaker: the available trucks could make only one of the 10,300 men strong divisions fully mobile. Additionally, the combat units often marched by foot to free space for transports. The ceiling for motorisation was also set by logistical realities.[11] According to a detailed agreement on logistical cooperation signed on 27 June 1941, the transport of fuel and other vital goods was under German authority until the railhead dropoff points.[12] Thus, when the *Torino* received additional vehicles in September, the Operations Office warned that the CSIR could not absorb more trucks due to the difficult supply situation.[13]

The different motorisation levels created a discrepancy between the *Pasubio* and the *Torino*, and the more mobile 3rd Divisione Celere (D.cl.) *Principe Amedeo Duca d'Aosta* (usually referred to as *Celere* or

---

[8] All following numbers are from USSME, *Le operazioni*, 531ff. The Italian Navy sent submarines and torpedo boats to the Black Sea. Their operations have been described as "very successful, far more so, in fact, than its less aggressive German counterpart", see Joel S.A. Hayward, *Stopped at Stalingrad: The Luftwaffe and Hitler's Defeat in the East, 1942–1943* (Lawrence: University Press of Kansas, 1998), 103–5.

[9] Schlemmer, "Italy," 135. The Italians had three (often incomplete) armoured divisions, three 'fast' divisions, two motorised infantry divisions, and several infantry divisions that were trained for motorised transport; of which some were already deployed on other fronts.

[10] The regiments are described in more detail in Luoni, *Pasubio*, 14–36.

[11] Likewise, the deployment of an armoured division would have consumed more fuel and supplies. As a rule of thumb, they needed three times the amount of an infantry division's supplies, Martin van Creveld, *Supplying War: Logistics from Wallenstein to Patton* (Cambridge: Cambridge University Press, 1977), 152ff., 185.

[12] ACS, T-821/200/IT 1382/936-941, Convenzione, 27 June 1941. On logistics see De Franceschi, *I servizi logistici*.

[13] ACS, T-821/20/IT 98/895-896, Concorso CSIR alla battaglia fra Nistro e Bug, 19 Aug. 1941. Yet, the *Torino* was stripped of many vehicles in favour of the other divisions; thus, it was arguably the least mobile formation and commonly functioned as a kind of corps reserve during the autumn battles.

sometimes PADA). The *Celere* included two cavalry regiments—the *Savoia Cavalleria* (subsequently *Savoia*) and the *Lancieri di Novara* (hereafter *Novara*)—a horse-drawn artillery regiment, and the fully motorised 3rd *Bersaglieri* Regiment.[14] The original idea behind the *celere* type divisions had been to form a unit for wide-ranging operational reconnaissance in mountainous or hilly terrain, hence the combination of horses and automotive vehicles to adapt according to altitude.[15] Yet, in the Russian plains this created a discrepancy in speed levels even within the *Celere*. The division also comprised the only armoured units, which were sent to Russia in 1941. However, the sixty light L3/33 tankettes of its tank battalion were plagued by mechanical breakdowns[16] and stood no chance against Soviet armour (which was not, in fact, their purpose). The light tanks were intended for reconnaissance and as support weapon against enemy infantry. Also the Germans deployed 281 outdated Panzer I units in Operation Barbarossa for similar tasks.[17] The Italian lack of independent armour meant, however, that there was no additional tool for breakthroughs or quick reserves. Thus, arguments that the CSIR's composition was flawed from the beginning, as it was not according to the combined arms doctrine, miss the point.[18] The CSIR was indeed a compromise between (political) ambition and the reality of the available means, but, as Schlemmer has pointed out, "the result of these efforts was definitely impressive"[19] (Fig. 5.1).

All of the CSIR's three divisions had been part of the Second Army during the brief campaign against Yugoslavia from 6–18 April 1941. The

[14] The *Bersaglieri* often marched by foot in order to free up vehicles for other duties, ACS, T-821/20/IT 98/901-905, Messe – Relazione, 23 Aug. 1941, f.902.

[15] USSME, *Le operazioni*, 74; see also Botti and Ilari, *Il pensiero*, 174ff.

[16] Twenty tanks had broken down by the end of August and could only serve as shop for spare parts, USSME, *Le operazioni*, 78; Albino Marsetic, *Dall'Adige al Don. Con il 79° reggimento fanteria in Russia* (Milan: Mursia, 2002), 43–44. The tank crews were sent back in 1942 to re-equip with the L6/40, Cappellano and Battistelli, *Light Tanks*, 38.

[17] David Stahel, *Operation Barbarossa and Germany's Defeat in the East* (Cambridge: Cambridge University Press, 2010), 107–8.

[18] USSME, *Le operazioni*, 77. Scotoni and Schlemmer also criticised the Italian high command for not foreseeing occupation duties—while arguing at the same time that the Italian units had no independent occupation area until the ARMIR was formed. Yet, also German infantry divisions had no special occupation sections, and security divisions were only formed subsequently.

[19] Schlemmer, "Italy," 141.

Second Army conducted most of the offensive operations on the Giulian front, but the divisions that later became part of the CSIR were deployed in the second line as army reserve. They were involved in the subsequent operations—the *Torino* arguably most—but hardly saw any combat.[20] Losses on the whole Giulian front amounted to 302 killed, wounded, and missing during the 'April War'[21] and several of the Second Army's divisions had been involved in more intense fighting than the three of concern here.[22] It is therefore difficult to label them the battle-hardened cream of the Italian Army. The 3rd *Bersaglieri* Regiment had seen severe fighting in the Abyssinian War 1935–1936, taken part in the occupation of Albania in 1939, and been deployed to the Alps in 1940—so there may have been some more experienced veterans.[23] For now, it is fair to assess that none of the CSIR's divisions had seen combat against a modern European army before it was deployed to the Eastern Front—a noteworthy contrast to many German divisions.[24]

A look at the deployment in Yugoslavia reveals continuity at the command level: the *Pasubio* under Major General Vittorio Giovannelli and the *Torino* under Major General Luigi Manzi were part of the corps commanded by Lieutenant-General Francesco Zingales, whereas the *Celere* under Brigadier-General Mario Marazzani formed part of another corps that was sent to the Giulian border.[25] Giovannelli, Manzi and Marazzani all kept command of their divisions until late 1942, and Zingales was envisaged to head the CSIR; after he fell ill, Giovanni Messe substituted

---

[20] [Lt. Col.] Salvatore Loi, *Le operazioni delle unità italiane in Jugoslavia (1941–1943)* (Rome: USSME, 1978), 56–66. On the April operations see ibid., 134ff.

[21] Loi, *Le operazioni*, 263. In the two other theatres (Zara front and Greek-Albanian) the losses were 32 and 3000 respectively.

[22] The *Torino* and *Pasubio* immediately redeployed to Italy, while the *Celere* was first assigned occupation duties and only returned to Italy from Bosnia in late June; departing to the Russian front between 20 and 25 July from Verona, ACS, T-821/20/IT 98/1001-1007, Gen. Marazzani – Impiego della divisione in Ukraina, Nov. 1941.

[23] The 1st, 2nd, 4th, and 5th *Bersaglieri* Regiments had shouldered the hard fighting against Greece in 1940–1941. The 3rd (and the 6th) only became involved in the brief and relatively calm campaign against Yugoslavia, Roggiani, *Bersaglieri*, 244–69.

[24] However, one could argue that the German infantry divisions had seen little combat in the French campaign and mainly occupied terrain conquered by armoured and motorised formations, Frieser, *Blitzkrieg-Legende*, 39.

[25] Loi, *Le operazioni*, 54.

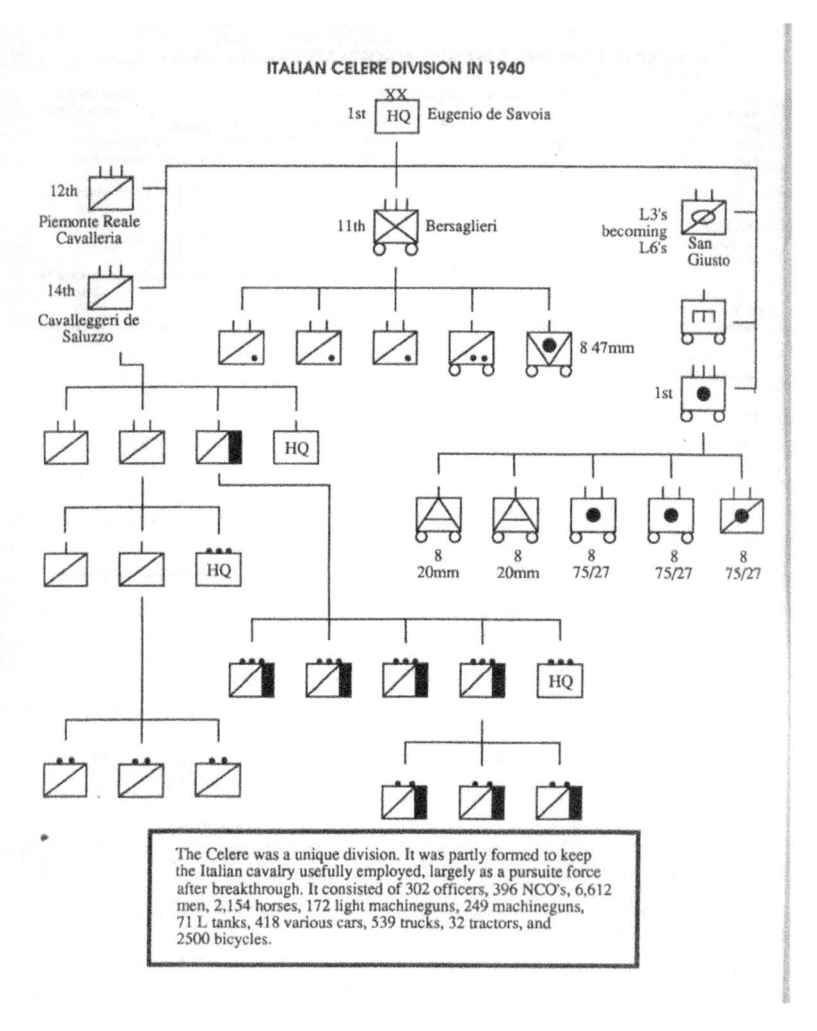

Fig. 5.1 Organisational scheme of a *celere* type division, here the 1st '*Eugenio di Savoia*' *Celere* division in 1940, from Greene, *Mare Nostrum*, 54

for him.[26] Messe had risen the ranks from simple soldier to general (and later Marshal of Italy) without attending a general staff course and was considered a 'soldiers' general'—though Mussolini, too, thought well of him.[27] He spent most of his time in elite units, and even managed to distinguish himself during the campaign in Albania and Greece. Several scholars have accredited the CSIR's successful track record to his actions; primarily his flexibility, eagerness to learn lessons, motivation of his men and determination to have his soldiers respected by the Wehrmacht.[28] The Germans noted how close he was to the soldiers: he visited the units on the frontlines, listened to their needs and rallied his officers around him.[29] His chief was initially Col. Guido Piacenza (later Col. Umberto Utili), the corps artillery was in the hands of Brigadier-General Francesco Dupont, and the engineers led by Col. Mario Tirelli. As mentioned before, the scholarship on Italian divisional commanders is underdeveloped. We will thus take a brief look at the CSIR's officers before later going to provide a more detailed assessment of their capabilities.[30]

Major General Vittorio Giovanelli (born 1882) was reactivated from reserve in 1940 and commanded the *Pasubio* until 4 December 1942. He was a highly experienced artilleryman, noted for his expertise on border fortifications.[31] Yet, it would be mistaken to jump to the conclusion that he was some old and hapless commander: rather, in March 1942 an Italian officer promotion board rated him markedly above average, contrasting him favourably with other divisional commanders.[32] Further

---

[26] Messe had been considered for commander even before Zingales' nomination, Longo, *Messe*, 118. It remained unclear how long he was to keep his command. Apparently, Mussolini was satisfied with his command and told him in late August that no one would substitute him, Messe, *Lettere*, 120.

[27] Schlemmer, *Italiener*, 22.

[28] Müller, *An der Seite*, 87; Schlemmer, "Italy," 145; Giusti, "Messe," 13.

[29] BA-MA, RH 31-IX/25, Fellmer to Tippelskirch, 10 Sept. 1942.

[30] Assessing the regimental commanders would be most useful; yet reliable data and parameters are difficult to establish. Again, further research is badly needed in order to differentiate between more and less capable Italian officers.

[31] BA-MA, RH 2/1672, fol.258.

[32] ACS, T-821/146/IT 2228/105. As in other armies, nepotism or personal animosities might of course have played in, but the ratings of 49 officers show a notable degree of nuances. They fluctuated between 60 and 83 points with an average between 74 and 77. Giovanelli scored 80. Also in subsequent cases where I cite this board, 'above-average' means 80 or higher. Umberto Utili received 82 in the colonel section, ACS, T-821/146/IT 2228/133.

notable officers included his chief, Lt. Col. Umberto Ricca, and the commander of the divisional infantry, Brigadier-General Aldo Princivalle.[33] The *Pasubio*'s 79th Regiment was headed by Col. Rocco Blasioli, the 80th by Col. Epifanio Chiaramonti and the 8th (Motorised) Artillery Regiment by Col. Alfredo Reginella.[34] In the *Torino*, the GOC was Major General Luigi Manzi, his chief Lt. Col. Umberto Scalcino, and Col. Ugo De Carolis head of the division's infantry. Manzi (born 1883) also came from artillery. In June 1943, German military intelligence sketched him as a "systematic, smart personality and strict superior. Has been very accommodating and amicable towards German officers."[35] The *Torino*'s 81st Infantry Regiment was led by Col. Carlo Piccinini, the 82nd by Col. Evaristo Fioravanti, the 52nd Motorised Artillery Regiment by Col. Giuseppe Ghiringhelli.[36] Brigadier-General Mario Marazzani (1887–1969), a cavalryman deriving from an old officer family, commanded the *Celere*. The Germans described him as a capable and calm soldier.[37] In March 1942, the Italian commission for officer advancement judged him well above average[38] and even proposed him for promotion due to his merits in war.[39] The deputy commander was Brigadier-General Gioacchino Solinas, and the chief Lt. Col. Dandolo Battaglini. The 3rd *Bersaglieri* Regiment was led by Col. Aminto Caretto (who was killed at the battle of Serafimovic in July 1942), the *Savoia* Regiment by Col. Weiss Poccetti, the *Novara* Regiment by Col. Egidio Giusiana, and the 3rd Horse-Drawn Artillery Regiment by Col. Cesare Colombo. Most of these nineteen key officers were made Knights

---

[33] Erstwhile GOC of 152nd Infantry Regiment *Sassari*, and chief of XI Corps; remained on the Eastern Front until 1943 and fought with the RSI after 1943.

[34] USSME, *Le operazioni*, 533–34.

[35] BA-MA, RH 2/1672, fol.311. Messe spoke less fond of him in captivity: "Manzi wasn't the right man. He was hesitant – he was clever, he was well liked by the division, but he wasn't the man we needed. I sent him away myself, not that he asked to go. He looked terrible when he left, he was weeping, he was absolutely done, he had given his all", TNA, WO 208/4185, S.R.I.G. no. 16, Conversation between Messe, generals Orlando and Berardi, and Lt. Colacicchi, 18 May 1943.

[36] USSME, *Le operazioni*, 534–35.

[37] BA-MA, RH 2/1672, fol.312. He had taught military history at the academy and served as military attaché in Poland between 1933–1937. He commanded the *Celere* until 1 November 1942, and became presidential adviser in 1947.

[38] ACS, T-821/146/IT 2228/100, and ibid., f.121.

[39] The Italian Army used this step (*Promozione per Merito di Guerra*) only in exceptional cases and it was a distinguishing achievement for every recipient.

of the Military Order of Italy for their services in mid-to-late 1942, but it is difficult to evaluate their qualities based on medals. Only those who fell in combat—De Carolis and Caretto—were posthumously awarded the Gold Medal of Military Valour.

The *Pasubio*, *Celere*, and *Torino* were distinguished from other Italian divisions in several ways. For one, they had no Blackshirt units. In normal binary divisions, the third infantry regiment was supplemented by a Blackshirt legion (two battalions). The only Blackshirt unit, the 63th *Tagliamento* Legion (hereafter *Tagliamento*) was assigned to the corps command with its three battalions to be employed independently. Its firepower had been augmented by adding one battery of 81 mm heavy mortars and one of 47/32 AT guns.[40] The CSIR's artillery has to be seen as a weak spot. The corps artillery had three batteries (36 barrels) of 105/32, two batteries (sixteen pieces) of 75/46 AA guns and two batteries 20 mm AA guns. The *Celere* possessed six batteries of horse-drawn 75/27, sixteen 20 mm AA guns and sixteen 47/32 AT guns. The *Pasubio* and *Torino* had three batteries (12 pieces) of 100/17 howitzers of Austrian-Hungarian origin, and six batteries (24 pieces) of the 75/27, which had been in service since the Italo-Ottoman War in 1911–1912. Based on experiences from the Greek front, the *Pasubio* and *Torino* were assigned one additional heavy mortar battalion and one battery 47/32 AT guns for their divisional artillery, which in both cases doubled the available barrels (bringing the 47/32 to 28 pieces in the *Torino*); also another battalion of 47/32 guns was assigned to the corps' artillery.[41] Thus, the CSIR's AT guns were effectively almost tripled—in total 92—(plus the ones on corps level) in comparison to what three normal infantry divisions would muster: clear evidence that the lessons-learned approach in spring 1941 had borne fruits and the *Comando Supremo* tried to assemble all available material.

Foreign Minister Ciano noted something that many historians seem to have forgotten: namely, that one should not compare Italian with

---

[40] USSME, *Le operazioni*, 75. The operations in Greece had exposed weaknesses in most Blackshirt formations. Yet, Ceva has argued that they were able to adapt and to learn, especially in Russia, see Ceva, "Fascismo," 392.

[41] USSME, *Le operazioni*, 75–76, 539. The *Pasubio* had twelve barrels less of the 47/32; in contrast, it had two batteries of 65/17 guns. Many of these additional forces were dragged out of units in Italy, thus there might have been different training levels and unfamiliarity between the formations.

German divisions, for at the level of equipment, the Italians will always look like a "poor cousin."[42] Still, one must not confuse the few panzer groups, *blitzkrieg* propaganda and Hitler's desire for a mechanised juggernaut with the Wehrmacht's bleak reality of horse-drawn guns and marching infantrymen. Stahel has called for the abandoning of the myth of a fully mobile and armoured Wehrmacht.[43] The vast majority of the *Ostheer* as well as other nations' contingents looked a lot like the CSIR— even if German infantry divisions had more vehicles and subsequently received large calibre AT guns. This should offer reason for caution when one reads (or writes) about the imperfect Italian preparations for the Eastern Front, as Schlemmer has also emphasised.[44]

What kind of enemy did the *Regio Esercito* expect to confront? The reports from their military attachés had kept them informed about ongoing developments in the 1930s, for instance Soviet armour doctrine and personnel changes.[45] Even before the first units reached the front, Colonel Giovanni Wiel, erstwhile military attaché in Moscow and later in the campaign head of the ARMIR's Information Section, warned of the Red Army's capable commanders and predicted resolute resistance.[46] One month after the start of Barbarossa, also Colonel Corrado Valfrè di Bonzo, the military attaché in Bucharest (who had earlier served in Moscow) compiled a thoughtful report, in which he complimented the improved Red Army leadership and the soldiers' resilience. He was also sceptical about any quick Soviet collapse.[47] In contrast, the ever-optimistic Cavallero and the military attaché in Berlin, General Effisio Marras, bought into the German narrative of a certain victory despite the delays, wear and tear and Soviet reinforcements.[48] Also Messe, who noted the sheer logistical problems at first hand, initially remained optimistic and

---

[42] Ciano Diaries, 26 June 1941.

[43] Stahel, *Operation Barbarossa*, 118–19. On the myth of superior German equipment see also Evan Mawdsley, *Thunder in the East: The Nazi-Soviet War 1941–1945* (London: Hodder Arnold, 2007), 26–31.

[44] Schlemmer, "Italy," 143.

[45] Longo, *L'attività*, 562–75.

[46] Cavallero Diary, 31 July 1941.

[47] Report printed in USSME, *Le operazioni*, 58–67.

[48] BA-MA, RM 11/61, Naval Attaché Rome (Löwisch) to Naval High Command, 26 Aug. 1941; Pelagalli, *Marras*, 108; Ciano Diaries, 23 June 1941.

clung to the belief that "things must go right at any cost."[49] Still, they were not alone in their optimism. After the Soviet-Finnish War in 1939 and the Wehrmacht's swift victories, most foreign observers expected the Red Army to collapse within weeks.[50] So, too, did the German high command where Hitler's optimism was shared, the enemy undervalued and a quick Soviet defeat expected, or—in the worst-case scenario—certain victory in the medium term.[51]

Italians to the Front

In the morning hours of 22 June 1941, the Wehrmacht commenced its momentous campaign against the Soviet Union: Operation Barbarossa. The Germans and their allies fielded 153 divisions with 3.7 million men, 625,000 horses, 4000 tanks, 7200 artillery pieces and 4400 combat aircraft against 186 Soviet divisions encompassing three million soldiers, 19,800 artillery pieces, 11,000 tanks and 9100 combat aircraft.[52] This turned the Eastern Front into the grandest land theatre of the Second World War. Yet, the attack remained a *va banque* gamble: the Germans were betting on a rapid victory and had few alternatives or positive prospects for a protracted campaign. Their misconceptions about space and time,[53] inadequate logistical preparation, belief in their operational supremacy, underestimation of the enemy and lack of motorisation and mobility were severe shortcomings for which even an excellent cooperation between armour and airpower could compensate only for a short while.[54] These flaws have been seen as classic defects of German military thought: searching for operational solutions to strategic problems.[55] The plan had been—simply put—to swiftly defeat as many Soviet forces

---

[49] Messe, *Lettere*, 117.

[50] Stahel, *Operation Barbarossa*, 148; Martin Kahn, "'Russia Will Assuredly Be Defeated': Anglo-American Government Assessments of Soviet War Potential Before Operation Barbarossa," *The Journal of Slavic Military Studies* 25, no. 2 (2012): 220–40.

[51] Johannes Hürter, *Hitlers Heerführer. Die deutschen Oberbefehlshaber im Krieg gegen die Sowjetunion 1941/42* (Munich: Oldenbourg, 2006), 282; Groß, *Mythos*, 232–33.

[52] Mawdsley, *Thunder*, 18–19; Stahel, *Operation Barbarossa*, 119.

[53] Bellamy vividly spoke of a 'funnelling out' effect as the front line became longer with every advance to the East, see Bellamy, *Absolute War*, 245.

[54] Groß, *Mythos*, 239ff.; Van Creveld, *Supplying War*, 150ff.

[55] Megargee, *Inside*, 117–41.

as possible near their spring-off positions and hope that this would have political consequences, i.e. a Soviet collapse—and, if this did not materialise, German forces were to advance to a vaguely defined line between Archangelsk-Astrakhan.[56] In the Baltic, Army Group North under Field Marshal Wilhelm von Leeb was pinned towards Leningrad, Army Group Centre (the most powerful) under Field Marshal Fedor von Bock marched through Belorussia towards Minsk and Smolensk; and Army Group South under Field Marshal Gerd von Rundstedt advanced through the heart of Ukraine.[57]

The jewels of the Wehrmacht were the four panzer groups that encompassed the armoured and motorised divisions. Through pincer movements they surrounded large swaths of the Soviet forces, with the bulk of the infantry divisions forming the static basis for these movements. One must not forget that the majority of the German *Ostheer* between 1941 and 1943 consisted of these 'ordinary' infantry divisions. Their number rose from 81 in June 1941 to 135 in June 1943 (around 60 per cent of all divisions), whereas the mighty armoured and motorised divisions remained around 25 (i.e. between 10 and 18 per cent of the total).[58] Germany's allies contributed around 700,000 soldiers to the operations in 1941, of which around half were Romanians, one-third Finns, nine per cent Italians, and seven per cent Hungarians.[59]

The early phase of the campaign brought the Wehrmacht overwhelming victories: the battles on the USSR's borders and the pockets of Bialystok and Minsk resulted in hundreds of thousands of Soviet prisoners, while 3990 Soviet combat aircraft were destroyed within the first two weeks.[60] The Red Army showed weaknesses in command and control (exacerbated by the fact that German special forces had cut its vulnerable landlines) and lacked radios in its tanks and aircraft, which hampered cooperation.[61] Yet, despite their great losses, the Soviets did

---

[56] Mawdsley, *Thunder*, 6–9.

[57] A concise history of operations up to September 1941 can be found in Mawdsley, *Thunder*, 59–87; Stahel, *Operation Barbarossa*.

[58] Hartmann, *Wehrmacht*, 79.

[59] David Stahel, "Introduction," in *Joining Hitler's Crusade: European Nations and the Invasion of the Soviet Union, 1941*, ed. David Stahel (Cambridge: Cambridge University Press, 2017), 1–14, here 12.

[60] Mawdsley, *Thunder*, 58–59.

[61] Bellamy, *Absolute War*, 199.

not collapse. They managed to safeguard vital industries (and Allied lease-lend support) and their ability to levy apparently endless new armies threatened to derail the half-baked German campaign plan. In fact, the end of July and the whole month of August brought bitter truths to the Wehrmacht. Dogged defence and repeated (costly) Soviet counter-attacks had stalled the onslaught and the Red Army improved its battlefield performance.[62] The German infantry divisions' strength had been reduced to an average of 40 per cent and the tank divisions' to 50 per cent.[63] And without any prospect of adequate replacements the Wehrmacht was being bled white. Some scholars, therefore, argue that Barbarossa had failed already by late August 1941.[64] At the same time, Hitler ordered parts of Army Group Centre to support the encirclement of the Soviet Fifth Army's east of Kiev, where the Germans captured an additional one million prisoners.[65] Hitler then focused on seizing Moscow.[66] But even as the march on the Soviet capital was still in full swing, Rundstedt's Army Group South simultaneously pushed—after relatively successful Soviet defensives in June and July—towards Kharkov, the resource rich Donets basin, and Rostov.[67] His army group comprised the First Panzer Group, the German Sixth, Eleventh, and Seventeenth Army, as well as the Romanian Third and Fourth Army, Slovak and Hungarian units—and soon the Italian corps.

The CSIR departed from Italy on 10 July and reached the assembly areas on the Dnestr via Hungary and the Carpathians around 5 August—often after lengthy foot marches of over 500 kilometres. Despite the glitches in assembling and in reaching the front, the Italians increased their marching speed to guard the flanks of the advancing German motorised and armoured divisions. German infantry divisions had their

---

[62] Glantz and House, *When Titans Clashed*, 74ff.; Hill, *Red Army*, 211ff.

[63] Stahel, *Operation Barbarossa*, 410, 419.

[64] Ibid., 441. Glantz argued that the Red Army only managed to seize the strategic defence in December, thereby creating the first turning point in the war, see David M. Glantz, *Barbarossa: Hitler's Invasion of Russia 1941* (Stroud: Tempus, 2001), 208.

[65] The best description is David Stahel, *Kiev 1941: Hitler's Battle for Supremacy in the East* (Cambridge: Cambridge University Press, 2012); Glantz, *Barbarossa*, 117–36.

[66] Glantz, *Barbarossa*, 213. The quarrels surrounding Hitler's decision cannot be recounted here; see exemplary Stahel, *Operation Barbarossa*, 425ff.; Megargee, *Inside*, 131ff.

[67] For the operations of Army Group South see Mawdsley, *Thunder*, 74–81.

own problems, too, in keeping pace with motorised formations,[68] but the Italian delay was also owed to insufficient communication equipment, logistical bottlenecks, Soviet air attacks[69] or simply bad weather.[70] Messe complained about the drop-off point allocated to his troops by German planners and tried to encourage the Wehrmacht to treat the CSIR like their own troops—but he also had cordial words about the German and Romanian allies.[71] Keitel told Cavallero on 25 August 1941 that the front was simply advancing too fast, that wear and tear had been higher than expected and that the Russians had further destroyed the already poor infrastructure in the border regions. In this context, he also told the Italians to think twice about their proposals to send another army corps by early September, as the shortage of transport would inhibit its useful deployment[72] (Fig. 5.2).

During the last stages of the battle of Kiev in August and September 1941, the Italians took part at the very southern wing of operations: first under the Eleventh Army, then under Ewald von Kleist's First Panzer Group (subsequently renamed First Panzer Army).[73] Messe noted the Eleventh Army's relative lack of success in achieving their aims. As reasons, he named the deficiency of armoured forces (dismissing the Romanian ones) and the "most tenacious resistance and fanatical counterattacks of the Reds" who never surrendered even in the most hopeless

[68] Groß, *Mythos*, 233.

[69] ACS, T-821/254/IT 3051/241, Bombardamento aereo, 31 Aug. 1941. Subsequent circulars tried to foster calm in the face of aerial attacks, ACS, T-821/254/IT 3051/353-354, Occultamento – Disciplina durante gli allarmi aerei, 7 Sept. 1941.

[70] BA-MA, RH 21-1/51, Kriegstagebuch des Panzerarmee-Oberkommandos 1, Band III, Feldzug in Russland, 1 Sept.–31 Oct. 1941 [hereafter KTB PzAOK 1, III], fos.8, 92, 113; BA-MA, MSg 2/4388, Distler – Als deutscher Verbindungsoffizier bei der italienischen Russland-Armee, n.d., fol.13 [hereafter cited as Distler – Verbindungsoffizier].

[71] ACS, T-821/20/IT 98/886-890, Messe – Relazione, 29 July 1941.

[72] DDI, IX:VII, doc.504, Meeting Keitel and Cavallero, 25 Aug. 1941.

[73] The Eleventh Army was moved to the Crimea in late September, while the Romanian Fourth Army was bled white in its onslaughts on Odessa, see Mark Axworthy, "Peasant Scapegoat to Industrial Slaughter: The Romanian Soldier at the Siege of Odessa," in *Time to Kill: The Soldier's Experience of War in the West*, eds. Paul Addison and Angus Calder (London: Pimlico, 1997), 221–32; DiNardo, *Germany*, 116ff. The First Panzer Group was formed of the German III and XIV Panzer Corps, the XIX Mountain Corps, and the Romanian Third Army, plus the motorised Slovak division and the Waffen-SS divisions 'Leibstandarte' and 'Wiking'.

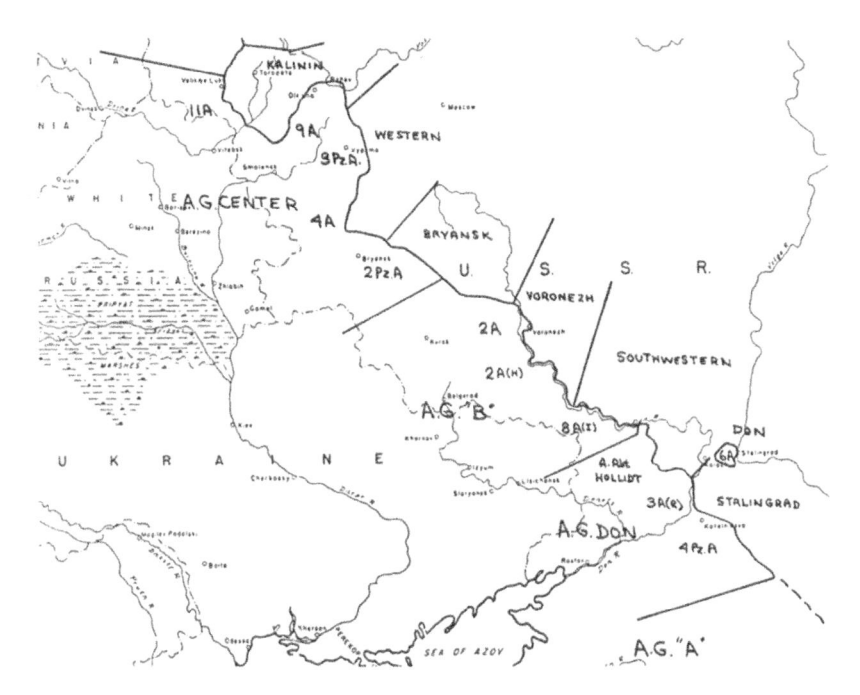

5 THE ITALIAN OPERATIONS ON THE EASTERN FRONT (1941)   101

Fig. 5.2 The theatre of operations. The order of battle shows the situation on 1 December 1942. The Italian Eighth Army is marked as '8 A (I)', from Glantz, *From the Don*, 11

situations.[74] The Eleventh Army was anxious to employ the CSIR[75] and requested the *Pasubio* (plus the 30th *Raggruppamento Artiglieria* with three groups of 105/32 guns, and one company of motorised *Bersaglieri*) to block the Soviet line of retreat on the right bank of the Bug. Messe hesitated to deploy the *Pasubio*. He wanted to prevent a

---

[74] ACS, T-821/20/IT 98/869-876, Messe – La manovra di Petrikowka, 2 Oct. 1941, quoted on f.889. Later he added two more points: bad weather had rendered many roads unpassable and the Germans had generally miscalculated the forces needed to conquer southern Ukraine, ACS, T-821/20/IT 98/891-894, Messe – Relazione, 4 Aug. 1941.

[75] Nonetheless, Messe described his first meeting with the Eleventh Army's GOC General von Schobert as very cordial, ACS, T-821/20/IT 98/867-868, Messe – Visite al Comando Supremo Rumeno ed al Comando della 11^ Armata germanica, 22 July 1941.

piecemeal deployment of his forces at all cost.[76] He also thought twice about splitting his units before the march-up was completed, as his intelligence reported strong Soviet rearguards waging fierce counter-attacks.[77] In the end, Messe gave way to German requests to demonstrate good will and the CSIR's own combat ability. The Wehrmacht had envisaged using the Italian divisions for mopping-up duties and only assigned them to new tasks after Messe hinted at the CSIR's mobility and usefulness in the ongoing operations.[78]

To fulfil this promise, Messe shifted resources within the CSIR: the *Pasubio* received the *Torino*'s vehicles (and more of the independent *autoreparti* from the Corps reserve) and successfully came through its baptism of fire on Russian soil on 11 August 1941. The *Pasubio* helped to seal off substantial enemy forces and took over one hundred prisoners during the so-called battle of the two rivers (Dnestr and Bug).[79] The operations have been described as a comprehensive success[80] and were complimented by the Wehrmacht.[81] Yet there are also other sources that should remind historians to be cautious about top-level praise—especially in coalition warfare. The German liaison officer to the *Pasubio* criticised the division's reliance on written orders instead of transmitting them in order to act more swiftly,[82] and listed further deficiencies in reconnaissance, concealment, marching discipline, medical services, flank protection, contact with neighbouring units, foresight in supply and the

---

[76] His decision might have been influenced by the substantial (and costly) operations of the Romanians against Odessa, Mark Axworthy, *Third Axis, Fourth Ally: Romanian Armed Forces in the European War, 1941–1945* (London: Cassell, 1995), 49ff.; Stahel, *Kiev*, 136–38.

[77] ACS, T-821/247/IT 2259/294-295, Notiziario sul nemico n.17/41, 11 Aug. 1941.

[78] ACS, T-821/20/IT 98/891-894, Messe – Relazione, 4 Aug. 1941, fs.892–93.

[79] ACS, T-821/20/IT 98/897-900, Messe – Relazione, 16 Aug. 1941.

[80] USSME, *Le operazioni*, 88–90. For a generally positive report on the *Pasubio*'s operations at this time see Gosztony, *Hitlers Fremde Heere*, 163–64. They also put great strain on the existing material; see the letter of a driver in one *autoreparto* dated 24 Aug. 1941, TNA, GFM 36/170, fos.31653-55.

[81] Giusti, *La campagna*, 102.

[82] A counter example is the attack by the *Torino*'s 82th infantry regiment on 19 November, which was launched near Rykovo from a defensive posture in bad weather based on a swift oral order, ACS, T-821/255/IT 3056/828-830, *Torino* to CSIR, 21 Nov. 1941.

employment of heavy weapons.[83] He praised the troops' heroic comportment in battle, but was critical of the fact that the divisional commander never went to the frontlines in order to improve his situational awareness. He argued: "regiments do not receive precise orders. It falls to the commander of the spearheading regiment to decide if he attacks or defends when making contact with (even numerically inferior) enemy forces. The Italian mentality will always make them favour the defensive."[84] The vague assessment about "Italian mentality" aside, the room granted for commanders on the spot to assess the situation and base their actions on this rather followed textbook *Auftragstaktik*. Nonetheless, this early report hints at weaknesses in the Italian divisions. It also included a remark that German advice was none-too-welcome among the Italian staff and that different mentalities and procedures in the two armies should therefore be acknowledged.[85] Yet, historians should also critically assess such low-level sources. In fact, Captain Becker's report was cited by DiNardo and Knox to demonstrate Italian deficits,[86] but its context has been overlooked: dating from 15 August 1941, it was probably the author's first assessment of the *Pasubio* after having spent only a few days with the division.[87] Many procedures were new to him and, additionally, this was the first real fighting for the *Pasubio* (after having just completed a long transport and tiring marches) on the Eastern Front, and indeed in the whole war. We should thus be cautious about citing this source for generalising statements about Italian military culture.

The CSIR subsequently operated under General Ewald von Kleist's First Panzer Group (renamed First Panzer Army in October). Kleist's orders were to cut off Soviet forces with mobile thrusts, but the German motorised units were already strained. In Giusti and Schlemmer's opinion, the CSIR's transfer to Kleist's group was a sign of German

---

[83] NARA, T-312/360/7934956-57, Cpt. Becker – Erfahrungsbericht Verb.Offz. *Pasubio*, 15 Aug. 1941.

[84] Ibid.

[85] Messe issued a circular on firing discipline that hints at some nervousness and ammunition wastage during the first combat operation, ACS, T-821/247/IT 2259/338-340, Messe – Disciplina del fuoco, 15 Aug. 1941.

[86] Knox, *Hitler's Italian Allies*, 115–16; DiNardo, *Germany*, 127, 239.

[87] The author could not establish further details on Becker. However, it is unlikely that he had been attached to the division before it reached the assembling areas (it would have been against common practice), thus in the best of cases he had served with the *Pasubio* for around two weeks.

confidence in its capabilities.[88] Messe realised the need for fast and independent movements in the coming operations,[89] but proudly noted the CSIR's control of a 150-kilometre frontline and the role it was assigned as Kleist's advanced flank guard.[90] In early September, the CSIR supported the Wehrmacht in crossing the Dnepr and lent successful artillery support to German units defending the bridgehead near Dnepropetrovsk.[91] Subsequently the *Pasubio* secured the road over the river for the *Torino*, *Celere* and German units, while Kleist's armour turned northwards.[92] The First Panzer Group praised the CSIR's backing for its offensives north of the Dnepr,[93] but nonetheless stripped the Italians of fuel for its own operations.[94] Messe, considered this to be a justified decision, which assisted the overall course of operations, but lamented that it reduced the troops' morale, given that they had wanted to take part in the battles. Messe also noted the stubborn Russian resistance and the difference of this theatre with its vast distances in contrast to prior more static campaigns.[95]

In September, the Italians continued to advance by foot[96] and launched an independently executed three-day manoeuvre that opened the way for German armour and contributed to the encirclement of five Soviet divisions. The CSIR helped to secure the crossing of additional forces across the Dnepr despite continuous Soviet artillery fire on the bridge.[97] The *Pasubio* first defended a bridgehead to guard the

[88] Giusti, *La campagna*, 102. In contrast, Scotoni held that operating within the most mobile formation of Army Group South only reduced the corps' already mediocre performance, see Scotoni, *Il nemico fidato*, 129.

[89] ACS, T-821/247/IT 2259/334-336, Messe – Orientamento e direttive per il futuro impiego, 14 Aug. 1941, f.335.

[90] ACS, T-821/20/IT 98/911-915, Messe – Relazione, 9 Sept. 1941, f.914.

[91] ACS, T-821/254/IT 3051/442, Mackensen to Messe, 9 Sept. 1941.

[92] ACS, T-821/20/IT 98/863-865, Messe – Relazione, 17 Sept. 1941.

[93] BA-MA, RH 21-1/51, KTB PzAOK 1, III, fol.75. Much to the Italians' satisfaction, ACS, T-821/247/IT 2259/487, Messe – Riconoscimento germanico azione *Pasubio*, 30 Aug. 1941.

[94] ACS, T-821/247/IT 2259/448-450, Messe – Promemoria, 27 Aug. 1941.

[95] Giusti, "Messe," 118.

[96] ACS, T-821/254/IT 3052/578, Messe to *Pasubio*, 17 Sept. 1941.

[97] ACS, T-821/254/IT 3052/784, Col. Tirelli to CSIR – Ponte sul Dniepr a Dniepropetrowsk, 29 Sept. 1941. The Wehrmacht warmly praised the Italian pontoon engineers for their assistance, ACS, T-821/255/IT 3053/31, Luschnig – Al comandante del II battaglione pontieri, 4 Oct. 1941.

Seventeenth Army's right flank[98] and then executed a pincer movement jointly with the *Torino* and parts of the *Celere*. By uniting their forces at Petrikovka, they blocked the Soviet exit route.[99] Despite difficult terrain, shortages of vehicles, dense Soviet minefields and fierce counter-attacks,[100] the Italians captured 7000 Red Army soldiers within four days (27–30 September) at the cost of 52 killed and 142 wounded.[101] Much to Mussolini's joy,[102] the Wehrmacht praised the CSIR's performance—not only did the Germans publicly do so for the benefit of the alliance, but the First Panzer Army also noted the CSIR's helpful contribution in its war diary.[103] Indeed, the repeated German requests for Italian help in river crossings hint at the excellence of its engineers.

Conquering the Donets Basin

When Army Group Center launched Operation Typhoon to conquer Moscow on 2 October 1941, the CSIR supported Army Group South's push over 300 kilometres towards the vital industrial centres in the Donets Basin. The First Panzer Army was intended to relieve pressure on the Eleventh Army by attacking the Soviet Ninth Army. The CSIR protected the First Panzer Army's left flank. The *Pasubio*'s 79th Regiment, Italian artillery (30th *Raggruppamento*), the *Tagliamento* Blackshirts, one company *Bersaglieri* and the German 198th ID jointly conquered the Soviet bridgehead at Pavlograd on 10–11 October.[104]

---

[98] In good cooperation with German forces, ACS, T-821/20/IT 98/869-876, Messe – La manovra di Petrikowka, 2 Oct. 1941, f.871.

[99] Detailed in USSME, *Le operazioni*, 97ff.

[100] ACS, T-821/254/IT 3052/792, CSIR to CS, 29 Sept. 1941; Marsetic, *Dall'Adige al Don*, 47ff.

[101] Other sources speak of 87 dead and 190 wounded Italians, Giusti, *La campagna*, 104, which probably included earlier casualties. Prisoner numbers are also difficult to assess. Some authors list 10,000, see Stahel, *Kiev*, 315.

[102] Ciano Diaries, 30 Sept. 1941.

[103] BA-MA, RH 21-1/51, KTB PzAOK 1, III, fol.79. Italian aircraft contributed vital reconnaissance during the operation, see USSME, *Le operazioni*, 102.

[104] This improvised Italian formation led the decisive push, USSME, *Le operazioni*, 107.

This highly successful attack[105] cleared the route to Stalino (today's Donetsk).[106] The only way in which the Italians could achieve their operational goals 150 kilometres eastwards was to concentrate all available vehicles on the *Pasubio* and *Celere*—at the cost of the *Torino*.[107] Fuel shortages, poor roads, destroyed bridges and mines obstructed speed and mobility. Mud and rain continued to thwart supplies,[108] which led to complaints about the unfulfilled German promises of sufficient provisions.[109] Notwithstanding the first serious problems with supplies, as well as the vast distances concerned (with most divisions scattered across large territories), the weather and the dogged Soviet resistance, the advance continued, with the men attempting to live off the land.[110] The onslaught on Moscow caused logistical bottlenecks on the whole front; Italian complaints thus raise the question of whether they had adequately grasped the overall situation and the importance of Operation Typhoon.[111] The Italian Ambassador in Berlin, Dino Alfieri, realised the failure of the German strategy as well as the need to resume the campaign in spring 1942—with all the problems this entailed.[112]

---

[105] Between 1 and 15 October, the Italians suffered seven dead and 77 wounded, capturing 531 Soviets, ACS, T-821/20/IT 98/925-929, Messe – Sintesi avvenimenti dal 1 al 15 ottobre, 17 Oct. 1941, f.928.

[106] ACS, T-821/254/IT 3052/34, CSIR to CS, 9 Oct. 1941; also ACS, T-821/255/IT 3052/44, Pasubio to CSIR, 10 Oct. 1941.

[107] Thus the *Torino* marched almost 1000 kilometres from the Romanian spring-off points to the Dnepr, Filatov, *La campagna orientale*, 47.

[108] ACS, T-821/255/IT 3053/99, *Pasubio* to CSIR, 12 Oct. 1941.

[109] ACS, T-821/20/IT 98/925-929, Messe – Sintesi avvenimenti dal 1 al 15 ottobre, 17 Oct. 1941.

[110] ACS, T-821/20/IT 98/939-949, Messe – Sintesi avvenimenti dal 15 ottobre al 10 novembre, 10 Nov. 1941, f.943. The *Celere* only carried food for two to three, thus delays of supply trains or of vehicles stuck in the mud could cause severe problems, ACS, T-821/20/IT 98/978-982, Gen. Marazzani – Relazione svolgimento attuale periodo operativo, 23 Oct. 1941.

[111] In Messe's opinion, the Germans did recognise the Italian efforts, but did not value their contribution sufficiently "in relation to the overall situation", ACS, T-821/20/IT 98/939-949, Messe – Sintesi avvenimenti dal 15 ottobre al 10 novembre, 10 Nov. 1941, cited on fs.946-47. While conquering the Donets basin and protecting the First Panzer Army's flank were important tasks, the push towards Moscow certainly ranked higher. But from a junior ally's point of view, things might have looked different.

[112] DDI, IX:VII, doc.681, Alfieri to Ciano, 24 Oct. 1941.

5 THE ITALIAN OPERATIONS ON THE EASTERN FRONT (1941)

In mid-October, the *Savoia* Regiment conquered Stalino[113] in cooperation with German mountain troops of the XLIX Corps against heavy resistance in this area.[114] Many of the following Soviet counter-attacks in the Donetsk basin had to be repelled without its own artillery, which was largely stuck in the mud.[115] After seizing Stalino, the CSIR independently conquered its new objectives in November: Gorlovka, Rykovo, and the important rail link at Trudovaya.[116] The *Pasubio* arrived from the North, while the *Celere* and *Torino* (slowly following by foot) pursued eastwards from Stalino towards Rykovo, before turning back to support the attack on Gorlovka, an industrial town of around 100,000 inhabitants. Largely lacking in artillery, the *Celere* and *Pasubio* attacked three Soviet divisions and four regiments on 1 November.[117] Messe's manoeuvre played out favourably. The Italian units jointly overcame the Soviets' "fanatic resistance"[118] at Gorlovka and conquered the town on 2 November after heavy street-to-street fighting.[119]

Thereafter, the Italians defended their newly gained positions and repelled three Soviet divisions near Nikitovka. Initially, the *Pasubio*'s 80th Infantry Regiment stood alone, and the situation became critical when it was surrounded and cut off from vital supplies.[120] In fact,

---

[113] The *Celere*'s cavalry could operate less troubled on the almost impassable roads, see USSME, *Le operazioni*, 110ff. In another encounter, the whole *Novara* regiment attacked 200 Soviets that were entrenched in a village with two 76 mm artillery guns. With a frontal dash and an enveloping manoeuvre, they were able to take over 100 prisoners, ACS, T-821/20/IT 98/978-982, Marazzani – Relazione svolgimento attuale periodo operativo, 23 Oct. 1941, f.981.

[114] BA-MA, RH 21-1/51, KTB PzAOK 1, III, fos.141, 147, not least due to partisan activity in the rear, ibid., fol.158. The German supply situation (fuel and ammunition) was also far from good, see ibid., fol.150. For a Russian view on the operations, [Gen.] Konstantin I. Provalov, *V ogne peredovykh liny* (Moscow: Voenizdat, 1981), 24ff., 49ff.

[115] BA-MA, RH 21-1/51, KTB PzAOK 1, III, fos.151–53.

[116] USSME, *Le operazioni*, 116ff.

[117] Ibid., 119.

[118] ACS, T-821/20/IT 98/939-949, Messe – Sintesi avvenimenti dal 15 ottobre al 10 novembre, 10 Nov. 1941, f.944. See also the description in the memoirs of a veteran, Marsetic, *Dall'Adige al Don*, 72–77.

[119] Based on the available evidence, the *Pasubio* seems to have run into serious trouble and the *Celere*'s help was much welcomed. See the messages by General Giovannelli to General Marazzani in ACS, T-821/20/IT 98/973, 18 Nov. 1941; Longo, *Messe*, 135.

[120] USSME, *Le operazioni*, 121–23; Marsetic, *Dall'Adige al Don*, 83ff. Parts of the 3rd *Bersaglieri* and the 79th regiment came to their rescue. The after-action report shows how badly pressed the 80th Regiment had been, ACS, T-821/20/IT 98/995-999, Col. Caretto – Relazione sull'azione di Gorlowka - Nikitowka, 14 Nov. 1941; also Roggiani, *Bersaglieri*, 284.

the defence of gained ground against superior forces became a recurring feature of the Italians' efforts—often with little artillery support[121] and in the face of Soviet armour.[122] The losses around Nikitovka amounted to 130 dead and 569 wounded; a substantial number, considering the forces employed in these operations.[123] Messe had already told the First Panzer Army in late October that his corps needed rest, but the Germans pressed for the continuation of the offensive.[124] The CSIR faced similar problems to all units on the Eastern Front: the men were exhausted and with every step forward, the front moved further away from the railheads, which meant that supplies had to be transported by truck. They thus became less reliable and especially vulnerable during the mud period (the so-called *rasputitsa*). The divisions were often stretched out over dozens (if not hundreds) of kilometres and their combat readiness invariably declined. Thus, Messe's insistence on a pause for regroupment and resupply was sensible, and his repeated telegrams show a desire to protect his troops from exhaustion. Indeed, his insistence on such a break was one reason why the Italian units resisted the first winter fairly well.[125]

The CSIR was granted a period of 'rest' after 15 November to improve its defensive positions, re-integrate the supply and artillery units, and distribute winter equipment and other badly needed replenishments

---

[121] ACS, T-821/255/IT 3056/831-835, Col. Fioravanti – Combattimento di Ubeschischtsche, 20 Nov. 1941, here f.833. Even regiments with artillery support encountered problems. An after-action report noted good fire direction, but also the ineffectiveness of small calibre guns against fortified positions, ACS, T-821/20/IT 98/989-994, Gen. Marazzani – Fatti d'arme di Gorlowka – Nikitowka, 18 Nov. 1941, f.994. The airforce was praised for its "great help" in reconnaissance and close air support with machine guns, see ibid.

[122] ACS, T-821/255/IT 3056/692, CSIR to CS, 13 Nov. 1941.

[123] As the artillery was largely stuck, the brunt of the fighting was again carried by the *Pasubio*'s 79th and 80th infantry regiments, the 3rd *Bersaglieri*, and the *Savoia* and *Novara* cavalry regiments – that is, in total, by less than 20,000 men. Messe judged the number of 2000 prisoners as "relatively small", but as an indicator of the toughness of the fighting, see ACS, T-821/20/IT 98/939-949, Messe – Sintesi avvenimenti dal 15 ottobre al 10 novembre, 10 Nov. 1941, f.949.

[124] USSME, *Le operazioni*, 123ff.

[125] The temperature fell to minus 20 °C in the first nights of November, ibid., 129.

after four months of incessant operations.[126] Only a mixed force—equalling one division—was deployed to assist the German operations. The First Panzer Army conquered Rostov on 20 November, but exhaustion and logistical difficulties had greatly reduced its effectiveness. The city was lost to the Soviets only nine days later, whereafter the Germans established themselves in winter positions along the river Mius. In pursuit of their successes, the Red Army also advanced further north, where it subsequently attacked various German corps, and ultimately also the CSIR, which held a frontline of 50 kilometres without any favourable natural obstacles to cling on to. The Soviets attempted to weaken the Italian defenses with constant mortar attacks and (night) infiltration.[127] At the same time, the Red Army started its counter-attack in front of Moscow on 5 December 1941.[128] It almost broke the German front completely: the main battle lines had to be taken back up to 170 kilometres and many units were cut off.[129] Thus, Army Group South resumed the offensive in order to relieve the pressure on the heavily battered Army Group Centre.

On 5 December, the CSIR joined the Seventeenth Army in the battle of Chazepetovka (continuing until 14 December) in order to close gaps in the frontline[130] and to secure better positions for the coming winter.[131] The *Pasubio* could hardly be considered ready for offensive actions, and of the *Celere*'s four regiments, only the *Bersaglieri* were considered combat-ready, which meant the *Torino* was assigned more tasks in the weeks that followed. Messe was very frank about the state of his troops in his messages to the First Panzer Army, and

---

[126] Messe extolled the CSIR and its persistent high morale. While his reports were full of eulogistic prose, he also spoke frankly about the men's needs and deeds, ACS, T-821/20/IT 98/939-949, Messe – Sintesi avvenimenti dal 15 ottobre al 10 novembre, 10 Nov. 1941, fs.946–47.

[127] See e.g. ACS, T-821/255/IT 3057/947, *Torino* to CSIR, 1 Dec. 1941.

[128] Mawdsley, *Thunder*, 106–7.

[129] Glantz and House, *When Titans Clashed*, 108ff.; Hill, *Red Army*, 265–323.

[130] Indeed there was a gap of twenty (!) kilometres to the neighbouring Seventeenth Army, USSME, *Le operazioni*, 134. Thus the Axis troops were lucky that a Soviet armoured attack hit the III Corps instead of this vulnerable spot, ACS, T-821/255/IT 3057/999, Fellmer (German liaison officer) to CSIR, 3 Dec. 1941. Messe warned the German commands that besides small calibre artillery, he had merely nine batteries of 105 mm guns and that his anti-tank pieces were "inefficient against heavy tanks", see ACS, T-821/255/IT 3057/1000-1002, Messe to First Panzer Army, 3 Dec. 1941, here f.1002.

[131] Detailed in USSME, *Le operazioni*, 135ff.

his tone became more concerned and critical.[132] Subsequently Kleist lauded the 3rd *Bersaglieri* and asked Messe to make five recommendations for the awarding of Iron Crosses.[133] This should make us question high-level praise and decorations, as in this case—the *Bersaglieri*'s valorous struggles aside—'political' motivations were clearly at work. Kleist obviously realised that he had to court his allies: especially as he needed the Italians, after a Soviet attack on Taganrog had forced him to divert German units to hold the Mius line.[134] Despite these different views, the CSIR mustered its last reserves to resume the attack at average temperatures of minus 20°C.[135] Messe had outlined the objectives, but left it to the division's commander to decide when and how to attack.[136] The cold prevented the machine guns from firing, which had a negative effect on the (relatively inexperienced) soldiers of the *Torino*— who suffered 29 killed, 123 wounded and 164 cases of frostbite on the first day of attack.[137] Still, the *Torino* was praised for its conduct against a well-prepared and fiercely resistant enemy that often preferred death to surrender.[138] After December 14th, the CSIR prepared winter positions, attempted to improve its logistics and erected defensive structures in and between settlements.[139]

Yet, the period of rest was brief. At Christmas the Soviets launched a large-scale attack at the interface of the CSIR and the German XLIX Mountain Corps.[140] Messe had been warned by his intelligence of an imminent Soviet attack. He had placed the *Celere* under German

[132] ACS, T-821/255/IT 3057/1000-1002, Messe to First Panzer Army, 3 Dec. 1941.

[133] ACS, T-821/255/IT 3057/1044, Messe to *Celere*, 5 Dec. 1941.

[134] See Kleist's order to the CSIR on 7 December 1941, printed in ACS, T-821/255/IT 3057/1085.

[135] USSME, *Le operazioni*, 136; ACS, T-821/255/IT 3057/1064, CSIR to CS, 6 Dec. 1941.

[136] ACS, T-821/255/IT 3057/1170, CSIR to *Torino*, 12 Dec. 1941.

[137] ACS, T-821/255/IT 3057/1053, *Torino* to CSIR, 6 Dec. 1941. In fact frostbite reached exceptional levels (915 men) during these operations, compare to other months in USSME, *Le operazioni del C.S.I.R. e dell'ARMIR*, 213.

[138] ACS, T-821/255/IT 3057/1163, CSIR to CS, 12 Dec. 1941. The head of the division's infantry, General Ugo De Carolis was killed on 12 December. The *Torino* had been assigned all available artillery from the *Pasubio* to master the challenges it faced, USSME, *Le operazioni*, 142.

[139] USSME, *Le operazioni*, 145ff.

[140] Ibid., 153ff.

command with a stead-fast order, and regrouped the *Pasubio* and *Torino* to counter possible breakthroughs, as a Soviet success would have opened the way to Stalino and threatened vital railway junctures.[141] On Christmas morning, the Red Army attacked with the 35th and 68th Cavalry Division and the 136th Rifle Division.[142] The real force levels are difficult to assess, but each cavalry division included one regiment of 64 BT light tanks.[143] The *Torino* managed to repel the attacks, while parts of the *Celere*'s sector were lost. The hard-tested 3rd *Bersaglieri* Regiment, two Blackshirt battalions and four artillery batteries secured a front of twenty kilometres against the better part of two Soviet infantry divisions.[144] One company of the *Tagliamento*—which had fought well before[145]—lost all its officers in defending Novo Orlovka against two Russian infantry battalions.[146] The XVIII battalion of the 3rd *Bersaglieri* repelled an attack of two infantry regiments and several cavalry squadrons at Ivanovsky.[147] In the end, the *Celere*'s sector held fast—not least due to relief attacks from the *Pasubio* and *Torino*.[148] The First Panzer Army also assembled the 318th IR, some *Bersaglieri* units, and German armour for a counter-attack, and managed to regain all the lost ground by 27 December.[149] In sum, the Christmas battle had been a great success: at the cost of 168 dead, 715 wounded, 207 missing, 305 frostbite, the Italians had defeated superior Soviet forces, which suffered over 2000 dead, and had captured 1200 prisoners, twenty-four 76 mm guns, nine AT guns as well as hundreds of rifles, automatic guns and vehicles.[150] The artillery had closely cooperated with the infantry, and the Italian ability not only to withstand the attack but to regroup and to counter-attack

---

[141] Longo, *Messe*, 148; Giusti, *La campagna*, 126.

[142] Ibid., 323, footnote 159.

[143] The Italian official history only states that Soviet armour was involved in the attack, without specifying numbers or tank types, see USSME, *Le operazioni*, 155.

[144] USSME, *Le operazioni*, 153.

[145] ACS, T-821/20/IT 98/951-953, Messe – Relazione 63^ Legione CC.NN., 18 Oct. 1941. These reports had been requested by the Chief of Staff of the MVSN and thus were possibly overly positive.

[146] USSME, *Le operazioni*, 155.

[147] Roggiani, *Bersaglieri*, 291ff.

[148] USSME, *Le operazioni*, 155–56.

[149] Ibid., 156; Roggiani, *Bersaglieri*, 298ff. Again the tank numbers were not specified.

[150] Giusti, *La campagna*, 127; USSME, *Le operazioni*, 159.

beyond mere tactical aims under enemy pressure shows what vital lessons the CSIR had learned after five months on the Eastern Front.

After the Christmas battle, activity along the front eased, but the Soviets continued skirmishes in January.[151] The CSIR was stretched to the limit and Messe demanded rest, more supplies and fresh troops to uphold operational effectiveness. The *Celere* in particular was in dire need of replacements and rest, but Kleist initially vetoed taking it out of line, for want of alternatives.[152] At the end of the first year in Russia, the CSIR had suffered 633 killed, 2496 wounded and 265 missing.[153] The Wehrmacht had 63,000 fatalities in July 1941 alone (i.e. amounting to the whole weight of the CSIR) and lost around 10,000 officers (between dead and wounded) during the first 50 days of Operation Barbarossa.[154] The motorised and panzer divisions bore the brunt of the casualties, as they were usually the first in battle.[155] In contrast to the Wehrmacht and the Red Army, the Italians were not the first line of advance during the breakthrough battles in June and July, and their overall strength was of course smaller.[156] In order to gain a better comparison one would have to look at a similar German (or Romanian) corps on that front sector, and its combat units. This would be useful for the purposes of assessing the scale of fighting the CSIR was involved in.[157] Yet, one has to bear in mind

---

[151] Ibid., 161–62. The Soviet actions caused 24 dead, 86 wounded, and 42 missing in the *Celere* alone.

[152] ACS, T-821/256/IT 3059/295, CSIR to CS, 14 Jan. 1942. Yet, some days later he shifted units to reinforce the *Celere*, ACS, T-821/256/IT 3059/44, First Panzer Army to CSIR, 25 Jan. 1942. In Berlin, Marras noted that the Germans had withdrawn the 16th Panzer Division and the Waffen-SS Division 'Leibstandarte Adolf Hitler', ACS, T-821/200/IT 1382/990-994, Marras – Questioni varie trattate con l'OKW, 29 Jan. 1942, f.991.

[153] These numbers only refer to direct combat losses, USSME, *Le operazioni del C.S.I.R. e dell'ARMIR*, 213.

[154] Stahel, *Operation Barbarossa*, 390. While 16,000 new officers were needed to fill these gaps, only 5000 replacements were at hand.

[155] At the end of August, the strength of Kleist's spearhead divisions was reduced by half, ibid., 416.

[156] The terrain also made the typical Soviet ambushes more difficult (in contrast to the dense woods and swamps in Army Group Centre's area of operations).

[157] The more numerous Romanian formations had lost 19,000 dead, 68,000 wounded, and over 11,000 missing from August to October 1941—mainly resulting from their onslaught on Odessa, Axworthy, *Third Axis*, 51ff.

that the *Pasubio*'s two infantry regiments and the *Celere*'s 3rd *Bersaglieri* Regiment had done the majority of the fighting (and dying). Especially the combat formations were exhausted after five months of incessant advancing and fighting[158]—a fate they shared with their comrades in the Wehrmacht. Yet, Italian soldiers were not granted home leave.[159] In comparison, German frontline troops were (at least theoretically) allowed fourteen days leave twice a year.[160]

Messe had asked for replacements on 3 December 1941: individuals for the existing units, the elite *Monte Cervino Alpini* Battalion, the 6th *Bersaglieri* Regiment, the 120th Motorised Artillery Regiment, and other supply and service units.[161] However, the level of reinforcements reaching the CSIR was very low and sparked repeated complaints: instead of the 7946 men requested, only 842 had arrived by 28 December, with another 2289 en route from Italy.[162] Messe also demanded several motorised reinforcements before the spring (foreseeing the logistic problems in the rainy period): i.e. one battalion each of M/13 medium tanks, light L 6/40 tankettes, and *semoventi*, as well as heavy 149/40 guns for the corps artillery.[163]

The Italians were repeatedly praised—on several levels and in different ways (not merely for propaganda or alliance purposes)—for their successes; also during the defensive battles around Christmas. Also several scholars have reached the conclusion that the Italians had "acquitted

---

[158] As Messe told the Germans, ACS, T-821/255/IT 3057/1000-1002, Messe to First Panzer Army, 3 Dec. 1941. The author could not identify more detailed casualty reports, but it would be useful to investigate this further. Roggiani spoke of over one hundred dead and 200 wounded and missing in the XVIII Battalion, Roggiani, *Bersaglieri*, 294. Thus, it had lost almost half its combat power.

[159] During the first nine months on the Eastern Front, only 340 men were granted temporary leave and 415 were repatriated for family reasons, see Longo, *Messe*, 146.

[160] Hartmann, *Wehrmacht*, 42. However, critical situations could delay such requests.

[161] ACS, T-821/256/IT 3059/99, CS to SUPERESERCITO, 2 Jan. 1942.

[162] ACS, T-821/256/IT 3059/170, CSIR to CS, 7 Jan. 1942. The 842 men had taken over one month to reach the front.

[163] ACS, T-821/256/IT 3059/40-43, Messe – Impiego CSIR campagna invernale e prossima campagna primaverile, 15 Jan. 1941. The ARMIR later gained three groups of 149/40 in the *9° Raggruppamento artiglieria d'armata*, see Finazzer and Riccio, *Italian Artillery*, 48–49.

themselves well during fall 1941"[164] and Schlemmer has argued that the CSIR, "on balance, was successful from the military perspective."[165] While the CSIR lacked the means to operate on the level of German armoured divisions, it fulfilled its assigned duties to the fullest. Problems in keeping pace and in close contact with the quickly moving fronts were normal[166] and do not appear to have been particularly severe in the Italian case. At the same time, it would be wrong to describe Italian actions merely as scuffling along behind German spearheads. The CSIR conducted independent manoeuvres on corps level, repeatedly formed ad hoc units for critical tasks, complied with all German demands (even if they deemed them wrong and suicidal), effectively managed to switch between defensive and offensive during mud and snow periods with precarious supply lines, and made good use of their limited air power. In short, the CSIR had fought a capable enemy in highly mobile operations over vast distances with all the logistical difficulties this implied.

Despite deteriorating sanitary conditions and increasing sickness rates,[167] the CSIR managed to adapt fairly well to its first Russian winter.[168] When Mussolini visited the front in late August, Messe warned him of the expected deficiencies in winter equipment, ammunition, petrol, vehicles, and other supplies. Messe was little convinced that Mussolini (or Cavallero) would take the promised steps and the CSIR

---

[164] Burgwyn, *Mussolini*, 120. DiNardo described their comportment as "reasonably well, despite the limitations under which the Italian troops labored", but wrongly argued the CSIR took not part in major action after 12 November, DiNardo, *Germany*, 127.

[165] Schlemmer, "Italy," 145.

[166] Stahel, *Operation Barbarossa*, 158ff.

[167] ACS, T-821/255/IT 3055/502-503, Stato sanitario delle truppe del CSIR, 1 Nov. 1941.

[168] The Italian official history (somewhat optimistically) claimed that all soldiers had been provided winter gear by the end of December, USSME, *Le operazioni*, 152. Messe held that frontline troops had received winter equipment at the end of November, once the logistical crisis had been overcome. This boosted the morale of soldiers who "saw and valued their superior winter equipment in comparison to the Germans – which the latter also acknowledged", see ACS, T-821/257/IT 3062/549-558, Messe to CS – La campagna invernale, 5 Mar. 1942, fs.552–53. The total numbers should always be seen in relative terms: initially, only sentries and patrols received full winter gear, as they actually needed them more than e.g. staffs; see TNA, GFM 36/170, Comando Supremo – Automezzi e parti di ricambio per il CSIR, 13 Oct. 1941. A mismatch between the soldier numbers and the material supplied did not automatically amount to an outright failure, and the logistical problems during October and November especially have to be borne in mind.

also perceived German reassurances as barely convincing.[169] Thus, besides relying on local goods and writing a memorandum in which he urged the acquisition of winter supplies and lubricants, he also acted quickly. He sent Colonel Della Porta on a special mission in late August 1941 to acquire horses, sledges, vehicles and clothes on the Romanian, Hungarian and Bulgarian black market.[170] The military attaché in Berlin, General Marras, translated and circulated German manuals on weapons maintenance in harsh winter conditions,[171] but Italians' own experiences (and tests) on how, for instance to keep machine guns working, were also directed to the CSIR.[172] The Italians also sent lubricants for artillery guns via planes in order to maintain their most essential firepower.[173] The late delivery was caused by logistical glitches—the demands had been made earlier.[174] Despite these preparations, frostbite still became a problem. But a detailed look at the cases of *congelati* show three noteworthy points: the officers shared their men's fate, the *Torino* had markedly higher numbers of cases (more than double the other divisions),[175]

[169] Longo, *Messe*, 137.

[170] ACS, T-821/247/IT 2259/448-450, Messe – Promemoria, 27 Aug. 1941, here f.450; ACS, T-821/258/IT 3064/15-29, Col. Caldarola – Accidenti da freddo nelle truppe del CSIR durante l'inverno 1941–1942, 24 Apr. 1942, here f.16. The material was also transported by air, ACS, T-821/255/IT 3036/911-917, Relazione sull'attività dell'Aviazione del CSIR fino al 15 novembre 1941, 24 Nov. 1941, here f.915. On the Italians' acquisition of goods in Romania see also TNA, GFM 36/31, Demetrescu to Pavolini, 29 Nov. 1941. See also Giusti, *La campagna*, 87. Longo cited a report from August, which mentioned German activities in Romania and Hungary. A certain competition over winter equipment seems to have taken place, Longo, *Messe*, 137–39; on the amount of material and Messe's initiative see ibid., 143ff.

[171] ACS, T-821/200/IT 1377/601, Manutenzione delle armi in caso di freddo, 7 Jan. 1942.

[172] ACS, T-821/200/IT 1377/597, Funzionamento armi automatiche, 2 Jan. 1942.

[173] ACS, T-821/200/IT 1377/635-636, Olio Fiat tipo Loocherd, 19 Jan. 1942; and ibid., f.641, Spedizione via aerea olio incongelabile, 15 Jan. 1942.

[174] The Italian sources show repeated earlier (fruitless) attempts to acquire more lubricants, see ACS, T-821/200/IT 1377/637, Grassi e lubrificanti per manutenzione armi, 13 Jan. 1942. Messe also asked for additional communications equipment, ACS, T-821/200/IT 1378/688, Richiesta stazione radio per il CSIR, 27 Feb. 1942.

[175] When the temperatures dropped to minus 31 °C on 6 December, the *Torino* was engaged in the aforementioned heavy fighting at Chazepetovka and had to search cover in the open plains for two hours, which resulted in around 700 cases of frostbite on this day alone, ACS, T-821/258/IT 3064/15-29, Col. Caldarola – Accidenti da freddo nelle truppe del CSIR, 24 Apr. 1942, f.17. Yet, the *Torino* also had an unsual high number of sick in October and November (which can be related to the fact that they covered the

and 571 Italians died from their wounds while around 40 per cent reported back for duty.[176] The severe winter hit all the invading forces hard. It is difficult to make precise comparisons, but the Wehrmacht, too, suffered badly from the cold[177]—and the Italian cases of frostbite do not appear significantly dissimilar.[178] The CSIR's activities demonstrate that the Italians did not just sit idle and that they were not overwhelmed by the Russian winter.[179] Nevertheless, the Italian soldiers were affected by over-optimistic campaign plans and inadequate preparations for winter positions before December. Messe had warned repeatedly about the need for rest and resupply, but his memoranda did not refer to the establishment of defensive positions for the coming winter.

Lessons Learned?

After the first winter in Russia, the Italians reassessed the overall situation and their past experiences. In spring 1942, Marras blamed the Wehrmacht's disregard for logistics, underestimation of the Red Army, and the weather, but also praised the Soviet combat proficiency and

---

vast distances almost entirely by foot), see ACS, T-821/256/IT 3059/207-219, Col. Caldarola – Situazione del servizio sanitario presso il CSIR, 10 Jan. 1942, f.215. In sum, the division had by far the highest number of non-combat related illnesses and the lowest number of recoveries: A staggering 43.8 per cent of the rank became ill, in contrast to seven per cent in the *Celere* (and among all rear units) and 20.5 per cent in the *Pasubio*.

[176] First-degree frostbite affected 18 officers and 1111 men, second-degree 48 officers and 1888 men, and third-degree 13 officers and 536 men; in total 79 officers and 3535 men of which 30 officers and 1605 recovered for service. A total of 1408 soldiers (including 35 officers) had to be sent home, the rest had perished, USSME, *Le operazioni del C.S.I.R. e dell'ARMIR*, 215, attachment 2; Giusti, *La campagna*, 134.

[177] The 253rd ID (part of Army Group North) had 1429 cases of frostbite, of which only 261 third-degree cases, Christoph Rass, *"Menschenmaterial": Deutsche Soldaten an der Ostfront. Innenansichten einer Infanteriedivision 1939–1945* (Paderborn: Schöningh, 2003), 155. But the different situational aspects, methods of counting and numerous variables make comparisons very difficult.

[178] Messe claimed (with a certain bias) that the Italian cases of frostbite had been "notably lower" in percentage than in German units, ACS, T-821/257/IT 3062/549-558, Messe to CS – La campagna invernale, 5 Mar. 1942, f.558. He also lauded the head of the medical services, Professor Caldarola, for his excellent work, see Messe, *Lettere*, 130.

[179] Messe also exchanged three high-ranked logistic officers whom he considered unsuitable, ibid., 124.

the importance of their counter-offensive.[180] Thus, he considered that the Soviets understood the two main factors—time and space—better than the Germans.[181] Marras' remarks on the fierceness of the campaign demonstrate the Italians' awareness (at the highest levels) of the brutalisation on the Eastern Front. He thought this conflict was "not only a total war, but a war of extermination. The Germans and Soviets are fighting for their existence and thus the fighting has reached levels of ferocity and destruction that have not happened in European wars for centuries. The mass killing of prisoners, the harsh treatment of civilians from both sides, the destructions, all form part of this kind of combat [...] a recurring phenomenon when two opposing ideologies" clash.[182] Interestingly, he did not count the Italians in this equation, nor Fascist ideology. As regards operations and tactics, Marras considered the German operational procedure of double envelopments as a failure, as it had not delivered the desired strategic results.[183] He praised the Wehrmacht for its skilful defensive actions, but hinted at the dangers of infiltration and static defense lines.[184] In an overall assessment of the Wehrmacht's operations in 1941, Marras again emphasised the continuing German underestimation of the Red Army (even after several months campaigning against them), warned of future Soviet winter attacks, and remained rather sceptical about successfully concluding the campaign in the coming year.[185] And indeed, the year 1942 turned out to be very different from what planners in Berlin and Rome had hoped for.

[180] ACS, T-821/252/IT 3033/15-28, [Marras] – La campagna invernale in Russia, [Spring] 1942, fs.15–16, 19–20. Messe also spoke critically of the German focus on operations and disregard for logistics, see ACS, T-821/257/IT 3063/957-959, Messe – Stralcio, 19 Apr. 1942.

[181] ACS, T-821/252/IT 3033/15-28, [Marras] – La campagna invernale in Russia, [Spring] 1942, f.21.

[182] Ibid., f.22.

[183] Ibid., f.23.

[184] Ibid., fos.25–26.

[185] ACS, T-821/252/IT 3033/29-42, [Marras] – Le operazioni germaniche nel 1941, Jan. 1942.

CHAPTER 6

The Italian Operations on the Eastern Front (1942)

At the end of 1941, the Soviet counter-offensives were in full swing. This period where the Wehrmacht suffered unexpected and painful setbacks and the Red Army maintained the initiative lasted until May 1942.[1] On 11 January, the First Panzer Army reminded all commanders and men of the seriousness of the current situation.[2] Messe considered none of his units fit for mobile operations.[3] But after his appeals to the Germans and the *Comando Supremo* had yielded no results, Messe could do nothing more than tell his men to hold out,[4] and he ordered support units to muster able men for combat duties.[5] In January, the *Celere* defended the important town of Voroshilova, despite little cover and housing, bad sanitary conditions, lack of reinforcements, insufficient crews to operate heavy machine guns—unsurprisingly, also official documents admitted for the first time a decline of morale.[6] On the 23rd,

---

[1] Mawdsley, *Thunder*, 118–48.

[2] ACS, T-821/256/IT 3059/34-35, First Panzer Army to CSIR, 11 Jan. 1942.

[3] ACS, T-821/256/IT 3061/821-827, Messe – Relazione morale e condizioni spirituali, 11 Feb. 1942.

[4] ACS, T-821/256/IT 3060/424-425, Messe to *Celere*, 21 Jan. 1942.

[5] ACS, T-821/256/IT 3059/38-39, Messe – Efficienza reparti in linea, 13 Jan. 1942.

[6] ACS, T-821/256/IT 3060/374, Gen. Marazzani to CSIR, 18 Jan. 1942; USSME, *Le operazioni*, 161–62.

© The Author(s) 2019
B. M. Scianna, *The Italian War on the Eastern Front, 1941–1943*, Italian and Italian American Studies,
https://doi.org/10.1007/978-3-030-26524-3_6

the town was lost and a costly counter-attack two days later failed.[7] Messe's warnings had been proven right—the men were exhausted.[8]

On 21 January, the Soviets launched a great offensive against the Seventeenth Army southeast of Kharkov. The attack also threatened the Italian rear. Some units were attached to German formations that operated against the 'Izyum bulge'.[9] The *Novara* Regiment and some engineer troops were deployed to defend the railway from Dnjepropetrovsk to Stalino (despite their poor state)[10] and subsequently fought under the so-called Mackensen group.[11] The 9th battery of the 8th Artillery Regiment (*Pasubio*) continued to fight with mixed German units under command of the 1st Mountain Division. Their cooperation appears to have worked very well: the battery successfully defended a village with one German company against Soviet tanks and one infantry battalion.[12] At Novaya Orlovka—at the intersection between the CSIR and the German XLIX Corps—the Italians deployed every available artillery piece to back the *Torino*'s infantry against five battalions of the Soviet 136th Rifle Division.[13] While Soviet morale and the appearance of their armour increased,[14] the Italians noticed their own lack of tanks, assault guns and AT guns, which put them at a great disadvantage. Thus, Messe sent a

[7] ACS, T-821/257/IT 3062/415-422, Messe – Sintesi avvenimenti dal 5 gennaio al 28 febbraio, 8 Mar. 1942, f.416.

[8] In another report Messe depicted the morale in rosier terms and emphasised the importance of officers as role models. But he hinted at problems with the postal service (in his view the German's fault), which he deemed fundamental to sustaining the men's morale, see ACS, T-821/256/IT 3061/821-827, Messe – Relazione morale e condizioni spirituali, 11 Feb. 1942, f.824; Messe, *Lettere*, 130.

[9] Detailed in USSME, *Le operazioni*, 162ff.

[10] ACS, T-821/256/IT 3059/55, CSIR to CS, 29 Jan. 1942.

[11] ACS, T-821/257/IT 3062/415-422, Messe – Sintesi avvenimenti dal 5 gennaio al 28 febbraio, 8 Mar. 1942, fs.419-20. Messe subsequently blocked German requests to send additional forces, ACS, T-821/257/IT 3063/1042-1043, Messe to Gen. Konrad, 22 Apr. 1942. Thus, congratulatory messages should be read with the subtext of alliance politics, see e.g. the warm words in ACS, T-821/258/IT 3064/316, Gen. Konrad to Messe, 17 May 1942.

[12] As noted in a German report that the head of the battery referred to, ACS, T-821/257/IT 3062/108-109, Lt. Palombo – Attività batteria, 24 Mar. 1942.

[13] ACS, T-821/256/IT 3059/62-65, Col. Utili – Azione nemica del 27 febbraio contro il caposaldo di Nowaja Orlowka, 12 Mar. 1942, here f.63. The Italians repelled the attack and reported 300 dead Soviets lying in front of their positions.

[14] Ibid., f.64.

message to the *Comando Supremo* in which he insisted (again) that "it is indispensable to possess tanks and self-propelled assault guns in this theatre to prevent severe consequences."[15] This frustration may have led to another development, as in this period Messe's documents show for the first time a narrative of desperate heroic gestures with inadequate material against a numerically superior enemy.[16]

After February, the situation in the Italian sector remained relatively calm until summer 1942—but several units under German command continued to be involved in heavy fighting.[17] On 22 March, the Italians launched an attack on Olichovatka to divert Soviet forces. The elite *Monte Cervino Alpini* Battalion had reached the CSIR in early March and immediately took part in the fighting.[18] Still, the following period was characterised by almost static fronts and preparations of defensive positions along 'fortified' villages and lines of trenches connecting them.[19] But even without large-scale operations in the CSIR's sector, the Soviets continued their "aggressive" patrolling and active skirmishing (including artillery and strafing from aircraft).[20] Messe thus highlighted the importance of patrols and observation to stay informed about enemy movements.[21] Yet, the drop in activity also provided time, which was used to reflect on the operations over the previous year so that valuable lessons could be drawn in preparation for the next contingents destined for the Eastern Front.[22]

[15] ACS, T-821/257/IT 3062/454, Messe to CS, 7 Mar. 1942.

[16] ACS, T-821/257/IT 3062/549-558, Messe to CS – La campagna invernale, 5 Mar. 1942, f.557; ACS, T-821/257/IT 3062/591-592, Messe – Relazione morale e condizioni spirituali, 3 Mar. 1942.

[17] Detailed in USSME, *Le operazioni*, 172ff.

[18] On this unit see Luciano Viazzi, *I diavoli bianchi 1940–1943. Gli Alpini sciatori nella seconda guerra mondiale. Storia del battaglione "Monte Cervino"* (Milan: Mursia, 1989).

[19] Detailed in ACS, T-821/257/IT 3062/254-256, Messe – Organizzazione difensiva settore CSIR, 18 Mar. 1942.

[20] ACS, T-821/257/IT 3063/646-655, Col. Utili – Situazione descrittiva avversaria alla data nel 1 aprile 1942, 2 Apr. 1942. A good impression is conveyed by the documents in ACS, T-821/258/IT 3064. Additionally, the food situation was so precarious that rations for rear troops had to be cut—thus one should be careful in labelling this as a calm period, ACS, T-821/257/IT 3063/717, Messe circular, 4 Apr. 1942.

[21] ACS, T-821/257/IT 3063/658-659, Messe – Attività esplorativa, 2 Apr. 1942.

[22] ACS, T-821/257/IT 3062/112-120, Messe to *Ufficio Addestramento*, 24 Mar. 1942. He also attached a detailed German document with information on the Red Army and captured Russian manuals.

Messe's memoranda, and their widespread circulation to units and the 'Training Section' of the General Staff, demonstrate the Italian ability to conduct an internal lessons-learned procedure and (critical) review of ongoing operations. In his writings, Messe emphasised the hard combat on the Eastern Front, and was full of praise for the Soviets' defence skills, their ability to adapt and fight back and their (surprising) counter-attack in winter, which had denied the invading forces the imagined and badly needed period of rest.[23] Thus, he indirectly recognised the Soviets' role in 'derailing Barbarossa' and did not blame the setbacks on 'General Winter'. Yet, Messe also highlighted the Red Army's weakness in coordinating artillery and infantry, as well as other tactical errors.[24] He praised the honest relations and good comradeship with German authorities,[25] but remained highly sceptical with regard to the possibility of sustaining a greater number of troops in the coming summer offensive. In Messe's opinion, the two main limiting factors—motorisation and logistics—had not changed substantially to cause optimism.[26]

On the other hand, Messe spoke in no uncertain terms about the CSIR's own shortcomings. He thought the defensive lines had not always been perfectly prepared and the piecemeal deployment of mixed calibres in villages had created a dispersion of forces.[27] Despite inadequate material to erect defensive positions, the idea had been to concentrate troops and supplies on villages, building trenches between them and improving roads in order to ease logistics and movement.[28] After a tour of inspection in April, Messe criticised the state of the defensive structures. While conceding troubles in gathering material and setting up

---

[23] Ibid., fs.113–14; ACS, T-821/257/IT 3062/549-558, Messe to CS – La campagna invernale, 5 Mar. 1942, f.550.

[24] ACS, T-821/257/IT 3062/112-120, Messe to *Ufficio Addestramento*, 24 Mar. 1942, f.116.

[25] ACS, T-821/257/IT 3062/549-558, Messe to CS – La campagna invernale, 5 Mar. 1942, f.555. As shown above, his remarks could be less cordial in daily messages during moments of crisis. This should not be surprising, however, and his positive tone here should be dismissed prima facie as tainted by the fact that he was reporting to the *Comando Supremo*.

[26] ACS, T-821/258/IT 3064/83-87, Messe to CS – Impiego del CSIR, 4 May 1942.

[27] ACS, T-821/257/IT 3062/382-384, Messe – Schieramento delle artiglierie, 9 Mar. 1942, f.383.

[28] ACS, T-821/257/IT 3062/549-558, Messe to CS – La campagna invernale, 5 Mar. 1942, fs.554, 556.

defence systems in severe climatic conditions, he pointed to poor positioning of machine guns, excessive concentrations of troops in villages and saw trenches and anti-tank positions as in need of improvement.[29] Interestingly, he concluded that "the majority of these shortcomings derive from the scant experience of the *ufficiali di complemento* – especially the young ones" who were tasked with supervising the defensive works.[30] Indeed, Messe had few positive words to say about the reinforcements: they were fresh, but of questionable quality, and incorporating them into the old formations became a lengthy process. Particularly the CSIR's infantry lacked experienced junior officers and the reserve officers were apparently inept at command.[31] Battalion commanders (all professional officers) were also short in supply and "not altogether excellent."[32]

Messe thus demanded closer guidance from battalion, regimental and even divisional commanders to improve defensive positions—which, of course, deprived them of time for other duties associated with their rank. On 12 May, Messe circulated directives to augment defensive lines (also by using rear troops) and reminded all subordinate units to employ their artillery to the very front to support the first trenches—especially against tanks.[33] He demanded that armoured attacks be immediately countered with concentrated fire from all available guns to prevent breakthroughs.[34] Messe also circulated German guidelines on fighting Soviet armour and created specially trained (infantry) anti-tank squads (one officer, one NCO and nine men) for each battalion, who received a two-week special training in rear areas.[35] The engineers were tasked to supply the infantry with improvised explosive devices, mines and other

---

[29] ACS, T-821/257/IT 3068/755-759, Messe – Organizzazione difensiva e lavori, 8 Apr. 1942.

[30] Ibid., f.759.

[31] ACS, T-821/258/IT 3064/83-87, Messe to CS – Impiego del CSIR, 4 May 1942, f.87.

[32] Ibid.

[33] ACS, T-821/258/IT 3064/209-211, Messe – Organizzazione difensiva settore *Pasubio*, 12 May 1942, f.210.

[34] ACS, T-821/257/IT 3068/755-759, Messe – Organizzazione difensiva e lavori, 8 Apr. 1942, f.757.

[35] ACS, T-821/257/IT 3063/1157-1159, Messe – Lotta anticarro, 29 Apr. 1942.

ad hoc means to resist enemy tanks.[36] Like other units, the engineers also received special anti-tank training (particularly the *guastatori* assault troops).[37] At the same time, Kleist provided six 75 mm anti-tank guns[38] to each Italian division and offered training courses to establish similar units to the German *Panzerjäger* (tank-hunting units).[39] Furthermore, Messe criticised the employment of (divisional) artillery as having been "always much greater than needed"[40] during the entire campaign. This caused logistical problems and harmed morale: for one, the gunners put strain on the materiel and used high quantities of ammunition (which could not easily be resupplied); secondly, the soldiers became accustomed to calling in artillery instead of relying on infantry support weapons.[41] He therefore reminded all units only to divert divisional artillery in direct fire support to the infantry if it was genuinely required and to improve patrolling for target-acquisition. These reports and efforts demonstrate again the Italians' recognition of their own weaknesses and their attempts to improve overall performance. In conclusion, Messe identified two main problems for the coming year: the difficulties in maintaining an increased Italian presence on the Eastern Front and the danger of Soviet armour. He had, however, limited leverage in both regards, as each depended on choices in Rome. Messe asked for reinforcements, materiel, tanks and artillery, but also realised that he had to improvise with the means at hand and he developed similar ideas to the Germans on how to confront the tank menace.

---

[36] Ibid., f.1158.

[37] ACS, T-821/344/IT 4590/998, Gen. Giovanelli – Corsi anticarro, 31 May 1942.

[38] The so-called 75/97/38, or 75/39 was based on the French 75 mm mod.1897 barrel, which was placed on the German PaK 38 carriage. Thanks to its high muzzle velocity, it could penetrate 120 mm armour plates and the Wehrmacht readily deployed the gun in the early stages of Barbarossa to meet the T-34, see Cappellano and Pignato, *Andare contro*, 174; Finazzer and Riccio, *Italian Artillery*, 102–4.

[39] ACS, T-821/258/IT 3064/512-513, Gen. Giovanelli – Pezzi anticarro 75 mm, 8 May 1942. The Italians intended to assign them to the divisions' artillery regiment and asked for especially suitable men—ideally volunteers—to man these guns. On these units see also Cappellano and Pignato, *Andare contro*, 283ff.

[40] ACS, T-821/257/IT 3062/399-401, Messe – Impiego dell'Artiglieria, 11 Mar. 1942.

[41] Ibid., f.400.

THE CREATION OF THE ARMIR

After the Soviet winter offensives, the front was stabilised in spring 1942. But the German *Ostheer* was badly mauled and in need of new men and material. By 20 March 1942, the Wehrmacht had lost 225,559 killed, 796,516 wounded and 50,991 missing.[42] All these losses in men, horses (250,814), vehicles and armour could not be made up. Hitler therefore welcomed new formations for the envisaged summer offensives in 1942; and "German requests for larger contingents of troops for the Eastern Front were most easily realised, relatively speaking, in the case of Italy."[43] Mussolini had constantly desired to send additional divisions (boasting as much as twenty) to augment the Italian participation.[44] Additionally, the CSIR had "merely" lost 1792 killed or missing and 7878 wounded (and suffering frostbite) by 30 July 1942—thus the vital political rationale for partaking in the campaign appeared to come at a very low cost.[45] While the pendulum swung in the Axis' favour in the sands of Africa, Mussolini felt comfortable in sending additional divisions to the East[46]— despite warnings from the *Comando Supremo* (to him and the Germans) about insufficient material and vehicles.[47] Messe had remained sceptical

[42] Bernd Wegner, "The War Against the Soviet Union 1942–1943," in *Germany and the Second World War. Vol. 6: The Global War*, eds. Horst Boog et al. (Oxford: Oxford University Press, 2001), 841–1215, here 872.

[43] Ibid., 906. On the other contingents' increases see DiNardo, *Germany*, 138–39.

[44] Cavallero claimed Italy could muster up to six new divisions, if Germany supplied the vehicles, see Ciano Diaries, 23 Oct. 1941; Cavallero Diary, 22 Oct. 1941. Yet, Cavallero remained sceptical about German promises and knew that domestic production could never achieve the desired motorisation numbers, ibid., 5 Mar. 1942. See also Schlemmer, "Italy," 146–51.

[45] Giusti's claim that thereby around one fourth of the CSIR had been lost gives an inadequate impression: wounded may have returned to their units while reserves that reached the CSIR made up the fatalities, Giusti, *La campagna*, 129. Still, as mentioned before, the casualty numbers need further scrutiny and detailed classification by unit. While the ARMIR divisions numbered 10–12,000 men, only around 6000 were effective combat troops; casualty figures have therefore always to be seen in perspective. For the number of combat soldiers, see USSME, *Le operazioni*, 228.

[46] He hoped the Germans might send armoured forces to the North African theatre in return, Burgwyn, *Mussolini*, 121ff.; USSME, *Le operazioni*, 181–83.

[47] Cavallero Diary, 21 Jan. 1942. In late January, the *Comando Supremo* had communicated its intention to send one additional corps and one *Alpini* corps to the Eastern Front as soon as possible (one in March and one in April). The Germans warned that the railway heads for unloading these troops would still be Christinovka (180 kilometres south of Kiev), i.e. a long way from the front. Additionally, the weather would be bad in spring

about deploying new divisions that could neither be sufficiently equipped nor supplied, but might cause setbacks that would undermine "the good name of the Italian soldier".[48] He therefore opposed the formation of an independent army, instead arguing for an exchange of the *Torino* and *Pasubio* and limiting the size of Italy's contingent[49]; thus he shared the opposition of many traditional Italian officers who saw this theatre as secondary (at the very best) and cautioned an ever-closer alliance with Germany.[50] But Mussolini overruled such opposition and the *Armata Italiana in Russia* (ARMIR, or Eighth Army) was formed in April 1942. The question of supreme command over this new formation had been raised in January.[51] The "elderly" and "mediocre" Italo Gariboldi (1879–1970)[52] was appointed on 2 April 1942—much to Messe's disgust.[53] The 63-year-old Gariboldi had never been an outstanding commander and Cavallero possibly appointed him to block further advancement of the successful and popular Messe.[54] His Chief of Staff

and German operations would not commence before June, see ACS, T-821/200/IT 1382/990-994, Marras – Questioni varie trattate con l'OKW, 29 Jan. 1942, f.992.

[48] USSME, *Le operazioni*, 195; Giusti, *La campagna*, 132ff. Messe thought a Soviet defeat less likely than a collapse of the Axis' supply system and troop exhaustion, Ciano Diaries, 4 June 1942.

[49] Giusti, *La campagna*, 132–37.

[50] Schlemmer, "Italy," 153.

[51] USSME, *Le operazioni*, 184.

[52] Burgwyn, *Mussolini*, 125.

[53] He repeatedly feuded with him until leaving the Eastern Front on 1 November 1942; according to one observer this was caused by his feeling of having been sacrificed (due to his often hard-nosed approach with the Germans), see TNA, GFM 36/240, Vidussoni – Appunto per il Duce, 24 Oct. 1942, fol.15. Yet, their relationship was very ambiguous. Gariboldi had been Messe's superior during the First World War, when the latter gained his fame as an *arditi* (stormtroop) commander and was proposed by Gariboldi for highest decorations, see AUSSME, Fondo Messe, b.X527, c.Proposte di Medaglia d'Oro, Italo Gariboldi – Relazione sull'azione del IX Reparto d'Assalto, 25 June 1923; on Messe's career in the First World War see Longo, *Messe*, 11–61. Gariboldi was arrested after 1943 and was lucky not to be executed by the RSI. After the Second World War, Messe included Gariboldi in an inner circle of generals that were meant to safeguard the prestige of the Italian Army, TNA, KV 3/266, fol.28a, Meeting by former generals, May 1947. Thus, their animosity should not be overrated; see also his positive remarks on Gariboldi in a letter to his wife, in Messe, *Lettere*, 144.

[54] Gariboldi's appointment was welcomed in Army circles, as he had been—like so many—a personal enemy of Cavallero, Ciano Diaries, 2 Apr. and 17 May 1942. More

was Bruno Malaguti (1887–1945), who had been decorated for bravery in the First World War (where he fought also on the Western Front and was part of the Interallied Control Commission for Germany), and later served mainly with the *Bersaglieri* and in staff roles.[55]

Between February and May, the new troops destined for the Eastern Front were intensively prepared for marching duties, manoeuvre warfare, river crossings and anti-tank defence—also on the basis of German and Italians experiences and memoranda that were circulated to the respective units.[56] The ARMIR included the former CSIR, which on 9 July became the XXXV Army Corps. In March, the *Celere* had been supplemented with the motorised 6th *Bersaglieri* Regiment, the 201st Motorised Artillery Regiment and support units (to the remaining 3rd *Bersaglieri*). The *Celere* thereby became a de facto (motorised) *Bersaglieri* division and arguably the most powerful Italian unit on the Eastern Front.[57] The LXVII *Bersaglieri* Battalion also contained the ARMIR's only armoured component: thirty-one L 6/40 light tanks and nineteen L 40 assault guns (with a 47/32 gun).[58] The *Novara*, *Savoia* and the horse-drawn artillery regiments were withdrawn from the division to form the so-called *Raggruppamento truppe a cavallo* (under

---

detailed on his appointment is Giusti, *La campagna*, 135–37. Why Messe left is also unclear (beyond his clear expression to do so). In a letter to Clara Petacci (probably in August 1942), he bitterly complained about being sidelined by Gariboldi and not having a position as primus inter pares in regards to other corps commanders. Messe praised his men and stated (in the hope that she would hand the letter to Mussolini) that he had done his duty as "soldier, citizen, and Fascist", but that he will not tolerate this situation to continue and ask for leave at the end of September after tiring fifteen months of service in Russia, see TNA, GFM 36/139, Messe to Petacci, n.d; also Messe, *Lettere*, 147–48 Further, he was destined for promotion and thus a new position had to be found for him even before he asked Cavallero for relief on 29 September, for thoughts on this matter see Cavallero Diary, 25 Sept. 1942.

[55] After offering resistance with his unit in September 1943, Malaguti was interned by the Germans and meant to be executed in the Fascist Salò Republic. He was liberated in April 1944 and died eight months later from the effects of his internment.

[56] USSME, *Le operazioni*, 194. Further preparations were vaccinations and allotment of winter equipment, see ibid., 184.

[57] In contrast, the 5th, 7th, 8th, 9th and 12th *Bersaglieri* regiments who fought in North Africa were also inserted in armoured (the *Ariete*, *Littorio* and *Centauro*) or motorised divisions (the *Trento* and *Trieste*), yet only with one regiment per division.

[58] Cappellano and Battistelli, *Light Tanks*, 40.

direct army command).[59] The II Army Corps under Lieutenant-General Giovanni Zanghieri (1881–1959) included the *Cosseria*, *Ravenna* and *Sforzesca* Infantry Divisions,[60] and the *Alpini* Corps, commanded by Lieutenant-General Gabriele Nasci (1887–1947), which consisted of the *Tridentina*, *Julia* and *Cuneense* (*Alpini*) Mountain Divisions. The *Alpini* Corps was only inserted in the frontline in September 1942. Additionally, the Eighth Army had the *Vicenza* Division under its direct command for rear-guard duties,[61] as well as additional Blackshirt troops,[62] artillery (the *9° Raggruppamento artiglieria d'armata* with modern 149/40 guns and 210/22 howitzers) and the Croat Legion.[63] The divisions of the *Alpini* Corps had been deployed against France in June 1940,[64] but only saw real combat in the Greek campaign—especially the *Julia*.[65] The *Tridentina* and the *Cuneense* reached the Albanian front in December 1940 and the divisions collected valuable experience up till spring 1941.[66] The divisions of the II Corps had even

[59] The most detailed account (without primary sources) is Giorgio Vitali, *Trotto, galoppo...caricat! Storia del Raggruppamento truppe a cavallo. Russia 1942–1943* (Milan: Mursia, 2010).

[60] The latter two were nominally mountain infantry divisions, but they possessed the same material like a regular infantry division. The only exception was the reduction of the machine gun battalion (one instead of two) in all three divisions.

[61] The division was deprived of an own artillery regiment and heavy mortars. It was commanded by the elderly General Etvaldo Pascolini (1884–1956).

[62] The *3 Gennaio* Blackshirt *raggruppamento* was set up on 15 April 1942 and led by Filippo Diamanti, see ACS, Fondo Diamanti, b.1, f.Camp. Russia, Diario Storico Raggruppamento CC.NN. Autocarrato *3 Gennaio* [hereafter cited as 'Diario Storico *3 Gennaio*'], 10 July 1942. Many Blackshirt formations were named after Fascist 'celebratory dates'. The 3 January 1925 marked Mussolini's seizure of absolute power after the Matteotti murder. The unit had conducted anti-partisan operations on the Balkans before.

[63] On the Legion see Müller, *An der Seite*, 106–12; Rory Yeomans, "Croatia," in *Joining Hitler's Crusade: European Nations and the Invasion of the Soviet Union, 1941*, ed. David Stahel (Cambridge: Cambridge University Press, 2017), 158–89.

[64] Faldella, *Le truppe alpine*, 1–28.

[65] Libero Porcari, "La 'Cuneense' sulle fronti di guerra," in *Gli italiani sul fronte russo*, ed. Enzo Collotti (Bari: De Donato, 1982), 261–92, here 268; Rasero, *Alpini della Julia*, 121ff.

[66] Faldella, *Le truppe alpine*, 47–115; Rasero, *L'eroica cuneense*, 225ff.; Rasero, *Tridentina avanti*, 235ff.

less experience and many units had been filled with conscripts who had never seen combat before.[67]

Material shortages had necessitated stripping Italian territorial divisions of some equipment, and pouring additional supplies into Russia. Yet, there were still painful deficiencies in anti-tank and anti-aircraft guns, and nor could general motorisation levels be improved.[68] The 229,005 soldiers (7000 officers) were equipped with 2657 light and 1742 heavy machine guns, 250 light and 600 heavy artillery pieces, 52 anti-aircraft guns,[69] 874 light mortars (45 mm) and 423 heavy mortars (81 mm), 278 Italian 47/32 and 54 German 75 mm anti-tank guns, 25,000 pack animals, 16,700 vehicles and 4770 motorcycles.[70] The air arm consisted of 23 reconnaissance and 41 combat aircraft.[71] If one compares this to the CSIR, the main parameters (men, horses, artillery) were more or less quadrupled, yet vehicle numbers only tripled, which reduced the overall mobility.[72] There were some additional imbalances: in contrast to the *Celere* and the *Pasubio*, the II and *Alpini* Corps' infantry had to rely mainly on their feet, and the XXXV Corps possessed 189 heavy mortars in contrast to the *Alpini* Corps' 72 and the II Corp's 153.[73] The same held true for the 47/32 anti-tank guns: the *Alpini* Divisions had two AT companies per division (in total 48 barrels), the XXXV had 28 guns across the divisions and the corps artillery another 80, the II Corps 22 throughout the divisions and 72 under corps command.[74] The most effective weapon against Soviet armour remained the artillery. Particularly the 36 modern 75/32 of the 201st Motorised Artillery Regiment (*Celere*) were intended for anti-tank roles, but these

---

[67] USSME, *Le operazioni*, 213.

[68] For the II Corps' problems and attempts to overcome shortcomings see ACS, T-821/373/IT 4883.

[69] The lack of aerial protection was repeatedly noted and enemy aerial supremacy was a continuous feature in the entire Italian sector—even if Soviet actions did not seem to have a severe impact on the early summer operations, see e.g. DS CS, VII:I, 30 May, and 7, 25, and 30 June 1942.

[70] USSME, *Le operazioni*, 187; Giusti, *La campagna*, 139.

[71] Ibid., 139.

[72] De Franceschi, *I servizi logistici*, 9; Schlemmer, *Italiener*, 30; USSME, *Le operazioni*, 194.

[73] Ibid., 188.

[74] Ibid., 189.

were in short supply, as were the modern 75/18 howitzers[75] and the 75/39—but at least this balanced the limited suitability of the 47/32 guns to some degree.[76]

The ARMIR was not meant to be an armoured army. Still, the absence of adequate mobile reserves was a disadvantage in defensive and offensive operations. In comparison, though German infantry divisions did not possess any tanks, they could usually rely on armoured reserves at the army or corps level. Thus, the ARMIR's fundamental weakness was its limited mobility and firepower, i.e. its scarce number of large calibre anti-tank, anti-aircraft and artillery guns. But the ARMIR was far from a hapless victim sent to the slaughterhouse—as was often claimed after the war. The Italians did their best to provide new materiel, the units were at high strength levels and fully operable despite shortcomings in motorisation—which also caused headaches to German infantry divisions in 1942.[77] Also Schlemmer reached the conclusion that the ARMIR mainly constituted a quantitative, and not a qualitative, improvement, but that "the *Comando Supremo* had done everything that was half-way reasonable (and perhaps even more) to make the Eighth Army into a field-ready formation."[78]

OPERATIONS IN SUMMER 1942: MARCHING TO THE DON

The German offensives in summer 1942 were expected to match the early successes of the previous year. Yet, the *Ostheer* had lost around 35 per cent of its manpower, lacked vehicles and ammunition, and the general staff judged only eight out of 162 divisions fully capable for offensive operations in March 1942.[79] The summer offensive was prepared

[75] The II Corps' artillery received all available 75/32 before being sent to Russia, Finazzer and Riccio, *Italian Artillery*, 26.

[76] Detailed USSME, *Le operazioni*, 190–93.

[77] On low battle-readiness of German divisions on 30 March 1942, see Wegner, "War," 877.

[78] Schlemmer, "Italy," 156.

[79] In September 1941, merely 134 out of 209 divisions were seen as fully operable, Bernd Wegner, "Vom Lebensraum zum Todesraum. Deutschlands Kriegführung zwischen Moskau und Stalingrad," in *Stalingrad: Ereignis—Wirkung—Symbol*, ed. Jürgen Förster (Munich: Piper, 1993), 17–37, here 23. On the lack of staff officers see Megargee, *Inside*, 127. A total of 41 of the around 65 divisions of Army Group South had been newly deployed to the East, Manfred Kehrig, *Stalingrad: Analyse und Dokumentation einer Schlacht* (Stuttgart: DVA, 1974), 26.

by smaller operations to improve the start-off situation for Army Group South. The Kerch peninsula was reconquered in May 1942, and this was followed by the seizure of Sebastopol in July 1942, which secured the Crimea for subsequent operations in the Caucasus and eliminated a possible threat on the flanks. The renewed battles for Kharkov, Izyum and Kupyank in May, and the following operations (Wilhelm and Fridericus II) in June provided spring-off positions for Operation Blue I, the great push towards the Don, which began on 28 June 1942.[80] The Italians remained part of Army Group South—whose 900,000 soldiers were subdivided in July 1942 (before Operation Blue II) into Army Group A and B, which marched towards Stalingrad and the Caucasus, respectively.[81] This splitting of Army Group South has been called a "fatal dissipation of forces"[82] and an ineffective attempt to achieve all Axis objectives at once: namely, both the oil in the Caucasus and the city of Stalingrad. Additionally, the Wehrmacht was unable to destroy either the existing Soviet forces or means of levying new troops. The scarcity of motorised and armoured forces was felt even more dearly as the Red Army abandoned its rigid resistance in favour of a more flexible defence. Evading encirclements through skilful withdrawals provided the time and means to assemble forces for a counter-offensive behind the Volga and the Don.[83]

The Fourth Panzer Army reached Voronezh on 5 July and advanced on Stalingrad together with the Sixth Army—whose left flank was covered by the Italians. The II Corps reached the assembling area near Kharkov in June and July (the *Alpini* arrived in August and learned that they would not be deployed to the Caucasus, but to the Don).[84] Gathering its forces proved (again) to be a slow and tricky affair.[85] Moreover, the advances brought the Italians from the densely inhabited industrial area of the Donets basin to the agricultural plains in the Don area, where their chances of living off the land and finding shelter were notably limited.[86] This increased the importance of unceasing

[80] Detailed in Bellamy, *Absolute War*, 447ff.; Wegner, "War," 942ff.
[81] Mawdsley, *Thunder*, 155ff.; Kehrig, *Stalingrad*.
[82] Wegner, "War," 974; Mawdsley, *Thunder*, 162–67.
[83] Bellamy, *Absolute War*, 471.
[84] USSME, *Le operazioni*, 217.
[85] The build-up is analysed in detail in ibid., 196–99.
[86] A good terrain description can be found in ibid., 38–43, 235ff.

supplies and material to erect defensive lines. While the II Corps was still overcoming problems of assembling its forces, the XXXV Corps, the *Sforzesca*, the *Raggruppamento a cavallo*, the *Monte Cervino* and most available artillery[87] started to advance to the Don under command of the German Seventeenth Army (on the flank to Army Group B) towards Voroshilovgrad (today's Luhansk/Lugansk) and Krasny Luch after 11 July.[88]

The Italians had to cross the Donets and pursue a withdrawing enemy (the Sixty-third Army). On 13 August, the ARMIR reached its assigned sector on the Don on the left flank of the Sixth Army's XVII Corps. The II Corps had mounted a foot march of 1100 kilometres (on average 32 kilometres per day) during which supply problems and partisans had caused minor delays.[89] Still, the advance to the Don had been relatively calm for the Italians. Now there lay ahead a period of cross-river infiltration and skirmishing. Only the *Celere* became involved in wider operations. It distinguished itself by eliminating a Soviet bridgehead near Serafimovich[90] at the end of July and withstanding the ensuing counter-attacks.[91] The battle included the first concentrated armoured attack—by 25 Soviet T-34 and 15 light T-18—on the *Celere* on 30 July. The infantry support weapons were useless, but the Italians targeted the accompanying infantry to stop the onslaught, and one 75/32 battery proved very effective at short range and destroyed twelve tanks—at very high costs.[92] Similarly, subsequent Soviet armoured attacks were countered primarily by targeting their accompanying infantry and employing artillery against isolated tanks. After five days of battle, the Italians had

---

[87] Gariboldi attached priority to artillery reaching the front, in order to support the expected offensives.

[88] On 23 July, the Eighth Army was gathered in force around Voroshilovgrad, USSME, *Le operazioni*, 204ff. The Soviets mined the territory and largely withdrew; still, the Italians took around 4000 prisoners, ibid., 207.

[89] Ibid., 208ff., 215.

[90] The Germans spoke of the battle of Kalac.

[91] The division had mastered 400 kilometres in four days to safeguard the threatened flank, Schreiber, "Italiens Teilnahme," 271; USSME, *Le operazioni*, 218ff.; Roggiani, *Bersaglieri*, 312ff. Also the *Sforzesca* was noted for her willingness to attack and pursue the enemy—albeit against weak forces, BA-MA, RH 31-IX/25, Fellmer to Tippelskirch, 24 July 1942.

[92] USSME, *Le operazioni*, 221. The official history does unfortunately not tell us what kind of tanks had been destroyed.

destroyed thirty-one tanks and two armoured fighting vehicles.[93] Until 21 August, the continued Soviet counter-attacks caused painful losses to the *Celere* and the German 79th ID, and the Red Army had gained critical bridgeheads on the right bank of the Don.[94] Some battalions were reduced to 200 men, and out of the *Celere*'s roughly 5000 men in combat duties 1082 (i.e. eighteen per cent) had been lost by 7 August.[95] Between 30 July and 14 August, the *Celere* reported 162 dead (eleven officers), 950 wounded (42 officers) and 89 missing. The division was subsequently withdrawn from the front line to rest and regroup—only parts of its artillery continued to fight under the German 79th ID. The test for the ARMIR came in the form of the so-called 'First defensive battle on the Don' between 20 August and 1 September 1942 when the Sixtythird Soviet Army assaulted the Italian XXXV and II Corps, based along the Don between the Kalitva and Choper rivers.

The 'First Defensive Battle on the Don' (20 August—1 September 1942)

The Soviet attack sought to obstruct the German advance to Stalingrad or at least force the Sixth Army to divert troops for flank protection.[96] The Eighth Army still formed part of Army Group B and bordered the Hungarian Second Army to its left and the German Sixth Army to its right (later the Romanian Third)—i.e. it was based to the north-west of Stalingrad. The ARMIR divided the first line of defence into three corps sectors: on the very left flank the II Corps (294th ID, *Cosseria*, *Ravenna*), the XXIX German Corps (*Torino*, 62nd ID) and on the right the XXXV Corps (*Pasubio*, *Sforzesca*); the remaining units were held in reserve. The Soviet Sixtythird Army consisted of four rifle divisions (1st, 153rd, 127th and 197th) in the first line and the 14th Guards and 203rd Rifle Division in the second.

The defenders faced several difficulties: the terrain was easy to penetrate and hard to defend. The enemy preparation zones were difficult

---

[93] Ibid., 225. The neighbouring Germans had destroyed sixteen; yet precise information is missing.
[94] Ibid., 225–33.
[95] Ibid., 228.
[96] Glantz and House, *When Titans Clashed*, 146–47.

to gain oversight over. Additionally, the ARMIR was holding a line of 270 kilometres, equalling a 30-kilometre sector per division, which Gariboldi considered impossible to defend, to supply or to reinforce.[97] Thirty-kilometre defence lines were double the length of the German norm and a Russian division usually had an attacking perimeter of three kilometres.[98] Thus, Gariboldi ordered active patrolling, augmented defensive lines as well as the allocation of reserves and supplies near the front.[99] The Italians created divisional reserves by deploying four battalions in their first line and two in reserve—i.e. each battalion held a seven-kilometre zone and was meant to receive all firepower possible from the regimental artillery to defend the first line and their improvised strong points.[100] In practice, the sheer length of the front rendered concentrated fire from all barrels improbable, and Gariboldi was well aware about the situation of reserves in mid-August 1942. He told his subordinate commands that the only available unit, the poorly equipped and trained *Vicenza*, could only contribute "good will."[101] Hitler had repeatedly asked to have the 22nd Panzer Division transferred as mobile reserve behind the ARMIR; it was, however, still engaged in battles, and could only be redeployed after 26 August.[102]

The Italians' operational concept (from 18 August) foresaw defensive positions (including two villages on high ground) with active counter-offensives, patrolling and additional defensive works to counter the threat

[97] BA-MA, RH 31-IX/11, Gariboldi to Army Group B, 31 July 1942, fol.247.

[98] BA-MA, RH 31-IX/74, Weitere Erfahrungen bei der Abwehr der russischen Großangriffe, 23 Jan. 1943, fol.9; Dmitry D. Lelyushenko, *Moskva-Stalingrad-Berlin-Praga: Zapiski komandarma* (Moscow: Nauka, 1985; first ed. 1970), 149. According to Italian doctrine, the theoretical defensive perimeter per division was three to five kilometres, USSME, *Le operazioni*, 189. The Soviet General Staff estimated that the average front line to be defended by one Italian (or Romanian) division in November was 15 kilometres; see Louis Rotundo, ed., *Battle for Stalingrad: The 1943 Soviet General Staff Study* (Washington: Pergamon-Brassey's, 1989), 70.

[99] See the general guidelines by Gariboldi in ACS, T-821/260/IT 3074/332-335, Gariboldi – Difesa del Don, 2 Aug. 1942. Yet, also the two German divisions within the ARMIR were holding frontlines of 65 (294th ID) and 55 kilometres (62th ID) respectively – albeit easier defendable terrain, USSME, *Le operazioni*, 239–40.

[100] Ibid., 240.

[101] Petacco, *L'armata*, 89.

[102] Geoffrey Jukes, *Hitler's Stalingrad Decisions* (Berkeley: University of California Press, 1985), 53, 55–57.

of armoured attacks from the east and north-east. Each battalion was ordered to send two companies to the main defensive line and hold one in reserve.[103] The deployment of anti-tank weapons was to be "decentralised and according to the terrain", while even divisional artillery (one 75/32 battery) was deployed on high ground near the front to provide close support to the main battle line (and the movement area).[104] Earlier orders and circulars further demonstrate the commanders' understanding of compact forward deployment and close artillery support to shield the infantry.[105]

German orders also envisaged the deployment of anti-tank guns near the front at vulnerable sites. These would attempt to destroy enemy armour by concentrated fire before they reached loopholes in the defence perimeters; some AT pieces were to be held as mobile reserves close to the main battle line.[106] In short, the Wehrmacht prohibited flexible operations and demanded rigid defences along the main battle line.[107] The terrain offered few opportunities for defensive positions and housing, while the Soviet side of the riverbank featured some dense woods and smaller hills.[108] Only a tight grip over the river, the creation of minefields or the destruction of villages and woods on the opposing bank could offer some improvement and help obstruct infiltrations. Additionally, the transportation and communications network was poorly developed and the few roads in the rear were not paved—a challenge for logistics on both sides of the front. Italian engineers and workers of the Organisation Todt constantly tried to improve them.[109] Further, the terrain was not ideal. According to David Glantz, the numerous deep gullies and gorges (*balkis*) had steep banks "well suited to serve as

[103] ACS, T-821/259/IT 3073/890-892, Ordine di operazione n.18, 18 Aug. 1942, f.890.
[104] Ibid., f.891.
[105] ACS, Fondo Diamanti, b.1, f.Camp. Russia, 'Diario Storico *3 Gennaio*', 16 Aug. 1942.
[106] ACS, T-821/259/IT 3070/650-652, XXXIX Army Corps order no.63, 11 Aug. 1942.
[107] Ibid., f.651.
[108] Detailed in USSME, *Le operazioni*, 235ff. The whole combat theatre lay between 50 and 250 metres above sea level. The important height near Verkhnyi Mamon was at around 220 metres altitude.
[109] Ibid., 238.

anti-tank obstacles or natural cover for anti-tank defences. Although the region appeared ideally suited for armoured operations, much of it was inaccessible for mechanised units and, moreover, severely compartmentalised."[110] Still, given the enemy situation, scarcity of reserves and the poor roads, one should ask if a rigid defence was in fact the only feasible (and possible) thing to do.

The 'First Defensive Battle on the Don' can be subdivided into four phases: first, the Soviet opening moves between 20–22 August, second the Italian counter-attack on 23 August, third the continued Soviet operations (24–25 August), and, lastly, the halt in their offensive up till 1 September. In early August, the Soviets had repeatedly attempted to locate weak spots on the Eighth Army's front, through active skirmishing and infiltration. The main attack was launched on 20 August against the XXXV Corps. The *Ravenna* and the *Sforzesca* were hard-pressed and the latter lost the town of Simofski.[111] The Soviets had attacked the Croat Legion the night before, and the whole 197th Rifle Division (828th, 862nd, 889th regiments) hit the *Sforzesca* at 2.30 a.m. after brief artillery preparation.[112] The *Tagliamento* was on the XXXV Corps' right flank and had the *Sforzesca* on its left. One battery of the 75/34 guns was used effectively against the Soviet onslaught.[113] Two batteries of the corps artillery's 105/28 pieces had been withdrawn from the front on 21 August due to a lack of ammunition and these were now badly missed.[114] Briefly before the attack, the Germans had stopped delivering fuel to the Eighth Army, which caused severe shortages[115] and repeated calls for aerial support did not yield the desired assistance.[116] Still,

---

[110] David M. Glantz, *From the Don to the Dnepr: Soviet Offensive Operations, December 1942–August 1943* (London: Cass, 1991), 24. Some gullies were so deep that armoured formations had to look for alternative routes, see Buttar, *Knife's Edge*, 150.

[111] In the end, the *Sforzesca* withdrew over ten kilometres under heavy casualties, DS CS, VII:I, 21 Aug. 1942.

[112] USSME, *Le operazioni*, 250.

[113] ACS, Fondo Diamanti, b.1, f.Camp. Russia, 'Diario Storico 3 Gennaio', 20 Aug. 1942.

[114] ACS, T-821/259/IT 3071/711, Unsigned letter, 21 Aug. 1942.

[115] ACS, T-821/456/IT 5474/332, Rifornimento carburanti, 18 Aug. 1942.

[116] ACS, T-821/259/IT 3069/570, Verbalizzazione – Lt. Col. Conti to ARMIR, 20 Aug. 1942.

the *Sforzesca* was ordered to gather all forces and defend its positions to the man.[117]

During the second night, the Soviets reinforced their foothold with two regiments. The Italians, too, poured in reserves (mainly the cavalry units of the *Raggruppamento a cavallo*).[118] The situation was "very serious" and the *Raggruppamento* was unable to hold a fourteen kilometre frontline.[119] On 23 August, the Italians tried to regain the lost positions on the river and assigned the (still severely weakened) *Celere* and the German 179th Infantry Regiment to support the counter-attack.[120] Despite its success, Messe noted many failings, which resulted in high casualties: poor use of mortars, poor concealment and insufficient use of terrain.[121] On the other hand, Messe's remarks on the Soviets' excellent use of mortars and the terrain sustain Glantz's argument that it was indeed possible to take advantage of the topography in erecting effective defences.

On 24 August, the Red Army continued its attacks—aided vital bridgeheads, which allowed the movement of troops and material across the Don. The *Sforzesca*—especially its vital artillery—was exhausted and the Soviets had as usual identified the junctions between divisions as weak spots. The *Sforzesca* and the *Celere* were in a precarious situation, but Italian demands to send reinforcements from XVII Corps (Hollidt) bore no results. The German's decision to place the *Sforzesca* under their direct command resulted in severe rows.[122] Messe was deeply offended by the German interference, especially during a crisis where the Italians defended their lines with desperate measures: some units had fixed their bayonets and the *Savoia Cavalleria* Regiment initiated a successful cavalry charge against Soviet positions at Isbushenskij on 24 August.[123] Indeed, this incident was seen as a turning point in Messe's relationship

---

[117] ACS, T-821/260/IT 3074/322, Messe to *Sforzesca* and *Pasubio*, 21 Aug. 1942.
[118] More detailed in USSME, *Le operazioni*, 254ff.
[119] ACS, T-821/259/IT 3069/567, Verbalizzazione – Utili to Malaguti, 21 Aug. 1942.
[120] USSME, *Le operazioni*, 262ff.
[121] ACS, T-821/260/IT 3074/438, Messe to *Pasubio* and *Sforzesca*, 23 Aug. 1942.
[122] USSME, *Le operazioni*, 271-74.
[123] Burgwyn, *Mussolini*, 127. German observers of the neighbouring XVII Corps noted that the "splendidly gallant attack" of the *Savoia* had destroyed the Soviet battalion, ACS, T-821/259/IT 3070/619, Phone call German Operations officer XVII Army Corps to DVK XXXV Corps, 24 Aug. 1942.

with the Germans, which had always been very ambivalent.[124] The liaison officer to his XXXV Corps, Major Reinhold Fellmer, observed as much: according to Fellmer, when Messe stopped wearing his Knight's Cross it cast dark shadows on the future of the Axis, as he was seen as the embodiment of a pro-German approach,[125] and vital in securing good relations through his charisma and authority.[126] In Rome, however, Cavallero told Mussolini that the German decision had been justified.[127] In any case, also subsequent counter-attacks against Soviet positions were thwarted by missing artillery ammunition,[128] but also nosedived with support of the Luftwaffe and other German units that were closely mixed with the Italians.[129] After ten days of battle, the ARMIR had suffered 883 dead and 4212 wounded—over half of the fatalities were men of the *Sforzesca*,[130] but other units also had notable losses.[131] The Soviets had slightly enlarged their footholds on the right bank of the Don at (Verkhnyi) Mamon and at Ogalev-Abrossimova, which became vital

[124] See also Schlemmer, "Italy," 145.

[125] BA-MA, RH 31-IX/25, Fellmer to Tippelskirch, 3 Sep. 1942.

[126] BA-MA, MSg 2/4388, Distler – Verbindungsoffizier, fol.52. Allegedly he had thrown his Knight's Cross (awarded 15 Feb. 1942) away and wrote a furious letter to Gariboldi, to the effect that the Germans withdrew their order. Yet, he continued to sport his German decorations and photographs show him wearing his Knight's Cross when he surrendered in Tunisia.

[127] DS CS, VII:I, 26 Aug. 1942.

[128] ACS, T-821/258/IT 3067/994, Messe to Gariboldi, 28 Aug. 1942.

[129] BA-MA, MSg 2/4388, Distler – Verbindungsoffizier, fos.42–43. The Luftwaffe repeatedly lamented bad marking of own Axis positions, and additionally, reconnaissance patrols on the ground were hindered by one's own prior extensive use of landmines, BA-MA, RH 31-IX/9, Malaguti to XXIX Corps, 21 Nov. 1942, fol.54; ACS, T-821/259/IT 3070/640, Hollidt circular to XXXV Army Corps, 1 Sept. 1942. On the other hand, tactical cooperation between Italian ground forces and the Luftwaffe also strengthened the defensive efforts, e.g. of the *Pasubio*, ACS, T-821/259/IT 3070/615, *Pasubio* to DVK XXXV Corps, 25 Aug. 1942.

[130] USSME, *Le operazioni del C.S.I.R. e dell'ARMIR*, 213, attachment 1. The losses were mainly in the 53rd and 54th infantry regiments and amounted at least to one entire battalion, ACS, T-821/260/IT 3074/211-214, *Sforzesca* to XXXV Corps, 7 Sept. 1942, here f.212.

[131] For the *Celere* see ACS, T-821/259/IT 3068/208. The *3rd Gennaio* had lost 458 of its 3000 men (46 killed, 272 wounded, 139 missing) between August 19 and 31, ACS, Fondo Diamanti, b.1, f.Camp. Russia, Comando '*3 Gennaio*', Relazione fatti d'armi 20/26 Agosto 1942, 12 Sept. 1942, fol.13; ACS, T-821/259/IT 3073/884, Perdite Raggruppamento CC.NN. '*3 Gennaio*': dal 19 al 31 agosto, more detailed on f.885.

springboards for the attacks in December.[132] The Red Army also had the advantage of occupying high ground—while Italian observation was hindered by dense woods on the Soviet-held left bank.

However, the Soviets had failed to split the Eighth and Sixth Armies and the ARMIR had stalled the attack largely with its own means. Italian counter-attacks failed even with German help. Yet, if the *Sforzesca* (and to a lesser extent the *Ravenna* and *Pasubio*) had stumbled on the first day, they had not fallen. The neighbouring German commands at the time (arguably) exaggerated the setback, as have later scholars[133]: the *Sforzesca* had repelled two initial attacks against it right flank by forces superior in number and materiel,[134] and immediately followed suit with patrols to scout possible routes for its own counter-offensives.[135] In fact, the offensive of the Sixty-third Army and the Twenty-first Army has been described (from the Soviet side) as slow, incomplete and little successful.[136] Yet, the Italian officers realised the weaknesses among their junior officers and NCOs, and the fact that a lack of clear orders had increased difficulties.[137] The Germans argued (with hindsight) that poor Italian scouting and observation had opened the way to overnight infiltration,[138] which then led to speedy Soviet surprise attacks, the elimination of ill-concealed heavy guns, and panic among the rather inexperienced infantry of the *Sforzesca*.[139] The Italian official history, however, argued

---

[132] Hamilton, *Sacrifice*, 73. The Germans blocked Italian proposals to eliminate it, see USSME, *Le operazioni*, 286, 454.

[133] Also the *Comando Supremo* in Rome perceived it merely as a local crisis, Cavallero Diary, 26 Aug. 1942. Particularly as at the same time, the question of Rommel's push towards Cairo hung in the air.

[134] Thus, the division did not crack "during the first assault", as claimed by Giusto Tolloy, *Con l'Armata italiana in Russia* (Turin: De Silva, 1947), 85.

[135] ACS, Fondo Diamanti, b.1, f.Camp. Russia, Comando '3 Gennaio', Relazione fatti d'armi 20/26 Agosto 1942, 12 Sept. 1942, fos.4–5, 9, 11.

[136] Kiril S. Moskalenko, *In der Südwestrichtung*, Vol. 1 (Berlin: Militärverlag der DDR, 1975), 339.

[137] BA-MA, MSg 2/4388, Distler – Verbindungsoffizier, fol.55.

[138] Defensive works (e.g. erecting minefields) were mainly done at night—due to Soviet observation, infiltration, and sporadic artillery fire.

[139] BA-MA, MSg 2/4388, Distler – Verbindungsoffizier, fos.40–41, 45, 55. In many instances the commanding officer reportedly attempted to stop retreating men at point blank, BA-MA, RH 31-IX/25, Joos to Tippelskirch, 25 Aug. 1942.

that while around half of the *Sforzesca*'s men had seen combat on the Western and Albanian front, they could not counter the Soviet numerical preponderance on 20 and 21 August with tactical skill alone.[140] Thus, inferior numbers, lack of airpower, fuel and reserves were cited as the main reasons for the initial setback. Moreover, the German liaison officer lauded the 3rd *Bersaglieri* Regiment, the *Tagliamento* Blackshirt Legion, the cavalry and the artillery for stalling the attack with "great bravery and dash", which had uplifted the whole corps' morale.[141] Our analysis should perhaps also include another, often-forgotten point: the skill and dash of the Red Army. Clearly, praise is due for these operations: the Soviets identified weak spots in the Axis defensive line, cleverly prepared the attack and tenaciously improved their positions across a formidable natural obstacle. Their night attacks and active skirmishing could hardly be stopped and were also loathed by the Wehrmacht.[142]

The Soviet footholds across the Don were obvious starting points for any coming offensive. Yet, both sides restricted their operations in this sector to river crossings, active patrolling and skirmishing (up to company-sized Soviet attacks), which remained part of their daily routine. On 18 September, Gariboldi informed the XXXV Corps that its current defensive line should be organised as winter position.[143] Thus, a period of two to three months of defensive preparations lay ahead of the ARMIR. The official history hardly dealt with these preparations, while other accounts often dismiss the Italian precautions as insufficient—at best. Did the ARMIR realise the coming challenges and the dangers of its positions? Or did it sit idle on the Don, only to be surprised by the Soviet onslaught in December?

---

[140] USSME, *Le operazioni*, 288–89.

[141] BA-MA, RH 31-IX/25, Tippelskirch to Army Group B, 29 Aug. 1942.

[142] The Red Army also placed great emphasis on snipers. The Fortieth Army, for example, trained 387 sharpshooters who reported 5500 killed enemy soldiers in three months, see Moskalenko, *Südwestrichtung*, 388.

[143] ACS, T-821/258/IT 3067/875, Gariboldi telegram, 18 Sept. 1942.

Preparing for the Second Winter—Sitting Idle on the Don?

The 'First Defensive Battle on the Don' had demonstrated the need for additional artillery and anti-tank weapons and the *Comando Supremo* immediately ordered more pieces to the Don front.[144] Yet, Italy's industrial output and the strategic situation did not allow large-scale reinforcements: after the defeat in the battle of El Alamein (24 October—4 November) vital resources were poured into Tripolitania and Tunisia. Further, the ARMIR's overall supply situation had already deteriorated during summer and the Italians blamed the Germans for not receiving more materiel, ammunition, food and petrol.[145] Now, even more Italians had to be supplied in a barely inhabited area, with poor roads, and railheads that were up to 130 kilometres from the frontline.[146] The problem, then, was not necessarily a lack of materiel or planning, but rather one of delivering the mass of goods to the front with limited cargo space, trains and trucks. Thus, in September the *Comando Supremo* despatched specialists to maintain vehicles and communication equipment,[147] easily erectable huts, plaids for the livestock, sanitary supplies to combat the cold, coats and furs and many other items.[148] Also thanks to a direct visit and the constant efforts of the Italian military attaché in Berlin,[149] the Eighth Army described the situation as "satisfactory" in October: the Germans had granted the number of trains requested, and 300,000 litres of fuel reached the ARMIR on a daily basis (out of 500,000 requested).[150] Yet, other sources show a notable decline of trains reaching the vital hub at Millerovo.[151] Still, the Germans considered,

[144] DS CS, VII:I, 30 Aug. 1942.

[145] BA-MA, RH 31-IX/11, Tippelskirch to Army Group B, 16 Aug. 1942, fol.106. The Italians passed the buck and stripped the Croat Legion off its fuel, which led to complaints from their part, see ACS, T-821/258/IT 3066/631, Croat Legion to XXXV Corps, 6 Sept. 1942.

[146] ACS, T-821/200/IT 1387/1065-1068, Sistemazione invernale 8^ Armata, 7 Oct. 1942.

[147] DS CS, VIII:I, 2 Sept. 1942.

[148] Detailed in ACS, T-821/200/IT 1386.

[149] Pelagalli, *Marras*, 193.

[150] ACS, T-821/200/IT 1387/1062, Sistemazione invernale 8^ Armata, 7 Oct. 1942.

[151] In August and September, 54 Italian and 36 German trains reached the ARMIR's railheads in Millerovo, in October 74 and 31, respectively, but in November only 43 and 28, ACS, T-821/200/IT 1387/1039, Trasporti ferroviari 8^ Armata, n.d.

for example, the Italian winter equipment "not bad"[152] and much of it arrived in time for the first snowfalls in early October 1942.[153] Several documents show a great alertness to procure additional winter gear. Thus, it seems unjustified to blame frontline commanders who could not control logistics or the home front. Commanders and planners of the ARMIR were aware of the precarious situation and the increased difficulties they faced in comparison to the previous winter.

In fact, the Germans had been expecting a Soviet offensive against their weaker allies or the vulnerable interfaces between the armies since late August–September 1942—particularly as the good infrastructure and woods on the Russian side benefitted the (concealed) deployment of reinforcements.[154] Not least thanks to liaison officers, the Italians were alarmed about this and issued repeated warnings about an imminent attack in November. Giusti has heavily criticised Gariboldi for his overconfidence and argued that the Italians had ignored signs of an impending offensive. However, in backing up her claims about the senior military's passiveness and sleepiness she mainly draws on memoirs.[155] This misapprehension fits the often-found stereotype about incapable—almost criminal—generals leading their poorly equipped men to the slaughterhouse.[156] The simple truth is that the ARMIR was in fact aware of a looming attack. But what measures did it take and how adequate were the preparations?

The sources clearly show Italian and German attempts to adapt to the situation the best they could. The ARMIR developed plans to counter possible attacks and divisional commands continued issuing warnings about their extended lines and lack of reserves[157]; appeals that Gariboldi

[152] BA-MA, MSg 2/4388, Distler – Verbindungsoffizier, fol.67.

[153] Trigg asserted that only 50 per cent of the 15,000 men in the *Ravenna* had winter coats (and only 3000 men in the *Cuneense*), but did not provide any source; see Trigg, *Death*, 141.

[154] In September, Russian defectors had warned about troop concentrations and new offensives, BA-MA, MSg 2/4388, Distler – Verbindungsoffizier, fol.65. The Soviets had started their preparations in August, USSME, *L'Italia nella relazione ufficiale sovietica sulla seconda guerra mondiale* (Rome: USSME, 1978), 146.

[155] Giusti, *La campagna*, 224ff.

[156] For example in Rochat, *Le guerre*, 392ff.

[157] ACS, T-821/258/IT 3067/975-976, Messe – Rioccupazione sponda destra Don, 15 Sept. 1942. Messe proposed to insert the *Tridentina* between the 298th ID and the *Pasubio*.

forwarded to Cavallero and Marras in Berlin who tried to reach agreements with German authorities.[158] In a circular to his division, General Marazzani, GOC of the *Celere*, outlined his ideas for a rigid defence of the few against the many.[159] He argued that neither the quantity of defences nor the terrain would stop the enemy, and thus good preparations, quick and independent decisions on the spot and the massing of forces at vital points would decide the outcome—and so, too, willpower and the readiness to die rather than retreat.[160] All available weapons were meant to support the 'line of defence', which was not, however, a static line, but a triangular connection of mutually supporting strongholds with a tactical defensive zone.[161] Italian reserves were held close to the main battle line, but the sheer length of the front line made a continuous observation of the Don impossible.[162] But given the low motorisation and poor roads, even reserves on corps level were expected to take four to five hours to reach under-threat sectors.[163]

How effective were these plans and preparations? The Fascist Party secretary, Aldo Vidussoni, visited the front extensively in early October and described morale and the sanitary conditions as very good (despite a severe lack of Red Cross nurses), but also noted some problems in completing preparations for winter and the defensive lines due to missing transport capacity and poor weather.[164] Still, he reported very few real complaints by the men, despite obvious calls for better rations and more cigarettes.[165] When the German liaison officer to the ARMIR, General Kurt von Tippelskirch, visited the Italian front, the *Pasubio*'s commander hinted at the rather theoretical German idea of defending the first line statically, given the scarce means available and the unsuitable terrain.[166] Tippelskirch, however, upheld the order, congratulated the Italians

[158] Cavallero Diary, 8 Oct. 1942; Pelagalli, *Marras*, 193ff.
[159] ACS, T-821/259/IT 3068/236-242, Gen. Marazzani – Note sullo schieramento e sistemazione a difesa, 14 Sept. 1942.
[160] Ibid., fs.236–37, 241.
[161] Ibid., f.237.
[162] BA-MA, RH 31-IX/16, Gariboldi telegram, 5 Dec. 1942, fol.250.
[163] ACS, T-821/259/IT 3068/220, Gen. Marazzani – Impiego reserve, 27 Oct. 1942.
[164] TNA, GFM 36/240, Vidussoni – Appunto per il Duce, 24 Oct. 1942, fos.12, 16.
[165] Ibid., fol.14. Yet, they might have been afraid to openly voice criticism.
[166] ACS, T-821/260/IT 3075/790-792, Gen. Olmi – Visita Generale v. Tippelskirch, 30 Sept. 1942.

for their work and argued that Romanian troops could fill the gaps.[167] Tippelskirch's reports to his German superiors were less rosy: he repeatedly stressed the need to augment defences and patrolling,[168] but also complimented the *Alpini* for having quickly erected suitable positions.[169] The improvement of their defensive works was considered as good, while there was little sign of enthusiasm for reconnaissance by force. Other German reports also repeatedly noted the low serviceability of Italian trucks,[170] and a lack of eagerness to gather intelligence on enemy movements and positions by active scouting.[171] But both German and Italian sources show not only that they had indeed noticed increased enemy activity since October,[172] but that they had attempted to counter it with improved patrolling,[173] river crossings,[174] and speeding up the construction of defensive measures, for which Gariboldi requested 18,000 POWs or civilians to add to the 7000 that had already been deployed.[175] Italian *coups de main* were often unsuccessful as the Soviets had a tendency to man their first trenches only thinly.[176] On the other hand, the less than 1000-men strong Blackshirt Legion *Montebello* had 47 dead

---

[167] Ibid., f.791.

[168] The Eighth Army had ordered six reconnaissance by force missions (in company strength) per month, while apparently each division did de facto less, BA-MA, RH 31-IX/15, German liaison with *Alpini* Corps, 13 Nov. 1942, fol.242.

[169] ACS, T-821/259/IT 3068/229-230, Gen. Marazzani – Visita del generale von Tippelskirch, 4 Oct. 1942. The *Alpini* Corps had been incorporated in the front line in September 1942 (north of the II Corps). As a rule of thumb, the Germans calculated 300 tons of material and 10-20 days time to prepare one kilometre of front line—i.e. 25 days to prepare ten kilometres with 4000 men, see [Lt. Col.] Eike Middeldorf, *Taktik im Russlandfeldzug. Erfahrungen und Folgerungen* (Berlin: Mittler, 1956), 143.

[170] As much as 40 per cent were deemed unsuitable for service in November, DiNardo, *Germany*, 148.

[171] This even held true for the *Alpini*, BA-MA, RH 31-IX/25, Fellmer to Tippelskirch, 4 Dec. 1942.

[172] ACS, Fondo Diamanti, b.1, f.Camp. Russia, 'Diario Storico 3 *Gennaio*', 1, 3, and 8 Oct. 1942.

[173] BA-MA, RH 31-IX/15, Tippelskirch to Army Group B, 9.11.1942, fol.277; BA-MA, RH 31-IX/15, Telegrams 29 Nov. 1942, fos.16, 24.

[174] See exemplary DS CS, VIII:I, 24 and 30 Oct., and 5 and 10 Nov. 1942.

[175] BA-MA, RH 31-IX/9, Gariboldi to Army Group B, 11 Oct. 1942, fol.250; ACS, T-821/260/IT 3074/112, *Sforzesca* to XXXV Corps, 25 Sept. 1942.

[176] ACS, T-821/259/IT 3068/214, Gen. Marazzani – Colpo di mano, 4 Oct. 1942.

and wounded from patrolling skirmishes in October 1942 alone,[177] and Italian files record daily occurrences of combat patrols, artillery fire and river crossings in the months prior to the Soviet offensive.[178] Therefore, it remains unclear if the Italian top-level documents give a distorted picture of the reality further down the command chain, if German units were indeed patrolling more actively, or if German accusations were simply a matter of expressing the desire to 'do more'—after all, the call for more patrolling and alertness is a one basic military demand, with constant possibilities for improvement. One should also note that the Soviets considered the Italo-German defences as very solid (they made no differentiation between the quality of Italian and German structures), well planned, built and concealed, and noted the difficulties in holding such a long front line (especially without operational reserves).[179]

Another aspect worthy of attention is the large-scale troop exchange the Italians started in October. All officers and men that had served in Russia since 13 December 1941 or earlier could ask for repatriation, and the old CSIR veterans indeed longed for replacement and rest.[180] The Germans estimated that around 60 per cent of the XXXV Corps' infantry was substituted in October and December.[181] While this did not affect the II and the *Alpini* Corps, Tippelskirch expected a notable decrease of the XXXV Corps' fighting power.[182] Besides Messe, also generals Giovanelli and Marazzani left their commands (of the *Pasubio* and *Celere* respectively). With hindsight, this has been painted as a cruel move by the generals, as if they were abandoning a sinking ship.[183] Yet the strain after fourteen months at the head of a division on the Eastern Front should

---

[177] ACS, Fondo Diamanti, b.1, f.Camp. Russia, 'Diario Storico *3 Gennaio*', 26 Oct. 1942.

[178] For example in DS CS, VIII:I, 2 and 7 Sept., and 6 Dec. 1942. For the *Alpini* Corps' front, see ibid., 13 Oct. 1942.

[179] Nikolai A. Fokin and Vladimir I. Sidorov, *Razgrom Italo-Nemetskikh voisk na Donu (Dekabr 1942 r.): Kratkii operativno-takticheskii ocherk* (Moscow: Voenizdat, 1945), 10–12.

[180] TNA, GFM 36/240, Vidussoni – Appunto per il Duce, 24 Oct. 1942, fol.15.

[181] BA-MA, RH 31-IX/35, fol.134.

[182] BA-MA, RH 31-IX/25, Tippelskirch to OKH, 16 Oct. 1942. On the other hand, the exchange of the 3rd *Bersaglieri*'s commanding officer has been described as positive development, Roggiani, *Bersaglieri*, 331.

[183] Messe's letters prior to his departure are filled with concerns about leaving his soldiers alone, see Messe, *Lettere*, 150ff.

not be underestimated[184] and command changes were normal procedures.[185] Likewise, relieving soldiers after fifteen months of incessant duty on the Eastern Front was sensible[186]: according to a report of the sanitary officers in the XXXV Corps in September 1942, 60–70 per cent of the men were emaciated, 70 per cent suffered from dysentery, 50 per cent from rheumatism and 30–40 per cent were deficient in vitamins.[187] Even if reinforcements were not battle-hardened professionals, they were not completely 'green',[188] and there was no other option: the *Celere*'s six *Bersaglieri* battalions numbered only 2000 men in early September.[189] Indeed, we should not overlook the Italian divisions' excellent strength levels after the substitutions. On 9 December 1942, the XXIX Corps reported that the German 298th ID had 404 officers and 12,257 others (and one Turkmeni regiment), the *Torino* 618 officers and 13,659 others, the *Sforzesca* 459 officers and 10,741 others and the *Celere* 515 officers, 11,872 rank, plus the Croat Legion of around one thousand men.[190] Furthermore, the Germans deployed the 27th Panzer Division[191] and the experienced 298th Infantry Division to support the Italians.[192]

[184] On Marazzani's exhaustion see TNA, WO 208/4185, S.R.I.G. no. 16, Conversation between Messe, generals Orlando and Berardi, and Lt. Colacicchi, 18 May. 1943.

[185] Post-facto memoirs have argued that Giovanelli's (and the regimental commanders') departure saddened the mood in the *Pasubio*, whose troops were closely attached to their senior officers, Marsetic, *Dall'Adige al Don*, 231–32.

[186] Those who were waiting for relief were not only unnerved, but also had—according to the Germans—only "limited interest" in personally contributing to the defensive works, BA-MA, RH 31-IX/15, Tippelskirch to Army Group B, 15 Nov. 1942, fol.240.

[187] Safronov, *Italyanski voiska*, 83.

[188] There are no reliable data for the reinforcements. They clearly had no Eastern Front experience, but their quality should not be dismissed offhand.

[189] USSME, *Le operazioni*, 295. Messe had highlighted in September that the *Celere* was reduced to 2000 men and the *Sforzesca* could not be considered as operational; thus he demanded to either withdraw these divisions or send *Alpini* units as supplements, ACS, T-821/258/IT 3067/983-984, Messe – 3^ divisione *Celere*, 9 Sept. 1942.

[190] BA-MA, RH 31-IX/18, XXIX Corps to Tippelskirch, 9 Dec. 1942, fol.14. The report was based on figures from 16 November. The Italian official history argues that the 298th was under strength with only two battalions in each of her three regiments and therefore not able to fulfil the assigned duties, USSME, *Le operazioni*, 297. Yet the German sources cited show different numbers.

[191] The division had suffered dearly before and only possessed 47 tanks, the equivalent of one tank battalion, Schreiber, "Italiens Teilnahme," 273.

[192] This 8th wave division had fought in Russia since 22 June 1941.

Despite the relative calm, the defensive works and arrival of new troops, the overall situation on the Don continued to worry Italian commanders. The danger of the Mamon bridgehead had been recognised, but the Germans dismissed an Italian proposal to advance across the river to form a defensive line running from Pavlovsk to (Verkhnyi) Mamon.[193] The foothold at Gorovka (Ogalev) remained in Soviet hands, but the *Pasubio* and the 62nd ID coordinated plans to defend the exposed bridgehead at Merkulov[194]—anticipating Soviet attacks against the vulnerable links between the corps sectors.[195] Messe wrote a detailed memorandum on the need to defend the Italian artillery (placed on the dominant hills), if needed with German armour, to prevent envelopment from east of Bolschoi.[196] Further, the XXXV Corps exchanged intelligence and information on suitable deployments with the Romanian I Corps in the neighbouring sector—a corps that had earlier occupied this same area,[197] but apparently refused to take over some parts of the Italians' right wing.[198] There appear to have been some quarrels with the Germans, too; for example the one between Marazzani and Brigadier-General Günther Blumentritt, who had been sent by General Hollidt, GOC XVII Corps, to make arrangements with the XXXV Corps. The Italians reminded him of his lower rank and Marazzani refused to accept his orders or be subordinated to him—he would accede only upon the presentation of a written order by General Hollidt.[199] While this can be read as an example of the Germans' arrogance toward their ally or as Italian sensitivity, it is also possible to identify a different cultural approach. Blumentritt, certainly a very confident staff officer, was used to a command system of joint responsibility and the custom of raising doubts when he disagreed with his commanding officer—a system that was less pronounced in the Italian Army.[200] Blumentritt later remarked

---

[193] USSME, *Le operazioni*, 454.

[194] ACS, T-821/259/IT 3069/330-331, Accordi *Pasubio* con 62^ divisione, 12 Sept. 1942.

[195] USSME, *Le operazioni*, 295.

[196] ACS, T-821/258/IT 3067/990-991, Messe – Difesa settore Bolschoj, 7 Sept. 1942.

[197] ACS, T-821/259/IT 3072, Exchanges Italian XXXV and Romanian I Corps, Oct. and Nov. 1942.

[198] Jukes, *Hitler's Stalingrad Decisions*, 80; Safronov, *Italyanski voiska*, 73.

[199] ACS, T-821/259/IT 3068/234, Gen. Marazzani to CSIR, 27 Sept. 1942.

[200] On joint responsibility and the 'General staff channel' see Megargee, *Inside*, 9, 64.

in Liddell Hart's *German Generals Talk* that the *Sforzesca* had run away, thus fostering a misleading image of the 'First Defensive Battle on the Don'.[201]

In conclusion, there were clearly German commanders who had little trust in Italian capabilities[202] and some friction, but such cases are and were an inevitable feature of war—not least among the Italians themselves[203]—and one should not assume an outright crisis between the Germans and their allies. Likewise, claims that the Germans and Italians "undervalued"[204] their enemy and were caught off guard lack credibility and can only be sustained if one ignores the available sources.[205] Forming operational reserves was a pipe dream—not simply because there were almost none, as became apparent during the Red Army's Operation Uranus in November—as fuel was scarce, means of communication and infrastructure were in an appalling state, and the weather and enemy airpower further hindered movements.[206] The Italians did take precautions, knew their weaknesses, and were well-informed what was coming at them[207]—there was simply not very much they could

---

[201] Giusti, *La campagna*, 221, 350.

[202] Wolfram von Richthofen, commander of the *Luftflotte 4*, noted in his diary on 29 November: "It looks as though the Russians are also going to hit the Italians; a bad thing, because they will probably run faster than the Romanians", cited in Hayward, *Stopped at Stalingrad*, 269.

[203] A lengthy memorandum by the Eighth Army's quartermaster, General Carlo Biglino, implies tensions between the army and corps level, as he repeatedly emphasised the need for a cooperative spirit, ACS, T-821/373/IT 4885/225-244, Gen. Biglino – Promemoria relativo al funzionamento dei servizi in Russia, 15 June 1942. Other observers judged the functioning of the Italian rear apparatus as rather good, see TNA, GFM 36/240, Vidussoni – Appunto per il Duce, 24 Oct. 1942, fol.6. There was little reason for Vidussoni to gloss over deficiencies and he was very critical of other organisational problems.

[204] Burgwyn, *Mussolini*, 202.

[205] See also the repeated claims by Hamilton of an alleged unpreparedness, e.g. Hamilton, *Sacrifice*, 67. Förster was more balanced in his judgment, arguing that the Germans and Italians expected the attack, but not the scale of the Soviet plans, Förster, *Risse im Bündnis*, 43.

[206] Limitations that became painfully clear when the *Julia* was transferred in mid-December, Hamilton, *Sacrifice*, 77–78.

[207] Soviet movements are described in detail by the XXXV Corps in ACS, T-821/22/IT 114. Also USSME, *Le operazioni*, 321ff.

do about it.[208] Similarly, German liaison officers and army commanders reported the looming offensive, the weak anti-tank capabilities of their allies and the need to form armoured reserves behind them, but Hitler overruled what he considered alarmist statements.[209]

[208] Even the often-criticised Blackshirt formations were not blind to the challenges they were facing, ACS, Fondo Diamanti, b.1, f.Camp. Russia, 'Diario Storico *3 Gennaio*', 19 Aug. 1942.

[209] Hildegard von Kotze, ed., *Heeresadjutant bei Hitler 1938–1943: Die Aufzeichnungen des Majors Engel* (Stuttgart: DVA, 1974), 132–33.

CHAPTER 7

The Battle on the Don, 11 December 1942–31 December 1943

On 19 November 1942, the Soviet offensive (Operation Uranus) spared the Italians, but targeted the neighbouring Romanian Third Army. It cut off 300,000 men of the German Sixth Army and the Fourth Panzer Army (and the Romanian Fourth) in the Stalingrad pocket. On the left flank of the Romanian Third Army, around 229,000 men of the ARMIR stood guard along the river Don northwest of Stalingrad.[1] At first it looked as if the Italians would not be embroiled in the battle. Thus, several German divisions operating with the ARMIR were redeployed to threatened zones. With them went most of the protection against enemy armour (their tanks and large-calibre anti-tank weapons), the second line of defence, and the only mobile reserves.[2] At the same time, the *Comando Supremo* was busy orchestrating the retreat from El Alamein through the cherished colony of Libya. But the hopes for a period of calm on the Eastern Front were dashed. On 2 December, the *Comando*

---

[1] The Italians never entered the city. Only a supply unit of 77 Italians was trapped with the Germans, and just two of these soldiers returned from Soviet captivity, see Alfio Caruso, *Noi moriamo a Stalingrado* (Milan: Longanesi, 2006).

[2] Only the 318th IR and 385th ID remained between (or behind) the *Cosseria* and *Ravenna*, and the severely weakened 27th Panzer Division stayed behind the Italian lines. Before, also the 294th ID, the 62nd ID and the 22nd PD had been in the ARMIR's rear, USSME, *Le operazioni*, 318f., 455.

© The Author(s) 2019
B. M. Scianna, *The Italian War on the Eastern Front, 1941–1943*, Italian and Italian American Studies,
https://doi.org/10.1007/978-3-030-26524-3_7

Supremo in Rome realised that an enemy offensive was imminent.[3] Even though this work deals primarily with the Italian forces, one must not forget the overall developments on the Eastern Front, where the fate of one or two (infantry) corps was just one of many events. This is an important context to take into account when we read of Italian calls for assistance and of the disappointment when they were not heeded.

Seeking to prevent relief for the forces encircled in the Stalingrad pocket, to ease supply lines in this sector of the front and to threaten the German Army Group in the Caucasus, the Soviets had prepared a new offensive plan. In late November, Army General Alexander M. Vasilevsky (1915–1959), the Chief of the General Staff, who had masterminded Operation Uranus with Army General Georgy Zhukov (1896–1974), and was now coordinator of all three fronts around Stalingrad, and the commander of the Southwestern Front Lt. Gen. Nikolai F. Vatutin (1901–1944), often regarded as one of the best Soviet commanders, set up a plan to destroy the ARMIR and the Army Detachment Hollidt along the Don and Chir between Novaya Kalitva and Nizhne Chirskaya.[4] This was approved on 2 December, as Operation Saturn. The plan foresaw two shock groups: the first included six rifle divisions and three tank corps of the First Guards Army, which were meant to attack towards Millerovo from the Mamon bridgehead; the second group, comprising five rifle divisions and one mechanised corps of the Third Guards Army was to push from east of Bokovskaya on the Chir westward to the important logistic hub (and headquarters of the ARMIR) Millerovo and there join forces with the first shock group. The Sixth Army (Voronezh Front) was meant to cover the Southwestern Front's right flank by advancing towards the vital railroad juncture at Kantemirovka, while the Fifth Tank Army would cross the Chir towards Tormosin and Tatsinkaya, after which the First and Third Guards Armies would jointly move towards Likhaya on the Donets.[5] During a second phase, the Second Guards Army, the "Red Army's strongest" formation,[6] and four tanks corps of the Southwestern Front were to exploit the breakthrough further towards Rostov to cut off the German retreat (Army Group A), and

---

[3] DS CS, VIII:I, 2 Dec. 1942.

[4] For Vasilevsky's account see Alexander Wassilewski, *Sache des ganzen Lebens* (Berlin: Militärverlag der DDR, 1977), 227ff.

[5] Glantz, *From the Don*, 12; USSME, *Le operazioni*, 335ff.

[6] Bellamy, *Absolute War*, 537.

disrupt Axis command and control and logistics. In short, the Red Army intended a flanking manoeuvre to the sea, similar to the German sickle cut in 1940.

However, strong German activities to relief the encircled troops forced the Soviets to alter their plan.[7] On 13 December, they decided to cut the second phase, and called the downsized operation 'Little Saturn'. The aim was still to disrupt German attempts to establish a land bridge to the forces in Stalingrad and to envelope the ARMIR and the Army Detachment Hollidt, but with lower ambitions. The Southwestern Front's forces were now redirected to the southeast to seal off Morozovsk and Tormosin—thereby thwarting efforts to relieve Stalingrad—instead of pushing towards Rostov after seizing Millerovo.[8] Simply put: instead of closing the door to German retreat, the plan now intended to narrow the exit corridor.[9] Even though the ambitions were lowered, the timetable was tightened and the armies expected to make faster progress than initially planned.[10]

In order to achieve this goal, Vatutin's Southwestern Front had three armies: the First Guards Army (formerly Sixtythird Army) entailed 110,700 men and 504 tanks in three tank corps (18th, 24th and 25th) and six rifle divisions under Lt. Gen. Vasily I. Kuznetsov (1894–1964), the Third Guards Army had 110,00 men and 234 tanks in one mechanised corps, several tank regiments and motorised brigades, and seven rifle divisions under Lt. Gen. Dmitry D. Lelyushenko (1901–1987), and the Fifth Tank Army fielded 90,000 men with 182 tanks, but hardly featured in the battles against the Italians, as it attacked German positions on the Chir river. Additionally, the Voronezh Front's Sixth Army with the 17th Tank Corps (which was allocated to the First Guards on the first day of operations) and five rifle divisions under Lt. Gen. Fedor M. Kharitonov (1899–1943) that totalled 60,200 men and 250 tanks, was intended to support the offensive.[11]

---

[7] Wassilewski, *Sache*, 238–42.

[8] Glantz, *From the Don*, 17.

[9] Even though the Soviets wanted to pursue the original plan, if the operations were to develop favourably, see Hill, *Red Army*, 416.

[10] Buttar, *Knife's Edge*, 149. The 17th Tank Corps would have to advance 150 kilometres in two days; 25th Tank Corps 250 kilometres in four days.

[11] All numbers from Glantz, *From the Don*, 28.

On 10 December, the ARMIR had four army corps in its sector. A list of opposing divisions or total force numbers often gives an inadequate impression, so we will instead compare combat battalions, artillery pieces and tank numbers.[12] In the very north, or left flank, the *Alpini* Corps comprised 26 infantry battalions and 216 barrels.[13] It was separated from the remaining Italian forces by the "narrow, but deep and fast-flowing" Kalitva river (which made it difficult to shift units).[14] The next formation was the II Corps that only had the *Cosseria* and *Ravenna* (plus the German 318th Infantry Regiment and later reinforcements) as well as engineer and artillery units, which amounted to 20 infantry battalions and 132 artillery pieces.[15] The XXXV Corps (formerly CSIR) consisted of the *Pasubio*, the 298th German ID and further artillery and Blackshirt formations (in total 20 battalions and 156 barrels).[16] The German XXIX Panzer Corps included the *Torino*, the *Celere*, and the *Sforzesca* (20 infantry battalions and 120 artillery pieces). It remained the only formation with assault guns and light tanks (around fifty). In total, the Eighth Army encompassed 86 infantry battalions, 156 artillery batteries with 624 guns of various calibres and fifty armoured vehicles. The only mobile reserve was the 27th Panzer Division—which, however, had just 47 tanks of various models and was already exhausted from prior combat.[17] It was thus too weak to be considered a real reserve force for an entire army, i.e. able to launch effective counter-attacks beyond the

---

[12] The average division strength in the Third Guards Army, for instance, was only around 7000 men, see Glantz, *From the Don*, 378.

[13] USSME, *Le operazioni*, 324. The Corps included the *Tridentina*, the *Julia*, and the *Cuneense* divisions, as well as additional artillery, the *Monte Cervino*, cavalry, and German artillery.

[14] Trigg, *Death*, 187.

[15] Ibid., 325. The *Cosseria* (89th and 90th infantry regiments, 108th Artillery Regiment, 318th German Infantry Regiment), the *Ravenna* (37th and 38th infantry regiments, 121st Artillery Regiment, and three German anti-tank companies), and additional artillery and Blackshirt units. The *Ravenna* received most of the Italian mechanised and armoured forces during these operations, see USSME, *Le operazioni*, 359.

[16] The 298th ID had three infantry regiments, one artillery regiment, and one anti-tank battalion.

[17] The Soviets could also count on adequate air and engineer support, USSME, *Le operazioni*, 327.

mere tactical level.[18] The 17th PD, initially intended as mobile reserve behind the ARMIR, had been ordered south to assist the relief attack on the Stalingrad pocket.[19] Another weakness was the 318th Infantry Regiment, whose 3000 men (many of them Ukrainians, former Russian POWs, or inexperienced over-aged men), had only arrived in late November to hold a eight to nine kilometre-long frontline, and were ordered by German commands—in spite of Italian protest—to deploy all its three battalions to the first possible line of defence instead of making use of the high ground and a defence in depth.[20] To make matters worse, the terrain in their sector benefitted Soviet infiltration and the deployment of tanks. The 318th IR was wedged between the *Cosseria* and *Ravenna*, but had lost direct connection with the *Ravenna* already by the 15th December before the main attack started.[21]

The Soviet forces operating against the Italian II Corps amounted to 90 infantry battalions, 25 motorised rifle battalions, 30 armoured battalions (754 tanks), 2065 artillery pieces, 300 anti-tank guns and 200 rocket launchers.[22] The counting in the Italian official history was rather precarious: it was not the entire Sixth Army that attacked (and neither did it attack at once) and not only the II Corps was hit.[23] Furthermore, not all Soviet formations were on full strength levels,[24] and the First Guards Army, for example, had been rebuilt for the third time in just a few months and always went into battle before it was fully ready.[25]

---

[18] Horst Scheibert, *Panzer zwischen Don und Donez. Die Winterkämpfe 1942–1943* (Friedberg: Podzun-Pallas, 1979), 147.

[19] Trigg, *Death*, 188. The 19th PD only reached the threatened sector on 25 December, see Glantz, *From the Don*, 403, note 63.

[20] Schlemmer, "Tedeschi a piedi,"135–36.

[21] Ibid., 137.

[22] Glantz, *From the Don*, 35–39. Even though artillery ammunition shortages and decentralised employment hampered its effectiveness.

[23] USSME, *Le operazioni*, 331. A detailed criticism can be found in Safronov, *Italyanski voiska*, 96–97; yet his counting shows a desire to make the Italians appear stronger and should be treated with caution.

[24] Konstantin K. Rokossovsky, ed., *Velikaya pobeda na Volge* (Moscow: Voenizdat, 1960), 312.

[25] Moskalenko, *Südwestrichtung*, 371.

There was nonetheless a vast imbalance of forces. In their main attacking perimeter, the Red Army's preponderance in numbers was enormous: its over 2000 artillery guns were opposed by 355, and the Italians had nothing to counter the 700 Soviet tanks—as most of their 47 light tanks were deployed in another sector.[26] The Soviets had ideal means for the three operational manoeuvres (preparation, penetration and exploitation). Further, Soviet artillery was more numerous, had wider ranges and multiple rocket artillery. In theory, it could therefore prepare the attack on ideal terms and lead an effective interdiction and counter-battery fire. Meanwhile the Italian ability to stop penetration by tanks (by active or passive means) was limited,[27] and no operational reserves were at hand to halt (or counter) the Soviet exploitation.[28] But what preparations had the Italian and German forces made?

Glantz has argued that the "German and allied defences were, for the most part, rigid and shallow"[29]—except in the areas opposite Soviet bridgeheads, especially in the Mamon zone stretching from Novaya Kalitva to Boguchar, where obstacles and good fire plans had been developed and the first defensive positions were five to six kilometres deep.[30] Glantz has provided a vivid description of the obstacles Soviet commanders faced in this sector, which further alludes to the preparations taken by the Italians:

---

[26] Glantz, *From the Don*, 29–31. The First Guards Army had the lowest artillery density of all armies on the Southwestern Front, see ibid., 35.

[27] A total 90 out of 114 Italian anti-tank guns were 47/32 guns, which were of limited use against T-34 and KV-1, while the mines often did not work. Yet, the Italians were not the only ones experiencing troubles with placing or clearing mines in the harsh climatic conditions, see the report in ACS, T-821/355/IT 4590/1022-1023, Gen. Tirelli – Sgombero campi minati, 17 May 1942. The Germans later blamed their ally for not laying all supplied mines, while the Italians countered they had received insufficient numbers, Pelagalli, *Marras*, 211.

[28] USSME, *Le operazioni*, 333; Trigg, *Death*, 187–88.

[29] Glantz, *From the Don*, 29.

[30] Ibid. Glantz added that the defences were "even weaker" in the area held by the Army Detachment Hollidt along the Chir—due to the arrival of the troops there in late November. The Russians concurred to this view, see Rokossovsky, *Velikaya podeba*, 342.

Regimental defences were 2-3 kilometres deep and consisted of platoon and company strong points prepared for all round defence. There were no second defensive positions or rear positions, and most sectors lacked any mobile reserve. Infantry platoons reinforced by anti-tank guns, mortars, engineers, and flame thrower elements usually manned strong points organised for all round defence supported by machine gun or rifle fire from adjacent trenches. Most strongpoints were located in villages or on heights and were constructed of earth and timber pillboxes. Anti-personnel and anti-tank obstacles and single and double rows of barbed wire covered the positions, and the defenders placed anti-tank mines on all armoured approaches to the strong points. Each strong point covered a distance of 1-1.5 kilometres, and multiple strong points covered one another throughout the depth of the tactical defence. Artillery was located along roads and near villages. Most anti-tank guns were located forward within each of the strong points or in the depth of the battalion defensive position.

The Italians and Germans created major strong points around larger towns, using stone walls and buildings in order to anchor the defence. One or two infantry companies with ten or sixteen mortars, and two to four batteries of 75 mm and 105 mm guns manned each major strong point. Artillery and mortar fire from division or corps artillery provided additional cover.[31]

The following maps demonstrate the Italian deployment according to circumstances and earlier (German and Italian) intentions: the divisional artillery (8th Artillery Regiment) was placed on high ground within two to three kilometres of the first trenches, thus it could lend direct fire support to the infantry. We should also note the infantry's tactical deployment: each regiment had two battalions deployed to the frontline and one in reserve (also to cover the artillery regiment). The same scheme was used further down the ladder: each battalion only used two companies to man the trenches and kept one as reserve.[32] Thus, there were second lines of defence, but no fortified positions other than the main battle line (Fig. 7.1).

---

[31] Glantz, *From the Don*, 29.
[32] See for example the *Pasubio*'s deployment, in Luoni, *La Pasubio*, 260, 265.

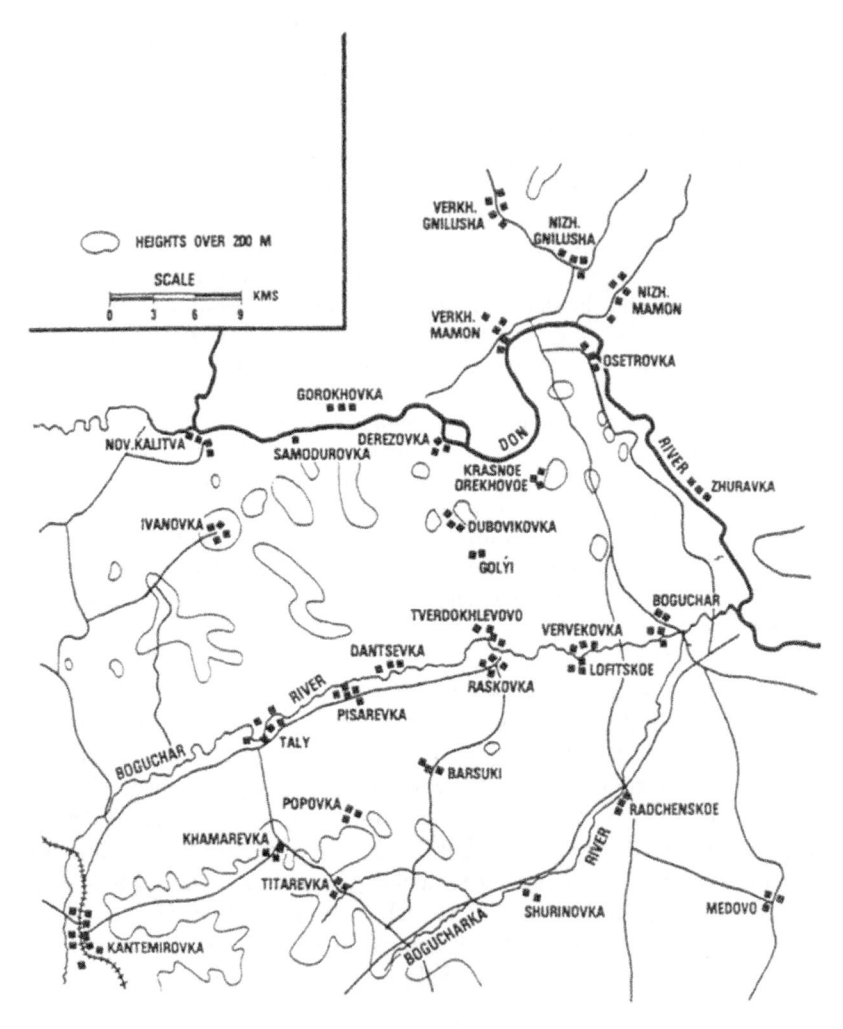

Fig. 7.1 Settlements and heights over 200 metres around the Mamon bridgehead, from Glantz, *From the Don*, 26

Scholarly opinions regarding the climatic conditions have varied. While most authors imply that it was always severely cold, Glantz has argued that "the weather in December 1942 in the great bend of the Don River was favourable for combat by warmly dressed troops. Temperatures ranged from 0 to 10 degree centigrade and never fell below minus 20 degrees centigrade. Snow cover was light (less than 15 centimetres), and there were no heavy snowdrifts. Consequently, road and cross country mobility was good for both sides."[33] While smaller rivers were frozen and could be traversed easily, engineering work was needed to secure the crossing of the 250–300 metre wide Don, whose ice layer was often thin or broken (or blown up on purpose by Italian or German forces).[34] Glantz thus dismissed arguments about 'General Winter' as the cause of the Axis' defeat, and Trigg has argued that the winter 1942–1943 was not as cold as the year before.[35] On the other hand, the Italian official history tells of a temperature drop to minus 30 °C in the night from 16 to 17 December.[36]

The Soviets deployed the Third Guards Army, under command of Lelyushenko, opposite the Army Detachment Hollidt, and their Sixth Army (Voronezh Front), under Kharitonov, against the Hungarian Second Army, the *Alpini* Corps and the left flank of the Italian II Corps (*Cosseria*), while Kuznetsov's First Guards Army faced the brunt of the II and XXXV Corps.[37] This deployment hints at the operational planning on army level that had begun on 14 December.[38] The First Guards Army was to breakthrough at the Mamon bridgehead, push towards Chertkovo and Degtevo, where it should join hands with the Third Guards Army (which was to attack in the Bokovskaya area, advance

---

[33] Glantz, *From the Don*, 24; the same argument is made by Filatov, *La campagna orientale*, 140.

[34] Glantz, *From the Don*, 24. The Soviets had crossed the Don in a nocturnal surprise attack in November with two companies, five tanks and several armoured cars, see Rotundo, *Battle for Stalingrad*, 108.

[35] Trigg, *Death*, 141.

[36] USSME, *Le operazioni*, 363.

[37] On further planning and preparations, see Glantz, *From the Don*, 18ff., 31–40; Fokin and Sidorov, *Razgrom Italo-Nemetskikh*, 14–41.

[38] Glantz, *From the Don*, 31–34.

further and then turn southwards), and afterwards develop the offensive towards Tatsinkaya and Morozovsk. The Sixth Army was to attack between Novaya Kalitva and Derzovka, and then proceed in southwestern direction (both phases were intended to cover the First Guards Amy's right flank). In the air, the attacking forces could count on the support of 72 bombers, 135 assault aircraft, 97 fighters and 106 reconnaissance and liaison aircraft that were based on newly constructed airfields close to the front.[39] While bad weather prevented their initial deployment on 16 December, they flew sorties before and thereafter, which often proved vital (with artillery support) for the success of ground operations. The First Guards Army assigned three additional tank corps (17th, 18th and 25th) to the first shock group (which already included the 24th Tank Corps) for breakthrough and exploitation on the sector borders between the First Guards and Sixth Army. These latter areas coincided with those largely held by the Italian II Corps near the Mamon bridgehead. Here, the German 318th Infantry Regiment remained between the *Cosseria* and the *Ravenna*. To the south (or right flank) were the 298th German ID at Boguchar and the *Pasubio*—which faced the Soviet bridgehead around Ogalev: the second crucial site of the coming operations.

After the large-scale build-up and intense practical exercises, the main attack had to be postponed to 16 December; the Red Army thus began a period of skirmishing and combat reconnaissance (up to battalion-sized operations). This period lasted from 11 to 15 December, and the second breakthrough phase from 16 to 18 December; the third phase, exploitation, began on 19 December.

During the skirmishing period, the Soviet forces (usually with several battalions) attempted to augment existing bridgeheads across the Don or establish new ones as spring-off positions for their tactical break-ins, envisaging rapid penetration with armoured and mechanised forces.[40]

---

[39] Ibid., 37–38; Rokossovsky, *Velikaya pobeda*, 331–32.
[40] Detailed in USSME, *Le operazioni*, 338–54.

After suffering heavy losses,[41] the Germans reinforced the forward positions of the *Cosseria* and part of the *Ravenna* with two regiments of the 385th ID on 15 December, and while the 387th ID hastened to reach Italian forward positions, one battalion of the 298th ID supported the *Pasubio*, and the 27th Panzer Division stood ready to support the *Ravenna*.[42] These actions showed that the main points of the coming attack would lie in the II Corps' sector (*Cosseria*, 318th IR, and *Ravenna*). One should not underestimate this phase of the battle: the Soviets managed to increase their footholds across the Don and cut off continuous defensive lines, for example between the 318th Infantry Regiment and the *Ravenna*.[43] The *Cosseria* was so weakened that the 385th ID was ordered to take over command over the division's 24-kilometre wide sector on 15th December and the *Cosseria* was to be taken out of the frontline once the situation had calmed down (Fig. 7.2).[44]

---

[41] DS CS, VIII:I, 11 Dec. 1942. The II Corps had suffered 82 dead, 212 wounded, and 139 missing (considered as dead) on 12 December alone; the XXXV Corps 230 dead and 596 wounded between 10 and 12 December, DS CS, VIII:I, 12 Dec. 1942. Enemy losses were reportedly higher, but in contrast to prior Italian casualty figure, the numbers of one day of 'skirmishing' show the intensity of Soviet actions.

[42] On the morning of 16 December, also the Group Schuldt (two SS police battalions) and the Group Fegelein (two SS battalions, one battery of self-propelled assault guns, and the 15th Police Regiment) reached the zone of Kantemirovka, where the 387th ID joined them on 18 December, Glantz, *From the Don*, 42.

[43] Counter-attacks by forces of the 318th IR and the *Cosseria* were initially successful, before they ultimately lost the ground late on 15th December and were cut off from the *Ravenna*, see BA-MA, RH 31-IX/35, Pertner – Gefechtsbericht *Ravenna*, 20 Mar. 1943, fos.60–74, here fol.62.

[44] USSME, *Le operazioni*, 356. The *Cosseria* was described as showing first signs of combat fatigue after five days and nights of attacks and counter-attacks, see BA-MA, RH 31-IX/35, Oberleutnant Salazer – Gefechtsbericht Division *Cosseria*, 18 Mar. 1943 [hereafter 'Gefechtsbericht *Cosseria*'], fos.76–81, here fos.77–78.

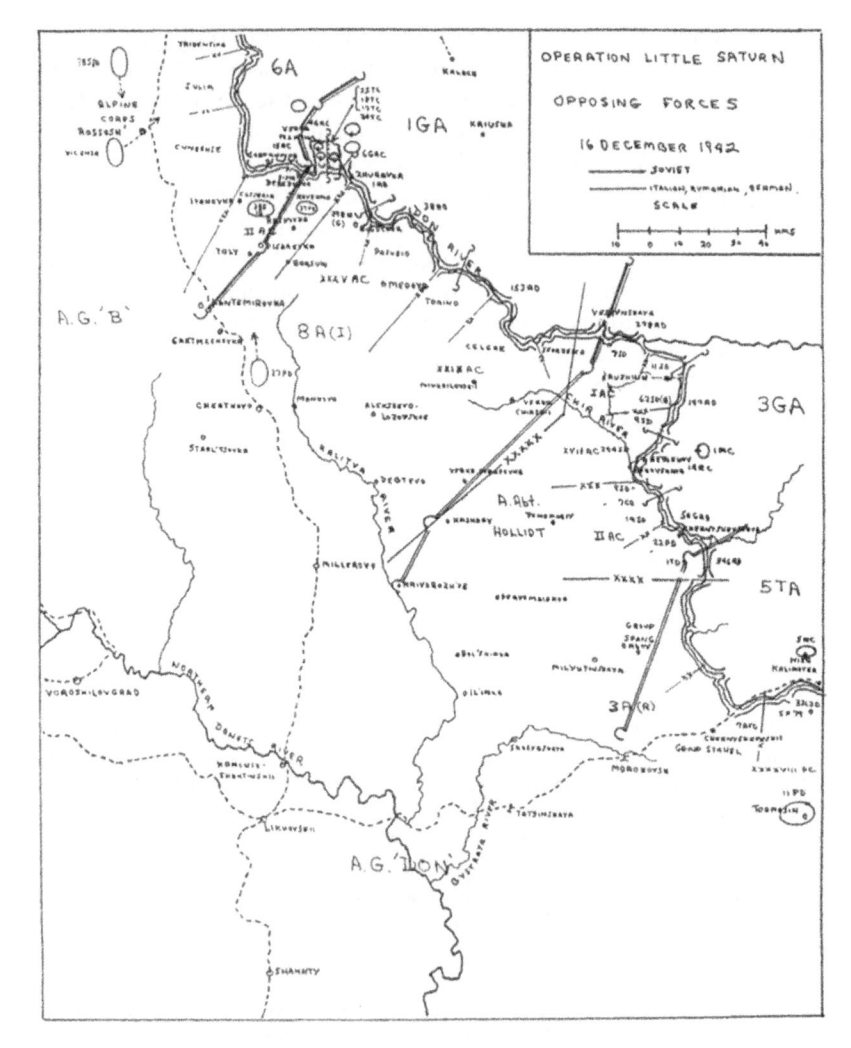

Fig. 7.2 Situation on 16 December 1942, from Glantz, *From the Don*, 43

Operation Little Saturn or the 'Second Defensive Battle on the Don'

At 8.00 a.m. on 16 December 1942, the Russians launched their assault with a ninety-minute artillery barrage throughout the First Guards Army's sector.[45] Heavy fog prevented Soviet, Italian or German aerial reconnaissance and close-air support; as visibility dropped under one hundred metres.[46] Yet, it also prevented the Soviet airforce from operating during the first half of the day[47] and hindered observation and the adjustment of Soviet artillery fire, which led to unaimed shelling and made the barrage less devastating as one could expect.[48] Additionally, the First Guards Army had the lowest number of tubes of all three attacking armies and did not concentrate its fire.[49] Many Axis defensive positions were thus left unscathed,[50] their defensive fire could not be suppressed and the coordination between Soviet infantry and artillery fire proved—just as in November[51]—unsatisfactory.

---

[45] USSME, *Le operazioni*, 356–62. The initial artillery shelling during Operation Uranus had been 80 minutes long and targeted first the main defence line and hereafter in a rolling barrage spotted targets and areas of enemy movement; see Rotundo, *Battle for Stalingrad*, 203ff. The Third Army started its artillery fire later in the hope that the fog would clear.

[46] DS CS, VIII:I, 16 Dec. 1942; Trigg, *Death*, 186.

[47] This fact is often stressed in Soviet depictions; yet their airforce had been very active in the days before, see BA-MA, RH 31-IX/35, Pertner – Gefechtsbericht *Ravenna*, 20 Mar. 1943, fol.62. Additionally, the air force is reported to have taken part in the battle after the middle of the day, see Rokossovsky, *Velikaya pobeda*, 344.

[48] The Third Guards Army reduced its artillery barrage to thirty minutes, Lelyushenko, *Moskva-Stalingrad-Berlin-Praga*, 151.

[49] Rokossovsky, *Velikaya pobeda*, 328–30.

[50] Glantz, *From the Don*, 42. Further, most Italian strongholds were on commanding heights that concealed much of the movements behind these first lines. A different view is held by Fokin and Sidorov. Based on an interview with Col. Mario Bianchi, the captured commander of the 37th Infantry Regiment (*Ravenna*), they claim that 25 per cent of this regiment had been "put out of action" after the artillery barrage, see Fokin and Sidorov, *Razgrom Italo-Nemetskikh*, 43, footnote 2.

[51] Rotundo, *Battle for Stalingrad*, 214.

Nonetheless, the infantry advanced against the largely intact Italian positions at 9.30 a.m. (while the artillery shifted fire to the second defensive line). The First Guards Army's commander (Kuznetsov) had allotted five rifle divisions and three tank corps to his 18-kilometre penetration sector, which "created tactical densities of one rifle division per 3.5 kilometres of front and six infantry support tanks and 75 guns and mortars per kilometre of front. In fact, Kuznetsov's superiority was 4:1 in battalions, 7.3:1 in machine guns; over 7:1 in artillery, and up to 10:1 in tanks."[52] Thus despite problems with artillery units (and ammunitions) reaching the front,[53] the density of guns and mortars was even greater than it had been during Operation Uranus in November,[54] and overall superiority was considerably higher than during the subsequent attacks in January.[55] Still, the Soviet infantry could not overcome the defensive lines of the II Corps who "did a creditable job of confining the attackers to penetrations of little more than three kilometres."[56] Especially the *Ravenna*'s 37th Infantry Regiment offered bitter resistance to the advancing infantry of the 41st and 44th Guards Rifle Divisions.[57]

With his infantry bogged down in "savage fighting"[58] Vatutin ordered Kuznetsov to send in his armour (the 17th Tank Corps

---

[52] Glantz, *From the Don*, 33–34.

[53] Additionally, the available ammunition stocks were at 40–50 per cent, see Rokossovsky, *Velikaya pobeda*, 330.

[54] See the numbers per attack zone and breakthrough sector of the Southwestern, Don and Stalingrad Fronts in Rotundo, *Battle for Stalingrad*, 322.

[55] For a comparison of the Fortieth Army's attacking sector, see Moskalenko, *Südwestrichtung*, 422.

[56] David M. Glantz and Jonathan M. House, *The Stalingrad Trilogy, Vol. 3: Endgame at Stalingrad. Book Two: December 1942–February 1943* (Lawrence: University Press of Kansas, 2014), 233.

[57] Rokossovsky, *Velikaya pobeda*, 344; Fokin and Sidorov, *Razgrom Italo-Nemetskikh*, 44.

[58] John Erickson, *The Road to Berlin* (London: Weidenfeld & Nicolson, 1983), 17.

possessed 168 tanks, and the 18th Tank Corps and the 25th Tank Corps 160 each).[59] The First Guards Army therefore had a tank density of almost 30 tanks per kilometre on its 18-kilometre wide breakthrough sector.[60] At 11.00 am, two brigades of the 18th and 25th Tank Corps advanced with some infantry that sporadically joined them on the way forward (one brigade of the 17 Tank Corps started 30 minutes later). Now one Italian passive anti-tank measure bore results: their mines.[61] Soviet engineers had cleared lanes, but many markers had been destroyed by the Red Army's artillery fire.[62] The 25th Tank Corps immediately lost twenty-seven tanks (German sources have identified them as T-34)[63] to exploding mines, and another four tanks of the 18th Tank Corps' attack brigade were destroyed.[64] Thus their attack had come to a halt after merely advancing one kilometre and had to be stopped.[65] If the Italian active anti-tank means had been stronger, the losses among the Soviet tanks (who lacked organised infantry support) might have even been higher. Despite these losses, around thirty Soviet

---

[59] His tanks had crossed the Don in the night from 15 to 16 December and taken position in the Mamon bridgehead around 7–10 kilometres away from the first Italian defensive line, see Rokossovsky, *Velikaya pobeda*, 340.

[60] Safronov, *Italyanski voiska*, 89.

[61] The Mamon bridgehead had been densely defended with mines. Over 4000 anti-tank mines were laid out in an area of two kilometres, Safronov, *Italyanski voiska*, 93.

[62] Glantz described the advance as "badly scouted", see Glantz, *From the Don*, 45; and, indeed, the transmission of information on mine fields was also criticised as a weakness in an internal Soviet study on the Stalingrad operations, Rotundo, *Battle for Stalingrad*, 269. On Soviet difficulties in removing mines and their tactical approach see ibid., 270ff.

[63] BA-MA, RH 31-IX/35, Pertner – Gefechtsbericht *Ravenna*, 20 Mar. 1943, fol.63. The Red Army repeatedly changed the organisation of its armoured formations. A new organisational table in July 1942 tried to standardise tank corps (which took time) by creating two brigades with one light and one medium battalion with T-60/70 and T-34 tanks, respectively; see Steven J. Zaloga and Leland S. Ness, *Red Army Handbook 1939–1945* (Stroud: Sutton, 2003), 71–79. The 17th Tank Corps, for example, had 98 T-34 and 70 T-70 at the beginning of operations; see Glantz, *From the Don*, 377.

[64] Glantz and House, *Stalingrad Trilogy*, 635, note 15; Glantz, *From the Don*, 45.

[65] Rokossovsky, *Velikaya pobeda*, 345.

tanks broke through towards Gadyche and Filonovo. The Germans sent the few tanks they had, who destroyed a large majority of these Russian tanks and helped repulse an attack on the vital hill 217.2; yet other armoured reserves could not assist the *Ravenna* due to lacking fuel.[66] Indeed, the German liaison officer at the *Ravenna* asked the neighbouring 298th ID and the 318th IR to strike the enemy in his flanks, but both units declined his requests for help.[67] The Soviets attacks had weakened the defenders, who hastily sought to assemble more reserves,[68] but had not achieved any breakthrough during three hours of fierce combat against dogged defence with counter-attacks and organised shelling from Italian-German positions.[69]

While the Russian armour in the First Guards Sector was bogged down, it was badly missing in the Sixth Army's area of operations (who had been forced to cede the 17th Tank Corps under Maj. Gen. P. P. Poluboyarov). Here, four rifle divisions (127th, 172nd, 350th, 267th and one tank regiment) had made good use of the existing bridgeheads at Samodurovka and Osetrovka and advanced with all the infantry support weapons they could drag along. They managed to penetrate the sectors of the *Cosseria* (and the 385th ID) and the 318th IR to a depth of 2–3 kilometres from Novaya Kaltiva to Derezovka, yet could not exploit their successes as the 17th Tank Corps was missing.[70] They were therefore still within the tactical defence zone of the Italian-German forces (Fig. 7.3).

---

[66] BA-MA, RH 31-IX/35, Pertner – Gefechtsbericht *Ravenna*, 20 Mar. 1943, fol.63

[67] Ibid., fol.64.

[68] USSME, *Le operazioni*, 360–61.

[69] Rokossovsky, *Velikaya pobeda*, 344–45; Fokin and Sidorov, *Razgrom Italo-Nemetskikh*, 45.

[70] Glantz, *From the Don*, 44.

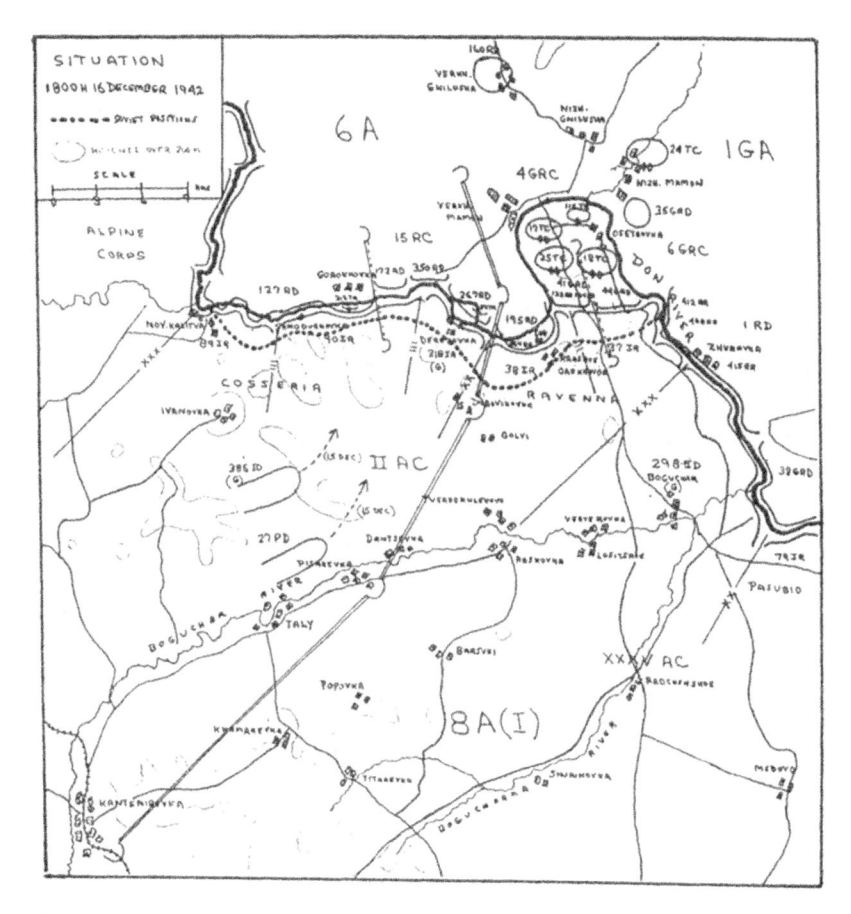

Fig. 7.3 Evening situation, 16 December 1942, from Glantz, *From the Don*, 43

Thus, on the first day, the battered *Cosseria* and *Ravenna* "did not run but fought back,"[71] and were supported by German troops. The First Guards Army had made little headway (the Third Army's attack had been even less successful)[72] due to dogged resistance of the defenders and their use of tactical reserves, but also due to a rather mixed Soviet performance, problems with artillery and airpower and unfortunate weather conditions. In the end, the Red Army's infantry had secured some success: also thanks to increased artillery shelling and air support, it was holding on to conquered ground in the enemy's tactical defence perimeter (2–3 kilometre deep in the First Guards Army's sector and 4–5 kilometres deep in the Sixth Army's), and continued to clear mines and to harass the enemy over night.[73]

The next day (17 December) proved to be decisive. Vatutin had ordered the First Guards Army to free pathways through the minefields over night and attack hill 217.2 and Filonovo at sunrise. The attack was to take place "at any cost" and the tank corps were to progress towards the Boguchar river to avoid being sitting ducks for the Luftwaffe in the Mamon bridgehead.[74] Indeed, the skies cleared, and the Red Air Force could lend strong support to the ongoing attack.[75] The Luftwaffe also tried to help the battered ground forces.[76] The Germans withdrew two wings (*Kampfgeschwader 27* and *Kampfgeschwader 51*) from Army Group Don (in total one third of General Hoth's available airpower for his relief attempt on Stalingrad) to support the ARMIR.[77] The offensive

---

[71] Trigg, *Death*, 187.

[72] Glantz, *From the Don*, 45–46.

[73] Rokossovsky, *Velikaya pobeda*, 345–46.

[74] Vatutin's order is printed in Fokin and Sidorov, *Razgrom Italo-Nemetskikh*, 133–34.

[75] The Seventeenth Air Army flew 645 sorties with enemy contact on 16 and 17 December alone, see ibid., 353.

[76] On 17 December, fifteen Soviet tanks were (reportedly) destroyed by Axis aircraft; see DS CS, VIII:I, 17 Dec. 1942; Hill, *Red Army*, 416.

[77] Hayward, *Stopped at Stalingrad*, 269. Much to the frustration of Wolfram von Richthofen, commander of *Luftflotte 4*, who thought that the Italians would run away in any case. He had served as air attaché in Rome, spoke Italian well, and had fought in the Spanish Civil War, where his opinion of the Italian military as unreliable and weak ally was formed, see James S. Corum, *Wolfram von Richthofen: Master of the German Air War* (Lawrence: University Press of Kansas, 2008), 126.

was launched against the whole front from Novaya Kalitva (*Cosseria*) to Boguchar (298 ID and *Pasubio*) and punched first holes in the defensive lines beyond mere tactical gains.[78] The Soviets improved their employment of armour in combination with infantry and artillery support. In all sectors, German and Italians were jointly trying to repulse the attacks, but the overwhelming numbers slowly wrestled them down. A first essential breakthrough happened between the 318th Infantry Regiment and the *Ravenna* near Dubikovka, where Italian forces had repulsed initial attacks of the 67th Tank Brigade.[79] The 318th IR dispersed, one of its battalions ceased to exist, and the remaining two were briefly encircled and had to fight their way out (towards the *Alpini* Corps and the XXIV Panzer Corps) under heavy casualties.[80] The Soviet 4th Guards Rifle Corps and the 25th Tank Corps pursued this success and raced to the Boguchar river in the second half of the day, where they were stopped by German reserves. On the very left flank, the 385th ID and the *Cosseria*, too, were overwhelmed. The German command ordered a retreat towards Ivanovka to cover the threatened connection to the *Alpini* Corps.[81] At the end of the day, it had become clear that the tactical defence zone had been lost and Soviet advances were up to 20–25 kilometres deep in the area around Mamon.[82] Thus they had created a dangerous bulge in the area between the *Cosseria*, the 318th IR and the *Ravenna*. Vatutin ordered the Sixth and First Guards to uphold the pressure throughout the night, and the Soviets slowly gained enough room to operate their armoured forces, which were to start full exploitation on the next day (Fig. 7.4).[83]

---

[78] Glantz, *From the Don*, 47–49; USSME, *Le operazioni*, 363–73.

[79] Aleksandr V. Kuzmin and I. I. Krasnov, *Kantemirovtsy: boevoi put 4-go gvardeiskogo tankovogo Kantemirovskogo ordena Lenina Krasnoznamennogo Korpusa* (Moscow: Voenizdat, 1971), 41. The Sixth Army reached a tank density of 31.6 per kilometre (including the 17th Tank Corps), Glantz, *From the Don*, 401, note 21.

[80] Schlemmer, "Tedeschi a piedi," 138.

[81] BA-MA, RH 31-IX/35, Salazer – Gefechtsbericht *Cosseria*, 18 Mar. 1943, fos.78–79.

[82] Rokossovsky, *Velikaya pobeda*, 347. This distance inlcudes, however, the way covered from their start off positions in the bridgehead.

[83] Glantz, *From the Don*, 49.

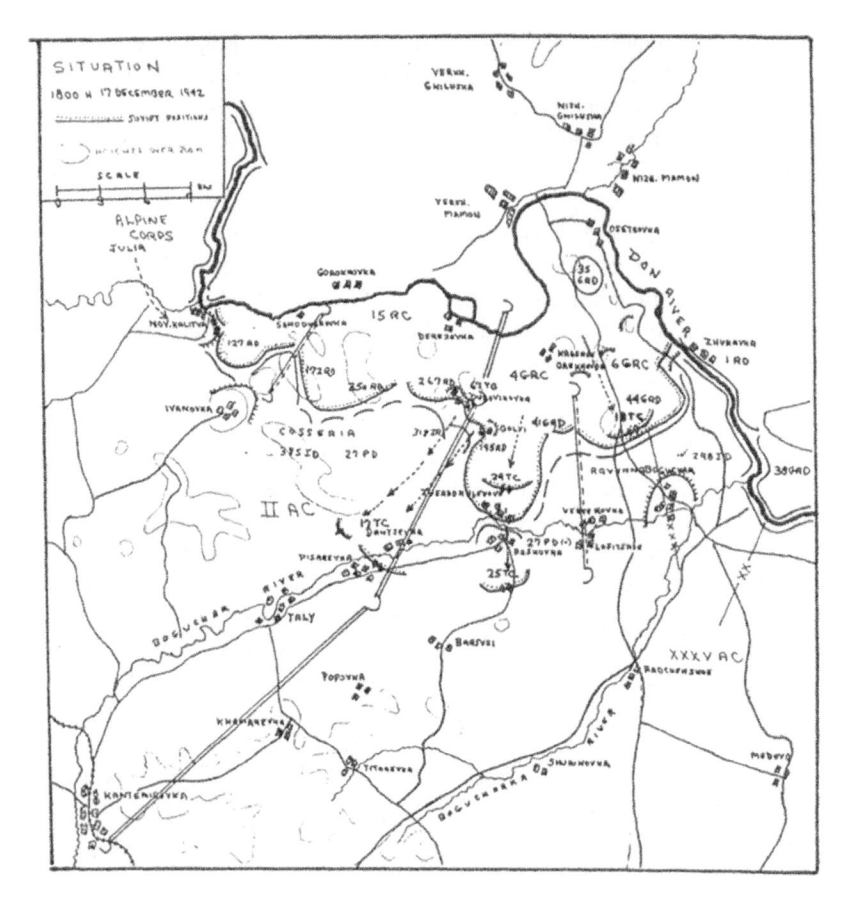

Fig. 7.4 Evening situation, 17 December 1942, from Glantz, *From the Don*, 48

On the morning of 18 December, Soviet rocket artillery fired against German and Italian units readying for the counter-attack (and those already attacking),[84] and the Soviets then pursued their offensive in the central sector of the Axis defensive positions in southern and southwestern direction towards Taly and the Boguchar river. There, two Italian infantry battalions defended their positions for one day against the 67th Tank Brigade to thwart their advance on Kantemirovka.[85] Yet the German and Italian second defence line on the Boguchar river was less strong (in fact mere ad hoc constructions)[86] and unable to withstand the powerful Soviet onslaught or was simply bypassed.[87]

On the very left flank of the Axis defence, the defensive line near Novaya Kalitva was holding, but Vatutin simply funnelled his armoured corps through the gap in the central part of the II Corps to exploit his successes with deep thrusts—threatening to outflank the remaining units on the Don. Afraid of being cut off by developments in their back, the (German) 298th ID started to withdraw—without informing the *Ravenna* to its left, which has been described as "a pattern that would be repeated in the next few weeks: German units withdrew repeatedly without informing neighbouring units from other nations."[88] Already by the 19th, the whole front line had been withdrawn by 40 kilometres[89] and Gariboldi planned to further give way until reinforcements arrived.[90] To make matters worse, the Third Guards Army slowly made progress on the 18th and had successfully penetrated German and Romanian defences south of the XXXV Corps (Figs. 7.5 and 7.6).[91]

---

[84] The Soviet artillery also caused disruption by interdiction fire, which undermined the Axis' command and control, see Rokossovsky, *Velikaya pobeda*, 348.

[85] Kuzmin and Krasnov, *Kantemirovtsy*, 42.

[86] Safronov, *Italyanski voiska*, 92–93.

[87] Glantz, *From the Don*, 51; USSME, *Le operazioni*, 375ff., 382f.

[88] Buttar, *Knife's Edge*, 159.

[89] The speed of the Soviet advance was similar, i.e. 20–25 kilometres a day for tank corps during Operation Uranus (the 25th Tank Corps had even reached an average daily rate of up to 50 kilometres), see Rotundo, *Battle for Stalingrad*, 112.

[90] Gariboldi in a phone conversation with Cavallero, in DS CS, VIII:I, 19 Dec. 1942. Cavallero was also very concerned with developments in North Africa in these days, see the lengthy meetings on 22 and 25 Dec. 1942, as well as his diary entries.

[91] Rokossovsky, *Velikaya pobeda*, 348–50.

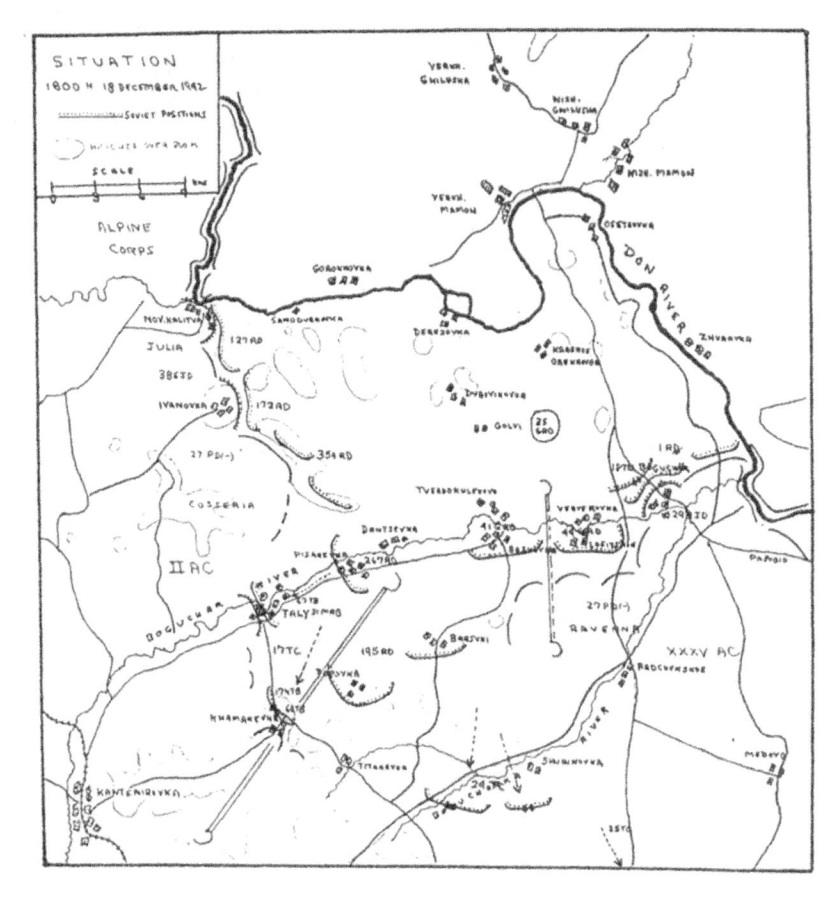

Fig. 7.5 Evening situation, 18 December 1942, from Glantz, *From the Don*, 50

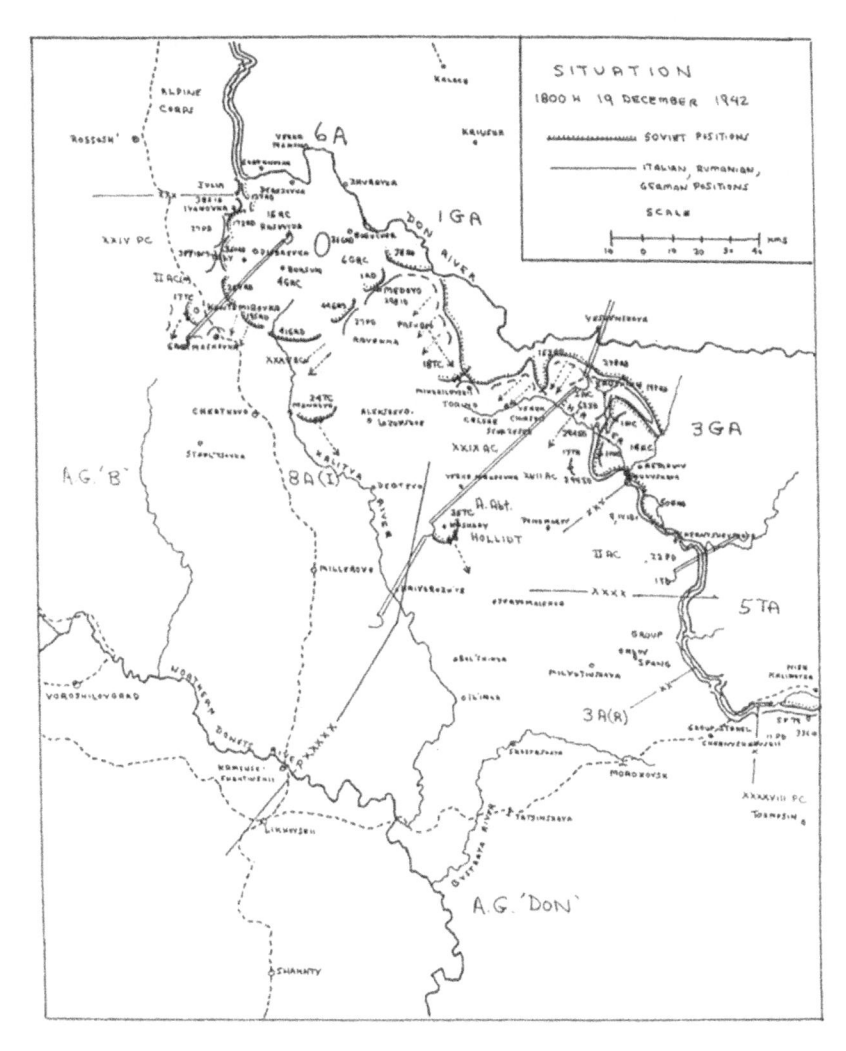

7 THE BATTLE ON THE DON, 11 DECEMBER 1942–31 DECEMBER 1943   173

Fig. 7.6   Evening situation, 19 December 1942, from Glantz, *From the Don*, 54

These break-ins led to the exploitation phase from 19 to 23 December.[92] Already by dawn, Kantemirovka had fallen. Hastily assembled SS troops, police units, and Italian remnants had defended it against two armoured brigades, which threatened the ARMIR's lines of communication.[93] Kantemirovka was a vital station on the only railroad that ran parallel to the Don from Millerovo to Rossosh.[94] It became a symbol for the Italian collapse and alleged unwillingness to fight. A report by Colonel Paoli in mid-February 1943, which did not deny instances of panic at Kantemirovka, claimed that the Germans had exaggerated this incident.[95] The official Italian history held that even though this was an inglorious episode "it was and remains an isolated case during the Italian campaign in Russia."[96] Another argument that the instance might have been exaggerated can be found in the internal Soviet general staff study. Here we learn that over 1000 Italians were killed in the fighting around Kantemirovka, while 1500 were captured.[97] This hardly constitutes a capture-kill ratio that implies that all Italians ran away or simply surrendered.

The First and Third Guards Armies staged wide-ranging manoeuvres with their motorised and armoured units towards Millerovo and Morozovsk—so fast that they ran into supply difficulties. The Luftwaffe inflicted painful losses on the 24th and 25th Tank Corps which also faced fierce Italian resistance on the ground. The Third Guards Army capitalised on their successes after "the Soviet 278th Rifle Division crushed defences of the Romanian 11th Infantry Division and drove it westward into the sector of the Italian *Sforzesca* Division. [...] Simultaneously, the Soviet 17th Guards Tank Regiment plunged through German defences north of Bokovskaya and occupied positions near Krasnaya Zarya in the German rear. It held these positions for two days thus blocking the orderly withdrawal of Romanian and German

---

[92] The rearguard fighting, withdrawal from the Don, and Italian role in defending Voroshilovgrad are retold in most detail in USSME, *Le operazioni*, 387–416.

[93] Glantz, *From the Don*, 56–57.

[94] See the map in ACS/T-821/200/IT 1387/1037.

[95] Pelagalli, *Marras*, 218.

[96] USSME, *Le operazioni*, 383.

[97] Fokin and Sidorov, *Razgrom Italo-Nemetskikh*, 87.

7 THE BATTLE ON THE DON, 11 DECEMBER 1942–31 DECEMBER 1943   175

units."[98] Many Italian and German units were encircled and captured (15,000 by 25 December)[99]; however, not all stragglers simply surrendered.[100] A significant number managed to return to their lines due to gaps in the Soviet front and the inadequate infantry support for their armoured formations.[101] In the evening of 22 December larger groups started surrendering, but this often depended on the attitude of their officers: some categorically rejected surrender offers by Russian emissaries, and ordered their men to continue fighting against the odds.[102] During the disastrous retreat—which included Romanian and Hungarian forces—allegations of uncomradely behaviour were traded, with each nation blaming the other for the defeat and ensuing chaos. But on many occasions, German and Italian units did fight jointly to defend strongholds or important towns, e.g. Meshkov, Arbuzovka and Chertkovo.[103] Even if this cooperation was far from flawless in the heat of battle and could only postpone the inevitable,[104] it still posed a threat to isolated Soviet units.[105]

Glantz's descriptions show what restricted chances the Italian, Romanian and Hungarian armies really had to withstand the Soviets'

---

[98] Glantz, *From the Don*, 62–63.

[99] Ibid., 62.

[100] 135 Italian stragglers were killed in combat near Malaya Losovka, see Nikolaj I. Afanasyev, *Ot Volgi do Shpree* (Moscow: Voenizdat, 1982), 87.

[101] Glantz, *From the Don*, 61.

[102] Afanasyev, *Ot Volgi do Shpree*, 90–91.

[103] Parts of the 298th ID and Italian troops from various units held Arbuzovka from 23 December until 25 December. Around 4000 of them launched a counter-attack in the night of the 24th only to be repelled under heavy casualties, see Fokin and Sidorov, *Razgrom Italo-Nemetskikh*, 68–69; see also Giorgio Scotoni, "La disfatta delle fanterie italiane sul Don nel dicembre 1942. 'Piccolo Saturno' e la battaglia di Arbuzovka," in *Battaglie in Russia. Il Don e Stalingrado 75 anni dopo*, ed. Olga Dubrovina (Milan: Ed. Unicopli, 2018), 221–33, here 226f. The 298th ID and mixed Italian units had resisted near Meshkov some days earlier, Glantz, *From the Don*, 61–62. The *Torino* had agreed to protect the rear during a joint retreat with the 298th ID—and did so tenaciously in cooperation with the Germans, BA-MA, RH 31-IX/35, Hammann – Gefechtsbericht *Torino*, 5 Mar. 1943, fos.19–31, here fos.24–25. Around 6000 German and Italian troops fiercely defended Chertkovo until 31 December, Afanasyev, *Ot Volgi do Shpree*, 92–95.

[104] For example, contradicting German orders had led to the loss of the *Sforzesca*'s artillery and vehicles, BA-MA, MSg 2/4388, Distler – Verbindungsoffizier, fos.73–74.

[105] Afanasyev, *Ot Volgi do Shpree*, 86.

armoured onslaughts.[106] Their options were limited: the frontline divisions from the central sector attempted to withdraw towards the south or southwest to evade encirclement. The Germans tried to prevent the fall of Tatsinskaya and Morozovsk—which would threaten the whole XXXXVIII Panzer Corps and a vital airfield—by sending the 19th Panzer Division to the Derkul river and the 3rd Mountain Division to Millerovo. The elite mountain infantry and additional armour was badly needed, as the 27th Panzer Divison had only ten effective tanks.[107] Yet, several steps to reorder German, Italian, Hungarian and Romanian units—and even successful local counter-attacks on over-stretched Soviet formations—could not reverse the overall development.[108] The subsequent retreat unfolded in two different sections. The southern group included the former XXXV Corps and parts of the German XXIX Panzer Corps, who came rather better out of the retreat than the northern group with the II Corps:[109] the XXXV Corps' divisions were described as "severely tested" on 15 January 1943, while the II Corps was "ineffective" (Figs. 7.7 and 7.8).[110]

[106] On 20 December, advancing T-34 s overwhelmed the 3rd *Bersaglieri* in Meshkov and two thirds of the regiment were killed or wounded, Roggiani, *Bersaglieri*, 334; Fokin and Sidorov, *Razgrom Italo-Nemetskikh*, 66.

[107] But the prolonged resistance and counter-attacks did help to halt the Red Army's offensive—until restocked formations resumed operations in mid-January, Glantz, *From the Don*, 58, 64.

[108] Ibid., 64–73.

[109] Giusti, *La campagna*, 251–56.

[110] ACS, T-821/2/IT 6g/939-945, Efficienza delle divisioni al 15 gennaio 1943, here f.943.

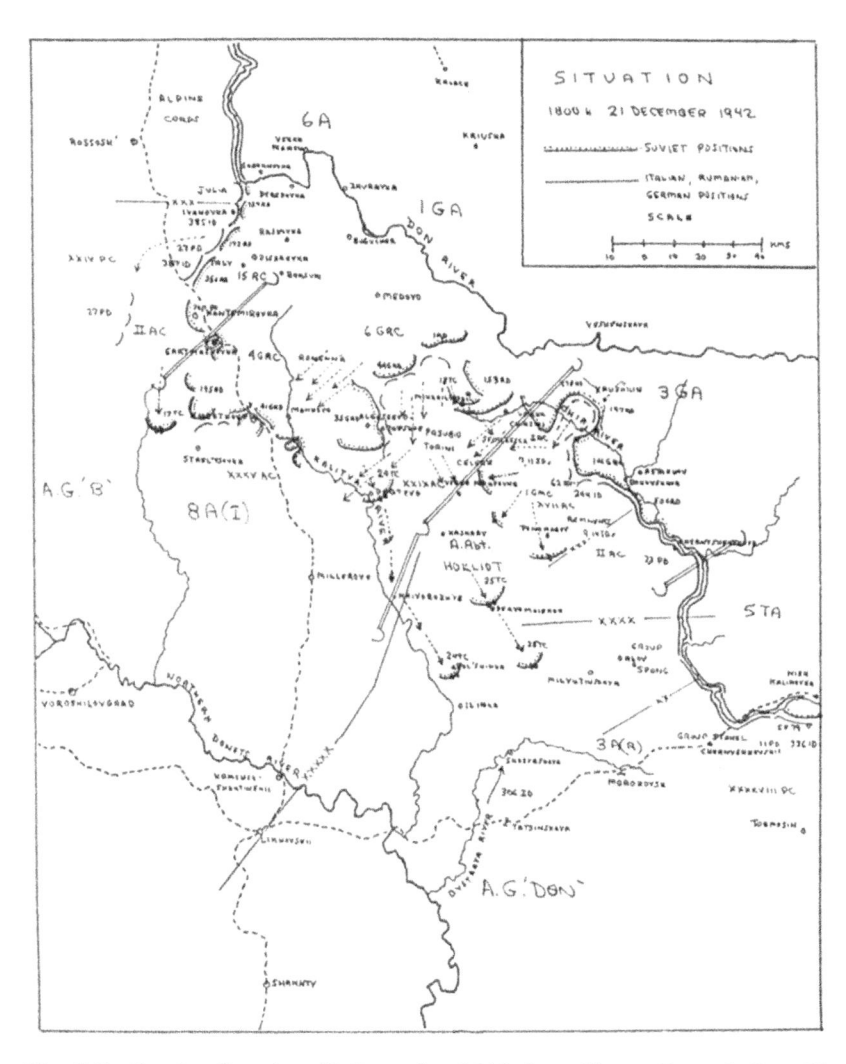

Fig. 7.7 Evening Situation, 21 December 1942, from Glantz, *From the Don*, 55

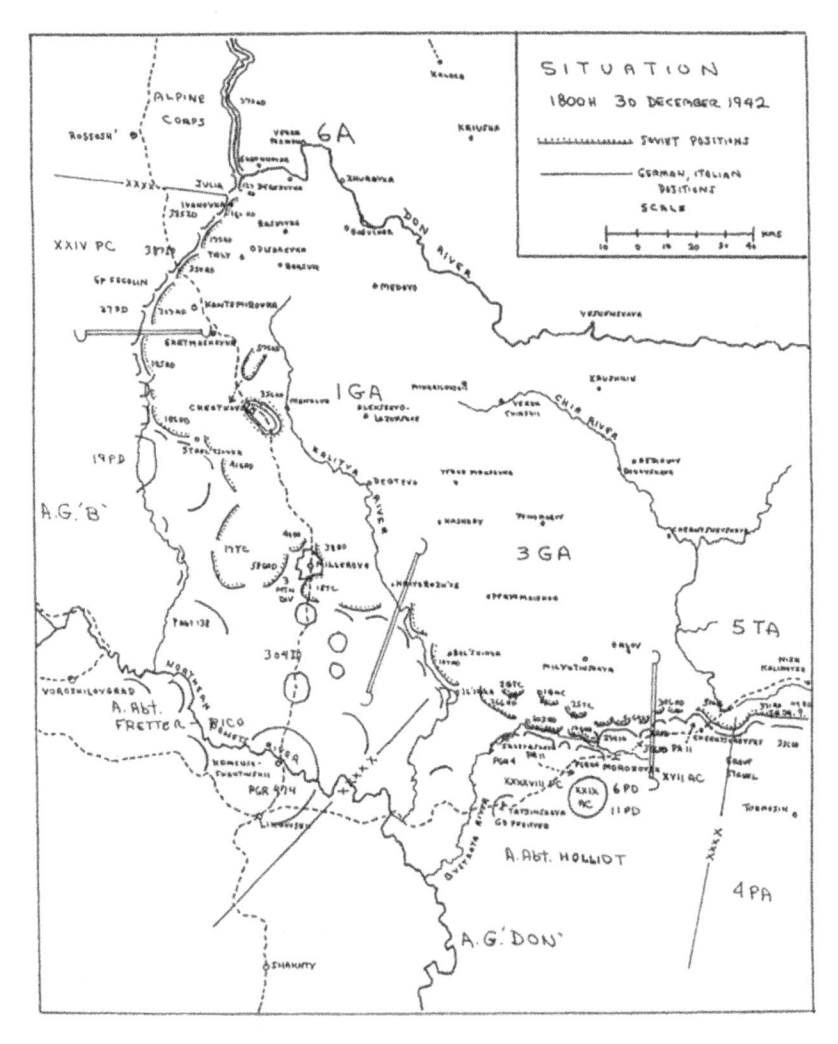

Fig. 7.8 Evening situation, 30 December 1942, Glantz, *From the Don*, 70

The *Alpini* Corps' Fate, January 1943

While the majority of the ARMIR's front was broken, the *Alpini* Corps (including the *Vicenza*) was left relatively unharmed until mid-January 1943. Yet, the general situation was deteriorating. The Soviet Voronezh Front launched an offensive against the Hungarian Second Army in the Ostrogozhsk and Rossosh areas, while the Southwestern and Southern Front advanced further south to clear Millerovo, Likhaya and Morozovsk of remaining Axis forces. The 'Ostrogozhsk-Rossosh' operation developed in the north from the vital bridgehead near Storoshevoye by the Fortieth Army under Lt. Gen. Kiril S. Moskalenko (1902–1985) against the Hungarian Second Army (mainly its II Corps), and was supported by the Soviet Third Tank Army's advance under Lt. Gen. Pavel. S. Rybalko (1894–1948) from the south towards Rossosh,[111] whose tanks "effectively guaranteed"[112] a breakthrough.

Thus, even though the *Alpini* Corps was not directly assaulted, the developments on its flank—particularly the deep thrusts by mobile Soviet forces—threatened its position. Indeed, fighting in their sector had previously been merely sporadic: besides the usual skirmishing, two Soviet regiments had attacked the *Tridentina* in the night of 16–17 January,[113] but otherwise only the *Julia* had taken part in major operations alongside the XXIV Panzer Corps and was praised for its conduct also by German war bulletins.[114] The low scale of combat prior to the retreat in January is critical for understanding the *Alpini*'s postwar narrative. Still, the *Alpini* are generally shed in better light than other Italian units—as the literature repeatedly claims that they "conducted themselves superbly"[115] and thus better than the II and XXXV Corps. Yet the *Alpini* Corps faced nothing similar to the onslaught that these latter corps experienced. We should not forget the simple fact that while the neighbouring corps were directly assaulted by far superior forces, the *Alpini* Corps was instead cut off by developments in other sectors before then trying

---

[111] Moskalenko, *Südwestrichtung*, 408ff.

[112] Buttar, *Knife's Edge*, 222.

[113] Rasero, *Tridentina avanti*, 384ff.

[114] DS CS, VIII:I, 29 Dec. 1942; USSME, *Le operazioni*, 428; Rasero, *Alpini della Julia*, 330ff.

[115] DiNardo, *Germany*, 154.

to evade encirclement. The operations in January can be subdivided into two phases: first the Soviet attacks (mainly on the Hungarian Second Army) and a second period with the *Alpini* Corps' withdrawal from 17 to 31 January.[116]

The XXIV Panzer Corps tried to prevent an encirclement of the *Alpini* Corps by aiding the Hungarian VII Corps (on the *Alpini*'s left flank).[117] But it had only four tanks, two assault guns, one battery of rocket artillery and five artillery pieces; and the 385th and 387th Infantry Divisions were also strained after severe combat in the preceding weeks.[118] Accordingly, none of the German counter-attacks that followed—either by the so-called Cramer Group (from the north) or the XXIV Panzer Corps—yielded any successes against vastly superior Soviet forces.[119] But the inevitable results were readily blamed on the allies. The *Alpini* Corps had initially agreed to hold their positions despite having already two Soviet tanks corps in their back.[120] Indeed, it was Lieutenant-General Nasci, commander of the *Alpini* Corps, who pressed the XXIV Panzer Corps to attempt a reconquest of Rossosh instead of falling back in northwesterly direction.[121] Thus, it is unsustainable to assert that the *Alpini* were purely lobbying for withdrawal.

In fact, the XXIV Panzer Corps began withdrawing on 15 January without informing the *Alpini* Corps, who had been more optimistic (than the Germans and Gariboldi) and ordered counter-attacks.[122] After the fall of Rossosh the coming day, confusion was mounting as Army Group B first prohibited any withdrawal of the *Alpini* Corps, before Gariboldi then issued a general order for retreat, which for the *Julia* and *Cuneense* meant abandoning much of their vehicles and heavy

[116] For a detailed description of the January operations, see Massignani, *Alpini e tedeschi*, 53–100; Hamilton, *Sacrifice*, 111–75; Giusti, *La campagna*, 256–61.

[117] The staffs of the *Alpini* Corps and the XXIV Panzer Corps were combined to improve overall coordination and command; which did not happen with the Hungarian Second Army, Hans Wimpffen, "Die Zweite Ungarische Armee im Feldzug gegen die Sowjetunion. Ein Beitrag zur Koalitionskriegführung im Zweiten Weltkrieg" (PhD diss., University of Tübingen, 1968), 231.

[118] USSME, *Le operazioni*, 423ff., 434. On the 385th ID, see Sigg, *Der Unterführer*, 311ff.

[119] Wimpffen, "Zweite Ungarische," 227ff.

[120] Ibid., 253–54.

[121] Ibid., 256.

[122] Buttar, *Knife's Edge*, 233.

weapons, and moving north of Rossosh.[123] After January 18th, the *Alpini* Corps and XXIV Panzer Corps were cut off from their lines of communication, supply and food reserves, surrounded by superior enemy forces and split into two groups.[124] Added to the cold, limited shelter, bad supplies, poor communication and general confusion, the rear area was already in the hands of Soviet armoured and mechanised units. Hence the operation was more a breakout from encirclement than a retreat. Wimpffen has argued—based on German sources—that the *Tridentina* and *Vicenza* started their movements in an orderly and efficient fashion, but as soon as they crossed paths with the XXIV Panzer Corps—and entered deep snow—the few suitable roads were plagued by traffic chaos and friction.[125] Also, the routes assigned for the *Julia* and *Cuneense* divisions crossed with around 10,000 German and Hungarian stragglers, which inevitably led to jams, chaos, and friction between the various formations.[126] The retreat was marked by a disorderly combat for the possession of villages and relied—on the Italian side—almost exclusively on infantry units of battalion size.[127] In the ensuing 21 larger skirmishes, the *Julia*, *Cuneense* and the *Vicenza* essentially ceased to exist, while the *Tridentina*—led by its commanding General Luigi Revèrberi and Lieutenant-General Nasci—maintained considerable cohesion and fought "brilliantly."[128] The *Tridentina* and the 385th ID managed to break out of encirclement (the Soviets had underestimated them and

---

[123] There was much controversy as to why the orders from Army Group B were not passed on earlier and why Nasci opted for a retreat from Rossosh over the open steppe at minus 40 °C. This is detailed in Burgwyn, *Mussolini*, 208ff.; Massignani, *Alpini e tedeschi*, 70–82, 120f. An initial preparatory order for withdrawal was wrongly translated by the Germans and thus interpreted as sign of independent action by the Italians, Wimpffen, "Zweite Ungarische," 223. The *Alpini* Corps has also been criticised because much of its artillery had been lost due to late preparations for withdrawal.

[124] Moreover, an early erroneous destruction of fuel at the XXIV Corps necessitated the abandonment of many vehicles, see Wimpffen, "Zweite Ungarische," 296.

[125] Ibid., 280.

[126] More detailed in Rasero, *Alpini della Julia*, 371ff.; Rasero, *L'eroica cuneense*, 345ff.

[127] Detailed in Hamilton, *Sacrifice*, 103ff.; USSME, *Le operazioni*, 433–50. The battles were often marked by sheer luck, as finding villages and evading Soviet columns decided over life and death, see Wimpffen, "Zweite Ungarische," 316ff.

[128] Schreiber, "Italiens Teilnahme," 277.

were caught-off guard) after a successful attack spearheaded by the *Tridentina* and four German assault guns.[129] In the end, however, only 27,500 of the 70,000 *Alpini* escaped from the 'Don pocket', of which around half had to undergo immediate medical treatment.[130]

After these disastrous retreats, the Eighth Army was dissolved on 31 January 1943. The *Comando Supremo* withdrew all remaining units by 22 May 1943,[131] which ended the Italian involvement on the Eastern Front.[132] The Italians were greatly concerned about the ever-increasing Soviet performance and morale,[133] and noted the German strategic crisis and the Wehrmacht's exhaustion.[134] But the remnants of the ARMIR were in no better shape. When General Marras visited the assembling area near Gomel between 9 and 14 March 1943, he initially refused to meet Italian soldiers. While the Germans "energetically" convinced him to do so, they noted the bad preparations that the Italian *Intendanza* had made for the retreat, but also an upswing of the soldiers' mood.[135] The ARMIR had lost 97 per cent of its artillery and 80 per cent of the vehicles and livestock. In total, 3010 officers (of 7130), 81,820 NCOs and men (of 221,875) were killed or missing, and 29,690 soldiers were

[129] Rasero, *Tridentina avanti*, 408ff.; Wimpffen, "Zweite Ungarische," 306ff.

[130] BA-MA, RH 31-IX/35, Salazer – Gefechtsbericht über den Rückmarsch des *Alpini*- und des XXIV Panzerkorps in der Zeit vom 14. bis 31. Jan. 1943 [hereafter 'Gefechtsbericht Rückmarsch *Alpini*'], 23 Mar. 1943, fol.91–101, here fol.100.

[131] The last battle involving Italian units was at Pavlograd on 10 February, Giusti, *La campagna*, 267; [Gen.] Mario Carloni, *La campagna di Russia* (Genoa: Effepi, 2010), 113ff.

[132] The dissolution of the Eighth Army had 'freed' 60,000 men for other duties, ACS, T-821/125/IT 1133/850-851, Colloquium Ambrosio and Sorice, 22 Feb. 1943. This number did not include the two divisions that had initially remained on the Eastern Front. Until April, the II Corps had been intended to remain in the East, Schreiber, "Italiens Teilnahme," 279. On the rallying of forces and repatriation, see also USSME, *Le operazioni*, 466–74.

[133] ACS, T-821/247/IT 2260/519-520, SIM Promemoria: URSS – Cenni sulla situazione militare, politica ed interna, 15 Aug. 1943.

[134] DDI, IX:IX, doc.503, Bova Scoppa (Bucarest) to Ciano, 15 Jan. 1943; Pelagalli, *Marras*, 196–206, 231ff.

[135] BA-MA, RH 2/2894, Massenbach – Bericht, fos.3, 8. Marras' descriptions of this visit are cited by Pelagalli, *Marras*, 225–26. In particular, bad quarters and the uncertainty about a subsequent deployment reduced the Italians' morale, BA-MA, RH 2/2894, Wochenbericht Italien, 5 Apr. 1943, fol.15.

wounded or suffered from frostbite.[136] This equalled to a casualty rate of 42 per cent for officers and 37 per cent among the ranks. Still, it is difficult to precisely calculate the combat-related deaths.[137] Around 70,000 men were captured during the retreat, of whom about 22,000 died on their way to a camp, 38,000 perished in captivity and only 10,032 survived.[138] In comparison, the Romanians suffered 155,010 dead, wounded and missing (over a quarter of their troops) between 19 November 1942 and 7 January 1943, and the Hungarians lost two-thirds of their force with 40,000 dead, 35,000 wounded and 60,000 captured.[139] However, the attacking Red Army also paid dearly for the success of Operation Saturn: over 80 per cent of the employed tanks were either destroyed or had to undergo repair, and infantry losses amounted to up to 70 per cent (for example in the 203rd Rifle Division).[140] The 'Second Defensive Battle on the Don' had been by far the bloodiest episode of the Italian operations in Russia. In the end, one-third of overall Italian military casualties during the *guerra fascista* (1940–1943) were suffered on the Eastern Front.[141]

Conclusion

Operation Little Saturn and the subsequent attacks on the Voronezh Front were a great success for the Red Army: they destroyed large numbers of German, Romanian, Hungarian and Italian units, drew in men and material from other sectors of the front (Stalingrad and Caucasus), and forced the Germans and their allies to abandon the lower Don and

---

[136] USSME, *Le operazioni*, 464.

[137] Burgwyn has argued—without primary sources—that around 25,000 of the 84,830 losses were combat-related, Burgwyn, *Mussolini*, 211.

[138] Ibid., 210–11.

[139] Dennis Deletant, "German-Romanian Relations, 1941–1944," in *Hitler and His Allies in World War II*, ed. Jonathan R. Adelman (New York: Routledge, 2007), 166–85, here 181 and footnote 685 on page 240. The Italian military intelligence concluded that without substantial German assistance, the Hungarian armed forces had no chance of regaining any significant combat strength, ACS, T-821/355/IT 4583/818-819, Gen. Carboni – Promemoria. Ungheria – Situazione militare, 31 Aug. 1943.

[140] Buttar, *Knife's Edge*, 212.

[141] Müller, *An der Seite*, 98; Rochat, *Le guerre*, 442. Rochat included those who died in captivity in the death toll of 80,000, which appears too low, however; see figures above.

the Donets.[142] The operations since autumn 1942 had demonstrated the Red Army's operational improvement—not only its preponderance in mass—at the end of its "learning year."[143] Had there been an alternative to defeat on the Don? Glantz has emphasised how strongly the Soviets dictated the course of events and argued that after the breakthrough on 17 December the lack of mobile operational reserves was particularly troubling for the footbound infantry units.[144] The Germans used the 6th, 11th and 19th Panzer Divisions to form ad hoc units in support of their (and the Italians') infantry—the Italians had no such flexibility or mobile reserves.[145] They could neither draw on mobility nor firepower on the ground and were also deprived of 'vertical artillery' from the skies for much of the time, which had been a vital factor in ending the Russian advance at the end of December.[146] The lack of mobile reserves meant that "once the defence was penetrated, only rapid withdrawal could ensue."[147] The Soviet general staff study emphasised the breakthrough phase as key moment of the entire offensive and the operational freedom it assured.[148] According to the Italian official history, the breakthrough and operational exploit was a foregone conclusion given the Soviets' numerical advantage of infantry, armour and artillery, the

---

[142] Hill, *Red Army*, 419.

[143] Mawdsley, *Thunder*, 217–22; Bellamy, *Absolute War*, 490–91; Glantz and House, *When Titans Clashed*, 120ff., 182ff. Still, the Red Army was no flawless fighting machine either. The offensive had started with bad intelligence, repeatedly revealed poor cooperation between infantry, artillery and armour (and the airforce), logistical problems, large gaps between formations resulting from troublesome command and control, and delayed and inaccurate artillery support during the penetration of the tactical defensive system during the first phase. Soviet losses were considerable: many tank and mechanised corps were reduced to 10–20 per cent (mainly due to tear and wear, but also enemy-inflicted losses) and the example of the 203rd Rifle Division – which was reduced from 8000 to 1000 men—was not uncommon. Yet, the Red Army started a rigorous lessons-learned approach and derived vital lessons from Little Saturn, see Glantz, *From the Don*, 74, 76–79; Fokin and Sidorov, *Razgrom Italo-Nemetskikh*, 107–9.

[144] Ibid., 77.

[145] Unfortunately, the lack of space and time (and primary sources) did not allow for more detailed studies on how individual units performed. Additionally, it is difficult to find suitable cases for comparisons.

[146] Buttar, *Knife's Edge*, 212.

[147] Glantz, *From the Don*, 29.

[148] Fokin and Sidorov, *Razgrom Italo-Nemetskikh*, 55, 104f., 109f.

excessive length of the front, the thinly manned Italian defensive lines, the few anti-tank guns, and the complete lack of mobility and operational reserves.[149] Additionally, this work flagged the failure to eliminate the Mamon bridgehead or to advance the defensive line from the north (Pavlovsk) as the Italians had proposed since August 1942, as well as rigid defensive orders, which had caused the late withdrawal of the *Alpini* Corps.[150] But were there any alternatives?

The Italian documents show that the commanders held similar ideas about static defence as the Germans. Thus, it is hard to credit the operational criticisms we often find: given the climate, infrastructure, the available materiel (and the enemy) the Italians could not simply regroup and wage daring operations by 'seizing the initiative'. The advancement of the first defensive positions to the Pavlovsk-Mamon line would have exposed these formations to Soviet assaults even further (and created the danger of having the Don in one's rear). Withdrawals were hampered by both the lack of serviceable vehicles and fuel shortages—and the impracticality of erecting new defensive lines. Only the creation of strongpoints in villages (as was often done) and all-round hedgehog defensives offered a feasible alternative. But even this option relied on the arrival of motorised and armoured reserves—which were missing on the entire front and could only achieve local successes during the stabilisation period in February and March 1943 (when also Soviet problems after far-flung advances had begun to show).[151]

The Soviet operations in winter 1942–1943 ended the Italian involvement on the Eastern Front. This moment has largely defined how the entire venture has been interpreted and judged until now: that is, as a futile, ineffective and tragic endeavour.[152] Only by incorporating a detailed discussion of the operations in 1941, the lessons-learned process, and the course of operations in 1942 can we adequately apprehend

---

[149] USSME, *Le operazioni*, 330, 463.

[150] Ibid., 433, 452–54.

[151] Glantz, *From the Don*, 193ff.; Förster, *Risse im Bündnis*, 97ff.

[152] It is notable that in contrast to the high command of the Hungarian Second Army, which openly accused its soldiers of cowardice in a circular (that was even read out to them), the Italian officers did not resort to such measures—also a contrast to General Luigi Cadorna's reaction after the rout at Caporetto in 1917. On the Hungarian case, see Wimpffen, "Zweite Ungarische," 333–37.

how the Italians fought on the Eastern Front. Yet, this is rarely done: in particular, the narrative of the 'tragedy on the Don' promoted in memoirs has blurred many of the facts about Italian combat performance before—but also during—winter 1942–1943. Consequently, two main topoi derived from the war on the Eastern Front:

1. The allegation of Italian military ineffectiveness
2. A multifold narrative of Italian victimhood.

The first point already became a contentious topic during the war and its impact went far beyond military circles. Messe's reaction to German circulars showed the immediate onset of a reciprocal blame game between Germans and Italians. As junior partners, the Italians were on the receiving end—especially after the narrative about Italians as 'eternal traitors' became even stronger following the events of September 1943. Schreiber has rightly pointed to the discrepancy between high politics and propaganda about Italian military ineffectiveness and the German liaison officers' actual post-battle reports.[153] It is difficult to establish an absolute measure for combat performance, since a large percentage of the documents were lost during the retreat. Here, we will instead look at the Wehrmacht's assessments of their allies at the time. The second topos is more of an Italian story. The Italians deemed themselves, victims of German uncomradely behaviour—having been deprived of food, assistance and vehicles by their supercilious Teutonic ally.[154] Reports to the *Comando Supremo* thus gathered together the 'evidence' of German misconduct. This narrative of victimhood was supplemented with a criticism of the Fascist regime and the top military leadership–particularly after 1943—and was interwoven with debates on Italian war crimes and the fate of Italian POWs in Soviet hands. Both of these narratives served to gloss over Italy's participation in a criminal war.

Thus, the next part will set straight some of the myths and provide some evidence, before looking deeper at the narratives of victimhood and how the myths and memories were created. This section will try to

---

[153] Schreiber, "Italiens Teilnahme," 283. Schreiber and Massignani used some of the reports in BA-MA, RH 31-IX/35, here fos.60–74, 127–33.

[154] Schreiber, "Italiens Teilnahme," 283–84.

answer the following questions: Did incapable officers command useless Italian formations and cowardly soldiers? Were the Italians 'lions led by donkeys' or even 'chickens led by donkeys' as some narratives suggest? How did the Italians react to the main challenge on the Eastern Front, i.e. stopping Soviet armour?

CHAPTER 8

The Italian Combat Performance: 'Chicken Led by Donkeys'?

Conventional wisdom about the Second World War has it that Germany's allies cracked on the Don, leading to the catastrophic defeat at Stalingrad.[1] If not their allies, then 'General Mud' or 'General Winter' were named as the reasons for failure.[2] These myths and stereotypes were nurtured by wartime propaganda, but the German and Italian memoir literature also besmirched the performance of the CSIR and ARMIR—and particularly that of the senior command. These over-generalising depictions of the Italians and other German allies are usually based on questionable sources and evidence. This section will first look at Soviet assessments of the Italians, then turning to a detailed analysis how the Germans rated the *Regio Esercito*'s divisions and commanders.

SOVIET ASSESSMENTS OF THE ITALIANS

One of the earliest evaluations of the Italian Army was an internal study that was completed in 1945. A General Staff directive of 9 November 1942 had laid out the need to collect 'lessons learned' and thus demanded a series of analyses of past battles. In total, the so-called 'Department of Research into and Appplication of Wartime Experiences'

---

[1] Wegner, "War," 1173ff.
[2] Stahel, *Operation Barbarossa*, 20; see also Jack Radey and Charles Sharp, "Was It the Mud?" *The Journal of Slavic Military Studies* 28, no. 4 (2015): 646–76.

© The Author(s) 2019
B. M. Scianna, *The Italian War on the Eastern Front, 1941–1943*, Italian and Italian American Studies,
https://doi.org/10.1007/978-3-030-26524-3_8

of the General Staff of the Red Army edited 26 studies, the last of which was completed in 1948.[3] Thus, these reports were intended as assistance for ongoing operations and thus arguably rather objective and also self-critical. The volume "Destruction of the Italian-German forces on the Don" praised the stubborn Italian (and German) resistance, their fierce counter-attacks, the high quality of the defensive works, the artillery fire plans and the extensive use of mines.[4] The authors, who based their report also on interviews with captured Italians, noted the chaos during the retreat, but in no way argued that the Italians had run away or had offered hapless resistance. Yet, this study was never published and remained the only volume decidedly focusing on the Italians for a long time.

From the Soviet point of view, the Italians were never the main enemy, and thus were, like the Romanians and Hungarians, mainly mentioned in passing—even though the Romanians received more attention due to their role in the battle of Stalingrad. In his memoirs, Nikita Khrushchev, described the Romanians and Italians as not standing up well to Soviet blows.[5] A mix of neglect and belittlement, as in German memoirs, can be found in postwar writings of senior leaders of the Red Army, which were published only after Stalin's death in 1953 and Krushchev's admission of Stalin's mistakes in 1956. Thus, one needs to bear the 'politics' of Soviet memoir literature in mind—both for internal reasons (creating a unifying narrative about the Great Patriotic War) and for countering international narratives dominated by German memoirs, in order to underscore one's great power status and the might of the Red Army (and of the enemies that one had defeated).[6]

Most of the memoirs of high-ranked generals hardly referred to the Italians. Rokossovsky did not mention them at all, and in his widely influential memoirs Georgy K. Zhukov merely put them in line with other satellite armies as less well armed, less experienced, less efficient

---

[3] Rotundo, *Battle for Stalingrad*, 1; Glantz, *From the Don*, 401, footnote 14. I would like to thank David Glantz for sending me a copy of this study.

[4] Fokin and Sidorov, *Razgrom Italo-Nemetskikh*, 10–13, 44–46, 54, 66f., 87f.

[5] In contrast he argued that the Hungarians had offered "very stubborn resistance", see Sergei Khrushchev, ed., *Memoirs of Nikita Khrushchev*, Vol. 1 (University Park: The Pennsylvania State University Press, 2005), 329.

[6] Seweryn Bialer, "Introduction," in *Stalin and His Generals: Soviet Military Memoirs of World War II*, ed. Seweryn Bialer (New York: Pegasus, 1969), 15–44, here 16ff.

and ascribed to the officers and men less interest in fighting, and to possibly dying, in faraway Russia than their Fascist leaders; yet he also mentioned the lack of operational reserves as reason for the downfall on the Don.[7] Vasilevsky made more detailed comments. He remarked that the Italians' entire frontline had collapsed only on the fifth day of operations as their command and control was hampered by deep armoured thrusts, which led to a disorderly retreat.[8] In context of the winter offensives, Vasilevsky stressed his concerns about German relief attempts (his elite Second Guards Army was sent to the Stalingrad front) and described the destruction of the ARMIR only as a first step of much wider and more ambitious plans.[9] Still, he considered the operations on the Don as "fundamental" for thwarting Manstein's relief attempts as it forced the Germans to shift reserves to this threatened part of the front.[10]

Only a few of the commanders who directly faced the Italians in Operation Little Saturn left written recollections. The Ukranian-born Lelyushenko, commander of the Third Guards Army, argued in his memoirs that not only the Italians and Romanians but the Germans too had been caught off guard by the scale and wide-ranging intentions of Operation Little Saturn.[11] He cited Manstein's memoirs in which he heavily criticised the Italians—without, however, further commenting on Manstein's accusations.[12] But overall, he did not subscribe to the tone and charges raised by many German commanders.[13] Unfortunately, two other main participants, Vatutin and Kharitonov were killed during the war. The commander of the Third Tank Army, Rybalko, died early and also Kuznetsov did not leave any memoirs. Moskalenko, commander of the First Guards Army between August and October 1942, who then led the Fortieth Army during the Ostrogozhsk–Rossosh operations, wrote

---

[7] Geoffrey Roberts, ed., *Marshal of Victory: The Autobiography of General Georgy Zhukov*, 2 Vols. (Barnsley: Pen & Sword, 2013), 1150–51.
[8] Wassilewski, *Sache*, 253.
[9] Ibid., 240–41.
[10] Ibid., 252–53.
[11] Lelyushenko, *Moskva-Stalingrad-Berlin-Praga*, 151.
[12] Ibid., 154.
[13] In fact, he was more interested in highlighting the high numbers of Germans that were captured; see ibid., 156.

about the Hungarians' lacking will to fight 'Hitler's war' and their low morale, but did not comment on the Italians.[14]

The memoir literature that appeared in the 1960s also fostered the cooperation between wartime commanders and historians. Marshal Rokossovky edited a volume on the Stalingrad campaign with several military historians in which they repeatedly mentioned the dogged Italian resistance and emphasised that the attack on Kantemirovka, where panic had struck Italian (and German troops), was a "great surprise strike in the back of the enemy."[15] There were other more academic studies. Afanasyev, who used Soviet archival material, emphasised the disarray of Italian formations during the retreat, but also their countless counter-attacks and fierce opposition; thus in no way portrayed them as ineffective and useless enemies.[16] Similarly, Kuzmin and Krasnov stressed the tenacious resistance of the II Corps and the defence of Taly.[17] One of the most popular books on the battle of Stalingrad was translated into Italian by the renowned Garzanti publishing house. Samsonov's focus on the Germans as main aggressors suited the overall Italian self-image. Further, he criticised the Wehrmacht generals for their self-exculpation after the war and questioned their master narrative that either Hitler or the German allies were to blame for defeat.[18] Likewise, his description of Operation Little Saturn was celebratory of the Soviet victory, without, however, disregarding the Italian resistance or speaking of a chaotic retreat.[19]

As mentioned above, Russian scholars have never devoted much attention to the Italian war effort. However, based on an analysis of all available writings, Scotoni reached the conclusion that the Soviets depicted the strong resistance and counter-attacks by Italian forces on the Don,[20] and also Filatov and Safranov were more balanced in their assessments of Italian fighting power. Safronov, who was also very critical of the Italian conduct, rejected the one-sided attacks by German officers in their memoirs and, for example, Liddell Hart's acceptance of such views.

[14] Moskalenko, *Südwestrichtung*, 396, 430ff.
[15] Rokossovsky, *Velikaya podeba*, 356.
[16] Afanasyev, *Ot Volgi do Shpree*, 85ff.
[17] Kuzmin and Krasnow, *Kantemirovtsy*, 41–42.
[18] Aleksandr M. Samsonov, *Stalingrado: Fronte russo* (Milan: Garzanti, 1961), 289ff.
[19] Ibid., 368ff.
[20] Scotoni, *L'Armata Rossa*, 29, 313.

Instead, Safronov argued, the truth probably lies somewhere in the middle of these one-sided depictions of the ARMIR as hapless fighting force on the one hand and the all-too positive portrayals in the Italian service histories.[21] Thus he demanded a more sober and objective view claiming two Italian divisions (the *Cosseria* and *Ravenna*) alone could not have defended their positions against two Soviet armies for one week. Yet, they also did not simply run away, but offered tenacious resistance (with the Germans) and inflicted heavy casualties on the Red Army.[22]

There are several conclusions that we can draw from this brief evaluation. Where the Italians were mentioned in Soviet accounts, they were depicted more favourably than in German memoirs. Subsequent scholarly work had increased this tendency. While we still need a thorough investigation of Russian primary material, for example to find out what the individual Soviet soldier thought of the Italians, it is fair to conclude that the fighting power of the ARMIR was in no way universally criticised. However, these glimpses cannot offer a full appreciation of the Italian's combat performance, but the vast German sources provide a detailed insight.

The Germans on the Italians

As mentioned earlier, an analysis of military effectiveness has to embrace several aspects: it can be subdivided into tactical, operational and strategic levels, and must always be seen in relative terms. It would be improper to juxtapose the Italian divisions to the fighting capacities of a German or Soviet armoured division. Rather, the appropriate comparison is with their infantry divisions that also stood little chance against motorised and armoured formations, and much like the Italian units, were also not meant to take on enemy armour by themselves. What follows is hardly an attempt to argue that the ARMIR was a flawless and efficient war machine. Rather, the author's intention is to provide more knowledge on how the Italian units performed in winter 1942–1943 and to warn about judgements with hindsight. We do, indeed, know about the Italian Army's imperfections today, but we must not forget

---

[21] Safronov, *Italyanski voiska*, 102.
[22] Ibid., 103.

that the Wehrmacht and the Italians noted many of them at the time as well. One liaison officer, for example, criticised the Italians' inadequate safety measures against attacks, little reconnaissance, poor placement and bad concealment of heavy infantry weapons and artillery, insufficient defensive works, linear defences, poor coordination between artillery and infantry and insufficient maintenance of weapons, materiel and uniforms.[23] However, it is 'Military 101' that no unit is ever perfect, and no patrolling ever sufficient—just as no boots or weapons are ever clean enough. Likewise, criticism on operational conduct is entirely normal and similarly took place within the Wehrmacht—one simply has to think of the frank tone of the after-action reports produced following the campaign against Poland in 1939.[24] German assessments, for instance identifying an inflexible Italian command system, must be analysed in context. The myth of mission command (*Auftragstaktik*) led to a special emphasis on this point—even in internal German reports.

Thus, the verdicts of different professional soldiers of various rank who served as liaisons to the *Regio Esercito*—and therefore had a vested interest in their operational effectiveness—provide an excellent source for re-evaluating claims about the Italians in the Second World War.[25] Schlemmer has used these liaison reports to analyse German–Italian relations and their perception of one another, but, not to look in detail at Italian combat performance.[26] On the other hand, Schreiber noted already in 1992 that the public impression of Italian military failure, as well as Tippelskirch's and the Wehrmacht senior leadership's observations, do not match the rather positive reports that came from the liaison officers attached to Italian units.[27] The liaison staffs were directly involved at the army, corps and divisional level at times of severe crises. Most had already served for several months with Italian units at the time

[23] BA-MA, MSg 2/4388, Distler – Verbindungsoffizier, fos.55, 76.

[24] Murray, "German Response," 286.

[25] Moreover, as most of the surviving Italian documents on this period are post-ex facto reports, Schlemmer, *Italiener*, 77. Regimental sources such as the *relazione* of the 5th *Alpini* Regiment have survived, but this latter was written in June 1943, and is therefore of limited value for assessing events during the retreat. It is, rather, a first document creating a narrative of victimhood, see ACS, T-821/230/IT 2009. Similarly, the papers of Lieutenant-General Nasci in the military archives contain largely post-ex facto documents, see AUSSME, Fondo Nasci.

[26] Schlemmer, *Italiener*, 70ff.

[27] Schreiber, "Italiens Teilnahme," 283.

of the winter retreat. Hence, their opinions were not based on first impressions, anecdotes, second-hand information in faraway headquarters or sporadic encounters. Obviously, outside assessments are never completely accurate, but they can offer a refreshing openness in terms of pointing the finger at shortcomings (without fear of superiors). Moreover, these liaison reports were internal documents, so they did not have to pay attention to alliance niceties and 'political' parlance.

Most studies on German–Italian relations and coalition warfare have only looked at the grand strategic, i.e. political level, and neglected the nitty-gritty of operational performance.[28] The cooperation on the strategic level was probably as much a double-faced sword as ever, while it generally worked better on the frontlines than in rear areas.[29] On the political level, Mussolini could neither hide his *schadenfreude* over German setbacks in Russia,[30] nor his disdain about broken promises. Field Marshal Keitel (unsurprisingly) lauded Italian operational conduct in a meeting with Ambassador Alfieri.[31] In private, he called the Italians "half-soldiers"[32]—but also argued that minor disagreements, particularly between the general staffs, were normal in coalition warfare.[33] Hence, the German–Italian coalition—which was a secondary factor for the daily life of Italian soldiers—was hardly at loggerheads before August 1942, when due to the military situation relations both became worse and necessitated greater cooperation.[34] Similarly to other theatres, on the Eastern Front the Italian senior command attempted to restrict German influence and preserve as much independence as possible, while at the same time longing for recognition from the Wehrmacht. This created an ambivalent love–hate relationship, but Messe, for example, also remarked

---

[28] An exception is Schlemmer, "Tedeschi a piedi."

[29] Massignani, *Alpini e tedeschi*, 136–37.

[30] Ciano Diaries, 20 Dec. 1941.

[31] The Italian official history noted also Keitel's praise for the CSIR in a conversation with Cavallero in Klessheim on 29 April 1942, USSME, *Le operazioni*, 186. But what else could he have done at a time when the Germans badly needed reinforcements? The value of such praise on the political-strategic level should be seen critically.

[32] Gosztony, *Hitlers Fremde Heere*, 166.

[33] DDI, IX:IX, doc.144, Alfieri to Ciano, 21 Sept. 1942.

[34] Müller, *An der Seite*, 92; Virtue, "Fascist Italy," 101ff.; Osti Guerrazzi and Schlemmer, "I soldati italiani," 413.

that sometimes the Germans appeared to value the CSIR's deeds more than the *Comando Supremo* in Rome did.[35]

As argued above, up to a certain point the Germans ran the logistics for the CSIR and ARMIR; after which the Italian service units funnelled supplies to the front. Logistics was also a chief reason for friction within the Wehrmacht. This was amplified by the traditional low importance (and prestige) of supply roles in the German military.[36] With a strong focus on operational excellence, the blame for setbacks and disregard for logistics went hand in hand. Indeed, Groß has demonstrated how German planners frequently overlooked the different speeds of infantry and armour, rendering cooperation between them difficult.[37] Thus, especially postwar memoirs that blame logistics for operational failures should be read in the context of the realities on the Eastern Front and the Wehrmacht's institutional bias towards supply duties.[38]

In order to improve logistical and operational cooperation the Germans and Italians had attached liaison staffs to each other's contingents since the beginning of the campaign.[39] Their number grew proportionately to the overall amount of Italian forces and formed an institutionalised structure also for the sake of keeping the smaller nations' contingents informed about operations in other sectors. The liaison staffs were meant to offer advice without having direct command authority (and while still being subordinate to German commands); thus, there was no unity of command or real jointness, not least

[35] Messe, *Lettere*, 145.
[36] Megargee, *Inside*, 123.
[37] Groß, *Mythos*, 230ff., 240.
[38] See e.g. the criticism in Giusti, *La campagna*, 140–43.
[39] Hans Doerr, "Verbindungsoffiziere," *Wehrwissenschaftliche Rundschau* 3, no. 6 (1953): 270–80; Schlemmer, *Italiener*, 52ff.; DiNardo, *Germany*, 105–6. The first Italian document indicating German liaison officers dates from 30 July, ACS, T-821/247/IT 2259/234, Messe– Ufficiali germanici di collegamento, 30 July 1941. Messe clearly stated these officers' tasks and limits. The Germans followed this practice with all their allies, usually sending more officers to their allies than receiving (which was quite normal, as they were the dominant ally). The Italians and Romanians had also exchanged officers on 20 July 1941 and two Romanians accompanied the CSIR, ACS, T-821/20/IT 98/867-868, Messe – Visite al Comando Supremo Rumeno ed al Comando della 11^ Armata germanica, 22 July 1941.

due to "differences in language, mentality and training."[40] In fact, the Wehrmacht had realised the extent to which cooperation depended on trust and personal relations: these were always better when no translators were needed, but few officers spoke Italian.[41] The Germans often looked down at their allies, and the fact that most liaisons were established in 1940 or in 1941—at the height of the Wehrmacht's successes and often in times of reverses of their allies—helped little to ease a patronising attitude.[42]

Major Hans-Wessel von Gyldenfeldt (1906–1978), who had worked under Rintelen in Rome and was employed in counter-espionage in the Federal Republic after the war, was deployed as liaison to the CSIR in July 1941; yet he soon fell out with Messe (especially during the 'First Defensive Battle on the Don') and was replaced by Major Reinhold Fellmer in October.[43] The German liaison mission to the Eighth Army (*Deutscher Verbindungsstab zum italienischen Armeeoberkommando 8*, or for short—also on the divisional and army corps level—*Deutsches Verbindungskommando*, DVK) had been created in June 1942. It was headed by Gyldenfeldt from 12 July 1942 until 28 August 1942. After the above-mentioned glitches—which hardly improved the Italians' relation with Gyldenfeldt—General Kurt von Tippelskirch (1891–1957) was appointed as the new head of the DVK to the ARMIR.[44] Tippelskirch had previously filled crucial positions in the German military intelligence, presiding over Foreign Armies East and Foreign Armies West as well as the military attachés between 1938 and 1941 (thus he also

---

[40] BA-MA, N433/8, Rintelen – Die Zusammenarbeit mit dem ital. Verbündeten, n.d., fol.4.

[41] In 1937, Marras noted that only around ten officers had a fair command of the language and even in 1942 there were only four generals who spoke sound Italian, Pelagalli, *Marras*, 16, 80, 194.

[42] Doerr, "Verbindungsoffiziere," 271. On the German view of the Spanish 'Blue Division', see Xosé M. Núñez Seixas, "Wishful Thinking in Wartime? Spanish Blue Division's Soldiers and Their Views of Nazi Germany, 1941–44," *Journal of War & Culture Studies* 11, no. 2 (2018): 99–116, here 103.

[43] ACS, T-821/20/IT 98/886-890, Messe – Relazione, 29 July 1941, here f.889; DiNardo, *Germany*, 127. The value of his reports from August 1942, which slur the Italian command system, should be read with this information in mind. The report is cited in Knox, *Hitler's Italian Allies*, 115.

[44] Ugo Cavallero's son functioned as Italian liaison to Army Group B—which was arguably a political appointment.

received rather negative reports about the *Regio Esercito* before the war).[45] Later he commanded an infantry division during the attack on the USSR, and operated as translator in important negotiations due to his language skills.[46] After the war, he wrote a prominent study on the Second World War, in which the Italian conduct on the Don received little approval.[47] He was a vital collaborator in the American Historical Division project, remained a leading figure in German veterans' circles,[48] and his views (and writings) influenced other German officers who were preparing their memoirs as well as Basil Liddell Hart.[49] Colonel Walter Nagel (1902–1975) became his Chief of Staff on 18 September 1942,[50] followed by then-Colonel Hans Speidel (1897–1984) in early January 1943.[51]

Tippelskirch was meant to take over command in times of crisis (with Italian consent) and was accompanied by around forty officers who were placed in liaison duties with other Italian formations. Indeed, Tippelskirch, who was not necessarily an Italophile,[52] tried to influence the thinking and orders of the Italian commands, and Speidel, too, later described his task as coordinating the defence and influencing operational and tactical decisions.[53] Tippelskirch appeared to be frustrated about the Italians' general bearing as well as their armament,

---

[45] Meier-Welcker, "Militärpolitik," 80.

[46] This primarily meant French, which he had learned in captivity during the First World War. We can only speculate about his Italian proficiency. An Italian source noted a brief speech he gave in Italian as something rather uncommon, ACS, T-821/260/IT 3075/790-792, Gen. Olmi—Visita Generale v. Tippelskirch, 30 Sept. 1942, f.792.

[47] [Gen.] Kurt von Tippelskirch, *Geschichte des Zweiten Weltkriegs* (Bonn: Athenäum, 1956), 108ff., 273–74.

[48] Howell, *Von den Besiegten lernen*, 282.

[49] On the contacts between Liddell Hart and Tippelskirch, see Searle, "A Very Special Relationship," 335, 352.

[50] Safronov, *Italyanski voiska*, 72. Gyldenfeldt introduced Nagel to his new tasks until November. Nagel had been assistant attaché in Moscow and knew Tippelskirch from prior positions in the Wehrmacht's intelligence section.

[51] Speidel later became Chief of Staff under Erwin Rommel and one of the most influential military personalities in the new German army after the Second World War.

[52] Pelagalli, *Marras*, 213. Yet, he had been in contact with the Italian attaché in Berlin before the outbreak of the war, ibid., 41. On his role prior to Barbarossa, see Megargee, *Inside*, 107ff.

[53] [Gen.] Hans Speidel, *Aus unserer Zeit. Erinnerungen* (Berlin: Propyläen, 1977), 138.

discipline and fighting spirit, thus arguing for stronger reserves behind the ARMIR and the establishment of joint formations led by German staffs on corps level.[54] Consequently, the Italians often perceived him as a watchdog and complained about his patronising attitude.[55] In fact, his personality seemed to have weighed down on the unity of command during the crisis in December 1942: Tippelskirch sent out orders to German units within the Eighth Army from the DVK without informing Gariboldi.[56] Tippelskirch's staff was proportionately increased: the intended strength of a DVK at an Italian division was one senior Captain or Major as head, one assistant officer, one translator (all three with knowledge of the Italian language), as well as two typists, three drivers and one motorcyclist—all this was increased at the corps and army levels.[57] In reality, however, none of the DVKs were at full strength, and the ideal manpower levels were even below requirements for calm periods. A retrospective German report claimed one would have needed liaison officers in each Italian regiment in order to reduce the friction in December 1942.[58] The Germans criticised some Italian officers' lack of will to cooperate and constantly tried to substitute the less cooperative ones. Due to professional pride and unwritten rules of alliance politics, the Italians were initially unwilling to accept too much advice from their ally—according to the German sources. Yet, one should realise what 'learning' meant in many cases: accepting the Wehrmacht's doctrines as the only valuable ones and throwing overboard one's own procedures (and training).

[54] Kotze, *Heeresadjutant*, 132; Safronov, *Italyanski voiska*, 74–76.

[55] Malaguti, the ARMIR's Chief of Staff, even told Gyldenfeldt that he was hoping Tippelskirch would be recalled to Germany, Safronov, *Italyanski voiska*, 76.

[56] BA-MA, RH 2/2894, Massenbach – Bericht, fos.9ff.; Messe, *La guerra*, 278ff. See also a report by Marras in Pelagalli, *Marras*, 194, 212–13; further Giusti, *La campagna*, 137; Scotoni, *Il nemico fidato*, 211–12. Also other armies noted the German tendency to use liaison officers to increase control and surveillance. This was eased by the fact that the DVKs were linked with an independent communication system and could directly report to Tippelskirch, Gosztony, *Hitlers Fremde Heere*, 248–49.

[57] BA-MA, RH 31-X/9, Vorschläge für die Aufstellung gemischter deutsch-italienischer Verbände auf Grund der Erfahrungen bei ital. Truppen in Russland u.a.d. Balkan 1941 bis 1943, 1 Dec. 1943, fol.4 [subsequently cited as 'Vorschläge']. The DVK to the *Alpini* was handed to Major-General Ernst Schlemmer (1889–1949) on 25 August 1942, who reportedly got on rather well with Lieutenant-General Nasci, see Safronov, *Italyanski voiska*, 74.

[58] BA-MA, RH 31-X/9, Vorschläge, 1 Dec. 1943, fol.5.

Indeed, the liaison staff continuously prompted the Italians to develop a lessons-learned procedure, support their infantry better,[59] and to communicate recent combat experiences to higher commands (as well as down the ladder).[60] Army Group B also sent a reminder to train troops during calm periods, to which the Italians politely replied saying that this procedure of constant development was also well established in the *Regio Esercito*.[61] Yet, Tippelskirch raised doubts and expected "nothing to happen."[62] The Wehrmacht also noted that Italian reports at divisional staff meetings often diverged from reality,[63] and acknowledged that direct criticism was an unsuitable approach.[64] Morale was deemed vital, so the Germans preferred to say a few niceties and award decorations.[65] But German sources also recognised their own arrogance *vis-à-vis* the Italian Army,[66] and DVK members admitted that many NCOs and simple soldiers of the Wehrmacht lacked respect for Italian officers.[67] Yet, the assertion that they were motivated by ideological feelings of superiority is probably (despite occasional racist remarks) an over-generalisation. The most dominant coalition partner always shows some arrogance, and the German reports were more a matter of professional soldiers assessing their comrades in arms.[68] The Wehrmacht's own self-esteem had probably reached its zenith in 1941 and remained strong in 1942.[69] Vice versa, the Italians attempted—sometimes by almost comical means—to prevent being seen as the junior partners,[70] but still felt controlled by

[59] BA-MA, RH 31-IX/14, Tippelskirch circular to liaison officers, 19 Oct. 1942, fos.237–38.

[60] BA-MA, RH 31-IX/11, Gyldenfeldt to Eighth Army, 18 July 1942, fol.338.

[61] BA-MA, RH 31-IX/9, Gariboldi to Army Group B, 16 Oct. 1942, fol.232. Gariboldi also ordered the troops to be trained in urban and forest combat, see BA-MA, RH 31-IX/13, Circular 27 Sept. 1942, fol.236.

[62] BA-MA, RH 31-IX/13, Tippelskirch to Army Group B, 19 Oct. 1942, fos.2–3.

[63] BA-MA, RH 31-X/9, Vorschläge, 1 Dec. 1943, fol.4.

[64] BA-MA, MSg 2/4388, Distler – Verbindungsoffizier, fol.5.

[65] BA-MA, RH 31-IX/25, Fellmer to Tippelskirch, 24 July 1942.

[66] BA-MA, RH 31-IX/14, Tippelskirch Memorandum, 1 Nov. 1942, fol.16.

[67] BA-MA, MSg 2/4388, Distler – Verbindungsoffizier, fol.4.

[68] Massignani, *Alpini e tedeschi*, 130ff.

[69] Megargee, *Inside*, 101.

[70] They informed the Germans in November 1942 (sic!) about the Italian custom that in a group of officers only the most senior returns a salute (to a German officer of any rank), which should not be seen as a special admiration for their allies, BA-MA, RH 31-IX/9, Malaguti to Tippelskirch, 10 Nov. 1942, fol.100.

the Germans and treated as second-class ally.[71] Even though the Italians sent telegrams that showed a certain wounded affection, it was impossible to reject organisational changes altogether. One example is anti-tank warfare—a difficult problem they shared with Germany's other allies (and the Wehrmacht's infantry divisions).[72] This case demonstrated the Italians' acknowledgement of their own shortcomings and willingness both to improve their doctrines and to listen to German advice—without embracing everything they were told or throwing their own experiences and operating procedures overboard.

Italian Anti-tank Warfare

During the Second World War the preferred method to destroy a tank was a mix between passive and active methods: anti-tank rifles, anti-tank guns and artillery, tank hunters (self-propelled guns), as well as aerial support and passive defences such as mines, were often much more efficient than risking one's own precious armour.[73] Anti-tank warfare should not, therefore, be considered the same thing as armour doctrine. As the Italians never sent tanks to the Eastern Front, their only way of effectively combatting Soviet armour was, in any case, restricted to their infantry support weapons and artillery park.[74] How did the Italians think they could master this challenge?

In the 1920s and 1930s, the debate in Italy on anti-tank measures entailed various different ideas: the use of artillery, aerial support, infantry support weapons, tanks and passive defence systems. Yet, stopping tanks with direct or indirect artillery fire became the most viable option.[75] Each infantry regiment was assigned one battery (with four pieces) of the remodelled 65/17 gun as direct firing support for the offensive, but also for defensive actions against tanks at distances below 500 metres, as the 1935 manual described it.[76] In 1940, there were

---

[71] TNA, GFM 36/240, Vidussoni – Appunto per il Duce, 24 Oct. 1942, fol.15.

[72] For Romanian problems, see Axworthy, *Third Axis*, 61.

[73] Ian Hogg, *Tank Killing: Anti-tank Warfare by Men and Machines* (London: Sidgwick & Jackson, 1996), 1–32.

[74] The few self-propelled assault guns (the L 6/40) had the same 47 mm cannon as the standard 47/32 AT piece.

[75] Cappellano and Pignato, *Andare contro*, 28ff.

[76] Ibid., 32–33.

still over 700 of the 65/17 pieces and it has been argued that these latter performed better than the 47/32 in anti-tank roles thanks to their greater calibre and better armour-piercing (AP) shells.[77] As outlined above, the 47/32 had been chosen for its low weight and versatility in mountainous terrain. It remained the main anti-tank weapon, even though it was obsolete by 1940.[78] The limited capabilities in destroying medium tanks meant that the Italian infantry had to rely on the divisional artillery. This even though Italian authors had warned about such a development in the 1930s and pointed to the need for better AT guns to protect the infantry.[79] Since 1928, Italian doctrine called for close artillery support in defence against armour, including a network of outposts and passive defences with interspersed (deep) areas for artillery pieces.[80] The 1937 doctrinal guidelines defined artillery as primary tool for assisting the infantry, and thus advocated a decentralised deployment of divisional artillery.[81] In defence, all artillery pieces—including anti-tank guns—were to concentrate predominantly on the area in front of the infantry defences, in order to prevent break-ins.[82] But the artillery corps continued to have its reservations about using its large calibre guns in AT roles—for it feared force dispersion and neglect of other tasks such as interdiction and counter-battery fire. Consequently, the general artillery doctrine in 1937 devoted only one page (of 124) to anti-tank defences, while a special nineteen-page booklet on the use of artillery against armour included concepts for direct fire against tanks.[83] In general, the artillery corps intended to use smaller calibres for direct fire and close infantry support—and the guidelines for the 47/32 were written accordingly.[84]

During the Spanish Civil War, the Soviet T-26B and BT tanks and armoured fighting vehicles were successfully combated by the 65/17

---

[77] Ibid., 33, 171. The AP shell was introduced in 1939. It could perforate 40 mm armour, given an impact angle of 30 degrees at 650 metres, which helped little against most its adversaries' armour during the war. More detailed in ibid., 39, 148ff.

[78] Ibid., 38.

[79] Ibid., 41, 51ff.

[80] Ibid., 65.

[81] Stefani, *Storia della dottrina*, II:I, 638–39, 650.

[82] Ibid., 643.

[83] Cappellano and Pignato, *Andare contro*, 69ff.

[84] Ibid., 72ff.

and 47/32, which increased the Italians' confidence in their materiel.[85] The Spanish imbroglio also demonstrated deficiencies in the cooperation between infantry and artillery. The latter had often been too slow for quick redeployments but was needed at short distance to protect the infantry.[86] Yet, this closeness exposed the guns (and supply units) to counter-battery fire and fast enemy formations. It seemed to justify the artillery's hesitation about providing close support with large calibre guns. Other lessons learned in Spain were the need to separate attacking enemy tanks from their accompanying infantry and the formation of specialised tank-hunting squads.[87] In February 1939, Lieutenant-Colonel Augusto d'Amico, who had served in Spain in 1937–1938 in various important roles, wrote a detailed lessons-learned memorandum. He stressed that anti-tank guns always had to be deployed to the first lines, the divisional artillery should be motorised in order to react faster, and he thus demanded a more flexible organisation of corps and divisional artillery.[88]

The Italians interpreted the German victory over France in 1940 as a clear sign of the superiority of mobile defence and manoeuvering in anti-tank warfare.[89] Thus, a light anti-tank rifle was proposed to secure the infantry's morale and 'punch'.[90] The initial German campaigns were widely discussed in various military journals,[91] and the authors thought about ways the infantry could use terrain, machine guns and AT guns to thwart enemy armour,[92] new means of forward artillery deployment, and the possibility of creating one anti-tank regiment in every corps, which

---

[85] Ibid., 63, 80ff. Only thirty of the new 47/32 could be deployed to Spain, see ibid., 83.

[86] Stefani, *Storia della dottrina*, II:I, 651.

[87] Cappellano and Pignato, *Andare contro*, 83.

[88] ACS, T-821/231/IT 2038/470-585, Lt. Col. Augusto d'Amico – Osservazione e constatazioni fatte nella guerra di Spagna, 1 Feb. 1939, fs.575–76.

[89] [Lt. Col.] Giovanni Gatta, "La difesa contro i carri armati ed il fucile anticarro," *Rivista di Fanteria* 7, no. 9 (1940): 393–407, here 404.

[90] Ibid., 407.

[91] A different view is held by Cappellano and Pignato, *Andare contro*, 97.

[92] [Col.] Mario Mori, "Come difendersi dagli attachi delle G.U. corazzate," *Rivista di Fanteria* 8, no. 4 (1941): 155–63; [Lt. Col.] Aldo Venier, "Fanteria moderna: Fanteria di qualità," *Rivista di Fanteria* 8, no. 7–8 (1941): 336–39.

could be flexibly employed.[93] The artillery also published another circular, which emphasised its own vital role in anti-tank warfare.[94] The defeat in the deserts of North Africa in winter 1940–1941 had exposed Italian weaknesses—only the 105/28 proved helpful against British Matildas.[95] Yet, sound criticism regarding the strategic error of failing to produce an adequate anti-tank gun should not be mixed with criticism of the operational and tactical means of countering this deficiency.[96] Carrier has shown that beyond the debates in military journals, the Italians managed to improve their training and consequently also their operational efficiency in the North African desert.[97] Thus, arguments that the Italians were surprised by Russian armour and suddenly woke up to the harsh realities of modern war are hardly convincing—in fact, the Wehrmacht had been unaware of the T-34's existence.[98]

How was anti-tank warfare conducted on the Eastern Front? In general, there were two ways of defending: either with a rigid linear front (similar to the First World War) or with a mobile front with tactical-operational manoeuvering. On the Eastern Front, Hitler overruled the OKH in winter 1941 by ordering a static defence and a linear frontline without deep defensive works.[99] The units sometimes used tactical leverage to conduct a mobile defence, and thereby upheld traditional German ideas that numerical inferiority could be outbalanced by manoeuvring. Manstein's counter-offensive in the Donets basin is a fine example of the possibilities of using operational defence even against superior forces.[100] Later counter-offensives, too, speak to the Wehrmacht's ability—always based on armoured divisions—in mounting swift

---

[93] [Col.] Italo Caracciolo, "I pezzi anticarro nella grande unità," *Rivista di Fanteria* 8, no. 3 (1941): 99–105.

[94] Cappellano and Pignato, *Andare contro*, 100.

[95] Ibid., 102.

[96] One missed opportunity was to develop the 75/32 earlier, see ibid., 152ff.

[97] Carrier, "Some Reflections." On improvements in anti-tank warfare in Africa and German material assistance see also Cappellano and Pignato, *Andare contro*, 105ff., 129ff.

[98] Ben H. Shepherd, *Hitler's Soldiers: The German Army in the Third Reich* (New Haven: Yale University Press, 2016), 116.

[99] Groß, *Mythos*, 243. On German tactical behaviour in defensive actions against the Soviets see Middeldorf, *Taktik*, 133ff. Yet Middeldorf speaks largely about 1943 onwards; thus a time when the rigid defence was changed in favour of a more flexible system.

[100] Groß, *Mythos*, 244–46.

and timely concentrations of forces for mobile defences.[101] Yet, this depended on the availability of mobile reserves and was clearly not the standard modus operandi of regular infantry divisions.

In spring 1941, Roatta's circular on Italian shortcomings had argued for a forward deployment of divisional artillery to guarantee direct fire support to the infantry.[102] Notwithstanding the Italians' additional training efforts in 1941, German memoranda, and their own experiences with Russian armour,[103] all these theoretical preparations could not paint over the fact that the CSIR still lacked suitable weapons to destroy Soviet medium and heavy tanks. The 47/32 gun was no match for the Soviet T-34: it could perforate 43 mm thick armour at 500 m with a ninety-degree impact curve, and 32 mm thick plates when the angle was decreased to sixty-degrees.[104] The T-34 had 45 mm plates on all its major parts and the turret, and its front plate had a thirty-degree inclination, which greatly reduced the impact of any shell. Yet, the gun's inability to pierce the front armour did not mean that it was wholly ineffective. Italian gunners—like their German comrades—found weak spots (under the turret) or targeted the tracks to disable Soviet tanks. The Italians—much like the Germans—had been impressed by the T-34 and Cavallero even envisaged it as a possible role model for a future successor of the (not yet built) Italian heavy P 40 tank.[105] Captured materiel was used for experiments to find weak spots and suitable ammunition.[106] Tests with captured T-34s showed that several hits at short distance (300–400 metres) with the 47/32 could indeed damage it.[107] Thus, it was not impossible to destroy them, but this required time and close range—a seldom-found luxury in war. Only the heavy artillery and the 75/46 anti-aircraft guns

---

[101] Ibid., 251.

[102] Cappellano and Pignato, *Andare contro*, 122–24.

[103] Ibid., 126, 137–40.

[104] USSME, *Le operazioni*, 78. The Germans also had troubles in destroying the T-34 as neither their Panzer III and Panzer IV (with a 50 mm and 75 mm gun, respectively), nor the assault gun (StuG III with the same 75 mm calibre) could penetrate the T-34 beyond distances of 500 metres (not to speak of the almost impenetrable KV-1), Stahel, *Operation Barbarossa*, 112–13. Captured French 47 mm anti-tank guns and the novel 50 mm pieces offered some improvement, ibid., 120, 165.

[105] Cavallero Diary, 3 Feb. 1942.

[106] Cappellano and Pignato, *Andare contro*, 128.

[107] Ibid., 179–80.

could knock out T-34 and KV-1 tanks (at very close distance).[108] During the battle of Serafimovich in July 1942, Italian artillery destroyed 33 Russian tanks (T-34s and BT-7s), mainly with German-supplied 75 mm and the 75/32.[109] Indeed, the modern 75/32 was employed effectively on the Eastern Front, but the low numbers prevented it having greater benefits. The extensively used mines were not always reliable, and so many of the Italian hand grenades were duds[110] that they demanded German ones in order "not to be absolutely inferior in close combat."[111] Additionally, the few Italian aircraft could not supply meaningful 'vertical artillery', which the Germans often relied on for their operations.

Both the Germans and Italians realised this weakness in AT capabilities and knew that the ARMIR could not repulse strong armoured enemy forces without help.[112] After August 1942, the Wehrmacht attempted—despite the desperate condition on the whole front—to improve the situation by exchanging information,[113] sending their own directives,[114] supplying guns[115] or providing additional training.[116] The Wehrmacht sent some highly proficient 75 mm AT guns to the Italians, which they made good use of,[117] and further pieces were sent (also large calibre anti-aircraft guns) as late as January 1943 in the case of the *Alpini* Corps.[118] Indeed, particularly the six divisions of the *Alpini*

[108] Ibid., 127.

[109] Ibid., 175.

[110] Hamilton, *Sacrifice*, 100. On mines see Cappellano and Pignato, *Andare contro*, 248–49.

[111] BA-MA, RH 31-IX/16, Malaguti to Tippelskirch, 27 Dec. 1942, fol.32.

[112] BA-MA, RH 31-IX/15, Tippelskirch to Army Group B, 25 Nov. 1942, fol.121.

[113] Cappellano and Pignato, *Andare contro*, 202.

[114] A translation of a German document (dating from 1 December 1941) on Red Army fighting techniques was widely circulated among Italian units from February 1942, ACS, Fondo Diamanti, b.1, f.Camp. Russia, 'Diario Storico *3 Gennaio*', Valore combattivo e metodi di lotta delle singole armi dell'Armata Rossa, 20 Feb. 1942.

[115] Like the Italians, the Romanians were meant to receive six large calibre anti-tank guns per division. In total, they had fourteen divisions, which complicated matters, BA-MA, RH 31-IX/72, Telegram 30 Aug. 1942, fol.62.

[116] BA-MA, RH 31-IX/14, Tippelskirch to Eighth Army, 20 Oct. 1942, fol.210.

[117] Report by the *Celere* artillerists, BA-MA, RH 31-IX/72, 11 Aug. 1942, fol.71.

[118] BA-MA, RH 31-IX/73, Telegram from 8 Jan. 1943, fol.5. In total, eighteen additional 50 mm PaK 38 pieces were intended for the *Alpini* Corps. The neighbouring divisions, however, declared that they could not spare any in the current crisis, BA-MA, RH

Corps and the II Corps lacked artillery and anti-aircraft guns and were highly vulnerable to aerial attacks.[119] Yet, the Italians tried their best to prepare their units for the Eastern Front. The *Cuneense* Division, for example, had received specialised anti-tank training before being sent to Russia,[120] and Italian orders for artillery deployment show a grasp of the situation.[121] Thus, the oft-levelled allegation that the Italians were positioning their units without considering reserves fails to grasp the realities on the ground. Still, the Commander of Army Group B, Maximilian von Weichs, insisted on sending experienced German officers to oversee anti-tank positions,[122] and Italian crews were meant to attend extra anti-tank schooling in Germany.[123] The ARMIR's chief of staff, Malaguti, sarcastically remarked that the Germans had "discovered America" (i.e. proclaimed a discovery which was in fact nothing new to the Italians) with their proposals and was annoyed by their constant tactical advice.[124]

The Italians had hedged their bets on amassing all available artillery to support not only the infantry, but also other artillery positions.[125] Their goal was to form one continuous main battle line with as many forces as possible in order to immediately block a Soviet attack.[126]

31-IX/72, Telegram by 19th Panzer Division, 10 Jan. 1943, fol.17. Furthermore, also ammunition stocks were low, ibid., Telegram 9 Dec. 1942, fol.50.

[119] BA-MA, N 433/4, Rintelen – Das italienische Expeditionskorps in Russland, 19 Dec. 1947, fol.2. The few large calibre AA guns available were mainly used in ground combat, BA-MA, RH 31-IX/16, Gariboldi to Army Group B, 27 Dec. 1942, fol.40.

[120] Massignani, *Alpini e tedeschi*, 129.

[121] BA-MA, RH 31-IX/9, Gariboldi memorandum, 12 Oct. 1942, fol.244. See also the general orders for the placement of reserves, in BA/MA, RH 31-IX/13, Gariboldi circular, 17 Sept. 1942, fol.419.

[122] BA-MA, RH 31-IX/72, Telegram, 7 Jan. 1943, fol.24; ibid., Telegram by Tippelskirch, 9 Jan. 1943, fol.22.

[123] BA-MA, RH 31-IX/74, Telegram from 7 Jan. 1943, fol.79.

[124] BA-MA, RH 31-IX/14, Summary of meeting between Tippelskirch and Malaguti, 14 Oct. 1942, fos.297–98. Malaguti even admitted of not having passed on Tippelskirch's last memorandum to his commanding officer (Gariboldi).

[125] Cappellano and Pignato, *Andare contro*, 129.

[126] Müller, *An der Seite*, 90. A view to which the Italians concurred, see Gariboldi's orders in BA-MA, RH 31-IX/16, Maßnahmen gegen Feindangriffe, 10 Dec. 1942, fol.156–57. Additionally, no regimental command was allowed to be more than three kilometres behind the front line so officers could lead and coordinate all divisional artillery, BA-MA, RH 31-IX/14, Tippelskirch to Eighth Army, 12 Oct. 1942, fos.351–52.

German experience had shown that the Russians only made a breakthrough with their tanks after eliminating all infantry units in the first lines; hence, the enemy's tactical scheme demanded the concentration of all anti-tank weapons, heavy machine guns and artillery in the front lines (often in villages that were fortified or at bigger strongpoints) under one single command; this would allow them to protect their own infantry—and use the opportunity to hit the enemy armour at close range.[127] The forward deployment meant that the artillery not only adjusted for curtain fire, but also concentrated its guns under regimental command or the corps artillery to block advancing Soviet columns.[128] Further, one also has to note the German intention to block a flexible Italian defence (in the tactical zone) as a means of fostering a psychological mindset that simply did not include any kind of retreat.[129] In conclusion, however, the Italians were aware of how to tactically deploy against the tank menace, exchanged information with the Germans and conducted joint efforts to improve their AT performance.

Given the absence of combat reports from December 1942, we have no detailed information on how Italian gunners confronted the attacking Soviet tank corps. However, the results during the first few days show that both the artillery and the passive defences were effective. According to Cappellano and Pignato, the Italian commands over-dramatised the tank threat and relied too much on possible German support.[130] Yet, given their inadequate infantry support weapons, the low efficiency of the 47/32, ammunition shortages, mine failures, the lack of aerial[131] or armour support and ultimately the number of Soviet tanks and their powerful counter-battery fire,[132] it is little surprising that the Red Army penetrated their defensive lines. Another indication that Italian

---

[127] BA-MA, RH 31-IX/72, Einsatz der Panzerabwehrwaffen, 16 Dec. 1942, fol.37. Light and medium calibre guns were to be placed on the flanks to be effective against the tanks' weaker side and rear armour. This tactical scheme was called *Pakfront* (or anti-tank gun front), when all guns concentretated their fire on one tank at the time, Bellamy, *Absolute War*, 580.

[128] Middeldorf, *Taktik*, 79, 82–83.

[129] Safronov, *Italyanski voiska*, 76.

[130] Cappellano and Pignato, *Andare contro*, 180.

[131] The low numbers of Italian combat and support aircraft could never outbalance the situation on the ground, Massignani, *Alpini e tedeschi*, 125ff.

[132] On the importance of fire dominance Middeldorf, *Taktik*, 139–40.

operations were not outright pitiable, and that tank-scares like the one at Kantemirovka were the exception, can be found in the German after-action reports on the Second Defensive Battle on the Don.

German Ratings of Italian Divisions

Even prior to December, the CSIR was not judged as a useless *bête noire*, as it received both praise and criticism.[133] A report by Major Fellmer, liaison to the XXXV Corps (the former CSIR), from summer 1942 shows this ambivalence in German assessments. He criticised the Italians' greenness in anti-tank warfare, poor weapon maintenance, bad communication and a hefty corps staff with over 150 officers. In the same report, however, the *Celere* was praised as "very well led" and neighbouring German divisions lauded its battlefield performance near Ivanovka on 14 July 1942; the *Sforzesca* was praised for very good marching discipline and eagerness to fight, whereas the *Pasubio* appeared to be lacking either.[134] All in all, the corps had shown its value, was deemed suitable for offensive tasks, and the Germans noted the Italians' disappointment that they were not part of the great offensive towards Stalingrad.[135]

The German combat readiness reports (*Zustandsberichte*) before the Soviet counter-offensives at the Don also deserve a closer look. Even though these reports have attracted some criticism as to their reliability, the commanders certainly had no interest in falsifying their combat readiness. Who would not yearn for more materiel, supply and reinforcements? Moreover, stating full combat readiness demonstrates self-assurance and willingness to fight. There is no such thing as 'ideal' combat readiness and these reports provide a useful litmus test. Particularly, the harsh realities on the Eastern Front inhibited ideal peacetime ration and supply levels—a fact that is often forgotten in Italian reports and secondary literature. Prior to the Soviet attack, the *Pasubio*, *Sforzesca* and *Celere* were not seen as fully-suited for offensive operations, while on 16 November 1942 Malaguti and Tippelskirch judged the other divisions (which had seen less combat in the preceding months) as fully

---

[133] Compare also Giusti's reference to Schlemmer on the early performance in her *La campagna*, 140.

[134] BA-MA, RH 31-IX/25, Fellmer to Tippelskirch, 7 Aug. 1942.

[135] BA-MA, RH 31-IX/25, Weekly report to Tippelskirch, 30 July 1942.

combat-ready for offensive operations.[136] The same held true for the *Alpini* Corps in early January 1943, i.e. before the storm gathered on their sector of the front.[137]

After the retreat from the Don, the Wehrmacht undertook a general evaluation of Italian combat performance on the Eastern Front, based on liaison reports.[138] The fact that they were written briefly after such a disastrous retreat would normally preclude positive assessments. At a political level, Hitler and Goebbels openly disparaged the Italian soldiers after the setbacks of winter 1942–1943.[139] When Ciano visited Hitler's headquarters two days after the start of Operation Little Saturn, one of his advisers who enquired about Italian casualties was told by the OKW that they had suffered "none at all", as they had allegedly "never stopped running."[140] A half-hearted press initiative spoke benevolently about the Italian conduct, but had little influence on German public opinion.[141] The public "blamed the Italian troops' low fighting power for the adverse developments in North Africa in early 1943"[142] and their jokes about unmilitary Italians reached Mussolini's ear.[143] Remarkably, frontline generals disagreed with such accusations: while Göring blamed the weather for the Stalingrad disaster, Hitler spoke about Italian and Romanian treason. General Rainer Stahel—who was awarded the Oak Leaves in January 1943—argued at this occasion that the Wehrmacht, too, was beset by the problem of untalented officers

---

[136] BA-MA, RH 31-IX/9, Malaguti to Army Group B, 16 Nov. 1942, fol.73.

[137] BA-MA, RH 31-IX/18, Tippelskirch to Army Group B, 11 Jan. 1943, fol.31. Except, of course, the *Vicenza* Division, which was never intended for anything but rear duties. The neighbouring XXIV Panzer Corps and the 19th PD were in a much worse state (after severe fighting), BA-MA, RH 31-IX/18, Tippelskirch to Army Group B, 10 Jan. 1943, fol.34.

[138] An overview of the fifteen reports can be found in BA-MA, RH 31-IX/35, fol.3.

[139] Gosztony, *Hitlers Fremde Heere*, 360. It took Ribbentrop until April 1943 to convince Hitler to award Gariboldi the Knight's Cross; see also Förster, *Risse im Bündnis*, 57.

[140] Hayward, *Stopped at Stalingrad*, 269.

[141] Pelagalli, *Marras*, 224.

[142] Kallis, *Nazi Propaganda*, 158.

[143] Ciano Diaries, 1 Apr. 1942.

as replacements, which in turn guided Hitler's fury against his own generals.[144] Likewise, Hitler told Admiral Horthy that the Hungarian Second Army had utterly failed,[145] and his outbursts against the Romanians severely marred relations with this vital ally.[146] In fact, as Field Marshal Friedrich Paulus did not commit suicide and Hitler of course refused to accept any blame for the Stalingrad disaster, the Germans' allies became obvious scapegoats.[147] Indeed, Hitler and the OKW started a reciprocal blame game with Mussolini and the *Comando Supremo*—and the German leadership criticised the ARMIR for easily collapsing and not offering more resistance.[148] All too often, only the German perspective is taken: but the Italians, Romanians and Hungarians obviously refused to accept culpability and either blamed the defeat on each other or on 'German ignorance'.[149] The leadership of the Hungarian Second Army had been fully aware that their withdrawal in January—if undertaken against Hitler's steadfast order but in accordance with everyone's view—would turn them into scapegoats for Army Group B, indeed noting that the "German press will write in one hundred years time" about the Hungarian responsibility for the crumbling of the southern front.[150] Still, given the dominant myth which the Germans themselves forged on the operations, i.e. that a failure of Hungarian forces had derailed their counter-offensive, the Italians and Hungarians resorted to blaming each other instead of correcting such distortions.[151]

In this context, a look at the German after-action reports can answer one further question: namely, did they slur the Italians as incapable

[144] Wassili S. Christoforow, Wladimir G. Makarow, and Matthias Uhl, eds., *Verhört. Die Befragungen deutscher Generale und Offiziere durch die sowjetischen Geheimdienste 1945–1952* (Berlin: De Gruyter Oldenborug, 2015), 30. I would like to thank Peter Lieb for pointing me to this reference.

[145] Wimpffen, "Zweite Ungarische," 346.

[146] Förster, *Risse im Bündnis*, 48–54.

[147] After the war, the 'allies broke on our flanks' narrative was supplemented, as leading Wehrmacht generals blamed Hitler in particular for the strategic disaster at Stalingrad, but Manstein, e.g. accused also Paulus; see Manfred Kehrig, "Stalingrad im Spiegel der Memoiren deutscher Generale," in *Stalingrad. Mythos und Wirklichkeit einer Schlacht*, eds. Wolfram Wette and Gerd R. Ueberschär (Frankfurt: Fischer, 2012), 205–13.

[148] Förster, *Risse im Bündnis*, 55ff.

[149] Gosztony, *Hitlers Fremde Heere*, 334.

[150] Wimpffen, "Zweite Ungarische," 227.

[151] Ibid., 38, 256–57.

soldiers and hold them responsible for the defeat (as later memoirs and scholars did)? As is so often the case with the Italian Army and the Axis alliance, sources below the top political level show a rather mixed picture. The German liaison officer to the *Sforzesca* lamented that not all vehicles had been destroyed during the retreat,[152] while the head of the DVK to the *Celere*, Lieutenant-Colonel Rehse, recounted the Italian artillery's valorous fight until the bitter end.[153] Rehse criticised, however, the poor positioning of the infantry during rear-guard actions (also in the case of the Germans), not least because of the high casualties among officers, who were then severely missed to uphold order during the retreat and to erect new positions.[154] The translator attached to the *Torino* mentioned traffic problems in his very benevolent report, blaming these also on German units.[155] He emphasised the wholesome cooperation during the withdrawal, despite the fact that on 23 December the *Torino* had lost all its regimental and battalion commanders and almost all its company leaders,[156] had not received food for five days and was later forced to abandon over 2000 sick and wounded on 15 January because of missing transport.[157]

The *Pasubio* also received a positive overall score sheet. This is rather surprising, as all staff and regimental officers, as well as 90 per cent of the rank-and-file had been replaced before the main Soviet assault in December.[158] The artillery was an exception—its officers had volunteered to remain on the Don. Thus, the German report described their conduct as yet another proof of the generally "excellent" Italian artillery, which had "stood its ground everywhere in Russia."[159] In general, the Germans deemed the artillery as the best branch of the *Regio Esercito*. The officers were hand-picked and often the finest of their annual cohort

---

[152] BA-MA, RH 31-IX/35, Joos – Rückzugskämpfe *Sforzesca*, 19 Nov. 1943, fos.5–11, here fol.8.

[153] BA-MA, RH 31-IX/35, Rehse – Gefechtsbericht *Celere*, Mar. 1943, fos.12–16.

[154] Ibid., fos.13–15.

[155] BA-MA, RH 31-IX/35, Hammann – Gefechtsbericht *Torino*, 5 Mar. 1943, here fol.24.

[156] See also the *Torino*'s own report, in BA-MA, RH 31-IX/35, fol.107.

[157] BA-MA, RH 31-IX/35, Hammann – Gefechtsbericht *Torino*, 5 Mar. 1943, fol.30.

[158] BA-MA, RH 31-IX/35, Eder—Several reports, n.d., fos.32–52, here fol.40.

[159] Ibid., fos.40, 44, 46.

at the academy.[160] Unsurprisingly, the Germans thought they held a qualitative edge over their comrades in the infantry.[161] Even though the Germans often criticised the artillery's cooperation with the infantry, they hinted at the constantly good results of the gunners, and also praised the pioneers and supply forces.[162] The account on the *Pasubio* also noted good cooperation with the neighbouring 298th ID, despite the usual remarks on the poor Italian communication equipment and sporadic instances of friction during the retreat.[163]

The *Ravenna* was complimented on its steadfastness (despite painful losses) near the Mamon bridgehead.[164] During the tumultuous retreat, staff officers attempted to reach troops that had been sealed off, and the Germans honoured General Francesco Dupont and his staff for energetically trying to set up defences at Taly.[165] Thus, the report concluded: "it is apparent that the *Ravenna* Division did not 'run away' on the first day, as often claimed particularly by the [German] 298th Infantry Division, but fought day and night between the 11th and 17th December 1942. A German division might have held out a few days longer, due to better materiel and weapons, but would have had to retreat as well."[166] It is interesting to note that the German report did not blame the *Ravenna* for giving way too easily but realised the material shortcomings faced and the immense pressure from the Red Army.

Yet, why did the *Ravenna* ultimately crack? The report described the almost complete lack of fuel, which inhibited the transportation of troops, the wounded, supplies and ammunition; and caused the loss of the division's artillery and vehicles.[167] Shoes were also seen as a major

---

[160] Artillery and engineer junior officers received an extra two-year course of training at their branch school of application, which apparently improved their wartime performance, Sullivan, "Primacy," 73.

[161] BA-MA, RH 31-X/9, Vorschläge, 1 Dec. 1943, fol.7.

[162] Ibid., fos.6–7.

[163] BA-MA, RH 31-IX/35, Eder – Several reports, n.d., fos.32–52, here, fos.32, 43.

[164] BA-MA, RH 31-IX/35, Pertner – Gefechtsbericht *Ravenna*, 20 Mar. 1943, fos.60–74, here fos.60–64.

[165] Ibid., fos.65–66.

[166] Ibid., fol.69. Also the 298th ID suffered such high casualties that it had to be regrouped as 387th ID.

[167] BA-MA, RH 31-IX/35, Pertner – Gefechtsbericht *Ravenna*, 20 Mar. 1943, fos.69–70.

deficiency. Yet, what was criticised was not the quality or quantity of the boots, but the poor care soldiers took of them.[168] The account further argued that the *Ravenna* had only six suitable 75 mm AT guns against Soviet armour and he dismissed the 47 mm as wholly unsuitable.[169] However, the most remarkable part concerned a decisive encounter during which the Soviet armour broke through the defensive lines. The *Ravenna* was short of anti-tank weapons and so the Germans had sent an anti-tank unit comprising two 88 mm and five 75 mm PaK 40 guns as support.[170] But the German unit was not under Italian command, which led to quarrels over its tactical deployment. The Italians wanted to position it near the frontline in order to concentrate fire on Soviet armour as soon as they reached the Italian minefields, and thus also cover their own infantry strongpoints. This was, after all, not only Italian protocol but also what German directives had told them incessantly. Yet, the German officers decided to place their guns well behind Italian infantry positions in order to counter possible Soviet breakthroughs—perhaps hinting at a lack of trust in the Italian infantry's combat skills.[171] When the Soviets attacked, their tanks fired on the Italian strongpoints and kept them in check, while the infantry cleared the mines and then advanced—without the Italian or German guns' lending support to the Italian infantry.[172] The Germans had obliterated their own guidelines and left the Italian positions unprotected. Therefore, the German (!) report concluded that the misplaced anti-tank weapons had led to the Soviet breakthrough, and considered this to be the decisive moment as the first (and main) defensive line was overrun.[173]

Despite this assessment, the rapporteur apparently remembered to think of his superiors and added the following passage: "it is clear that

---

[168] Allegedly the soldiers wore their shoes for two or three months without using shoe cream and fats; this dried them up and destroyed the leather, BA-MA, RH 31-IX/35, Pertner – Gefechtsbericht *Ravenna*, 20 Mar. 1943, fos.70.

[169] Ibid.

[170] Ibid., fol.71.

[171] One could argue, in defence of the German officer on the spot, that he perhaps lacked the transport or fuel to move his large calibre pieces and thus decided for a more backward placement. Moreover, the unit had arrived only the day before.

[172] BA-MA, RH 31-IX/35, Pertner – Gefechtsbericht *Ravenna*, 20 Mar. 1943, fos.71–72.

[173] Ibid., fol.72.

the German soldier is superior to the Italian in every regard [...but] one must not forget that the German soldier is better armed, equipped, trained and fed. This does not justify, however, that the German soldier deems and treats his ally as merely half a soldier."[174] The many quarrels between the *Ravenna* and the 298th Infantry Division led him to believe that this experience and uncomradely behaviour left a bad memory among the Italian soldiers.[175] Indeed, General Marras too had noted Tippelskirch's and the 298th division's tendency to blame Italian units.[176] Two things stand out here: both the German ability for critical self-assessment, and the benevolent tone in which the rapporteur described the Italian operations. The reports were far from one-sided slurs about poor Italian performance. Wartime British evaluations, too, reached similar conclusions. The *Pasubio* was said to have seen "more active service than most Italian divisions and maintained a good record throughout", while the *Torino* was ascribed a "good war record," and the *Sforzesca* and *Ravenna* were deemed "of average standard."[177]

Of all Italian units, the *Cosseria* probably received the most negative balance sheet. The report argued that their front had collapsed due to very strong enemy forces, but also a deficit in strongpoints (which were not properly linked with trenches), little cover for their own artillery, inadequate protection against cold, poor anti-tank training, little ammunition for artillery and bad cooperation between the artillery and infantry.[178] Thus, the division's retreat itself was sketched as unorganised, and the soldiers failed to set up new defensive positions despite the personal courage and efforts made by their commanders.[179] In contrast, the same German liaison officer emphasised the combat value of the *Julia*, which he thought to be composed of much better soldiers than the *Cosseria*.[180] The account cited numerous successful counter-attacks and good cooperation with German tanks and self-propelled assault

---

[174] Ibid., fol.73.

[175] Ibid., fol.74.

[176] Pelagalli, *Marras*, 209.

[177] TNA, WO 208/4550. See the sections on the *Pasubio, Torino, Sforzesca,* and *Ravenna*.

[178] BA-MA, RH 31-IX/35, Salazer – Gefechtsbericht *Cosseria*, 18 Mar. 1943, fol.80.

[179] Ibid., fos.79, 81.

[180] BA-MA, RH 31-IX/35, Salazer – Gefechtsbericht *Julia*, 18 Mar. 1943, fos.84–89, here fol.88.

guns, whose support made the *Julia* tenaciously resist and willingly attack Russian armour—despite inadequate anti-tank training.[181] The reports on the *Alpini* should be read with caution. For the Germans, the attacks in December had already confirmed all their stereotypes about their allegedly unreliable allies.[182] Even though the *Alpini* Corps did not crack at first, it had been well aware of its dangerously exposed position, and yet requests for withdrawal were dismissed.[183] Thus, it is plain wrong to claim that no precautions were taken for an eventual retreat.[184] Before the January offensive, the defensive works erected by the *Alpini* were deemed as good or even very good; and Lieutenant-General Nasci was acclaimed for his frontline inspections, tactical skill and close cooperation with the Germans.[185] The German after-action report vividly portrayed the sufferings during the retreat, with marching times of 12–15 h per day, covering 300 kilometres over open ground with almost no food and shelter. Nasci was praised for his attempts to get his men back to safe areas and his leadership in the battle for Nikolayevka.[186]

The Germans subsequently wrote two memoranda to summarise what had happened. The report by Major Schlubeck focused mainly on the II Corps and XXXV Corps. Schlubeck criticised the *Ravenna* for the deficient coordination between its few anti-tank crews, infantry and commanders, but warmly described the *Pasubio* and *Torino*'s fierce resistance up till the order for retreat was given on 19 December.[187] The report argued that a feeling of helplessness against enemy armour had shattered

[181] Ibid., fos.85–86, 88.

[182] Massignani, *Alpini e tedeschi*, 133.

[183] Burgwyn, *Mussolini*, 207–8.

[184] For the accusation, see e.g. Tolloy, *Con l'Armata*, 167; who likened this to the defeats at Custozza and Caporetto.

[185] The defensive works are described in BA-MA, RH 31-IX/25, Reports to Tippelskirch, 29 Oct. and 6 Nov. 1942, in contrast to report from 23 Oct. 1942. On Nasci, see BA-MA, RH 31-IX/25, Fellmer to Tippelskirch, 16 Oct. 1942.

[186] BA-MA, RH 31-IX/35, Salazer – 'Gefechtsbericht Rückmarsch *Alpini*', 23 Mar. 1943, fos.95–96, 99. Nasci had experienced the Greek campaign in 1940 and had opposed the withdrawal upon the Greek counterattack, thereby gaining a reputation as steadfast officer, DS CS, II:I, 23 Nov. 1940. See also W. Faccini and G. Ferrari, "Gabriele Nasci. Generale degli Alpini," in *Studi Storico-Militari 1991* (Rome: USSME, 1993), 363–544.

[187] BA-MA, RH 31-IX/35, Schlubeck – Auszug und Schlussfolgerung aus den Gefechtsberichten, 12 Apr. 1943, fos.118–21, here fos.118–19. The *Ravenna* had reportedly been attacked by around 200 enemy tanks.

their inner cohesion. Previously, the Italians had been optimistic and showed "no defeatism" despite their bad materiel, inadequate weapons and the poor state of defensive works.[188] The main reason for this was identified in the "excellent" conduct of the commanding officers, who assured cohesion among their men through personal leadership; thus, the report concluded: "one cannot say that the officers have failed."[189]

The second conclusive memorandum was written in November 1943, hence, after the Italians had signed the armistice with the Allies and long after the events on the Don. Besides the reports on the *Cosseria* and the *Julia*, First Lieutenant Salazer, a translator in the DVK to the *Alpini* Corps, also wrote the brief on the *Alpini* and this conclusive report, since many higher-ranked liaison officers had been killed or captured. He criticised the *Sforzesca*'s performance in August, and particularly the lower officer ranks.[190] In general, he cast the Italians as unprepared for the winter attacks, as they were "not used to Russian winters."[191] Yet, Salazer seems to have omitted the experience the Italians' had gathered since August 1941 and the fact that most Italian soldiers were trained for Alpine combat or were in fact mountain troops.[192] Thus the oft-nurtured stereotype of Italians being 'snow shocked' in Russia is hardly convincing. Additionally, the Italians had closely studied the winter campaign in 1941–1942 and noted the skilful Soviet attacks, the chaos in the rear and dangers of static defence lines—exactly the scenarios that were repeated in winter 1942–1943.[193] However, also the close observation of ongoing campaigns could not prevent another defeat.

First Lieutenant Salazer credited tactical successes largely to the DVK and German leadership,[194] but admitted that the *Celere*, *Torino* and

---

[188] Ibid., fol.120.

[189] Ibid., fos.119–20. Particularly the high combat losses of the *Torino* were taken as evidence of the officer's heroic leadership from the front. The report also entailed minor criticism of the junior officers.

[190] BA-MA, RH 31-IX/35, Salazer – Zusammenfassung der Gefechtsberichte, 12 Nov. 1943 [herafter 'Zusammenfassung'], fos.127–33, here fol.127.

[191] Ibid., fol.128.

[192] The Germans had noted in earlier assessments that most Italian troops were trained for combat in Alpine regions under severe conditions, BA-MA, RH 2/1892, Das italienische Kriegsheer, Jan. 1940, fol.5.

[193] ACS, T-821/252/IT 3033/15-28, [Marras] – La campagna invernale in Russia, [Spring] 1942, here esp. fs.19, 21–26.

[194] BA-MA, RH 31-IX/35, Salazer – Zusammenfassung, 12. Nov. 1943, fol.131.

Pasubio had—by and large—held their lines until the order for retreat was given; thus even the critical Salazer added: "despite all shortcomings and deficiencies that have erupted during the operations, it is not only exaggerated but plain wrong to uphold the claim that the Italians merely ran away."[195] He particularly approved of the *Torino*, *Tridentina* and *Julia*. He still deemed Italian divisions, like the Romanians and Hungarians, weaker than their German counterparts, but thought it possible to improve their value by deploying them jointly with (or next to) the Wehrmacht.[196] As reasons for this inferiority he named the bad NCOs, and above all deficiencies in anti-tank guns and anti-tank training (this, apart from his racial remarks about inferior bodily and moral characteristics of the Italians).[197] Still, Salazer concluded, one should acknowledge the many positive aspects of the Italian engagement as well as the officers' heroism and tenacity of the men.[198]

In conclusion, the majority of the Italian divisions deployed to the Don were depicted rather well. None had cracked easily or 'run away' as later accounts often suggested. The Italian formations were overwhelmed, much like the Germans and other satellite armies, by superior Soviet arms and numbers. Beyond these situational factors, they also suffered from homemade shortcomings, such as a rigid command, bad materiel and inadequate anti-tank training. The Italian soldiers were no 'chickens', but were they 'lions' led by donkeys? It is intriguing to further look at the Italian officers; especially as research on German divisions has shown the vital nexus between the GOC and the divisions' leadership culture and operational effectiveness.[199] Postwar scholarship and most memoirs were very critical of the senior leadership and helped feed to a 'lions led (or even abandoned) by donkeys' narrative. And yet, we repeatedly find difficulty in locating primary sources for such assessments—other than sporadic anecdotal evidence or reciprocal blame-laying in generals' memoirs.

---

[195] Ibid., fos.129, 132.
[196] Ibid., fos.132f.
[197] Ibid., fol.133.
[198] Ibid.
[199] Hartmann, *Wehrmacht*, 135ff.

GERMAN RATINGS OF ITALIAN OFFICERS

To look at Italian sources alone might provide a biased picture. But what do German sources tell us? Were the Italian officers as incompetent as many authors would have us believe? These German sources can help us discredit some myths, as they provided a very balanced and, indeed, rather positive picture of the Italian officer corps. As well as the liaison reports, this sections also draws on a file from the German military archives in which 547 Italian officers—mainly colonels and generals—were described on index cards.[200] The information therein regarded their position and career, and also featured a little sketch on their character and abilities. General Enno von Rintelen, military attaché since 1936 (and his aide Friedrich-Karl von Plehwe), authored many evaluations on Italians serving in Rome, while liaison officers and *Fremde Heere West* (the military intelligence branch observing western armies) also provided many assessments. Thus, one cannot claim that Rintelen—who was sometimes perceived as pro-Italian—had fostered biased assessments without actually having seen these officers in the field. Of these 547 officer ratings, around fifteen per cent are without comment; of the rest, two-thirds are mainly positive, whereas really negative characterisations are very much the exception. However, the few that do exist are usually cited in order to confirm existing stereotypes—sometimes even inaccurately.[201] In addition, the officers concerned were either seen as incompetent by the Italians themselves or were not field commanders, but rather had 'political' roles, like Ugo Cavallero, Ettore Bastico (1876–1972), or Giuseppe Castellano.[202] Likewise, Italian officers

---

[200] BA-MA, RH 2/1672. The Germans had started this system of evaluating Italian officers during the Abyssinian War, see BA-MA, RH 67/37, Fischer – Zusammenstellung über die höheren Stäbe in Ostafrika, 2 Apr. 1936. The Italians edited a similar, but shorter, file on the Germans. It was started during the French campaign, but only half-heartedly updated and included very few detailed descriptions. It is found in ACS, T-821/475/IT 5982.

[201] The slating of General Giuseppe Castellano for example, is taken from the American *The Saturday Evening Post* of September 1944 and is not a German remark. Compare BA-MA, RH 2/1672, fol.157, to Jürgen Förster, "Die Wehrmacht und die Probleme der Koalitionskriegführung," in *Die "Achse" im Krieg. Politik, Ideologie und Kriegführung 1939-1945*, eds. Lutz Klinkhammer, Amedeo Osti Guerrazzi, and Thomas Schlemmer (Paderborn: Schöningh, 2010), 108–21, here 119–20.

[202] Also the frequently panned Graziani received much better ratings than one would expect. General Hans Röttger ascribed him highest leadership qualities and operational talent, even during the days of the RSI, BA-MA, N/422/10, Notizen und Ausarbeitungen

branded as anti-German on their index card could still receive good assessments as military leaders—and vice versa, being inclined towards the Axis did not automatically lead to a good evaluation. Hence, the Germans appear to have regarded this list as register of military capabilities and not a matter of personal favours, animosities and the like. At the same time, there was no need to soft pedal criticism: the index cards were for internal German use. In sum, these files constitute an exceptionally objective and frank view from numerous perspectives.

Messe was described as the most capable of all Italian generals on the Eastern Front. He was portrayed as a man with quick apprehension, who handed out clear orders, and did not shy away from personal responsibility or sending away officers that he thought unsuitable for their tasks.[203] One report therefore concluded: "put in a German uniform, everyone would have believed him to be a German general."[204] When he was recalled to Italy, the German liaison officer noted the troops' longing for his strong character and leadership.[205] His Chief of Operations and later Chief of Staff, Colonel Umberto Utili, was depicted as a very clear-minded and smart officer.[206] Messe's successor, Francesco Zingales, was seen as ambitious, not very pro-German and with "average military skills."[207] Indeed, an Italian advancement board voted unanimously against promoting him in March 1942[208]; thus reached similar conclusions to the Germans.

Gariboldi had earned a reputation as highly uncooperative partner in North Africa, which was confirmed in Russia, but the prior experience

---

einzelner Kapitel zu Röttiger „Der Feldzug in Italien", 1948, fol.43; see also BA-MA, RH 2/1672, fol.266A.

[203] Schlemmer, *Italiener*, 22.

[204] BA-MA, MSg 2/4388, Distler – Verbindungsoffizier, fol.16.

[205] Additionally, also his chief of staff and many other experienced officers had left their units, BA-MA, RH 31-IX/25, Fellmer to Tippelskirch, 5 Nov. 1942.

[206] BA-MA, MSg 2/4388, Distler – Verbindungsoffizier, fol.36. The same argument was made by Fellmer, in BA-MA, RH 2/1672, fol.523. Utili became a hero during the so-called War of Liberation between 1943–1945 and always remained close to Messe—who held the commemorative speech at his funeral, see AUSSME, Fondo Messe, b.X(27), c.11, Letter by Edmondo De Renzi to Messe, 28 Sept. 1953.

[207] BA-MA, RH 2/1672, fol.545.

[208] ACS, T-821/146/IT 2228/102.

possibly also influenced how the Germans viewed him.[209] Already on 20 December 1942, Cavallero noted the tendency even within the Italian Army to blame the setback on Gariboldi.[210] After the retreat, General Marras visited the front between in March 1943. The German Captain von Massenbach accompanied him and subsequently wrote down his impressions of senior Italian officers. He described Gariboldi as an "old, white-heared gentlemen, very quiet, lacking any dash; making a completely apathetic and resigned impression."[211] His Chief of Staff, Bruno Malaguti, however, was generally rated much more positively—even after the retreat.[212] Massenbach described him as loyal, very efficient (drafting all important orders himself) and as a human control centre of the army whose door and ears were always open.[213] So, too, an Italian officer promotion board rated him as clearly above average.[214] Thus, all negative remarks on Gariboldi aside, his chief seemed to have been an excellent choice.

The II Corps' command received less cordial remarks. The commander, Giovanni Zanghieri, was thought to be a pessimistic royalist and poor soldier.[215] Tippelskirch even described him as "completely useless and insignificant."[216] Gariboldi, too, deemed Zanghieri's orders too complicated and he allegedly never checked if they were actually carried out.[217] His will to cooperate with the Wehrmacht was regarded as badly as that of his chief, Colonel Ugo Almici, who was portrayed as "very nervous" and almost "hostile" in his bearing towards the Wehrmacht.[218] The corps' divisional commanders were rated better. In the *Ravenna*,

[209] BA-MA, MSg 2/4388, Distler – Verbindungsoffizier, fol.5. Ironically, many Italians considered him as too soft on the Germans, see TNA, GFM 36/240, Vidussoni – Appunto per il Duce, 24 Oct. 1942, fos.15–16.
[210] Cavallero Diary, 20 Dec. 1942.
[211] BA-MA, RH 2/2894, Massenbach – Bericht über Reise mit General Marras zur 8. ital. Armee vom 9. bis 14.3.1943 [hereafter cited as 'Bericht'], fol.7.
[212] BA-MA, RH 2/1672, fol.302.
[213] BA-MA, RH 2/2894, Massenbach – Bericht, fol.7. He even ascribed him a great sense of humour.
[214] ACS, T-821/146/IT 2228/109.
[215] BA-MA, MSg 2/4388, Distler – Verbindungsoffizier, fol.7. Zanghieri only arrived in Russia in summer 1942, but had been a widely respected figure and military writer before.
[216] BA-MA, RH 2/2894, Massenbach – Bericht, fol.7.
[217] BA-MA, RH 2/1672, fol.547.
[218] Ibid., fol.6.

the GOC Edoardo Nebbia was reportedly very proficient[219] and his chief of staff (and successor as GOC), Francesco Dupont, was described as "active, able, [with a] can-do personality. Good and thoughtful organiser and commander [... who had] shown his superiority *vis-à-vis* other Italian divisional commanders in Russia, and demonstrate[d] a particularly positive attitude in cooperating."[220] In a discussion with other German officers after (!) the retreat, the highly critical Tippelskirch called him the "best Italian divisional commander on the Eastern Front", and stressed that he had taken good care of his soldiers.[221] His operations officer and divisional staff were complimented, despite criticising the fairly bloated staff (twenty-five officers).[222] In fact, the accusation of bloated Italian staffs has often been raised. However, German infantry divisions also had around twenty officers in their staff. To assess this claim one would have to know the exact force levels and the number of staff officers to make comparisons to German divisions. Vidussoni, too, criticised the high number of officers (often without combat experience) in the ARMIR's staff (240) and in the *Alpini* Corps (100), and the long distance of their headquarters to the front (several dozen kilometres).[223] Still, even if one takes these numbers and—bearing in mind that the Italians only had one army in the East—one should also compare it to the German case. In an exemplary depiction of the German Eighteenth Army command staff in 1941, Hürter accounted for up to 100 officers, 130 NCOs, 25 civil servants and several hundred further members of the Wehrmacht, and showed that its headquarters—once the frontline had become static—was 45 kilometres to the rear.[224]

The commander of the *Sforzesca*, General Carlo Pellegrini, was praised as an experienced trooper and colonial officer, who was widely respected

---

[219] Ibid., fol.364. Nebbia left for North Africa and assumed command of the X Corps during the battle of El Alamein.

[220] BA-MA, RH 2/1672, fol.199.

[221] BA-MA, RH 2/2894, Massenbach – Bericht, fos.7–8.

[222] Ibid.

[223] TNA, GFM 36/240, Vidussoni – Appunto per il Duce, 24 Oct. 1942, fol.13.

[224] Johannes Hürter, "Die Wehrmacht vor Leningrad. Krieg und Besatzungspolitik der 18. Armee im Herbst und Winter 1941/42," in *Der deutsche Krieg im Osten 1941–1944. Facetten einer Grenzüberschreitung*, eds. Christian Hartmann, Johannes Hürter, Peter Lieb, and Dieter Pohl (Munich: Oldenbourg, 2009), 95–153, here 98.

and close to the needs of his men.[225] His chief, Giovanni Fiore, the son-in-law of the Fascist *quadrumvir* Cesare Maria De Vecchi, was cast in a less positive light. The Germans had noticed certain deficiencies in his handling of infantry units (as an artillery man) but noted that he held firm in times of crisis.[226] General Michele Vaccaro was seen as idle and corpulent, but nonetheless a courageous soldier and skilful tactician.[227]

In the *Alpini* Corps, the average ratings were even better. The commanding general Nasci was praised as extremely capable and close to his men, with a good performance during the operations in January.[228] The *Julia*'s chief of staff, Michele Molinari, was also deemed diligent and thorough.[229] General Reverberi (*Tridentina*) was praised as a good soldier,[230] and the GOC of the *Cuneense*, Emilio Battisti (1889–1971), has been described as an exemplary leader—riding on horseback at the head of his troops during the retreat, and thus spreading confidence through his calm leadership.[231] This backs up claims that the men had full confidence in their officers.[232] Nasci, Reverberi and Battisti stayed at the front with their men—refusing to be flown out—and personally led counter-charges in contested villages.[233] The (then) Colonel Mario Carloni was repeatedly mentioned as brave and excellent commander, who was very friendly towards Germany and proficient even in desperate situations.[234] Carloni commanded the 6th *Bersaglieri* Regiment (*Celere*),

[225] BA-MA, MSg 2/4388, Distler – Verbindungsoffizier, fol.10.
[226] Ibid., fol.10.
[227] Ibid., fol.7. Vaccaro was responsible for the division's infantry.
[228] BA-MA, RH 2/1672, fol.360.
[229] Ibid., fol.346.
[230] Ibid., fol.429.
[231] Hamilton, *Sacrifice*, 124. Knox, on the other hand, argued that Battisti "gave up any semblance of command during the retreat from the Don" and relied on Nuto Revelli—a rather dubious crown witness, Knox, "Italian Armed Forces," 171, 179.
[232] Porcari, "La 'Cuneense,'" 284.
[233] Hamilton, *Sacrifice*, 134; Petacco, *L'armata*, 142, 145.
[234] BA-MA, Rh 2/1672, fol.150; BA-MA, MSg 2/4388, Distler – Verbindungsoffizier, fos.79–80. Carloni was one of six Italian holders of the German Cross in gold. After the 8 September 1943, he fought for Mussolini's RSI, was later found guilty for war crimes (having shot an Allied POW), and demoted to Colonel. In his memoirs, Carloni made counter-arguments to the narrative of Revelli and others. Jointly with other generals, among which also Emilio Battisti, he edited several accounts on the Russian campaign, see e.g. Emilio Battisti, Mario Carloni, Guido Caromio, Umberto Guglielmotti, and Armando Odenigo, *Italianzy kaputt? (Con l'Armir in Russia)* (Rome: CEN, 1959).

which formed the rear-guard from mid-December and then fought together with many *Alpini* units. Despite the chaotic retreat and heavy losses, Carloni's men continued to fight as a cohesive force jointly with German units,[235] and reached Gomel in good order.[236]

In conclusion, the German after-action reports and other miscellaneous assessments only cast Gariboldi and the II Corps' command in a negative light, while most other remarks on the senior leadership were positive. Nonetheless, the caricature of Italian generals as corpulent, lacking imagination and detached from reality (and the front lines) remains an enduring myth. In many instances, 'funny' depictions of the Italians as militarily useless clowns are readily taken at face value, without any proper reflection on the source.[237] Hence, allegations of military amateurishness—whether advanced by the Germans, in Italian memoir literature, or by serious scholars—should be reconsidered.[238] We should not forget that the more senior officers in particular had all seen combat during the First World War (mainly in mountainous regions), and held various decorations for bravery. For example, Malaguti had received one Bronze and three Silver Medals for Military Valour, and Battisti had been decorated for service in the First World War, in the Italian colonies, in the Spanish Civil War and on the French and Albanian fronts. In fact, one could accuse them rather more of militarism—fighting almost incessantly in wars since 1911—than of inexperience. Yet another stereotype has it that they rested on their laurels after 1918 and indulged in wine

---

His memoirs were first published in 1956 and subsequently reprinted, inter alia by rightwing publishers, see Carloni, *La campagna di Russia*.

[235] BA-MA, RH 31-IX/35, Schlubeck to Steinbauer, 16 Feb. 1943, fos.110–11. The Italian 75/18 pieces continued to fight even when they ran out of armour-piercing ammunition. His own report can be found in BA-MA, RH 31-IX/35, fos.113ff.; and in his memoirs, Carloni, *La campagna di Russia*, 63ff.

[236] ACS, T-821/354/IT 4511/647-661, Lt. Col. Manaresi – Rapporto sull'invio del 9º treno A.P.E. in Russia (febbraio-marzo 1943), 24 Mar. 1943, f.656.

[237] See the classic caricature e.g. in Alfio Caruso, *Tutti i vivi all'assalto. L'epopea degli alpini dal Don a Nikolajevka* (Milan: Longanesi 2003), 22. Even highly respected historians have uncritically cited an assessment by Léon Degrelle (sic!), who slandered the Italians in his post-war memoirs, Müller, *An der Seite*, 86.

[238] Schlemmer has argued in several articles that the Italian officers on the Eastern Front proved to be open-minded, flexible and capable to learn, e.g. Schlemmer, "Zwischen Erfahrung und Erinnerung," 431.

and pasta.[239] To be sure, colonial experiences differed from armoured warfare on the Eastern Front; but as shown above, the Italians were precisely aware what adaptation was necessary—not least thanks to their experience in very diverse military conflicts, on each occasion demanding learning on the spot.

As the liaisons' after-action reports have shown, the German view of the Italian battalion, regimental, and divisional commanders was very positive. On the other hand, NCOs and junior officers were rated less favourably. In fact, experienced German officers likened the chaotic behaviour during the retreat to the French Army in 1940[240] and complained incessantly about the lack of NCOs and junior officers, who were not there to uphold discipline during the retreat.[241] Was it not, then, this group who had not learned their lessons and failed their men? Given that most of the memoir literature was written by the lower ranks of junior officers (or reserve officers), NCOs and soldiers, we should also ask if their narrative of abandonment and sacrifice was instrumental in brushing over their own mediocre military track record and looking for scapegoats further up the chain of command.

Similarly, German assessments of Romanian officers were better than conventional wisdom has it.[242] A sheet from July 1942 rated the commanders of the Third Romanian Army, the subordinated army corps and divisions—including commanding generals, chiefs of staff and operations officers. In total 61 officers were assessed. Only one was rated as poor, the vast majority as good and several as very good or excellent.[243] Most Romanian divisions were rated positively and capable of operating independently, or were even deemed suitable for difficult tasks before the Stalingrad disaster.[244] Thus, the stereotypes about the Romanian Army

---

[239] See the rather odd comment in Knox, "'Totality' and Disintegration," 83.

[240] BA-MA, MSg 2/4388, Distler – Verbindungsoffizier, fol.77.

[241] Italian reports criticised rear units for their insufficient "military spirit", Pelagalli, *Marras*, 212.

[242] For some thoughts on comparisons of Romanian and Italian performances, see Harward, "First Among Unequals," 456ff.; Axworthy, "Peasant Scapegoat," 221–32. Axworthy cited the numbers of Knight's Cross (*Ritterkreuz*) holders as an indicator for a better Romanian battlefield performance. Yet, scholars have been sceptical of taking the Knight's Cross as measurement for combat performance, Töppel, "Das Ritterkreuz."

[243] BA-MA, RH 20-17/766, Stellenbesetzung der 3. rum. Armee, 30 July 1942.

[244] BA-MA, RH 20-17/766, Gefechtswert der großen rum. Verbände, 30 July 1942.

should also be reconsidered[245]; and a closer look at the German liaison reports on Hungarian units would be another fruitful step. Maybe the Germans were wrong in their assessments, but their one-sided and discourteous criticism came only with hindsight at a point when scapegoats were needed. Moreover, those closest to the events wrote the most balanced and positive critiques. German appraisals and criticism of their allies should thus be read carefully within the context of military operations, the character of the individual providing the rating, and their date.

A memorandum on the employment of mixed German and Italian units in December 1943 argued that a vast majority of the senior officers (above the rank of major) had proficiently worked towards common objectives in Russia,[246] and despite shortcomings they had cooperated "with great trust and a lot of good will."[247] The content and tone of this report is all the more important for the fact that it was written after both the dramatic retreat in Russia and 8 September 1943. It hints at the pragmatism of coalition warfare below the strategic political level. Like earlier reports, the memorandum noted the soldiers' loyalty and bravery (when properly led), the importance of providing the men with direct role models and of improving officer-to-man relations, as well as the need to use their strong national pride as motivation.[248] The NCOs were painted as lacking authority, failing to create cohesion and overburdened with administrative work. The junior officers fared little better. They were portrayed as "unmilitary and dependent", poorly schooled, without feelings of responsibility or closeness to their soldiers.[249] Thus, the memorandum made two suggestions for the future employment of Italian forces—even envisaging joint regiments.[250] This document shows not only the intimate knowledge the Germans had acquired about weaknesses in the *Regio Esercito*, but also their deep thinking about coalition warfare on the tactical level, and the fact that as late as December 1943, the judgements on the Italians were more balanced than may be expected.

---

[245] On the genesis of this perception, see Harward, "First Among UnEquals."
[246] BA-MA, RH 31-X/9, Vorschläge, 1 Dec. 1943, fol.2.
[247] Ibid., fol.3.
[248] Ibid.
[249] Ibid., fol.2.
[250] Ibid., fos.6–8.

To conclude our remarks on operational performance: we should not take too seriously anecdotal evidence and the derogatory remarks about the Italians as generally bad soldiers. Rather, it is important to use the available sources to focus on tangible operational and tactical criticism. An analysis of German after-action reports and various officer assessments leads to a more balanced picture. First, the Italian infantry divisions were notably lacking in the necessary equipment and training to effectively combat Soviet tanks. Yet they did successfully fight against the Red Army—even if they attacked with manageable armoured forces. The 'tank scare' at Kantemirovka was an exception. The Italian Army proved capable of learning the hard lessons on the Eastern Front and in many instances cooperated well with German units. Second, Italian troops did not run away in the face of the enemy, but faltered under the immense pressure of Soviet attacks, like the neighbouring German, Romanian and Hungarian units. Further research will have to show when and under which circumstances comparable German divisions crumbled. Third, the battalion, regimental and divisional commanders were persistently complimented for their professionalism and operational conduct. The Italian artillery in particular was lauded. Thus, a 'lions led by donkeys' narrative does not fit the Italian performance.

CHAPTER 9

Narratives About Victimhood: Evil Germans, Good Italian Occupiers and Evil Soviets?

Besides the question of combat performance and officers' capabilities, three other fields need connecting: the question of German behaviour *vis-à-vis* their ally, the Italian occupation and the fate of prisoners in the Soviet Union. These issues were used in political quarrels after 1945 in order to create or to deride narratives about victimhood. A little clarification is needed on each of these three fields in order to debunk these myths and the paradigms of victimhood that still persist in secondary literature.[1] The most immediate accusation concerned the Germans, who had allegedly abandoned the Italian units on the Don. This accusation turned the Italian soldiers into victims in the 'public sphere'. Second, 'official Italy' and the Army denied any misconduct on Russian soil, whereas the Soviets and Italian Communists argued otherwise. Third, the fate of the Italian prisoners of war was politically instrumentalised. For anti-communists, the poor treatment of Italian POWs and the involvement of exiled Italian Communists in interrogations remained a thorny issue and added another aspect of victimhood. Thus, the following section first looks at the narrative of German cruelty towards their allies, then at the Italian involvement in crimes on the Eastern Front, before turning to the fate of the Italian prisoners.

[1] E.g. in Hamilton, *Sacrifice*. See also the remarks in Evan Mawdsley, "Sacrifice on the Steppe: The Italian Alpine Corps in the Stalingrad Campaign, 1942–1943. By Hope Hamilton," *War in History* 20, no. 1 (2013): 133–35.

© The Author(s) 2019
B. M. Scianna, *The Italian War on the Eastern Front, 1941–1943*, Italian and Italian American Studies,
https://doi.org/10.1007/978-3-030-26524-3_9

Victims of Their Teutonic Ally?

The setbacks in North Africa in autumn and winter 1942—with the loss of Italy's settler colony in Libya and the US intervention in the war—and the coming fall of Tunisia led to a severe crisis. The critical food situation led to strikes, the population became ever more concerned about Italy's fortune in the 'German war', and protests slowly grew.[2] It became clear that either Sardinia or Sicily would be targeted next, thus bringing the war to Italian soil. While the countries resources were strained already and her forces spread over the Balkans, the relations with the Germans soured notably in spring 1943.[3] The retreat in Russia further dampened the mood—also within military circles.[4] In a conversation with Speidel on 31 January 1943, Gariboldi reportedly predicted that Italy would not be able (and willing) to uphold her alliance with Germany for more than six months.[5] In May 1943, the *Regio Esercito* compiled reports to show not only that the Germans had never supplied them the necessary material and left them in the lurch, but that they had also maltreated them.[6] Many Italian soldiers, too, felt abandoned by their own commands and placed at the mercy of the Germans.[7] Thus, the 'retreat from the Don' became a cornerstone of the 'evil German' narrative. Other scholars have already discussed the mutual accusations and Italian attempts to counter them.[8] Yet, it is fundamentally important to understand *why* these after-action reports were written,[9] and put the 'retreat from the Don' in

---

[2] Avagliano and Palmieri, *Vincere*, 211ff. Already before the December retreat, the Germans noted that the setback at El Alamein had resulted in "defeatist talk" and a generally depressed mood, BA-MA, RW 5/v.424, Defaitistische Propaganda in Italien, 27 Oct. 1942, fol.3.

[3] The Italian diplomatic service in France even withheld information on sabotage and partisan activities from their allies, ACS, T-821/354/IT 4513/676, Puti (Paris) to Barbuscio Rizzo (Rome), 14 June 1943.

[4] Giannuli, *Le spie*, 218–19.

[5] Speidel, *Aus unserer Zeit*, 141.

[6] Schreiber, "Italiens Teilnahme," 283–84.

[7] According to an intelligence assessment of the ARMIR, Cavallero Diary, 27 Jan. 1943.

[8] Osti Guerrazzi and Schlemmer, "I soldati italiani," 413.

[9] Mussolini had always attempted to proof Italy's trustworthiness and reliability in order to counter prejudices about the Italian 'treason' in 1915 that were still virulent in Germany, see Woller, *Mussolini*, 175–76; König, *Kooperation*, 295ff.; Rusconi, *Deutschland/Italien*, 151ff.

wider context with the 'evil German' narrative that the Italians embraced after the war. At the same time, a vital change had occurred at the top of the Italian Army.

On 1 February 1943, Vittorio Ambrosio (1879–1958) replaced the Germanophile Cavallero as Chief of Staff of the General Staff. Ambrosio was a traditional cavalryman. He was devoted to the House of Savoy and had kept his distance from the Fascists, but had nonetheless risen through the ranks as staff officer without holding prominent 'political' positions or vital field commands.[10] He switched positions with Roatta in January 1942: the latter took over command of the Second Army in Slovenia, while Ambrosio became Chief of Staff of the Army.[11] He had witnessed first-hand that the fortunes of war were turning. While he was Chief of Staff of the Army, Mussolini had only received him once, but with Cavallero on the way to the exit door, the dictator called in a strategic meeting on 26 January. Ambrosio gave a grim outlook for 1943, criticised again the deployment of forces to the Russian theatre (which he had opposed), and hoped to end this commitment altogether as he did not consider the Germans capable of turning the tables soon—especially as the likeliness of an Anglo-American landing in the West increased.[12]

The reverses fuelled Ambrosio's opinion that the war was lost and by March 1943 he was convinced that the Germans were the real enemy.[13] His closeness to Marshal Caviglia—a key figure in gathering opposition to the Axis and a possible successor to Mussolini—and Badoglio made him a crucial part of the events that led to the toppling of Mussolini and the armistice on 8 September 1943.[14] Upon taking his up his role as

[10] Cecini, *I generali*, 142–57. He became commander of the Second Army in 1938, but the campaign against Yugoslavia included little fighting and subsequent anti-partisan actions were different to e.g. leading an army against the British or Russians. On his time on the Balkans see Osti Guerrazzi, *Italian Army*, 31–50.

[11] This *reenvirement* was motivated by Cavallero's desire to get rid of the so-called 'Spanish group' of generals Roatta, Gambara and Bastico; according to Cecini, *I generali*, 146.

[12] Deakin, *Brutal Friendship*, 162. He stressed this point again in two memoranda for Mussolini in late February and urged to reinforce the Balkans and the Mediterranean, see ibid., 166ff.

[13] Knox, "'Totality' and Disintegration," 94.

[14] Cecini, *I generali*, 148ff. On his relations to Caviglia see Pier Paolo Cervone, *Enrico Caviglia, l'anti Badoglio* (Milan: Mursia, 1992), 214ff. On Badoglio, Pieri and Rochat, *Badoglio*, 767ff. Also other widely respected officers in retirement, such as General Francesco Saverio Grazioli, who was considered a Russia expert, wrote memoranda to

head of the *Comando Supremo* in February, Ambrosio had surrounded himself with men he trusted (generals Ezio Rosi, Antonio Sorice, Castellano and Roatta) and wanted to know which further officers he could count on.[15] In March, he therefore asked all surviving generals, colonels and staff officers[16] for detailed reports on the happenings in North Africa and Russia—even those scattered across the various hospitals.[17] Ambrosio clarified his intentions in a letter to Gariboldi: he asked for precise and confirmed information about the German conduct before and during the retreat, cases of non-cooperation, as well as on failed assistance and the theft of Italian vehicles and materiel during the retreat.[18] Some of the replies only arrived in May and June and often did not include exactly what had been asked for; others, like General Nasci, came to see Ambrosio personally.[19] In his *relazione*, Major-General Carlo Pellegrini, GOC of the *Sforzesca*, did not expressly focus on relations with the Germans. Yet, he mentioned the good cooperation with the XXIX Corps' commander during the joint retreat.[20] General Fabio Martorelli instead hinted at the Italians' low training standards and poor armaments, which he saw—together with the extensive front line and inadequate reserves—as the chief reason for the defeat.[21] The *Celere*'s deputy-commander and an Italian liaison officer to the German Army Group advanced similar arguments about overstretched defensive lines and arrogant allies—emphasising the harsh German conduct during the

Mussolini, which showed their sceptical view of the situation of the Axis and their urge to focus on the defence of the Italian peninsula, see TNA, GFM 36/217, Gen. Grazioli – La situazione della guerra ai primi di febbraio 1943, 10 Feb. 1943. Grazioli had suggested the conclusion of a separate peace treaty with the USSR to Mussolini, see ibid., Gen. Grazioli – Pro-memoria per l'Eccellenza il Capo del Governo, 5 Dec. 1942. An idea that Mussolini raised with Göring and told Ciano to communicate it to Hitler as well, Ciano Diaries, 16 Dec. 1942. On Grazioli, see Cecini, *I generali*, 173–87; Giannuli, *Le spie*, 201.

[15] Mussolini resisted some of the appointments; see IWM, EDS AL 2763/4, Ambrosio Diary, 4 Feb. 1943.

[16] ACS, T-821/355/IT 4573/698, Promemoria per l'Ecc. Vecchiarelli, 20 Mar. 1943.

[17] Many of these letters and lists of officers can be found in ACS, T-821/355/IT 4573.

[18] ACS, T-821/355/IT 4573/696, Ambrosio to Gariboldi, 13 Mar. 1943.

[19] IWM, EDS AL 2763/4, Ambrosio Diary, 1 Apr. 1943. Gariboldi and Zanghieri, too, visited Ambrosio, see entries for 3 and 15 Apr. 1943.

[20] ACS, T-821/355/IT 4552/466-467, Promemoria, 29 May 1943.

[21] ACS, T-821/355/IT 4572/666-667, Promemoria, 23 Apr. 1943.

retreat, which they thought motivated by their belief in an early Italian withdrawal that had left the responsibility for restabilising the front to the Wehrmacht.[22] The *Torino*'s chief of staff, Lt. Col. Turrini, argued that the Germans had been bad comrades in arms—never aiding the Italians with food or transport during the retreat and treating them like "dead weight that should be left to its fate."[23] Further, he argued that the 298th ID never even attempted to understand Italian viewpoints or needs, disparaged the liaison officer, tended to see Italian units as militarily incapable and used them as scapegoats—a view supported by General Zingales, the XXXV Corps' commander.[24] Indeed, the Italian ambassador in Berlin, Dino Alfieri, also stressed the German tendency to blame Italian and Romanian forces for the recent setbacks in Russia, and even though this attitude was not new, he now demanded a stronger reply by hinting at German failures to supply fuel and other materiel.[25]

These reports formed the background for the Italian talking points in preparation of the conferences held with the German political and military leadership in spring and summer 1943; indeed, they have to be understood in the context of the Italians' re-evaluations of their general strategic position.[26] The *Comando Supremo* almost exclusively blamed the rout on the Don on the Wehrmacht: this latter had not heeded Italian warnings about overextended fronts or their demand for supply additional anti-tank guns, material for defensive works, mines, transport vehicles and fuel. The repeated reassignments of sectors and the poor German organisation of occupied territory were seen as further causes of defeat.[27] All Italian corps had suffered from very late orders for withdrawal, which—combined with missing fuel—had led to the loss of

---

[22] ACS, T-821/355/IT 4572/673-674, Promemoria, 11 May 1943.

[23] Ibid.

[24] ACS, T-821/355/IT 4572/679-683, Promemoria, 1 June 1943.

[25] Deakin, *Brutal Friendship*, 205. The Germans had allegedly even tried to film fleeing Italian units, see ibid.

[26] See e.g. the memoranda by General Giuseppe Castellano in February 1943, ACS, T-821/128/IT 1154a. This was extended to demands to all service chiefs to send their strategic assessment, ACS, T-821/211/IT 1581/715, Ambrosio to Riccardi, Fougier and Rossi, 7 Feb. 1943.

[27] ACS, T-821/355/IT 4528, Principali questioni che potrebbero essere trattate con la parte Germanica, Fronte Russo – 8^ Armata, 21 Mar. 1943, fs.17–20.

the *Alpini* Corps' artillery and vehicles.[28] The liaison officers' role was especially criticised: in the Italian view they had acted rather as control officers.[29] In conclusion, the reports that Ambrosio had asked for, were less self-critical than, for example, General Marras' *relazione*.[30]

The reports should be treated with caution. Zingales, for example, was known as anti-German[31] and a negative depiction of the Wehrmacht after a crushing defeat was arguably little surprising. In December 1946, Gariboldi went so far to declare that the Germans had first not foreseen the strong Soviet resistance, but then blamed the Italians for their own battlefield failure.[32] Giusti has used General Lerici's after-action report to describe flaws in officer training, logistics and operational command. Yet, she used his report (to Gariboldi) from 28 January 1943 to assess operations in 1941; and to support her argument that the Russian campaign had been the ultimate proof of Italian unreadiness for war and exposed more general defects in the armed forces.[33] Lerici's criticism is certainly interesting—even though it is not as pronounced as she makes us believe and lacks context. However, one must not forget that Lerici himself was rated as a rather average officer by a promotion board in March 1942,[34] and had an interest in a self-exculpating account.

Beyond these high-level after-action reports, two generals were selected to question survivors of the retreat in various hospitals across Italy, on these same issues. They mainly found junior officers, and only some from the higher ranks (around 500 in total),[35] most of whom had suffered from frostbite.[36] The majority of the officers questioned described the Germans as arrogant, ungenerous and often brutal towards the Italians—in short, exceptionally bad allies. The chief accusations were

---

[28] ACS, T-821/355/IT 4528, Principali questioni che potrebbero essere trattate con la parte Germanica, Il ripiegamento del C.A. Alpino, 21 Mar. 1943, f.23.

[29] ACS, T-821/355/IT 4528, Principali questioni che potrebbero essere trattate con la parte Germanica, Il ripiegamento del II e XXXV C.A., 21 Mar. 1943, fs.21–22.

[30] Pelagalli, *Marras*, 209.

[31] BA-MA, RH 2/1672, fol.545.

[32] Burgwyn, *Mussolini*, 221.

[33] Giusti, *La campagna*, 118–20.

[34] ACS, T-821/146/IT 2228/105.

[35] ACS, T-821/355/IT 4575/735-736, Promemoria, 22 Apr. 1943.

[36] ACS, T-821/355/IT 4575/737-747, Gen. Granati – Relazione sulla visita compiuta ad ufficiali reduci dal fronte russo [hereafter 'Relazione'], 16 Apr. 1943.

an unwillingness to share shelter or food (which forced the Italians to steal) and quarrels (and even the use of force) to prevent Italians from using sledges or vehicles. Only a minority confirmed close and good relations—especially during combat and on the front—and praised the German fighting skills.[37] Yet, even those speaking benevolently about the Wehrmacht's military skills, agreed that a majority of the German soldiers were hostile towards their allies and behaved ruthlessly against Soviet civilians and prisoners.[38] In contrast, Italian relations with the Soviet population were cast in a much more favourable light. Clearly, the wounded officers were slightly biased after the retreat, trying to make sense of the defeat, and some were still shell-shocked.[39] Being questioned by high-ranked officers in hospital meant that certain things were muted while others were accentuated—even though General Orlando Granati argued they had talked as if they were among themselves.[40]

However, a high-ranking Fascist party official gathered similar impressions during a trip to the remnants of the Eighth Army in February and March 1943. Lt. Col Angelo Manaresi argued that the Germans did not treat the Italian soldiers as equal to their own, did not offer any help during the retreat, and were similarly cold and distant with regard to the Hungarians and Romanians.[41] He warned that the returning soldiers might unleash a "surge of aversion for the Germans."[42] Soldiers' letters from the front showed not only the low point of relations in February 1943,[43] but the reversal of enemy and ally: depictions of friendly Soviet civilians and evil Germans became "the predominant theme in correspondence from Russia."[44] It is important to note that all the future topoi of the postwar debates are already present in these reports: the evil German ally, good behaviour *vis-à-vis* the Soviet civilians, and even

---

[37] Ibid., f.741.

[38] Ibid., fs.742, 746. Major Serano (Part of the *Torino*'s 52nd Artillery Regiment) defended harsh German actions against Italian formations that had "ceased fighting and whose officers were – due to exhaustion – not up to their duties any more", ibid.

[39] ACS, T-821/355/IT 4575/737-747, Gen. Granati – Relazione, f.746.

[40] Ibid., f.738.

[41] ACS, T-821/354/IT 4511/647-661, Lt. Col. Manaresi – Rapporto sull'invio del 9° treno A.P.E. in Russia (febbraio–marzo 1943), 24 Mar. 1943, fs.655, 659.

[42] Ibid., f.660.

[43] Pelagalli, *Marras*, 218.

[44] Cavallo, *Italiani in guerra*, 184.

the desire to take up arms against the Germans after the happenings in Russia.[45] Indeed, the victim narrative went beyond the military sphere. "When the Germans threw the blame for the break in Russia and the collapse at Stalingrad upon the Italians the Duce's indignation mingled with that of the rest of Italy. The country was quickly exasperated by the news of how the retreating Germans monopolised the tanks and lorries and left the Italians in the lurch."[46] This mood was conveyed in many memoirs—as will be described below—and formed the starting point for an alleged desire to fight against the Germans to avenge their 'treason' in Russia.[47]

What was true in these accusations of uncomradely German behaviour? Many were reported with hindsight, after the Axis had 'broken'. Additionally, most documents were lost during the retreat, which makes it almost impossible to assess what really happened. Even before the winter retreat, German reports had emerged claiming that Italian soldiers were throwing away their weapons and material,[48] or were selling their equipment to the local population.[49] After the retreat, many of these German allegations were handed over to General Marras.[50] The Italians immediately tried to prove these stories wrong,[51] and indicated that the *Sforzesca* had followed direct German orders to destroy all weapons and vehicles that could not be carried with them.[52] It could not be established whether the Germans actually took pictures of exhausted Italians during the retreat—this seems hardly credible.[53] Yet, it fuelled the 'evil German' stereotype in postwar memoirs.

On the other hand, there are some foundations for the Italian claims. German sources reveal Wehrmacht soldiers stealing from Italian

---

[45] ACS, T-821/355/IT 4575/737-747, Granati – Relazione, f.747.
[46] Wiskemann, *Rome-Berlin*, 291; Avagliano and Palmieri, *Vincere*, 247ff.
[47] Tolloy, *Con l'Armata*, 207.
[48] BA-MA, RH 31-IX/16, Report, 19 Dec. 1942, fol.75.
[49] As for example in Dnepropetrovsk, which fuelled partisan activity, BA-MA, RH 31-IX/12, Telegram, 7 Sept. 1942, fol.36.
[50] BA-MA, RH 2/2894, Head of Liaison Staffs Berlin to Military Attaché Rome, 8 Mar. 1943, fol.4.
[51] BA-MA, RH 31-IX/12, Malaguti to Tippelskirch, 30 Sept. 1942, fol.37.
[52] Burgwyn, *Mussolini*, 205.
[53] Tolloy, *Con l'Armata*, 177.

magazines[54] and an SS unit refusing to take Italian wounded on their half-empty lorries.[55] However, friendly fire accidents occurred on both sides, and scholars have raised doubts that the Italians were merely victims.[56] Massignani has exposed Italian misbehaviour and use of force to get their way in the struggle for survival during the retreat.[57] The GOC of the XXIV Panzer Corps—Colonel (posthumously General) Eibl—died under mysterious circumstances on 20 January and German sources mention several cases of aggressive Italian behaviour *vis-à-vis* the Wehrmacht.[58] In the rallying areas and during transports back to Italy, the soldiers' discipline was not always at its best: the Wehrmacht complained about grave misconduct towards Soviet civilians in February and March 1943,[59] and small-arm ammunition was withheld on train journeys after shooting incidents in late spring 1943.[60]

In conclusion, it is fair to assess that—quite naturally—a certain degree of friction occurred during the withdrawal in winter 1942–1943. Similar reports and bitter memories emerged, for example, between Hungarians and Germans.[61] The Germans had, however, not willingly abandoned the Italians on the Don. But the self-victimisation served another purpose: it glossed over painful questions of the Italians' own performance by pointing at the Germans (instead of poor materiel); this also suited the postwar narrative about the 'evil German ally'.[62] After the war, the question of how this narrative was perpetuated and defended remained vital for the Italian Army. But to what extent had the Italians been involved in Hitler's war of extermination? Did they forge the 'evil German' image merely to whitewash themselves?

[54] BA-MA, RH 31-IX/9, Eighth Army to German liaison officers, 13 Nov. 1942, fol.88.

[55] BA-MA, MSg 2/4388, Distler – Verbindungsoffizier, fol.89. If this was a case of the Wehrmacht blaming the Waffen-SS for wrongdoings could not be assessed, but it should not be excluded.

[56] Corni, "Briefe von der Ostfront."

[57] Massignani, *Alpini e tedeschi*, 135. See also Hamilton, *Sacrifice*, 84, 87; Schreiber, "Italiens Teilnahme," 283–85.

[58] His report is printed in Schlemmer, *Italiener*, 146–52; also Buttar, *Knife's Edge*, 244–45.

[59] Ben H. Shepherd, *War in the Wild East: The German Army and Soviet Partisans* (Cambridge: Harvard University Press, 2004), 175.

[60] BA-MA, RH 2/2894, Wochenbericht Italien, 17 May 1943, fol.23.

[61] Wimpffen, "Zweite Ungarische," 346ff.

[62] See again Focardi, *Il cattivo tedesco*.

Victims of Defamation? The Italians and the War of Extermination

In order to understand postwar allegations of Italian criminal behaviour it is useful to investigate the current state of the historiography. The issue of Italian occupational methods has only aroused academic interest during the last twenty years, and many scholars have finally debunked the myth of the Italians as *brava gente* who allegedly never committed any wrongdoing. Undoubtedly, the Italians were no saints and did take part in a war of aggression that resulted in the death of millions of soldiers and innocent civilians. Yet, the existing works show that Italian crimes against civilians were on a much lower scale in comparison to German, Romanian and Hungarian acts. Indeed, two recent books on the Eastern Front, which also consulted Russian sources, have repelled tendencies to draw an equals sign between the Italian conduct and the German *Vernichtungskrieg*.[63] Thus, the following section will look at the role of ideology before analysing the Italian treatment of civilians, prisoners of war and partisans.

Occupation policies and war crimes are inherently related to the question of the Army's relation to Fascism, especially as the *Regio Esercito* upheld an alleged 'apolitical' stance during and after the war.[64] A common narrative therefore portrayed the Italians as trapped in an ideological war between Nazism and Communism—as Marras's above-cited report highlighted already in winter 1941–1942. Recent scholarship has questioned this 'apolitical' framing. Osti Guerrazzi has emphasised the closeness of Italian generals—if not to Fascism—to monarchist and anti-Communist ideas long after 1943.[65] Yet, a monarchist army was per se nothing extraordinary, and Knox has argued that in the Italian case, the strong loyalty felt to the monarchy served as a restraining element between 1940–1943 and ultimately benefitted Mussolini's ousting.[66] Thus, the regime's criminal character should not automatically be linked to the Army, let alone each individual soldier. It is also

---

[63] Scotoni, *Il nemico fidato*; Giusti, *La campagna*. Stramaccioni only briefly referred to Russia and criticised the Italian treatment of prisoners, without providing new evidence, Stramaccioni, *Crimini di guerra*, 47–49.

[64] Botti and Ilari, *Il pensiero*, 436ff.

[65] Osti Guerrazzi, *Noi non sappiamo odiare*, 297–304.

[66] Knox, "'Totality' and Disintegration," 81.

problematic to follow Bartov's arguments on the Wehrmacht's radicalisation to confront German and Italian behaviour. There were important differences between the two regimes and the armed forces. Beyond the fact that Italian soldiers never swore their oath to Mussolini—but to the King—the regime was far more willing to strike compromises, there was less ideological propaganda within the *Regio Esercito*, and there was no large-scale increase in the officer corps with younger and more fascist men.[67] In sum, the King remained the point of loyalty and Mussolini "failed to dominate the internal mechanism of the royal armed forces"[68]; much to the dissatisfaction of fascist hotheads such as Roberto Farinacci who vehemently asked for a stronger indoctrination of the *Regio Esercito* in 1939.[69] Thus, how widespread was fascist ideology within the Army?

In a conversation with the German military attaché on 1 December 1939, the Deputy-Chief of the Army's General Staff, General Roatta, claimed that it would soon be necessary for the Europeans to unite in fighting 'Russian Bolshevism'.[70] Yet, Rintelen thought as late as June 1941 that a war with Russia would not arouse great enthusiasm in Italy.[71] As documents of the Fascist secret police (the OVRA) have shown, many Italians were surprised by the German attack on the USSR and believed in a rapid victory, but this did not alter the often-unsympathetic view of their ally.[72] Osti Guerrazzi and Schlemmer have argued that Italian public opinion perceived Barbarossa "without a doubt" as an ideological war and soldiers returning from the front knew of the ongoing war of extermination—but were also appalled by German methods.[73] Yet, the effect of propaganda on the home front and the actual behaviour of soldiers in the field should be analysed separately, in order to avoid any conjecture. Inflammatory speeches and the conviction that they were waging a crusade against Bolshevism do not mean that Italian soldiers plundered and murdered their way through Russia. Further, it is fruitful to have the Soviet propaganda in mind. While the non-German invaders were less focused on and less targeted by its organs, the Romanians

---

[67] Ibid., 101ff.; Ceva, "Fascismo," 385.
[68] Knox, "'Totality' and Disintegration," 90.
[69] TNA, GFM 36/170, Farinacci to Mussolini, 13 Sept. 1939.
[70] BA-MA, RH 2/2936, Rintelen to Tippelskirch, 1 Dec. 1939, fol.2.
[71] BA-MA, RH 2/2936, Rintelen to Gen. Matzky, 6 June 1941, fos.218–19.
[72] Giannuli, *Le spie*, 92–94.
[73] Osti Guerrazzi and Schlemmer, "I soldati italiani," 399–403.

and Finns, for example, were more likened to the cruel German enemy. As Berkhoff pointed out, "in total contrast, the Italians received a good press," and the Italian people (that were separated from the Fascists) were even praised.[74] This, in turn, would allow Italian writers after the war to gloss over the Italian role in the invasion and occupation of the Soviet Union, and refer to the *brava gente* image.

In Italy, Fascist authorities used anti-bolshevism and anti-semitism in all press organs, and were supported by the Catholic press' idealisation of the war as a modern crusade to liberate the oppressed peoples of the Soviet Union.[75] In doing so, the propaganda could build on dystopian narratives of the Soviet Union that had been formed during the 1920s and 1930s, and the anti-Communist rhetoric employed during the Spanish Civil War. This, however, included already the idea of liberating the Ukrainians.[76] The efforts of Italian propaganda were not restricted to the home front. The field chaplains (around 200) carried this message to the men.[77] Also soldiers' newspapers on the front, especially the weekly *Dovunque* that was issued since January 1942,[78] spread anti-Communist and anti-Slav propaganda.[79] Scholars are still divided to what extent this had an effect on the men. Virtue has argued these themes and wordings are found in the mens' letters, and that especially Catholic soldiers were inclined to support anti-Communist rhetoric.[80]

---

[74] Karel C. Berkhoff, *Motherland in Danger: Soviet Propaganda During World War II* (Cambridge: Harvard University Press, 2012), 196; on the other nations see ibid., 194ff.

[75] Quinto Antonelli, "Fronte russo. Le forme della propaganda," in *Battaglie in Russia. Il Don e Stalingrado 75 anni dopo*, ed. Olga Dubrovina (Milan: Ed. Unicopli, 2018), 167–82. Scotoni has argued that the corps was even meant to be called *Corpo Anticomunista italiano* (CAI)—but could not provide evidence for this claim, Scotoni, *Il nemico fidato*, 137.

[76] Olga Dubrovina, "Immagine del nemico. Meccanismo della costruzione," in *Battaglie in Russia. Il Don e Stalingrado 75 anni dopo*, ed. Olga Dubrovina (Milan: Ed. Unicopli, 2018), 159–65.

[77] Maria Teresa Giusti, "'Restare vivo è molto difficile…'. Gli italiani sul fronte orientale e l'immagine del nemico," in *Battaglie in Russia. Il Don e Stalingrado 75 anni dopo*, ed. Olga Dubrovina (Milan: Ed. Unicopli, 2018), 81–109, here 103–4.

[78] Virtue, "We Istrians," 291–92.

[79] On propaganda material see Quinto Antonelli and Sergej I. Filonenko, *"Vincere! Vinceremo!" Cartoline sul fronte russo (1941–1942)* (Trento: Fondazione Museo storico del Trentino, 2011). For the home front's view of the Russians, see Giannuli, *Le spie*, 97–102.

[80] Virtue, "We Istrians," 282, 293; Duggan, *Fascist Voices*, 373.

Duggan has demonstrated the existence of Fascist beliefs and expressions in soldiers' letters, described the often-racist depictions of the locals, and argued that "even when direct contact with ordinary Russians led to a revision of stereotypes, there was rarely any sign of unwillingness to call into question the campaign."[81] Giusti, on the other hand, has argued that the men on the front remained relatively unaffected by political propaganda; even if they half-heartedly repeated its parlance in their own letters,[82] and initially believed in the regime's propaganda, reality soon led them to understand the similarities between Russian peasant life and their own homes.[83] A conclusion that is also upheld by Antonelli[84] and by Filatov,[85] and also Virtue who acknowledged that "among soldiers' letters, praise of the occupied civilian population as 'affable, hospitable, and kind' was most common after the disaster on the Don."[86] This ambivalence was also present on the official level where the Ukranians were considered in particular as 'worthwhile' for liberation. Despite the 'civilizing mission' and crusading rhetoric on the political level[87]—as well as the anti-Bolshevism, anti-Slavism and anti-Semitism inherent in the press[88]—ideology seems to have played a small role for the Italian Army's actual conduct of operations.

Virtue has demonstrated that one colonel of the 3rd *Bersaglieri* Regiment and a senior officer (Roberto Lerici) of the *Torino*'s 81st Infantry Regiment employed anti-Bolshevik crusade rhetoric in two

---

[81] Ibid., 376. Yet Duggan's reference—beyond his own sources—to Nuto Revelli as proof of Fascist sympathies and ideological racism *vis-à-vis* locals is somehow problematic (as will be described below).

[82] Giusti, *La campagna*, 94, 159–67. An opposite view is held by Osti Guerrazzi and Schlemmer, "I soldati italiani," 408–9.

[83] Giusti, *La campagna*, 164; also Della Volpe, *Esercito e propaganda*, 89ff.

[84] Antonelli, "Fronte russo," 181–82.

[85] Filatov, *La campagna orientale*, 53, 57ff. Some of his claims based on Soviet interrogations of prisoners should be considered more carefully. What else should Italian POWs have told the Soviets? It was clearly not a good idea to stress one's hatred of Communism and belief in ultimate Fascist victory.

[86] Virtue, "We Istrians," 293.

[87] Scotoni, *Il nemico fidato*, 125ff.

[88] Mario Isnenghi, "La campagna di Russia nella stampa e nella pubblicistica fascista," in *Gli italiani sul fronte russo*, ed. Enzo Collotti (Bari: De Donato, 1982), 377–423; Osti Guerrazzi and Schlemmer, "I soldati italiani," 391ff.

reports stemming from June and October 1942, respectively.[89] Were the senior officers setting the tone and attempting to instil ideological hatred into their soldiers' minds? The CSIR's first order of the day emphasised the Italian Army's role as a bulwark against Bolshevism and was signed by its intended commander General Zingales.[90] Yet, the second, issued by Messe, made no references to Bolshevism or ideology.[91] Indeed, Zingales may have been an exception and to cite the first order alone is to fail to analyse the whole picture. After he was appointed as new commander of the XXXV Corps in November 1942, Zingales proclaimed in a speech to the *3 Gennaio* Blackshirts: "This war is a continuation of the March on Rome; it is our war, a war for you Blackshirts."[92] The Italian Fascists obviously framed the war in Russia as a fight against Communism,[93] but we still need research into whether the Blackshirts behaved differently to regular army units.[94] Zingales' audience might have influenced his choice of words, but they stand in stark contrast to Messe's farewell address to the Blackshirts several weeks earlier.[95] Messe emphasised their qualities as warriors, but did not refer to 'Fascist values'. He further lauded them as volunteers who were willing to pay a blood price—but above all encouraged them to have good relations with other units.[96] Thus, Messe did not even use ideologically coloured language in an informal farewell speech to Blackshirts; historians should, therefore, carefully weigh postwar Communist newspapers' claims

[89] Virtue, "We Istrians," 290–91.

[90] ACS, T-821/247/IT 2259/120, Zingales– CSIR- Ordine del giorno n.1, 8 July 1941.

[91] ACS, T-821/247/IT 2259/279, Messe– CSIR- Ordine del giorno n.2, 4 Aug. 1941.

[92] ACS, Fondo Diamanti, b.1, f.Camp. Russia, 'Diario Storico *3 Gennaio*', 5 Nov. 1942.

[93] Diamanti had told his men that service on the Eastern Front was a honourable duty for "legionnaires and fascists", thereby he also making references to the Blackshirts' service in the Spanish Civil War, ACS, Fondo Diamanti, b.1, f.Camp. Russia, doc. vari, Letter, 5 Nov. 1942.

[94] Scotoni held that they fulfilled the same duties and were only used for propaganda acts, such as tearing down Communist symbols, Scotoni, *Il nemico fidato*, 138. The Blackshirts were the only units with real volunteers; thus, we should not exclude clear anti-Communist sentiments, Filatov, *La campagna orientale*, 35.

[95] Compare Zingales' speech on 5 November to Messe's on 11 September 1942 in ACS, Fondo Diamanti, b.1, f.Camp. Russia, 'Diario Storico *3 Gennaio*'.

[96] Ibid., Messe speech, 11 Sept. 1942.

about Messe's supposed use of ideological language.[97] Further, even when Messe sent his comments on combat morale to Rome in winter 1941–1942, the subsection on propaganda did not include references to anti-Bolshevism or similar ideas to raise soldiers' morale.[98] Nor did his telegram to Mussolini, in which he summarised the CSIR's operations (and attempted to gain additional materiel).[99] Also the Secretary of the Fascist Party, Aldo Vidussoni, who visited several units down to company level in early October, criticised the work of the propaganda sections of the Eighth Army and demanded a rapid improvement to infuse more ideological fervour.[100] Particularly as he reported the "Fascist spirit widespread among the men, but not so much among the officers."[101]

Indeed, it is intriguing to analyse the language of Italian military documents. In circulars to lower divisional commands, General Marazzani, for example, argued for a heroic defence to the last man against the 'Russian hordes', yet did not employ other ideological semantics.[102] Many other documents are instead full of references to duty, heroism and the *Patria*.[103] In contrast, a congratulatory message from General Hoth to Messe (on the bold assistance of Italian aircraft) included the ominous

[97] The time period might also play a role. Messe became more distant from Mussolini and the regime as the war progressed and the chances of victory diminished, Giusti, "Messe," 19ff. For his use of fascist parlance and enthusiasm for Mussolini in letters to his wife in 1940 and early 1941, see ibid., 29–30, 40; Messe, *Lettere*, 93–94. His letters in 1942 show a notable decline in sympathy for the regime, repeatedly stressing his loyalty to the *Patria* above else, see e.g. ibid., 144. He hardly used the term 'bolsheviks' in his letters; if so, it was in context of describing harsh actions by the Soviet government against its own population, see ibid., 117–18. Yet, these letters were edited by his son, so caution is advised as to their reliability and we should complement them with other sources.

[98] ACS, T-821/256/IT 3061/821-827, Messe– Relazione morale e condizioni spirituali, 11 Feb. 1942, f.825.

[99] ACS, T-821/255/IT 3057/1042, Messe to Mussolini, 5 Dec. 1941. Messe spoke in derogatory terms of the low professional and cultural standards of Soviet officers. Yet, he compared them to Italian NCOs – which was certainly no praise for them, ACS, T-821/257/IT 3062/112-120, Messe to *Ufficio Addestramento*, 24 Mar. 1942, f.116.

[100] TNA, GFM 36/240, Vidussoni – Appunto per il Duce, 24 Oct. 1942, fos.13, 16.

[101] Ibid., fol.16.

[102] ACS, T-821/259/IT 3068/236-242, Gen. Marazzani– Note sullo schieramento e sistemazione a difesa, 14 Sept. 1942, fs.241–42.

[103] See e.g. the laudatory message from Messe to the *Pasubio*, which contained hopes for new victories, ACS, T-821/20/IT 98/971, Messe to Giovanelli, 18 Nov. 1941; also ACS, T-821/257/IT 3062/549-558, Messe to CS – La campagna invernale, 5 Mar. 1942, f.558.

'struggle against Bolshevism' trope.[104] Hoth was no exception among German senior commanders, who by and large accepted the dictum of an ideological struggle and embraced the new ideology (and clearly the parlance).[105] Italian senior officers seem to have differed in this regard as the use of ideological parlance of which we have some proof was not as widespread as one would have thought. Thus, we should also reconsider whether anti-Bolshevik propaganda was actually vital to securing good morale[106]; and maybe look at different moments of the Italians' deployment: Virtue has hinted at a process of increasing brutalization and politicisation.[107] Yet, in evaluating such documents it is important to assess the Italian occupation methods on the Eastern Front, in which rhetoric and actions were not always identical.

The Treatment of Civilians and Prisoners

Giusti has identified varying concepts of occupation as the explanation for the different behaviour of the Wehrmacht and the Italian Army. While the German *Lebensraum* model envisaged total submission and extermination based on racial hierarchies, the Italian *spazio vitale* bet on including locals. In short, this was to be a 'civilizing mission' that could not work if 'barbarian' violence was systematically employed.[108] Scotoni and Virtue have listed similar reasons for the Italians' less brutal occupational policies: their aims in the conquered territory were not as wide-ranging, the influence of ideology was less, and propaganda prompted the soldiers to see the Soviet populace (especially the Ukrainians) "in a generally positive light."[109]

[104] ACS, T-821/257/IT 3062/107, Hoth to Messe, 25 Mar. 1942.
[105] Hürter, *Hitlers Heerführer*, 372–76; Shepherd, *Hitler's Soldiers*, 122–23.
[106] For this argument see Osti Guerrazzi and Schlemmer, "I soldati italiani," 406ff.
[107] Virtue, "We Istrians," 298.
[108] Giusti, *La campagna*, 189, 198.
[109] Scotoni, *Il nemico fidato*; Giusti, *La campagna*, 191. Her reliance on memoirs for factual claims about the Italian troops' behaviour *vis-à-vis* the civilian population is, of course, problematic, ibid., 192ff.; Virtue, "Fascist Italy," 68, 108ff., 116. The author contrasts the content of Italian propaganda to Bartov's main argument of ideology and barbarisation regarding the German case, Bartov, *Hitler's Army*. However, Bartov's claims have also been disputed, see in general Christian Hartmann, Johannes Hürter, and Ulrike Jureit, eds., *Verbrechen der Wehrmacht. Bilanz einer Debatte* (Munich: Beck, 2005); Neitzel and Welzer, *Soldaten*, 321ff.; Shepherd, *Hitler's Soldiers*, 188–89.

In sum, Italian designs and goals, and not the soldiers' supposed humanism, set the tone for their behaviour.[110]

Italian occupation policies were also defined through the general framework of Axis cooperation: German authorities controlled the rear (until the ARMIR was formed) and captured suspects had to be handed over.[111] The Germans readily made clear that they would be directing the course of action in the newly conquered territories, not least to secure supplies.[112] The CSIR—merely a corps—had no independently controlled rear area and the Germans fulfilled policing roles. A circular transmitted to the CSIR demanded severe punishment for any civilian outrage and regarded occupied territory as an operational area. It also explicitly asked for the rapid employment of Soviet POWs in support of ongoing operations.[113] By and large, the Italians complied with German demands in regards to forced labour, the treatment of partisans, Russian POWs,[114] commissars and the Jewish population, which were mostly handed over to German authorities.[115] There is no evidence, however, that Italian units carried out the infamous Commissar Order.[116]

[110] Roatta complained about the lack of caution Italian soldiers had shown in their close relations with civilians of newly conquered territories before the Russian campaign, ACS, T-821/354/IT 4507/589-601, Roatta – Addestramento e operazioni, 28 July 1941, f.599.

[111] On the general organisation of the Italian rear see Emilio Tirone, "La politica italiana verso la popolazione civile e i prigionieri di guerra sul fronte russo," in *Battaglie in Russia. Il Don e Stalingrado 75 anni dopo*, ed. Olga Dubrovina (Milan: Ed. Unicopli, 2018), 189–212, here 191ff.

[112] The literature on German occupation policies is vast, see Dieter Pohl, *Die Herrschaft der Wehrmacht. Deutsche Militärbesatzung und einheimische Bevölkerung in der Sowjetunion 1941–1944* (Frankfurt: Fischer, 2011); Mawdsley, *Thunder*, 228–32; Shepherd, *Hitler's Soldiers*, 274–96.

[113] ACS, T-821/247/IT 2259/428-432, Direttive sulle potestà militari, sulla sicurezza e amministrazione nei territori conquistati ad est del Nistro, [transmitted] 23 Aug. 1941.

[114] Initially the CSIR was envisaged to transfer them to camps in Italy, but soon the Germans requested the handover of all captured Soviets, Giusti, *La campagna*, 237. Still, there are Italian propaganda videos from the Eastern Front that show the employment of Soviet POWs for assistance duties (e.g. at airfields, which violated conventions).

[115] Schlemmer, *Italiener*, 32–38.

[116] Virtue, "Fascist Italy," 50. Commissars were meant to be immediately handed over to the Germans, ACS, T-821/247/IT 2259/428-432, Direttive sulle potestà militari, sulla sicurezza e amministrazione nei territori conquistati ad est del Nistro, [transmitted] 23 Aug. 1941, here f.432; BA-MA, RH 31-IX/11, Gyldenfeldt to Eighth Army, 16 July 1942, fol.357. Most Commissars were shot by members of German motorised and armoured formations, i.e. those units who were most likely to encounter them first, Felix

Likewise while Italian soldiers were not actively engaged in shooting or rounding up Jews, despite passively observing their capture and maltreatment, the compilation of lists played into the hands of the German authorities.[117] Yet there is no evidence of contacts with the *Einsatzgruppen* operating behind the front where the CSIR was employed in 1941 or of involvement in their actions. This does not preclude, however, Italian knowledge of the ongoing executions,[118] which also visitors were fully aware of.[119]

Situational aspects were also important. The Italians suffered from the harsh climate and faced difficulties in living off the land.[120] When logistic bottlenecks increased as early as August 1941, the Wehrmacht's motorised and armoured divisions relied almost completely on the requisition of local resources and the Italian forces following behind consequently found less goods.[121] German authorities attempted to regulate what the Italians requisitioned, but could not prevent uncontrolled food requests.[122] While this soured relations with the local population, it also cast the troops in a poor light and endangered discipline.[123] The Italians, still, were generally "not regarded as terrible looters during

---

Römer, *Der Kommissarbefehl: Wehrmacht und NS-Verbrechen an der Ostfront 1941/42* (Paderborn: Schöningh, 2008). Kleist's First Panzer Group killed the highest number of Commissars and Römer showed that half the divisions under its command were directly involved—yet, he could not find evidence for the involvement of Italian units, ibid., 244, 391. I would like to thank Felix Römer for this information regarding the Italian divisions.

[117] Virtue, "Fascist Italy," 62; Schlemmer, "Die comandi tappa," 522. Schlemmer could demonstrate that 200 Jews had been handed over to German authorities, which has to be placed in contrast, however, with over 200,000 Jews where the Romanians either shot themselves or handed to the Germans, DiNardo, *Germany*, 133.

[118] Most detailed in Scotoni, *Il nemico fidato*, 130–34, 138. Helmut von Alberti, liaison to the CSIR, also held positions as local commander of Dnepropetrovsk, Taganrog, and Novorossisk, where thousands of Jews were executed, ibid., 133.

[119] See the reports in TNA, GFM 36/240, Vidussoni – Appunto per il Duce, 24 Oct. 1942, fos.8–9.

[120] Virtue, "Fascist Italy," 11.

[121] ACS, T-821/247/IT 2259/448-450, Messe– Promemoria, 27 Aug. 1941, here f.449.

[122] NARA, T-312/360/7934956-57, Cpt. Becker – Erfahrungsbericht Verb.Offz. *Pasubio*, 15 Aug. 1941, fol.2.

[123] BA-MA, RH 31-IX/25, Heidkämper to Tippelskirch, 27 Aug. 1942.

the war,"[124] or as prone to rape (as much evidence about the Romanians and Hungarians indicates).[125] Nevertheless, the Germans reported "rather unpleasant instances in regards to behaviour towards the civilian population" by the XXXV Corps (former CSIR) when it moved eastwards after a long winter rest,[126] and the Italians were involved in oppressive measures such as the burning of villages, shooting innocents, forced prostitution and pillaging.[127]

However, Messe's circular to divisional commands in September 1941 already shows an important difference from German orders. He cautioned against close contacts with the population, arguing that this might diminish the troops' combat morale and alertness: he reminded his subordinates that "a victorious army is not meant to win affection in occupied countries, but it is essential to inspire appraisal, respect, distance, which implies prestige."[128] Partisan groups in the Donets basin were indeed organised by local Communist Party functionaries and NKVD agents—it thus made sense to warn of Communist activities and was not an example of blind ideological fury.[129] In an early circular on possible Soviet paratrooper drops, Messe also warned about contacts with the Jewish population—citing prior attacks on Axis forces.[130] These fears of partisan warfare were reinforced by testimonies of captured armed civilians,[131] and the killing of wounded Italian soldiers, probably by NKVD forces, around Christmas 1941.[132] Yet, cautioning contacts with civilians (especially Jews and Communists), or attributing acts of sabotage to them is still different from executing them—as the Romanians did at the same time. Moreover, the scholars who refer to such documents as proof of a war of extermination run the danger of

---

[124] Virtue, "Fascist Italy," 39–40.

[125] Karel C. Berkhoff, *Harvest of Despair: Life and Death in Ukraine Under Nazi Rule* (Cambridge: Harvard University Press, 2004), 217.

[126] BA-MA, RH 31-IX/25, Wessel to Tippelskirch, 30 July 1942.

[127] Burgwyn, *Mussolini*, 217; Giusti, *La campagna*, 199ff.; Scotoni, *Il nemico fidato*, 213–14.

[128] ACS, T-821/254/IT 3051/449-450, Messe– Schieramento delle truppe e contatti con gli indigeni, 11 Sept. 1941, quoted on f.450.

[129] Scotoni, *Il nemico fidato*, 171ff.

[130] ACS, T-821/247/IT 2259/188, Messe– Difesa antiparacadutista, 25 July 1941.

[131] ACS, T-821/247/IT 2259/296, Lt. Ferrarese – Paracadutisti in civile, n.d.

[132] Tirone, "La politica," 190–91.

blurring committed crimes with speculative assumptions. Several scholars have cited severe orders issued by the Italian commands. However, as Burgwyn has observed in relation to an Italian threat to shoot one hundred hostages for every killed Italian soldier: "no proof has yet emerged that the Italians actually carried out their side of this infamous bargain."[133] In fact, meagre primary material has made it difficult to provide reliable numbers on the scale of Italian measures, but harsh orders should not be mistaken for atrocities actually committed.[134] Consequently, Soviet postwar accusations were themselves moderate: only 36 Italians were charged with war crimes,[135] and the files show a notable difference between the German and Hungarian actions on the one hand, and the Italians' on the other: only five per cent of 175 asserted war crimes in the Voronezh area were associated with Italian (*Alpini*) troops.[136] Also Italian diplomatic reports trying to investigate the German occupation regime found that the civilians were hostile towards their Teutonic ally, but rather indifferent towards the Italians.[137]

The Italian Army never received a *carte blanche* for criminal behaviour like Hitler's soldiers, and "the Italians did not become more brutal to local civilians"[138] even after the defeat on the Don. In fact, while we should not see them as saints, they were also no marauding juggernaut on their retreat, as Berkhoff noted that even "when they passed through Ukraine again in the summer of 1943, they looted German supplies, which the authorities refused to share with them, offered natives to work for food, sang for food (thus earning the nickname of 'Running

[133] Burgwyn, *Mussolini*, 219.

[134] Schlemmer provided the number of twelve executions in one district, Schlemmer, "Die comandi tappa," 528, and named other instances without providing figures over a longer period, see also Schlemmer, *Italiener*, 35ff.

[135] Scotoni, *Il nemico fidato*, 286ff.; Giusti, *La campagna*, 203–8. Giusti cited one allegation of 615 executed civilians under the watch of one Italian captain, but she did not follow it up further. This would have constituted a very substantial war crime and needs further investigation. One has to note, however, that the high number, e.g. of executed Hungarian generals, also owed to the Cold War situation and the purges by the new regime in Budapest.

[136] Scotoni, *Il nemico fidato*, 270ff.

[137] Schlemmer, "Die comandi tappa," 529–30. Parts of the reports, which obviously are less convincing in their claims that the more objective Soviet ones, are printed in ibid., 532–46.

[138] Virtue, "Fascist Italy," 26–27, 156ff.

Tenors'), distributed Soviet leaflets, and even traded away their weapons. City dwellers fed them even though they had little themselves."[139]

Messe, too, criticised the Germans' occupation methods and missed opportunities, for instance in exploiting Ukrainian nationalism,[140] and other Italian sources show a strong disapproval of German policies even before the setbacks of winter 1942–1943.[141] However, describing Messe's criticism as proof of "a complete incomprehension between the allies on occupation strategies"[142] would be too simplistic. Also 'the Germans' adopted varying policies and their treatment of civilians, POWs and partisans depended more on time and circumstances than Giusti suggests. A German Infantry Division commander of Army Group Centre who faced well-organised partisans in the immediate rear of the frontline was likely to take a different approach than his comrades in the relatively calm Ukraine, where the partisan movement only gained strength in early 1943, and the population remained passive with a tendency for collaboration.[143] Therefore, only focusing on the Italian corps can lead to distorted pictures.

The memoir literature was—unsurprisingly—full of stories of cordial relations between Italian soldiers and civilians.[144] Still, academics should be careful to take such documents at face value: memoirs, but also letters captured by the Soviets, should be questioned for their usefulness as source. Mistreating civilians or shooting prisoners was hardly a suitable

---

[139] Berkhoff, *Harvest of Despair*, 217.

[140] Giusti, *La campagna*, 195–97. The Italians trained around 80 Cossacks under command of a former Tsarist colonel at Millerovo in Autumn 1942, see TNA, GFM 36/240, Vidussoni – Appunto per il Duce, 24 Oct. 1942, fol.20; also Piero Crociani, "Cosacchi in grigio-verde," in *La campagna di Russia. Nel 70° anniversario dell'inizio dell'intervento dello CSIR*, eds. Antonello Biagini and Antonio Zarcone (Rome: Nuova Cultura, 2013), 201–14.

[141] See the report (probably by Marras), in ACS, T-821/456/IT 5469/222-233, Fronte dell'Est, 24 Oct. 1942; Pelagalli, *Marras*, 164ff.; Giannuli, *Le spie*, 201–2.

[142] Giusti, *La campagna*, 199.

[143] Especially in the countryside, see Berkhoff, *Harvest of Despair*, 114ff.; also Pohl, *Herrschaft*, 291; Oleg Zarubinsky, "Collaboration of the Population in Occupied Ukrainian Territory: Some Aspects of the Overall Picture," *The Journal of Slavic Military Studies* 10, no. 2 (1997): 138–52.

[144] See e.g. Marsetic, *Dall'Adige al Don*, 64–65. The men were sometimes surprised by Soviet hospitality—even during the retreat from the Don—which, they argued, would not be offered by Italians on this scale to foreign soldiers, Cavallo, *Italiani in guerra*, 184.

topic for the loved ones at home. Yet, Scotoni has demonstrated—based on Russian sources—that the *Alpini* did not rule with excessive force in their occupation zone around Voronezh: they stripped civilians of material for their defensive works and employed forced labour, yet they relied on cooperation with local authorities to normalise daily life.[145] This practise was generally followed in Italian occupation areas and included the election of representatives, the strengthening of jurisdiction,[146] as well as sanitary and spiritual assistance.[147] Indeed, Soviet interrogations of civilians in the Voronezh rayon after its liberation found that Italian troops had committed only five per cent of the around 175 cases of plundering and violence against civilians, prisoners and partisans (the Germans committing 60 per cent and the Hungarians 35 per cent).[148] It clearly shows again that Italian units did commit war crimes, but on a far lesser scale than German or Hungarian soldiers in the same area. In sum, it is therefore more than problematic to simply add the Italian behaviour on Russian soil as another example of ruthless Italian occupation policies (next to the African colonies and Yugoslavia).[149] These cases varied and we should differentiate to improve our understanding of occupations.

The treatment of Soviet prisoners was the Wehrmacht's first widely documented war crime.[150] How did the Italians handle captured Red Army's soldiers? Atrocity stories spread to the Italians and spurred a belief that the Soviets took no prisoners.[151] This might have led to a lower willingness to give quarter in the heat of battle; yet we lack reliable

---

[145] The Luftwaffe had heavily bombarded Voronezh and subsequent German ground operations further devastated the city—resulting in the second highest death toll any city suffered (after Stalingrad), Scotoni, *Il nemico fidato*, 265.

[146] Ibid., 204–24, especially 208, 210.

[147] Tirone, "La Politica," 194–97. In the area around Rossosh, the Italians were lucky to be deployed in a very religious and monarchist zone, see Virtue, "We Istrians," 295.

[148] Sergey I. Filonenko, "Popolazione locale ed occupazione sul Don tra il 1942 ed il 1943: Contrapposizione ed antagonismo," in *La campagna di Russia. Nel 70º anniversario dell'inizio dell'intervento dello CSIR*, eds. Antonello Biagini and Antonio Zarcone (Rome: Nuova Cultura, 2013), 137–47, here 145.

[149] See Amedeo Osti Guerrazzi, "Italians at War: War and Experience in Fascist Italy," *Journal of Modern Italian Studies* 22, no. 5 (2017): 587–603, here 590.

[150] Mawdsley, *Thunder*, 237–40.

[151] Tolloy, *Con l'Armata*, 92–93.

sources to make any convincing claims.[152] The Italians had to hand over prisoners to German authorities, yet no shootings during surrender or briefly after their capture are documented; while this, of course, is rarely the case in such situations.[153] In spring 1942, the CSIR circulated a directive to treat Soviet POWs and deserters benevolently in order to ease their surrender and acquire an additional workforce; thus, despite references to humanity and justice, this directive clearly had practical use.[154] Only when the Italians started to independently administer their rear area in summer 1942 did they preside over own prisoner camps and used captured soldiers as forced labour.[155] The two initial camps were later extended (to ten) and encompassed up to 15,000 prisoners, who often came from German captivity.[156] Joint control over prisoners made the Italians complicit in maltreatment, but it is difficult to establish more information.[157] Only a minority of prisoners in Italian hands was employed as forced labour: 3200 men (of 15,000) had to fulfil some kind of duties and twenty per cent of these were assigned to defensive works.[158] Overall, the treatment appears to have been relatively mild[159] and mortality rates appear to have been lower than in German camps; even though they also rose to fifteen per cent during winter despite Italian measures to improve the prisoners' conditions.[160]

---

[152] Argued e.g. by Giusti, *La campagna*, 240–41. Osti Guerrazzi and Schlemmer cited an order by General Zanghieri in which he demanded that no prisoners should be taken, yet both scholars did not further analysis this question, ibid., "I soldati italiani," 410.

[153] Giusti, *La campagna*, 236–37.

[154] ACS, T-821/258/IT 3064/91-92, Col. Utili– Trattamento dei prigionieri di guerra e disertori sovietici, 1 May 1942.

[155] Giusti, *La campagna*, 236ff. The Italians had employed Soviet prisoners for labour since winter 1941, but on a lesser scale, see also Tirone, "La politica," 199–200.

[156] The camp numbers depend on the method of counting, i.e. if only those camps in the rear or also the ones close to the front are included, for the differentiation see Scotoni, *Il nemico fidato*, 224ff.

[157] Medical and nutritional supply was above the levels of German camps, Virtue, "Fascist Italy," 51–55; Giusti, *La campagna*, 240–41.

[158] Scotoni, *Il nemico fidato*, 228. Yet, the Italians also employed forced labour that they received from the Organisation Todt.

[159] Tirone, "La politica," 201ff.

[160] Scotoni, *Il nemico fidato*, 229, 232, 235.

Engaging the Partisans

Besides general relations with civilians and regular soldiers, the existence of partisans especially affected occupation practices during the Second World War. During the advance in 1941, the CSIR encountered almost no insurgents, yet maintaining control over the lines of communication and fear of subversion remained pre-eminent concerns.[161] Soviet stragglers and individual partisans occasionally attacked Italian units,[162] and twenty civilians who were suspected of forming a partisan unit were captured near Gorlovka in November.[163] Yet, in total 'only' 27 partisans were shot by Italian units in 1941, while of 2652 arrested and interrogated suspects only 249 were handed to the Germans—the rest were left unharmed.[164] Indeed, the industrialised Donbas area was not necessarily textbook guerrilla terrain. The few acts of resistance were sporadic raids, sabotage and propaganda[165]—much in contrast to the grander operations in the rear of Army Group Centre and Army Group North.[166] Still, this did not prevent the German authorities from running a ruthless occupation regime in the Donbas.[167]

In January 1942, when the Soviets created the Izyum bulge, the CSIR was ordered to control informants, agents and partisans behind the front. Initially it was mainly the *Carabinieri* who extended their tasks as military police to 'robustly' guard the rear.[168] In a circular to CSIR formations, Messe ordered an end to quarrels over responsibilities and reminded his men that in face of the spy and partisan threat only results counted.[169] Thus, he clearly referred to the idea of 'military necessity', but his order can hardly be interpreted as offering any wide-ranging *carte blanche*. In essence, he urged good cooperation over

---

[161] On the persisting fear over paratrooper drops see BA-MA, RH 31-IX/9, Gariboldi telegram, 2 Nov. 1942, fol.158.

[162] ACS, T-821/255/IT 3053/102, *Pasubio* to CSIR, 12 Oct. 1941.

[163] ACS, T-821/255/IT 3056/804, *Pasubio* to CSIR, 18 Nov. 1941.

[164] Giusti, *La campagna*, 183. It is unclear what happened to these 249 persons.

[165] Scotoni, *Il nemico fidato*, 173–84.

[166] Shepherd, *War in the Wild East*, 84ff.

[167] Scotoni, *Il nemico fidato*, 179ff.

[168] A detailed study on the *Carabinieri*'s action could shed further light on the Italian occupation approach.

[169] ACS, T-821/256/IT 3060/535, Messe– Repressione attività di informatori del nemico e di partigiani, 26 Jan. 1942.

common goals and not ruthless extermination. The rhetoric of military necessity should therefore be understood within the situational context and judged in terms of the evidence of the actual deeds that followed such orders. As described above, the units had hardly any combat power left in January 1942 and were in dire need of reinforcements and supplies. Thus, an upheaval at their back was equivalent to cutting their lifeline. Messe therefore reminded all rear units that they were part of another kind of front and asked them to combat partisans wherever necessary.[170] In order to control the rear areas, the Italians scouted villages for able-bodied men who had not been residents before 22 June 1941 and interned them. The Italians also interrogated captured female and under-age informants—but the sources do not reveal their ultimate fate.[171] Everyone who was suspected of espionage—including women and children—was to be handed over to the German Secret Field Police (*Geheime Feldpolizei*, or GFP) and could only be executed with the GFP's consent.[172] On the other hand, Italian units might have ignored their orders and shot partisans and suspected civilians instead of handing them to the GFP—like other German allies did[173]—but there are so far no documents hinting in this direction.

In summer 1942, regular formations became involved in anti-partisan operations in order to combat the rising threat—in what now became an Italian-administered rear area.[174] The Italian Army was unprepared for counter-insurgency warfare in Russia, but received some information and memoranda from German authorities.[175] Italian directives emphasised upholding good relations with civilians and strict discipline to prevent

---

[170] ACS, T-821/256/IT 3060/599-601, Messe– Difesa retrovie, 30 Jan. 1942.

[171] They were interrogated, but the report does not state what happened to them afterwards, ACS, T-821/257/IT 3062/63, Attività C.S. [Counter-Espionage], 27 Mar. 1942.

[172] ACS, T-821/256/IT 3060/536-537, Maj. Bianchi – Attività di partigiani e spionaggio nemico, 16 Jan. 1942.

[173] Krisztián Ungváry, "Hungarian Occupation Forces in the Ukraine 1941–1942: The Historiographical Context," *The Journal of Slavic Military Studies* 20, no. 1 (2007): 81–120, here 86–88.

[174] On the organisation see Gentile, "Alle spalle dell'ARMIR," 162–64; Schlemmer, "Die comandi tappa," 514ff. For the Italian rear organisation in November 1942, ibid., 528.

[175] Stefano Basset and Filippo Cappellano, "L'esercito italiano e la guerra antipartigiana in Russia (1941–1943)," in *Battaglie in Russia. Il Don e Stalingrado 75 anni dopo*, ed. Olga Dubrovina (Milan: Ed. Unicopli, 2018), 119–43, here 120–21.

excessive violence and alienating popular support.[176] Locally recruited police and militias were also to be strictly supervised by Italian authorities so that they would not undermine overall strategy.[177] Initially, the *Vicenza* Division and the *Carabinieri* passively assisted German units.[178] In September, the so-called *Nuclei Cacciatori* (hunter squads, around 30 men strong), were formed as mobile direct action groups.[179] While they were designed to hunt out partisans, their relation to civilians was more ambiguous—even though they were (formally) not allowed to kill witnesses, for example.[180] What they did (or report back) in practice, is difficult to establish, but due to the low partisan activity they never really started a toxic spiral of violence and counter-violence.[181]

In summer 1942, the overall level of partisan activity in the area where Italian troops were based remained comparatively low (and thus also Italian casualties), though some attacks were reported near Kharkov, Voroshilovgad and Millerovo.[182] When the Italians reached the Don, the valleys on the riverbank bore the danger of surprise attacks and all villages within five kilometres of the river were evacuated, as the very high steppe grass provided sufficient cover for surprise night attacks.[183] Indeed while the terrain did not offer large swathes of dense forests or swamps, it did not entirely preclude partisan operations. However, the 165 partisan groups (each with 20–25 fighters) that had been formed by Soviet state organs in autumn 1941 in the Voronesh province had not

[176] Giusti, *La campagna*, 185–86.

[177] BA-MA, RH 31-IX/13, Gariboldi circular, 1 Sept. 1942, fos.164–66. On the employment of Russian forces under Italian command see Crociani, "Cosacchi in grigio-verde." In total, 2423 locals served in 249 police formations that helped Italian forces in the rear areas, Basset and Cappellano, "L'esercito," 132.

[178] Scotoni, *Il nemico fidato*, 186ff.

[179] The regular frontline formations had to send detachments of sixty men to form these squads, Schlemmer, "Die comandi tappa," 524ff. Service in these units was meant to constitute a "title of honour", BA-MA, RH 31-IX/13, Direttive per l'azione dei nuclei cacciatori, 15 Sept. 1942, fol.71.

[180] Scotoni, *Il nemico fidato*, 239–40.

[181] See Basset and Cappellano, "L'esercito," 137–41.

[182] The Italians estimated around 250 partisans near Kharkov, an important logistical hub, ACS, T-821/373/IT 4885/214-217, Comando II Corpo d'Armata, 18 June 1942; BA-MA, MSg 2/4388, Distler – Verbindungsoffizier, fos.8, 18, 23, 29; Virtue, "Fascist Italy," 122, 138ff.

[183] BA-MA, MSg 2/4388, Distler – Verbindungsoffizier, fos.33, 63–64.

been trained continuously, as the risk of an occupation had been judged as an unlikely scenario.[184] These groups had less training and were less prepared to wage a partisan war. Additionally, many men deserted when the occupation started, communication was difficult and only some (untrained) locals could be recruited so that the total number of active partisans in summer 1942 was less than 500.[185] The local Soviet commands thus demanded an increase of recruitment and activities, and the number of forces behind the Italian lines on the Don increased after August. Despite organisational problems and difficulties in recruitment, they were ready to strike when the Red Army came closer and, until then, they kept a very low profile and restricted themselves to sabotage, reconnaissance and propaganda.[186]

Indeed, the Italian official history noted an increase of partisan activities in the rear between August and December 1942,[187] but the frontline divisions' daily reports show little 'bandit activity'.[188] The latter may not be wholly surprising, as the *Vicenza* and smaller units under Army command were tasked with anti-partisan operations. The *Vicenza* reported that one of their companies had been attacked by strong partisan formations 50 kilometres south-west of Starobelsk on 23 November, suffering eighteen killed, six wounded and one missing.[189] But the Eighth Army's accounts reveal rather limited partisan activity. All Italian reports on anti-partisan activities were sent through the German liaison to Army Group B. For the period between 10–26 December 1942 the Chief of Staff, General Malaguti, reported one partisan killed, five captured and an additional 830 suspects that were held in custody[190]; between 28

[184] Vladimir V. Korovin, "Azioni militari dei partigiani sovietici contro gli eserciti tedeschi, italiani e ungheresi negli anni 1942–1943," in *Battaglie in Russia. Il Don e Stalingrado 75 anni dopo*, ed. Olga Dubrovina (Milan: Ed. Unicopli, 2018), 39–71, here 41–42.

[185] Ibid., 44.

[186] Ibid., 47–48, 68. On preparations and activities before the December attack, see ibid., 50ff.

[187] USSME, *Le operazioni*, 323. The same argument is made in Giusti, *La campagna*, 187. Some partisan formations had been revealed and captured, Scotoni, *Il nemico fidato*, 190.

[188] ACS, T-821/259/IT 3068.

[189] DS CS, VIII:I, 25 Nov. 1942. Also possibly inflated numbers of killed partisans, have to be treated with caution, as they could be intended to report 'successes'.

[190] BA-MA, RH 31-IX/19, Malaguti to Army Group B, 28 Dec. 1942, fol.3.

November and 10 December 1942 he listed thirteen killed partisans, 19 captured (of which two were executed) and 37 suspects[191]; from 6–27 November 1942 five partisans were killed in the Eighth Army's area of responsibility, 46 captured (of which 19 executed) and "32 suspects and fifteen lost Russian soldiers captured and sent to concentration camp."[192] Between 26 September and 5 October 1942, the XXIX Army Corps reported eighteen killed partisans.[193] In sum, the available records confirm 40 killed partisans in the entire Eighth Army's zone of responsibility in late 1942—in an area of 265 cities and 476,000 inhabitants.[194] Other numbers paint a similar picture. From July 1942 to March 1943, the *Carabinieri* checked 3700 civilians of which 900 were arrested and sent to the ARMIR's camps and another 940 individuals were captured during operations (89 partisans and 16 paratroopers); whereas own losses of the *Carabinieri* amounted to nine killed, four wounded and eighteen missing.[195]

Even suspects convicted of weapons possession and propaganda activities were sentenced to yearlong forced labour but not executed.[196] Are these numbers reliable or did the Italians suppress information? Clearly, some documents might be missing and some shootings may not have been reported. Yet, the Italians never had any scruples about openly reporting figures of killed partisans in other theatres.[197] Thus maybe the *relazione* did not "aim to confirm the low intensity"[198] of fighting, as some scholars have argued, but showed the reality, i.e. a generally low

---

[191] BA-MA, RH 31-IX/19, Malaguti to Army Group B, 17 Dec. 1942, fol.7. At the cost of one Italian dead.

[192] BA-MA, RH 31-IX/19, Malaguti to Army Group B, 28 Nov. 1942, fol.13. In this context, 'concentration camp' simply means a collection camp. The Italians lost eighteen men (three officers) in this period.

[193] BA-MA, RH 31-IX/19, Ditfurth [?] to Eighth Army, 7 Oct. 1942, fol.30.

[194] Schlemmer, "Die comandi tappa," 518. On the low activity in the *Alpini*'s sector see Scotoni, *Il nemico fidato*, 236ff.

[195] Giusti, *La campagna*, 187.

[196] Scotoni, *Il nemico fidato*, 246.

[197] The daily summaries for the *Comando Supremo* frankly listed those numbers, e.g. for the Slovenian theatre.

[198] Gentile, "Alle spalle dell'ARMIR," 166.

intensity of fighting, which is also confirmed by research on Soviet partisans, who had chosen a wait-and-see approach in this area.[199] Partisan activities intensified after the Soviet attack in December 1942 and irregular forces harassed the Italians during their retreat.[200] The *Ravenna*, for example, reported as many as one thousand partisans near Taloj,[201] the *Cuneense* was attacked near Annovka,[202] and the Gomel area was full of partisans, which obstructed movements and threatened logistics.[203] Burgwyn has argued that partisans killed over 4000 Italians and captured around 7000.[204] Russian sources mention one incident where 800 partisans captured around 4000 stragglers before handing them over to the Red Army.[205] Giusti even maintained—based on Russian sources—the partisans had joined hands with advancing regular units (and civilians) in killing or capturing 11,000 *Alpini* in ten days.[206] The Italians might have mistaken some attacks from regular units during this chaotic retreat, but one should not dismiss these reports offhand, as Russian sources have documented how partisans and regular units operated jointly.[207] Indeed, partisans operated with civilians and regular troops in Pavlograd in February 1943. The Italians had to use artillery to clear the city,[208] and Colonel Carloni, who led the attack,

---

[199] Scotoni, *Il nemico fidato*, 237. Further, one joint attempt of German, Hungarian, and Italian troops to hunt down partisans in December failed utterly, see Jörn Hasenclever, *Wehrmacht und Besatzungspolitik in der Sowjetunion. Die Befehlshaber der rückwärtigen Heeresgebiete 1941–1943* (Paderborn: Schöningh, 2010), 433.

[200] Scotoni, *Il nemico fidato*, 244ff.; Burgwyn, *Mussolini*, 219; Virtue, "Fascist Italy," 141f.; Hamilton, *Sacrifice*, 133.

[201] For the *Torino* see BA-MA, RH 31-IX/35, Hammann – Gefechtsbericht *Torino*, 5 Mar. 1943, fol.22; The *Ravenna* in BA-MA, RH 31-IX/35, Pertner – Gefechtsbericht *Ravenna*, 20 Mar. 1943, fos.65, 67.

[202] USSME, *Le operazioni*, 436.

[203] ACS, T-821/354/IT 4511/647-661, Lt. Col. Manaresi – Rapporto sull'invio del 9° treno A.P.E. in Russia (febbraio–marzo 1943), 24 Mar. 1943.

[204] Burgwyn, *Mussolini*, 219.

[205] Lelyushenko, *Moskva-Stalingrad-Berlin-Praga*, 157.

[206] Giusti, *La campagna*, 187.

[207] Scotoni, *Il nemico fidato*, 249ff. Also the Hungarian Second Army was assaulted by civilians, partisans, and regular forces—not least after requisitioning houses and forcefully taking food and other vital resources, Wimpffen, "Zweite Ungarische," 294.

[208] BA-MA, RH 31-IX/35, Schlubeck to Tippelskirch, 18 Feb. 1943, fol.108. Detailed in Scotoni, *Il nemico fidato*, 192ff.

reported that the "numbers of partisans is so enormous that their deployment rather appears to be an uprising."[209]

Italian crimes against civilians and partisans (these two should not be mixed) arguably reached their highest point during this period, but in sum it is fair to assess that—while the overall numbers remain imprecise—they were comparatively very low.[210] At the same time, one has to contextualise the crimes—which does not excuse them—with the Italians' bad operational situation: the retreat in face of an overwhelming enemy in wintertime with a chaotic rear resulted in a struggle for survival that produced a toxic combination. While this made killing partisans (out of sheer cruelty) the least of priorities, it might explain (but not justify) ruthless behaviour *vis-à-vis* civilians in a struggle for survival. Memoir statements on apparently mild reactions during the retreat need to be treated with great care, of course. Schlemmer's justified criticism of the violent rhetoric in one of General Nasci's orders should be put in context and only judged upon actual actions: for a commander to put the welfare of his troops over that of civilians was neither surprising, nor an isolated phenomenon or per se criminal.[211] Moreover, even in Pavlograd—arguably the largest battle where partisans fought side by side with regular Soviet forces—the Italians appear not to have been involved in the brutal reprisals after the recapture of the city.[212]

In conclusion, the Italians did resort to violence against non-combatants on several occasions, but on a limited scale and "with important exceptions, [they] exhibited little enthusiasm in aiding the Germans in the mass killing of innocents."[213] Both the structure and the situation worked to restrain Italian conduct, while the low influence of ideology also had an important effect. Given the Italians' overall casualty numbers up till December 1942 and the limited partisan activity, it is fair to assess that situational factors prevented an escalation and reactions always remained proportional to the threat.[214] As it stands, there is more than a grain of truth in Virtue's assessment that "the lack of partisan warfare

---

[209] BA-MA, RH 31-IX/35, Col. Carloni – Gefechtsbericht. Brückenkopf Pawlograd – Dnjepropetrowsk, 17 Feb. 1943, fos.113–15, here fol.115.

[210] Scotoni, *Il nemico fidato*, 247ff., 251ff.

[211] Schlemmer, "Die comandi tappa," 523.

[212] Scotoni, *Il nemico fidato*, 200–2.

[213] Burgwyn, *Mussolini*, 220.

[214] As argued by Scotoni, *Il nemico fidato*, 191.

in Italian zones of occupation was more a cause of the moderate behaviour of Italian soldiers than a result of it."[215] Moreover, Messe repeatedly criticised the harsh German approach and lack of 'carrots' being offered to Ukrainian nationalists.[216] Counterfactuals about different behaviour in face of a serious partisan threat cannot be fully answered, but one should not assume that the Italians would have behaved similarly restrainedly in face of an organised partisan war, mounting casualties and poor supply situation.[217] Comparative views underline the importance of situational factors; and thus further counter the 'Bartov argument'. The restrained Italian reactions to limited threats prevented a spread of violence and, therefore, a vicious cycle of reprisals, counter-reprisals and crimes like the ones in the Balkans.[218] At the peak of the repression in Slovenia, Italian forces killed around 2000 partisans in July and August 1942 alone.[219] Yet, also here, behaviour depended on circumstances. While the Italians were ruthless on the Greek mainland, the islands remained places of relative calm and a 'light' occupation.[220] In comparison, Italy's allies also behaved differently according to situational factors. In 1941–1942, the Hungarian Army had two occupation zones: the area around Poltava was so calm that it was "little different from peace time", while the second zone, at the southern exit of the Brjansk Forest, was a hotbed of

[215] Virtue, "Fascist Italy," 9.

[216] Basset and Cappellano, "L'esercito," 128–30.

[217] It would be interesting to analyse whether Italian soldiers refrained from anti-partisan duties and which consequences they faced—given that Italian military justice was rather lenient between 1940 and 1943 (especially in comparison to 1915–1918) there certainly was some leverage. On the military justice see Giorgio Rochat, *Duecento sentenze nel bene e nel male. La giustizia militare nella guerra 1940–1943* (Udine: Gaspari, 2002). Also Knox, *Hitler's Italian Allies*, 34.

[218] Giusti, *La campagna*, 186. Leading scholars have found similar results for the Balkans: the Italians were certainly no saints, but the sheer existence of harsh orders (such as the infamous "3C" circular in Yugoslavia) was no proof that a war of extermination followed; and differentiations must be made regarding their victims or enemies, as partisans and civilians were not in the same category. Indeed, while Italians employed similar measures they differed in "frequency and intensity" to the Germans', Rodogno, *Fascism's European Empire*, 415; Agarossi and Giusti, *Una guerra*.

[219] Rodogno, *Fascism's European Empire*, 339. On the escalation of violence from July onwards see Osti Guerrazzi, *Italian Army*, 92ff.

[220] For this argument see Paolo Fonzi, "The Italian Occupation of Crete During the Second World War," in *Italy and the Second World War: Alternative Perspectives*, ed. Emanuele Sica and Richard Carrier (Leiden: Brill, 2018), 51–75.

insurrection, and the ruthless Hungarian slaughter and pillaging in this latter area even appalled German authorities.[221] Thus, one should think twice about accusing the Italians' rear and supply system of incompetence, as they seem to have forestalled worse cases of pillaging and deteriorating morale that—in the Hungarian case—increased the probability of reprisals against innocent civilians. Ungváry has explained the Hungarian crimes south of the Bryansk Forest mainly in terms of situational factors.[222] Similarly—even though as part of Army Group North—the Spanish 'Blue Division's' occupation policy has also been described as rather a reaction to situational factors than driven by ideology.[223]

In sum, ideology played a small role in the Italian conduct on the Eastern Front and the scale of violence against civilians, prisoners and partisans was limited—particularly in contrast to Hungarian, Romanian and German actions.[224] Such comparisons have no intention of absolving the Italians as good-hearted people who never committed war crimes. Yet their actions have to be contextualised and the pendulum cannot simply swing from decade-long overlooking of crimes to a blurring of

[221] In spring 1942, the three divisions killed the same number of partisans as the entire Army Group Centre. The Hungarians also shot uniformed paratroopers, which was not common, and referred to collective reprisals without German orders, i.e. escalating on their own watch, Ungváry, "Hungarian Occupation," 84, 100, 113, 119. Later occupational methods on Polish territory were much more lenient, see ibid., 111; Krisztián Ungváry, "The Hungarian Theatre of War," in *Germany and the Second World War. Vol. 8: The Eastern Front 1943-1944*, eds. Karl-Heinz Frieser et al. (Oxford: Oxford University Press, 2017), 846–959, here 850ff.

[222] Besides strong partisan activity, the bad state of Hungarian troops—training levels, malnourishment, and medical supplies—also spurred violence, Ungváry, "Hungarian Occupation," 112, 116; on this case, see also Truman O. Anderson, "A Hungarian *Vernichtungskrieg*? Hungarian Troops and the Soviet Partisan War in Ukraine, 1942," *Militärgeschichtliche Mitteilungen* 58, no. 2 (1999): 345–66.

[223] Xosé M. Núñez Seixas, "Good Invaders? The Occupation Policy of the Spanish Blue Division in Northwestern Russia, 1941–1944," *War in History* 25, no. 3 (2018): 361–86. For similarities between the Spanish and Italian cases, see Xosé M. Núñez Seixas, "Unable to Hate? Some Comparative Remarks on the War Experiences of Spaniards and Italians on the Eastern Front, 1941–1944," *Journal of Modern European History* 16, no. 2 (2018): 269–89.

[224] Schlemmer, "Das königlich-italienische Heer," 174. The Romanians, for example, had a much more pronounced anti-semitic demour, see Dennis Deletant, *Hitler's Forgotten Ally. Ion Antonescu and His Regime, Romania 1940–1944* (New York: Palgrave Macmillan, 2006), 127ff.; Axworthy, *Third Axis*; also Ungváry, "Hungarian Occupation" on the situational factors.

facts that forges an Italian war of extermination that did not exist. This would additionally distort and ignore the nuances that decades of scholarship on German occupational policies have created.

The 'disaster at the Don' narrative included countless examples of Russian civilians inviting Italian soldiers into their *izba* (village huts) and providing them with food and shelter (in a sense as payback for their good conduct on the way to the Don).[225] Thus, the memoir literature seems to have neglected the partisan threat and simply converted to the tale of peaceful coexistence with the local populace, which was not always accurate. This gains additional importance given that much of the memoir literature was later linked to the Italian partisan war, and therefore the negative connotations of partisan activity were deliberately overlooked. The nasty facets of criminal Italian behaviour were thus mentally fixed on the march to the Don, i.e. the '*guerra fascista*', and could then be used as an allegation against the top military authorities. We should not forget that the accusations put forth against the senior leadership did not essentially concern its criminal rhetoric, but rather military ineffectiveness and its sacrificing of its own men by sending them into battle with bad equipment. Yet, another facet of victimhood was also hotly debated and became a problem for Rome's postwar relations with the Kremlin: Italian prisoners in Soviet hands.

VICTIMS IN SOVIET CAPTIVITY

When the ARMIR was defeated on the banks of the Don and decimated during the retreat in the steppes, the Soviets captured over 70,000 Italians. Around 22,000 were either shot immediately or died on their way to the camps, another 38,000 perished in captivity (mainly in the first six months of 1943), and only 10,032 returned to Italy in 1945–1946.[226] The mortality rate of those who reached the camps was a staggering 56.5 per cent—in contrast: the overall Hungarian death rate in Soviet camps was 10.6 per cent, the Romanians' 29.1 per cent, the

---

[225] Faldella, *Le truppe alpine*, 180; Giusti, *La campagna*, 255.

[226] In addition to the ARMIR soldiers, the Soviets also sent captured Italian Military Internees (IMI) from Germany and RSI diplomats to their POW camps in 1945, which has led to some problems in providing exact figures, Burgwyn, *Mussolini*, 210–11; Elena Agarossi and Victor Zaslavsky, *Togliatti e Stalin. Il PCI e la politica estera staliniana negli archivi di Mosca* (Bologna: Il Mulino, 1997), 163.

Finns' 16.9 per cent and the Germans' 14.9 per cent.[227] In total, more than 80 per cent of Italians who fell into Soviet hands did not survive the war. In comparison, over 98 per cent of captured Italians survived British, French and American prisons,[228] and even the 600,000 Italians who fell into German hands after the *8 settembre* had similarly low mortality rates.[229]

What were the reasons for these extraordinary mortality rates in Soviet camps? Certainly, the time of capture played a role.[230] In a harsh winter climate, while major operations were still ongoing, the Soviets faced many supply problems and had to handle the numerous prisoners from the Stalingrad pocket. Even though Italians prisoners were in general treated better than German prisoners, there were instances where Italians were killed instead of captured or, indeed, shot after falling into Soviet hands.[231] Many soldiers perished (or were further weakened) on their way to the camps—often stripped of their winter clothing by the Soviets.[232] The camps were characterised by poor sanitary and lodging conditions, little food and resulting high mortality rates, until the disorder improved in spring 1943.[233] The lack of spiritual assistance or contact with families, as well as noted cases of brutal attacks on prisoners, added to the detrimental effects of hard labour.[234] But beyond the situational problems, the Soviets generally had low regard for prisoners

---

[227] Giusti, *I prigionieri*, 97. This, however, does leave out the vital factor when they were captured.

[228] Bob Moore, "Enforced Diaspora: The Fate of Italian Prisoners of War During the Second World War," *War in History* 22, no. 2 (2015): 174–90, here 175ff.; Flavio Conti, *I prigionieri di guerra italiani 1940–1945* (Bologna: Il Mulino, 1986); Giusti, *I prigionieri*, 97.

[229] Hammermann has calculated that 19,714 Italians (of 600,000) died from forced labour and malnourishment, and poor conditions – thus, the IMI had a mortality rate of around three per cent. See Hammermann, *Zwangsarbeit*, 584.

[230] Those Germans who fell into Soviet hands during the battle of Stalingrad had similarly high death rates, due to the harsh transports and generally poor conditions in winter 1942–1943, see Rüdiger Overmans, *Soldaten hinter Stacheldraht. Deutsche Kriegsgefangene des Zweiten Weltkriegs* (Munich: Propyläen, 2000), 89, 131.

[231] Buttar, *Knife's Edge*, 189–90.

[232] Giusti, *I prigionieri*, 34.

[233] Ibid., 43, 59–109.

[234] Roberto Morozzo della Rocca, *La Politica estera italiana e l'unione sovietica (1944–1948)* (Rome: La Goliardica, 1985), 108.

and the camp system was just beginning to be organised.[235] Thus, the mortality rates in winter 1942–1943 resulted more from neglect and the chaotic POW system than a Soviet desire exterminate the Italians.[236] A memorandum of the Italian General Staff's Information Office from 29 January 1946, which was based on prisoners' narratives, arrived at the conclusion that near the combat zones the Italians were treated viciously, but matters improved as soon as they reached the rear.[237]

Whereas Italian soldiers in Western captivity were motivated to join the Allied war effort after 8 September 1943, the exiled Italian Communists fulfilled the Soviets' desire to re-educate prisoners. Under the tutelage of Palmiro Togliatti they tried to indoctrinate the soldiers with lectures and other means.[238] For this purpose, the Communists also founded the *L'Alba* news sheet, which was first published under Togliatti's control on 15 February 1943.[239] In sum, they were not very successful: some prisoners signed up out of opportunism, while those resisting these initiatives—as in British or US camps—were not necessarily all dyed in the wool Fascists, but may instead have been considering their standing as soldiers if they returned home as 'collaborators',[240] or else were simply not attracted by Communism.[241] Morozzo della Rocca has described the Communist propaganda as intense, but not harshly imposed.[242] Yet, the Italian exile Communists did nothing to ease the prisoners' fate either.

[235] Giusti, *I prigionieri*, 45ff.

[236] Morozzo della Rocca, *Politica*, 94. Prison camp number 188, for example, held 2500 prisoners on 1 May 1943, but at the end of month a mere 160. The cause for this drop was probably a mixture of relocations, malnutrition, and diseases, Agarossi and Zaslavsky, *Togliatti e Stalin*, 162–63. See also Giusti, *I prigionieri*, 68ff.

[237] As cited in Morozzo della Rocca, *Politica*, 107.

[238] Agarossi and Zaslavsky, *Togliatti e Stalin*, 166; Giusti, *I prigionieri*, 111ff.

[239] Ibid., 137ff.

[240] Especially soldiers from Northern Italy feared reprisals against their families from German or RSI authorities, Moore, "Enforced Diaspora," 180.

[241] Only 31 officers who had collaborated were investigated after their return and some were downgraded by Italian counter-intelligence, Petacco, *L'armata*, 208; Giusti, *I prigionieri*, 148–56. In contrast to the captured Wehrmacht officers, who founded the anti-Hitler National Committee for a Free Germany (NKFD) which included both Communists and non-Communists, the Italians never formed a similar organisation in captivity—despite some ideas in this regard, ibid., 142ff.

[242] Morozzo della Rocca, *Politica*, 108.

On the other hand, the hunger strike of one general seems to have improved the men's conditions.[243] The officers in the *Alpini* Corps had paid a particularly high price.[244] The three captured generals Umberto Ricagno, Emilio Battisti and Etvaldo Pascolini were spared the marches to camps. After long interrogations in Moscow they were deported to camp Cernzi, where all Axis generals were held in better facilities—according to common practice and conventions. After *8 settembre* the Italian officers politely asked to be separated from the Germans, and were transferred to camp Suzdal. In this old monastery near Moscow they, too, were indoctrinated and interrogated by the Italian exile Communist Paolo Robotti. Soon, after generals Battisti and Ricagno returned from Soviet internment in March 1950, they were appointed to head the Bologna and Bari Territorial Commands respectively, which the British thought to be "somewhat strange appointments" after seven years of captivity.[245] Battisti later became involved in political debates about the campaign on the Eastern Front, published on his time in Soviet captivity and ran for the neo-Fascist MSI.[246] Still, the generals' alleged cowardly behaviour remained a hallmark of the Eastern Front memoir literature. According to this myth, the Italian generals had waited in safe positions until they were captured, leaving their men in the lurch, and then spending a relatively calm time as prisoners. Bearing in mind the positive German ratings of the senior officers, the generals' refusal to be flown out, their repeated leadership at the top of their troops, and their behaviour in captivity, we should reconsider this myth.

Indeed, the period of captivity became a contested issue during the repatriations in 1945 and 1946 as it influenced the overall memory and

---

[243] Petacco, *L'armata*, 215–16.

[244] Eight out of twelve regimental commanders had been killed or captured, one of six generals died in battle, three were captured, and two led their troops out of encirclement. In contrast, all 21 generals of the II and XXXV corps reached Voroshilovgrad, two of the twenty regimental commanders fell in battle, and four were taken prisoner. All numbers in Petacco, *L'armata*, 154.

[245] TNA, FO 371/96269, WT 1191/2, The Italian Army in 1950, 8 Jan. 1951, fol.5.

[246] His publication with Carloni and others shows that some officers were arguably closer to Fascism than others (or had developed very strong anti-Communist tendencies during the Russian campaign), and that they remained in contact with influential in far-right circles. The publication referred to is Battisti, Carloni et al., eds., *Italianzy kaputt*.

narrative of the *campagna di Russia*.[247] The Italian exile communists—who flocked back to Italy—were probably the best informed about the prisoners' conditions. Yet, they preferred to remain silent to uphold the ideal of a socialist paradise in Stalin's Soviet Union—a myth the returning POWs might shatter.[248] Thus, they attempted to stall the repatriations. But the Kremlin decided on a gesture of goodwill (which was also meant to raise Communist popularity in Italy) and started repatriations even before the Americans and British released their prisoners.

The political Right and large parts of the media waged massive campaigns and instrumentalised the prisoners' fate for their political goals. Yet, one should acknowledge that both political sides took a clear stake in these debates: whereas the Right used a fervent anti-communism (against Togliatti and the Soviets in general), the political Left caricatured every defender of the Italian POWs as fascist. Additionally, the very emotional and accusational memoirs did not contribute to a sober analysis.[249] The debates added to the self-victimisation in the public discourse, but combined with the Left's attacks against the senior military leadership it merged topics of military honour and victimhood. By attacking the Communist Party one could defend the military's performance, the *brava gente* narrative, and the victim status of the troops who had returned from Soviet captivity. Thus, the Russian campaign could be linked to the general memory of captivity and imprisonment, which remained a widespread topic in the collective memory.[250] Yet, Moore made a thought-provoking observation how the fate of prisoners in the USSR was muted by the *Resistenza* myth:

> The nascent Italian Republic had to establish an acceptable narrative for its existence within the Western orbit. This involved talking up the resistance to fascism (although only to an extent, in order to avoid allowing communism too great a role) but also meant that the fate of the Italian prisoners in the hands of the Western powers was essentially marginalised as something of an embarrassment. In contrast, the relatively small numbers of Italians in Soviet hands could be seen as fitting into a Cold War agenda,

---

[247] These debates will be described in more detail below. The vast majority of Italian soldiers had returned by 1946, Giusti, *I prigionieri*, 165ff.
[248] Petacco, *L'armata*, 163, 220ff.
[249] Morozzo della Rocca, *Politica*, 99.
[250] Rochat, "La prigionia," 381–402.

especially as their fate was uncertain and many had not been returned at the end of hostilities. However, the political prominence of the Italian Communist Party (PCI) in the postwar era prevented them from becoming too much of a political weapon, whereas the Italian forces seized by the Germans could be seen as reinforcing the country's victimisation at the hands of the Nazis, while at the same time underplaying the country's role as an Axis ally.[251]

However, the prisoners became only one piece in the memory and the contested narrative of the campaign in Russia. The analysis of the different topoi of victimhood shows their interrelatedness: Being a victim of the Germans served the Italian master narrative after 1943 and 1946, the Army's supposedly apolitical stance remained a dictum during the Cold War, and the troops' relatively mild behaviour on Soviet soil, as well as the prisoner issue, became hotly debated topics. These, in turn, were all related to the myths about poor operational performance and bad officership. Memoirs shaped much of the collective memory and held the upper hand in shaping public discourse. Therefore, the next section will examine the main currents and narratives deriving from these memoirs. This will help us to understand the political infighting about POWs, senior officers and the Italian involvement on the Eastern Front, which functioned as a proxy war over general questions of Italy's role in the Second World War.

[251] Moore, "Enforced Diaspora," 189.

CHAPTER 10

Shaping the Myths: Memoirs, the Army and the *Alpini*

The operations in Russia have been distorted for decades by the Italian (and German) memoir literature.[1] The output is unparalleled by any other aspect of the Fascist War of 1940–1943.[2] In 1965, Rochat listed 49 books that were largely written from the 'bottom' of the Army.[3] By 1985, over 100 memoirs had been published, a figure that has today probably reached 200.[4] The following will look closer at the most important memoirs, their authors and contextualise their narratives. Basically, the memoir literature wants us to believe three things[5]:

1. The Italian soldiers were primarily victims, i.e. of the weather, the Fascist regime, poor materiel, incapable senior commanders, the Germans, and they were caught up in the brutal ideological war in the East (between Communism and Nazism).

---

[1] As pointed out by Schlemmer, *Italiener*, 3ff. The role of publishers would also deserve a closer look, Mondini, *Alpini*, 160.
[2] Morozzo della Rocca, *Politica*, 99.
[3] Rochat, "Memorialistica."
[4] Rochat, *Le guerre*, 397.
[5] Osti Guerrazzi and Schlemmer created a slightly different combination, see their "I soldati italiani," 387; for a collection of topoi, see also Safronov, *Italyanski voiska*, 14.

2. In contrast to the Germans, the Italians always had good relations with the Soviet populace, i.e. were *brava gente*, and fought a 'normal' war.
3. The Italian Army was militarily inefficient, mainly due to the poor leadership of the senior command and the general military 'unpreparedness' for war.

Mario Rigoni Stern (1921–2008), Nuto Revelli (1919–2004), Giulio Bedeschi (1915–1990), Giusto Tolloy (1907–1987), Eugenio Corti (1921–2014) and Egisto Corradi (1914–1990) wrote the most important accounts in terms of circulation and impact. Giulio Bedeschi's *Centomila gavette di ghiaccio* sold 1.1 million copies by 1979 and Mario Rigoni Stern's *Il sergente nella neve* almost half a million.[6] Rochat credited this success to the mythical images of the frozen steppes and the superhuman status attributed to the Red Army, which eased the way for arguments about inferiority of numbers and materiel as the reason for defeat.[7] The campaign was mainly looked at in terms of victimhood, sacrifice, betrayal and retreat. Indeed, many book titles already condense this narrative.[8] The first 18 months of the campaign took on only secondary importance, as the story was instead habitually told from the end. This muted the earlier period, i.e. the Italian participation in a criminal war, but also successful operations. In contrast to German propaganda of Stalingrad as heroic sacrifice to the last man,[9] the Italian memoirs emphasised the retreat and only minor episodes were—for specific reasons (see the part on Nikolayevka below)—portrayed as last stands. This hints at both the authors' intentions and the ideals that influenced the common narrative in the civilian sphere. The retreat from the Don was framed similarly to the abandonment myth regarding El Alamein.[10] Yet, unlike the North African memoir literature, the works on the Eastern Front were much more critical towards the military leadership itself. Particularly Gariboldi, the general staff, and the rear command were

[6] Numbers in Morozzo della Rocca, *Politica*, 99.
[7] Rochat, *Le guerre*, 398.
[8] See, e.g. Piero Fortuna and Raffaello Uboldi, *Il tragico Don. Cronache della campagna italiana in Russia (1941–1943)* (Milan: Mondadori, 1980), or the highly successful Egisto Corradi, *La ritirata di Russia* (Milan: Longanesi, 1964).
[9] Kallis, *Nazi Propaganda*, 128–29.
[10] Corni, "Wüste bis zum Don."

strongly attacked.[11] At times, this 'donkey' narrative was even widened to incorporate the First World War. The slaughter of hundreds of thousands was allegedly repeated between 1940 and 1943 with an "army [that] was armed, dressed, and directed like 24 years earlier."[12] It is also imperative to note that this narrative—which often has a clear political message—was not wholeheartedly embraced by the Italian Armed Forces and unsuitable for their memory. Rochat noted the memoirs' moral message, but argued that this did not entail political positions.[13] Such an assessment requires further scrutiny, especially as the memoir writers also effectively became the historians of the campaign.[14] The prime counterexample to Rochat's claim can be found through an analysis of the life and work of Giusto Tolloy.

Giusto Tolloy: Staff Officer Turned Socialist

Tolloy's memoirs became one of the most pronounced criticisms of the Italian involvement in the East, particularly due to his political career after 1945. Born in Trieste, he had fled from his native city during the First World War, and later volunteered to become a professional officer, where, according to his own account after the war, he was less exposed to Fascist ideas.[15] Tolloy has thus been painted as an archetypical protagonist of a generation that was betrayed by Fascism and forced to fight an 'unwanted war' (*guerra non sentita*).[16] He left the military academy in Modena with flying colours,[17] but was very negative about his experience there, criticising his peers' lack of drive to become real soldiers—for Tolloy, they were more interested in the petty nineteenth-century ideal

---

[11] Carlo Vicentini, *Noi soli vivi. Quando settantamila italiani passarono il Don* (Milan: Mursia, 1997), 66, 73; Gianluca Cinelli, *Nuto Revelli* (Turin: Aragno, 2011), 33.

[12] Vicentini, *Noi soli vivi*, 323.

[13] Rochat, "Memorialistica," 473.

[14] Osti Guerrazzi and Schlemmer, "I soldati italiani," 387.

[15] Dino Mengozzi, "Una testimonianza. Da militare di carriera all'impegno antifascista," in *Il prezzo della libertà. Giusto Tolloy* (Reggio Calabria: Città del Sole, 2015), 18–20.

[16] Roberto Pagan, "Introduzione," in *Il prezzo della libertà. Giusto Tolloy*, ed. Roberto Pagan (Reggio Calabria: Città del Sole, 2015), 5–13, cited on 7–8.

[17] Ibid., 9.

of an officer.[18] His first mission was on the Greek front during the spring offensive in March 1941. Thus, he did not witness the disastrous events the preceding winter,[19] but he depicted his deployment as a first sign that he was punished for his anti-fascist ideals.[20] In Greece, he was not only appalled by Italian casualties, but was (apparently) also critical of his own superiors and had early clashes with "arrogant" German soldiers.[21] Yet, his criticism of the military operations needs to be put into perspective. Tolloy was serving at the front for the first time, while his division (the *Bari*) had coped with the difficult challenges on the Epirus front since November 1940. Therefore, his outrage and his reaction to the losses suffered—which were lower than in autumn and winter 1940—should be seen in context. It is also important to note that he linked his narrative of abandonment and abuse by Fascism not only to the Russian theatre, but also to the botched campaign against Greece. Yet, when disaster struck, he was—like in Russia—not necessarily suffering in the trenches.[22]

In Russia, Tolloy served as major in the ARMIR's logistics command, a deployment that he interpreted as yet another punitive measure for his political ideas.[23] While he habitually perceived himself as victim, it is important to note that he served—again—in the rear and did not share the frontline hardships. Still, his admirers saw his role as a "privileged observer" as another argument why his analysis of the Italian general staff was so accurate, as he had witnessed the alleged logistical chaos, the high command's incompetence, the opportunism and their closeness to the Fascists and Germans.[24] Thus, his lack of frontline experience was turned to his advantage. After the retreat in Russia, he witnessed the *8 settembre* in Rome, which he later claimed had completely shattered his belief in the *Esercito* and the King. Hereafter, Tolloy fought

---

[18] Roberto Pagan, ed., *Il prezzo della libertà. Giusto Tolloy* (Reggio Calabria: Città del Sole, 2015), 30, 75–81.

[19] Ibid., 83–84.

[20] Ibid., 84, 87.

[21] Ibid., 89–93.

[22] Tolloy arrived at Durazzo on 14 March and served in the 47th *Bari* Infantry Division, witnessing first-hand the futile attacks near Komarit, where he was apparently in the first lines. It is unclear, however, what exactly his role was.

[23] Ibid., 95.

[24] Pagan, "Introduzione," 11–12.

with the 'Garibaldi' partisans in the Emilia-Romagna from late spring 1944 onwards. Around this time Tolloy also started his political career. He was a founder of the *Partito Italiano del Lavoro*, which merged with the Socialist Party (PSI) right after liberation. He then pursued a party career in Bologna. After becoming a member of parliament in 1948, he remained his party's expert on defence matters, and even headed the Senate's Defence Committee.

His diary on the Russian campaign was first published clandestinely in occupied northern Italy at the end of 1944 and reprinted in 1947. In the preface, Tolloy extolled the *Resistenza*, linked it to the volunteerism of Mazzini and Garibaldi, and expressed his hope for societal change—expressing his faith as "a convinced Marxist."[25] Already in February 1946, he had published a mini-series of eight articles in the Socialist newspaper *Avanti!*—as many individuals in the PSI had pushed him since November 1945 to write more on his experiences.[26] Thus, if one simply looks a little closer at Tolloy's vita and his writings, it is impossible to support Rochat's claim that the memoirs were apolitical.

Tolloy intended to show three things: the failure of the Italian Army's senior leadership, their indifference towards the fate of their men, and their closeness to Fascism.[27] Tolloy portrayed them as discreditable serfs of the Germans, caught in theories and careerism, detached from the realities of war and the men's hardships on the front.[28] The personnel changes in October and November 1942—after 15 months of incessant service on the front—were in Tolloy's view an evident sign that Messe and the general staff officers had abandoned a sinking ship.[29] The strong criticism of the general staff was, however, not accompanied by a critical re-examination of his own track record as a major in the general staff, about which we learn nothing in his memoirs. But even Tolloy admired the Italians' fight with inadequate means against the Red Army.[30] Additionally, Tolloy claimed that despite the Fascist ideological

---

[25] Tolloy, *Con l'Armata*, 8.

[26] Pagan, *Il prezzo*, 147. The articles are printed in ibid., 153–78. In fact, he had been in close contact with Pietro Nenni (1891–1980), the head of the Italian Socialist Party, before and during his partisan activity, ibid., 115.

[27] Ibid., 148ff.

[28] Tolloy, *Con l'Armata*, 18–22, 104–5, 122–23, 138–41.

[29] Ibid., 143.

[30] Ibid., 170.

propaganda, the Italian soldiers had behaved generously in the occupied territories, and relations with the Germans had been much worse.[31] Thus, while he viciously attacked the senior officers, he also defended the simple soldiers.

The 'evil German' is a key topos in his memoirs, particularly in the discussion of the retreat from the Don. He claimed that the 298th Infantry Division's withdrawal had happened without informing the Italians, and subsequently the Italian officers abandoned their soldiers to save their own skins.[32] Hence, Tolloy depicted the simple soldiers' "abandonment" as a typical sign of an unjust society, where the "innocent were dying and the culprits saved themselves."[33] Yet, he did not stop there. He deemed such circumstances so widespread in other parts of Italian society that it would lead to a class struggle and revolution like in the Russia of 1917, redeeming society of injustice.[34] This included a desire to combat the Germans, i.e. augment the strength of the *Resistenza* and provide it with a *raison d'être* and inclusive narrative for former Italian soldiers—like Tolloy—to whitewash themselves after having fought for Fascist goals.

After the article series in *Avanti!* it was foreseeable that the reprint of his diary in 1947 would arouse public attention. The political Left celebrated the book as a sincere and objective criticism of the Army's moral and professional deficiencies.[35] Yet, reviewers also highlighted the contrast between the Teutonic fury and the benevolent Italian soldier. His attacks were all the more painful and thus all the more propagandised by the Left, as he had himself been a staff officer and could (with some right) claim to be able to criticise the military leadership on the basis of his professional background. Tolloy also repulsed accusations about Soviet abuse of Italian prisoners, dismissing these as stereotypes about 'Soviet barbarism' akin to Fascist propaganda.[36] It has been argued that his memoirs and the debates surrounding his arguments (for over

---

[31] Ibid., 56.

[32] Ibid., 173–77, 180–81, 225–26.

[33] Ibid., 181.

[34] Ibid., 181–82. He argued that all men and nations that had been betrayed by the Germans now formed (writing in April 1943) a "gigantic spearhead of the Red Army" in Nazi occupied territories, ibid., 208.

[35] For mainly positive reviews, see Pagan, *Il prezzo*, 187–214.

[36] Ibid., 152.

fifteen years) not only made his career, but also transformed him into the prime target of the political Right, Fascist nostalgics and defenders of the Italian Army,[37] such as Messe, who transformed the charges against him personally into an insult against the whole Army and thereby the *Patria*. Indeed, Tolloy repeatedly clashed with Messe in the postwar period.[38] Tolloy's diary was published (openly) around the same time as Messe's memoirs on the Eastern Front and the books can be seen as antipodes: Tolloy writing a *j'accuse* and Messe a self-defence of the senior Italian leadership. They both shared, however, a benevolent depiction of the simple soldiers: Tolloy described in almost romantic tones the process of enduring hardships to then create a better world, whereas Messe's account highlighted the heroism and combat performance. Hence, despite similarities, there were important differences, which show the Italian Army's specific emphases in remembering the Eastern Front and its distinct narrative.

THE ARMY'S VOICE

Only a few senior officers wrote memoirs about their experiences in the *campagna di Russia*. The great exception was Messe's memoir (*La guerra al fronte russo*, 1947), which augmented his standing and gave distinct leverage to his views. Messe believed that the "tragic retreat" had only happened after the Third Romanian Army and the Second Hungarian Army had given way.[39] Thus much like the Germans, he chose to blame others. In his memoirs, Messe portrayed his troops' bravery, good-heartedness and their apolitical attitude,[40] while describing the Italians as sandwiched between German and Soviet cruelties.[41] Messe thus helped cemented the postwar *brava gente* narrative of Italians as good-hearted soldiers who did no harm to the Russian populace

---

[37] Pagan, "Introduzione," 12.

[38] Pagan, *Il prezzo*, 148.

[39] AUSSME, Fondo Messe, b.X27, c.AA, Messe to Zigiotti, 9 Jan. 1963.

[40] He even included the Blackshirts in this narrative and had also extolled their performance during the war, see his description of Diamanti and his men, in ACS, Fondo Diamanti, b.1, f.Camp. Russia, 'Diario Storico *3 Gennaio*', Assessment by Messe, 31 Oct. 1942.

[41] Cecini, *I Generali*, 340.

and behaved in stark contrast to the Germans.[42] Besides Messe, Mario Carloni,[43] Colonel Mario Odasso,[44] General Umberto Salvatores' description of the 6th *Bersaglieri*[45] and Alberto Massa Gallucci's reminiscences about the POW period are standout works,[46] while other key officers did not publish anything.[47] The former general, Emilio Faldella, devoted little space to the Russian front and backed the usual narratives: the Germans had not realised how scarce Italians' means were and threw them into a battle they could only lose, while the conduct *vis-à-vis* the civilian population had been marked by warmth and generosity.[48] But Faldella emphasised that the crises on the Don were solved not least by the Italians' sacrifices.[49] Given the low output and meagre influence of former Italian commanders, it is misleading to argue that much of the narrative was cemented by "self-representations of senior officers,"[50] when in fact only Messe's memoirs had any impact.

But what about official publications? Similar to General Ambrosio's attempts to shed more light on the retreat (and leave the responsibility at the Germans' doorstep), the Italian Army was keen to tell *its* story about the happenings in Russia—particularly on the Don. The *Ufficio Storico* published two relatively short accounts: the first in 1946 covered the happenings on the Don in winter 1942,[51] while the second published a

---

[42] Messe, *La guerra*, 85ff.

[43] Carloni, *La campagna di Russia*.

[44] [Lt. Col.] Mario Odasso, *Col Corpo alpino italiano in Russia* (Cuneo: Panfilo, 1949).

[45] [Gen.] Umberto Salvatores, *Bersaglieri sul Don* (Bologna: Compositori, 1958). He had commanded the regiment as colonel and his book had three reprints.

[46] [Gen.] Alberto Massa Gallucci, *No! Dodici anni prigioniero in Russia* (Milan: Rizzoli, 1958). He had been operations officer of the *Pasubio*'s divisional staff when he was captured near Millerovo on 21 Dec. 1942; he was promoted to General after the war.

[47] Utili's posthumously published memoirs, for example, only dealt with the 1943–1945 campaign in Italy—i.e. the struggle against the Germans and Mussolini, see Umberto Utili, "*Ragazzi, in piedi!...*" *La ripresa dell'esercito italiano dopo l'8 settembre* (Milan: Mursia, 1979).

[48] [Gen.] Emilio Faldella, *L'Italia e la seconda guerra mondiale. Revisione di giudizi* (San Casciano: Cappelli, 1963), 239–40.

[49] Ibid., 275.

[50] Osti Guerrazzi and Schlemmer, "I soldati italiani," 387.

[51] USSME, *L'8ª Armata Italiana nella seconda battaglia difensiva del Don* (Rome: USSME, 1946).

year later was devoted to the operations up till October 1942.[52] Its name itself was rather telling: 'The Second Defensive Battle on the Don' can be seen as an attempt to play down Italy's role in invading the Soviet Union and to evoke the image of the defensive on the Piave or on the Isonzo during the First World War. Rochat has argued that the 1946 volume had no anti-Soviet tone, but rather an anti-German one.[53] Indeed, these works have to be seen in the context of the emerging victim narrative.[54] Despite blaming the Germans, they nonetheless emphasised the Italian soldiers' skills and in no way accepted representations of them as hapless victims.

Hereafter, there was a long break in official publications. In 1975, a volume edited by colonels Constantino De Franceschi and Giorgio De Vecchi was devoted to logistics on the Eastern Front,[55] and the same authors provided a detailed description of the whole campaign two years later.[56] This sought to put the Italian participation "in the right light" as General Bovio later claimed (as head of the historical office),[57] as particularly the supply and the functioning of the rear apparatus were repeatedly attacked in memoirs. The USSME also published a collection of relevant excerpts from the Soviet 'History of the Great Patriotic War'. The volume defended the Italian performance, and for instance, also Messe personally, against allegations of criminal behaviour.[58] The official publications therefore show a clear reactive intention against various allegations. However, they never had a strong influence on the public memory or the general narrative. Nor were these bulky operational histories popular on the book market. Yet, they were reviewed

---

[52] USSME, *Le operazioni del C.S.I.R. e dell'ARMIR*. For the USSME works, see also Bovio, *L'Ufficio*, 91–92. The USSME also 'supported' other publications, e.g. Luoni, *Pasubio*.

[53] Rochat, "Memorialistica," 468.

[54] Schreiber, "Italiens Teilnahme," 283–84.

[55] De Franceschi, *I servizi logistici*. This volume was attacked in the memoir literature for listing all kind of unnecessary deliveries, but overlooking the failure to supply the men adequately, see, e.g. Vicentini, *Noi soli vivi*, 64.

[56] USSME, *Le operazioni*.

[57] Bovio, *L'ufficio*, 91.

[58] USSME, *L'Italia nella relazione ufficiale sovietica*; on the Don front in general, ibid., 156–82; on Messe, ibid., 159.

(unsurprisingly) with great acclaim in the *Rivista Militare*,[59] where the campaign was widely discussed. In fact, a look at this semi-official discourse in the *Rivista Militare* is vital to understanding the Army's narrative and memory.

THE DEBATE IN THE *RIVISTA MILITARE*

The *Rivista Militare* was the leading military journal from 1856 to 1918. It was recreated for a spell between 1927 and 1933, but the Fascist regime disliked its often-critical viewpoints and banned it. It was relaunched in January 1945 with eleven issues per year, a number that later fell.[60] It remained the prime outlet for the Army's officers to debate current and past issues. Further, its aim was to improve the armed forces' dialogue with civil society and to increase their prestige domestically and abroad.[61] Other formats destined for the rank-and-file, such as the biweekly *Corriere Militare* (renamed *Il Quadrante* in 1966), and publications by other branches or units could not be included, but would merit a closer look in future studies.[62]

The campaign in Russia was discussed in early issues of the *Rivista Militare* that appeared while the Second World War was still raging. General Pietro Maravigna described the German attack as a foolish bid for *Lebensraum* with insufficient resources, whose defeat was predictable; the Italian involvement was left wholly unmentioned.[63] Maravigna looked at the operational history with greater detail in two subsequent articles. He noted the brutal character of the war and repeated his arguments about German strategic errors without, again, mentioning the CSIR.[64] The first

---

[59] A. Borrozzino, "L'8ª Armata italiana nella 2ª battaglia decisiva del Don. *SME Ufficio Storico*," *Rivista Militare* 2, no. 12 (1946): 1525–26.

[60] [Lt. Col.] Pier Giorgio Franzosi, *I cento anni della Rivista Militare* (Rome: Tip.Reg., 1976), 11ff.; Ada Fichera, *La pubblicistica della difesa in Italia: riviste militari di ieri e di oggi* (Rome: Ministero della Difesa, Commissione italiana di storia militare, 2012), 9–29.

[61] Fichera, *La pubblicistica*.

[62] The *Biblioteca centrale* in Rome holds microfilm copies of both magazines.

[63] [Gen.] Pietro Maravigna, "Perchè e come la Germania attaccò la Russia nel 1941," *Rivista Militare* 1, no. 4 (1945): 401–17.

[64] [Gen.] Pietro Maravigna, "La condotta delle operazioni durante l'offensiva tedesca sul fronte russo (1941–1943)," *Rivista Militare* 1, no. 6 (1945): 625–47; the second part, ibid., "La condotta delle operazioni durante l'offensiva tedesca sul fronte russo (1941–1943)," *Rivista Militare* 1, no. 7 (1945): 758–74.

article including the Italian role was published by an *Alpini* Lieutenant in January 1946. It centred on the retreat in January 1943, described the suffering in the cold, the hopeless situation against enemy tanks, the good relations with the Soviet populace and the evil German ally.[65] Also other articles confirm Rochat's claims about an anti-German tone in early publications. Major Romolo Guerico, argued that the Wehrmacht generals had realised their errors in 1944 and saw this as proof that one could not speak of a failure of Germany's allies on the Don.[66] Guerico even stated his desire to tell the 'true story' before incorrect narratives could spread.[67] While this does not speak for the objectivity of his article, it reveals something much more significant in this context: namely, that the Italian Army was aware that the struggle over the interpretation of recent events had already started and that it was falling behind.[68] Therefore, subsequent articles highlighted not only the suffering, but also the good performance and tenacity of the Italian divisions.[69] The operations in December 1941 and summer 1942 were also discussed in order to showcase good combat performance.[70] The first USSME publication on the Second Battle of the Don was published in late 1946 and was positively reviewed, as it supported the general trend of the *Rivista Militare*.[71] In fact, an analysis

[65] [Lt. (*Alpini*)] Silvano Fincato, "Attraverso la sacca. Memorie di un alpino nella campagna di Russia," *Rivista Militare* 2, no. 1 (1946): 95–110; the second part was published one month later, ibid., *Rivista Militare* 2, no. 2 (1946): 208–25.

[66] [Maj. (*Bersaglieri*)] Romolo Guerico, "Responsabilità germaniche nelle operazioni che condussero al ripiegamento invernale 1942–43 nella campagna di Russia," *Rivista Militare* 2, no. 2 (1946): 143–68, here 161f., 167.

[67] Ibid., 168.

[68] [Maj. (Infantry)] Luigi Forlenza, "Accuse e difese degli ufficiali," *Rivista Militare* 2, no. 5 (1946): 497–502.

[69] [Lt. Col. (Artillery)] Filippo Acquistapace, "La divisione alpina 'Tridentina' nella 'battaglia del Don,'" *Rivista Militare* 2, no. 8–9 (1946): 986–1004; [Lt. Col. (*Bersaglieri*)] Romolo Guerico, "La 3^ Divisione Celere 'Principe Amedeo Duca d'Aosta' nella seconda battaglia difensiva del Don (Dicembre 1942–Febbraio 1943)," *Rivista Militare* 9, no. 6 (1953): 669–89.

[70] [Lt. Col. (Infantry)] Pietro Pallotta, "Una divisione ternaria all'attacco – Chazepetowka 5–14 dicembre 1941," *Rivista Militare* 9, no. 3 (1953): 367–71; [Lt. Col. (Infantry)] Pietro Pallotta, "Motorizzati contro corazzati (Serafimowitsch 30 luglio–8 agosto 1942)," *Rivista Militare* 9, no. 12 (1953): 1202–6; [Lt. Col.] Gualtiero Stefanon, "Il forzamento del fiume Dnjeper nel 1941," *Rivista Militare* 24, no. 9 (1968): 1099–116.

[71] A. Borrozzino, "L'8ª Armata italiana nella 2ª battaglia decisiva del Don. SME Ufficio Storico," *Rivista Militare* 2, no. 12 (1946): 1525–26.

of the journal's review section shows which narratives were approved or disapproved.

Two very early works received rather negative evaluations. Tolloy's book was heavily criticised as an unfounded attack against the officer corps and general staff.[72] In short, the reviewer, Luigi Mondini, found it virtually useless and devoid of any factual substance.[73] Eugenio Corti's memoirs were portrayed as juvenile hot-headedness and an expression of (understandable) frustration about chaotic organisation, bad materiel and insufficient preparation. But while the reviewer seconded these criticisms, Corti's allegations against the simple soldiers were immediately countered.[74] Other memoirs, e.g. those by the *Alpini* Egidio Franzini or Mario Barilli, were better received. Barilli was complimented for presenting the infantry's heroic deeds,[75] and Franzini's depictions of the disrespectful German ally, his time as Russian prisoner, and even negative remarks on the rear organisation were welcomed as honest accounts.[76] Surprisingly, the prisoner of war issue received rather little attention in the *Rivista Militare*,[77] much like—rather less unsurprisingly—occupation policies and anti-partisan operations. The first general overview on the Russian campaign by the former journalist Aldo Valori similarly excluded these issues. His book was praised for highlighting the soldiers' sacrifices and their heroic

---

[72] L. Mondini, "Con l'armata italiana in Russia. *Giusto Tolloy*," *Rivista Militare* 4, no. 2 (1948): 198–99.

[73] Mondini had served as military attaché in Athens between 1938 and 1940, then commanded a division on the front, before becoming deputy chief of staff of the Eleventh Army in occupied Greece. After the war, he became the first head of the *Ufficio Storico* (1945–1949) and subsequently directed the military academy in Modena. He also wrote a book on the Greek campaign—in which he vehemently defended the military—and a hagiography of Pietro Badoglio in 1963.

[74] G. Occhialini, "I più non tornano. *Eugenio Corti*," *Rivista Militare* 4, no. 2 (1948): 200–1.

[75] F. Runcini, "Alpini in Russia sul Don. *Mario Barilli*," *Rivista Militare* 10, no. 5 (1954): 545–48.

[76] G. Occhialini, "In Russia (Memorie di un alpino redivivo). *Egidio Franzini*," *Rivista Militare* 4, no. 4 (1948): 471–72.

[77] An exception was a simple review, see A. Barbato, "Dodici anni prigionia nell'URSS. *Enrico Reginato*," *Rivista Militare* 23, no. 4 (1967): 519–20. The first detailed article was only published after the collapse of the USSR, see [Ambassador] Ettore Baistrocchi, "Militari italiani in unione sovietica," *Rivista Militare* 48, no. 6 (1992): 90–103.

combat—also over the fifteen months before the retreat on the Don.[78] Reviews on works in the late 1950s and 1960s confirmed this trend: some criticism was accepted, but outright denigrations of the Army or the simple soldiers were strongly rejected. At the same time, the narratives of retreat, suffering and disloyal German allies were always flanked by positive accounts of Italian combat performance. The latter especially was a narrative the *Rivista Militare* welcomed (after all, it was a military publication), particularly when it was supported by claims of good Italian conduct *vis-à-vis* the civilian population.[79] The ideal form therefore became a mix between glory and tragedy,[80] while narratives of pure victimhood or hapless *brava gente* were never accepted.

The USSME works in the 1970s drove a number of other articles that looked at operational matters.[81] They lauded the USSME studies as thorough analyses of the Italian soldiers' valorous struggle in a war they never 'wanted', but nonetheless fought tenaciously with inferior materiel.[82] They thus linked the general master narrative on the Italian Army in the Second World War to the specific case of the Eastern Front. General Antonio Saltini devoted a whole article on the decision to participate in the campaign. He exclusively blamed Mussolini and did not discuss the military's own role in decision-making.[83] Other articles emphasised the shared fate of the ARMIR's neighbouring armies against

---

[78] "La campagna di Russia. CSIR – ARMIR: 1941–1943. *Aldo Valori*," *Rivista Militare* 6, no. 12 (1950): 1339–40.

[79] "Ritorniamo sul Don. *Franco La Guidara*," *Rivista Militare* 21, no. 4 (1965): 658–61; V. Baldieri, "Con la Divisione 'Ravenna' 1939–1943. *Giulio De Giorgi*," *Rivista Militare* 29, no. 11–12 (1973): 1332–34. See also M. Furesi, "Bersaglieri sul Don. *Umberto Salvatores*," *Rivista Militare* 14, no. 11 (1958): 1678–80; E. Fasanotti, "Atti di leggenda – Russia 1942–1943. *Zanotti Morino*," *Rivista Militare* 24, no. 12 (1968): 1579–80.

[80] See the review by Rinaldo Cruccu, who took part in several USSME works, "Franco La Guidara: 'Ritorniamo sul Don fino all'ultima battaglia'," *Rivista Militare* 33, no. 2 (1977): 133.

[81] The work on logistics was published in a condensed version in the *Rivista Militare* as [Brigadier-Gen.] Vittorio De Castiglioni, "I servizi logistici italiani al fronte russo, 1941–1943," *Rivista Militare* 32, no. 2 (1976): 26–37.

[82] [Brigadier-Gen.] Vittorio De Castiglioni, "Dal Dniester al Don," *Rivista Militare* 34, no. 8 (1978): 74–82, here 82.

[83] [Lt. Gen.] Antonio Saltini, "L'intervento militare italiano in Russia," *Rivista Militare* 31, no. 4 (1975): 89–93.

overwhelming odds,[84] and were accompanied by more specific studies that re-evaluated operational performances.[85] General Aldo De Carlini analysed the *Ravenna*'s operations in January 1943 in order to cast light on what he perceived as a nebulous memoir-driven narrative that framed the retreat only as an inglorious tragedy—excluding the actual operations during and after the retreat.[86] De Carlini also criticised some of the tactical choices on the Don—this, notwithstanding his claim that the scale of the Soviet attack and inadequate Italian means had precluded any chance of a successful defence.[87] Colonel Bonabello wrote a general appreciation of the ARMIR's performance and proposed its honourable conduct as an example for young Italian soldiers (this, in 1984).[88] The number of articles steadily declined in the 1980s and 1990s, also owing to a general change in the *Rivista Militare*: events in the Second World War received less attention as the journal changed its character. Yet, the 1970s and early 1980s had led to a notable re-evaluation: the Germans received less blame, the Italian operational performance was much more accentuated, and victimhood was substituted with a narrative of glorious defeat.

An analysis of the *Rivista Militare* shows that the official military voice promoted a different view on events than the master narrative set out in the memoir literature. Tolloy's work, for example, was a clear non-runner. Other articles in the *Rivista Militare* reflected criticisms of the general shortcomings, but repelled attacks on the officer corps and the simple soldiers' performance. It would be wrong to claim that the Italian Army perpetuated any narrative of 'total victimhood'—important nuances were made. Despite the early attention to the 'evil German' narrative and incessant emphasis on Italian inferiority in face of the Soviet onslaught, discussion of valorous combat was always a central theme. However, even during this early period, other articles in the *Rivista*

---

[84] De Castiglioni, "Dal Dniester al Don," 79.

[85] A mixture of memoir and re-evaluation was [Gen.] Aldo Beolchini, "La Sforzesca nella prima battaglia difensiva sul Don," *Rivista Militare* 39, no. 1 (1983): 99–120.

[86] [Lt.Gen.] Aldo De Carlini, "Le operazioni della Divisione di fanteria Ravenna sul fiume Donez nel gennaio 1943," *Rivista Militare* 33, no. 3 (1977): 33–44. De Carlini had been a company commander in the 37th Infantry Regiment of the *Ravenna* and subsequently fought as partisan in northern Italy.

[87] Ibid., 42–44.

[88] [Col.] Pietro Bonabello, "L'8ª Armata italiana nella 2ª battaglia difensiva del Don," *Rivista Militare* 40, no. 1 (1984): 129–42, here 142.

Militare celebrated the post-1943 fight against the Germans—especially the battle of Monte Lungo.[89] The Army worked keenly to safeguard its reputation as a valorous fighting force. Thus, memoirs that attacked the institution's very backbone (its officer corps) or portrayed it too much as a hapless victim were reviewed notably more coldly, or indeed not discussed at all.[90] Thus, it is only partly right to see the Italian Army as the driving force behind the establishment of a victim narrative and one must not blur the differences between memory and commemoration in the civilian and military spheres. Like the memoir literature, the articles in the *Rivista Militare* also focused strongly on the *Bersaglieri* and even more so on the *Alpini*. Particularly their tale of the retreat provided a common ground that allowed its story to be related to the most powerful myth: Italy's 'rebirth' during the *Resistenza*.

The Don, the *Resistenza* and the *Alpini*

Nuto Revelli was a key figure in relating the *Alpini* to positive aspects of the recent war. In 1939, he had joined the military academy and departed as young *Alpini*-Lieutenant to Russia in July 1942. After returning to Italy, he fought with several partisan groups in the Cuneo region.[91] His first book, *Mai tardi* (1946), told his story on the Eastern Front 'from below', and "was full of sarcasm about the vainness of the regime's rhetoric and the military culture."[92] Revelli launched several attacks on the Army as an institution full of nepotism and corruption and as a partner of the Fascist regime.[93] He would later go on to criticise all forms of bureaucracy and state authority.[94] In his "irate" books,[95]

---

[89] [Cpt.] Giorgio Anselmi, "M. Lungo: Gloria d'Italia," *Rivista Militare* 2, no. 1 (1946): 9–16.

[90] "Ritirata in Russia. Stefano Dotti," *Rivista Militare* 13, no. 5 (1957): 813. Revelli and Rigoni Stern's works received almost no attention. On the other hand, the memoirs of notable German commanders (Manstein and Guderian) were even serialised in parts. Soviet views were also included and criticism of Italian behaviour—if raised—eagerly countered.

[91] During this time, he also wrote the lyrics to a famous partisan song, the *Badoglieide*, a sarcastic attack on Badoglio's role during Fascism, and indirectly against the whole Army leadership.

[92] Cinelli, *Revelli*, xxxvi.

[93] Ibid., 18ff.

[94] Ibid., xlv.

[95] Schlemmer, *Italiener*, 4.

he described the Army as an incapable force, fleeing, and retreating, and named its officers and the Germans as the chief reason for the defeat.[96] *Mai tardi* did not arouse much attention upon publication. Only by incorporating his diary into the book *La guerra dei poveri* (1962) and with the subsequent reprint of *Mai tardi* in 1967 did Revelli secure his place as a leading author on the *campagna di Russia*. His second book was even more 'dangerous' for the military. In *La guerra dei poveri*, Revelli looked back at his life: growing up in Fascist Italy, volunteering for Mussolini's war, and then fighting as a partisan. He told his readers a powerful story of resurgence, overcoming his personal moral crisis as an officer of a beaten army by way of his service in the *Resistenza* and the new political ideals. Revelli always depicted anti-heroes who strove for peaceful individualism and defended, similarly to Tolloy, the 'little man on the street' who was abused by 'the system'. This was a view he repeatedly conveyed in far-left newspapers,[97] and in a late book where he contrasted 'two' Italian wars, i.e. the Fascist War and the partisan war after 1943.[98] Revelli thereby attacked the whole military establishment—especially those without a *Resistenza*-alibi.[99] His closeness to grandees of the *Resistenza* and the political Left further increased his opposition to the postwar *Esercito*. Revelli's close friend, the *Alpini* veteran and important writer, Mario Rigoni Stern, also desired to give a voice to the unknown heroes (or rather, victims) who had coped with everyday suffering in wartime. Indeed, Rigoni Stern forged a narrative in which the soldiers' enemies were not to be found in the opposing trenches, but in the upper echelons of their own state and army.[100] These books were designed as, and are still seen as, counter-narratives to the official service histories.[101] Rigoni Stern and Revelli not only wrote down their own experiences, but also engaged 'academically' in oral history projects, in which, their own narrative was further perpetuated.[102]

---

[96] Nuto Revelli, *Mai tardi. Diario di un alpino in Russia* (Cuneo: Panfilo, 1947), 219.

[97] Mario Passi, "Revelli: le voci di un'odissea bianca," *L'Unità*, 10 Feb. 1992.

[98] Nuto Revelli, *Le due guerre: guerra fascista e guerra partigiana* (Turin: Einaudi, 2003).

[99] Cinelli, *Revelli*, xxxvi.

[100] Folco Portinari, "Introduzione," in *I racconti di guerra*, ed. Mario Rigoni Stern (Turin: Einaudi, 2006), v–xxiii, here xiii–xiv.

[101] Cinelli, *Revelli*, xxxviii.

[102] On Revelli's oral history projects, see ibid., 77ff.

Therefore, citing their books as 'eye-witness' accounts is highly problematic and should be stopped.

Giulio Bedeschi was the third *Alpini* veteran to have a major literary impact. After his service on the Eastern Front, Bedeschi had commanded a Fascist formation in the Civil War. Still, he became a vital figure in making the narrative of victimhood (minus the slanders against the high command) acceptable to the postwar Army. He won important literary prizes for his *Centomila gavette di ghiaccio* (1963), and his edited volumes of veterans' miscellaneous reminscenses also became bestsellers.[103] Bedeschi published in the *Rivista Militare*,[104] as his narrative was within the Italian Army's accepted bounds—in contrast to Revelli or Tolloy. Bedeschi, Revelli, and Rigoni Stern all became vital voices for the *Alpini* myth and helped to cement a 'good military' narrative around them.[105]

Despite his harsh criticism of the military elites, even Revelli's early work shows an undeniable pride in being an *Alpini* officer.[106] Revelli portrayed the *Alpini* as markedly anti-Fascist and the "non plus ultra of the good-hearted Italian soldier."[107] The highly critical Tolloy, too, emphasised the *Alpini's* democratic spirit, a discipline that was not just military, and their good and caring officers, but argued that these values had decayed in the years preceding the war.[108] The *Alpini's* 'sacrifice on the Don' became idealised as a first rite in the resistance against the Fascist regime and the Germans; this allowed for a 'happy ending', and satisfied feelings of revenge, as the Italians fought 'at home' (again with less means than their enemy) the 'same' Germans who had (allegedly) abandoned them on the Don.[109] Obviously, not everyone joined the resistance, but the image of a simple tellurian peasant soldier defending

---

[103] His *C'ero anch'io* (I was there as well) volumes included mixed second-hand accounts of soldiers and officers. For the Russian campaign, Giulio Bedeschi, *Fronte Russo: C'ero anch'io* (Milan: Mursia, 1982).

[104] Giulio Bedeschi, "Alpini sul fronte russo nella seconda guerra mondiale," *Rivista Militare* 30, no. 6 (1974): 75–82; Giulio Bedeschi, "Il corpo d'armata alpino sul fronte russo," *Rivista Militare* 39, no. 2 (1983): 39–48.

[105] Their writings in relation to the *Alpini* myth are analysed in greater detail in Mondini, *Alpini*, 157–218.

[106] Cinelli, *Revelli*, 29; also Mondini, *Alpini*, 179ff.

[107] Osti Guerrazzi and Schlemmer, "I soldati italiani," 390.

[108] Tolloy, *Con l'Armata*, 206–7.

[109] Notably, e.g. in Nuto Revelli, *La guerra dei poveri* (Turin: Einaudi, 1962), 312; Oliva, *L'alibi*, 84ff.

the homeland against the Germanic invader was a common one, and it also evoked myths and memories of the First World War.[110] Thus, there was a mixture of romanticising mountain and country life and the fight against oppression for newfound ideals. The government had betrayed the *Alpini* in Russia and on the *8 settembre*, therefore it could or even had to be substituted with new ideas.[111] Yet, the nexus between the *Alpini* myth of the Eastern Front, the War of Liberation and the *Resistenza* has been ignored. In fact, these two *lieux de mémoire* are intrinsically linked. This also played into the traditional *Alpini* myth. The *Corpo Alpino* was founded in 1872 as an elite formation for the defence of the borders with France and Austria. From the very outset, it blended romantic ideas of mountaineering and peasant life in the mountains. At least since the First World War, the *Alpini* have gained a mythological status in Italian society. The *Alpini* symbolised a cohesion based on values and social and regional background rather than military drill—thus turning them into elite soldiers of a peculiar kind, who were perceived differently to other soldiers, and closer to civilian culture.[112]

So why did the brief deployment in Russia became the focal point of the *Alpini*'s memory of the Second World War? In short, because of the lack of alternatives and the aforementioned mental mindmaps they could refer to. The campaigns against France and Greece and the occupational duties in the Balkans gave little chance for glory, and only one battalion had fought in the battle of Keren in Italian East Africa.[113] Thus, even though the *Alpini* had only reached the Russian front in late August 1942, their employment had to be interpreted in order to make any sense of it. For an elite formation, it was difficult to blame defeat on their training or look for tactical and operational shortcomings. Thus, the narrative of a 'sacrifice in the steppe' was promoted. *Alpini* memoirs and writings (even by scholars) claimed that the *Alpini* Corps had been foolishly deployed (and thus sacrificed) in the plains and not, as envisaged, in the Caucasus, where the nasty Wehrmacht had sent their

---

[110] Especially Nuto Revelli, *La strada del davai* (Turin: Einaudi, 1966).

[111] This narrative is particularly pronounced in Nuto Revelli, *Il mondo dei vinti* (Turin: Einaudi, 2005).

[112] De Marco, *Il mito*, 56ff.; Oliva, *Storia degli Alpini*, 3–4, 10–11; Mondini, *Alpini*, 63ff.

[113] On Keren, see Faldella, *Le truppe alpine*, 163ff.

own mountain units.[114] Hamilton stated that their material and communications equipment did not really work,[115] and General Faldella endorsed these rather bizarre claims about faulty radios and artillery guns that were purely designed for mountain warfare.[116] It is astonishing that an elite formation (which praises itself for its versatility and adaptation) placed so much emphasis on the fact that it had only been trained for mountain warfare and thus could not adequately fight in the plains.[117] Another Italian general even claimed that the deployment to the Don had itself caused a "psychological trauma" to the *Alpini*.[118] It was linked to the myth that the Germans had deliberately sacrificed the *Alpini* Corps to save their own forces (i.e. the XXIV Corps).[119] Yet, the *Alpini*'s deployment or 'sacrifice on the steppe' was not uncommon, as the Germans employed their own as well as Romanian mountain troops in similar fashion.[120] Secondly, the Wehrmacht did not willingly sacrifice the *Alpini* Corps to cover the XXIV Panzer Corps' retreat. Rather,

[114] Vicentini, *Noi soli vivi*. In a meeting with Mussolini on 28 January 1942, Göring had remarked that the *Alpini* divisions would render great services, especially in the Caucasus; without, however, outlining details on operational deployment, see DDI, IX:VIII, doc.211. Likewise, Hitler to Ciano in November 1941, USSME, *Le operazioni*, 183. Hitler repeated the intention to deploy the *Alpini* jointly with German mountain troops in August 1942, DDI, IX:IX, doc.21. Yet, as Marras had already noted in in January 1942: it would also depend on the Romanian presence and logistics, ACS, T-821/200/IT 1382/990-994, Marras—Questioni varie trattate con l'OKW, 29 Jan. 1942, f.993. Interestingly, the Italian dictum that one's forces should not be split hardly featured in the postwar debates, although this played a vital role in all discussions about the possible deployment of the *Alpini* in the Caucasus, see Cavallero Diary, 30 July 1942. Indeed, sending the *Alpini* Corps might have led to a substitution with a German corps or break-up of the Eighth Army; Gariboldi was already not amused when the two other corps were ordered to advance on the Don in July, as this disunited the Eighth Army. Likewise, he had been sceptical about incorporating German units in the ARMIR for the same reasons, Scotoni, *Il nemico fidato*, 149; Cavallero Diary, 30 July 1942. Thus, the whole 'wrong deployment' story of the *Alpini* Corps is a double-edged sword, to say the least.

[115] Hamilton, *Sacrifice*, 29–31.

[116] Faldella, *Le truppe alpine*, 211.

[117] See, e.g. in Oliva, *Storia degli Alpini*, 196ff. The Italians' complaints were apparently so strong that Hitler felt the need to explain the *Alpini*'s deployment to the Fascist Party's secretary, see TNA, GFM 36/240, Vidussoni – Appunto per il Duce, 24 Oct. 1942, fol.17.

[118] [Maj. Gen.] Antonio Saltini, "L'intervento militare italiano in Russia," *Rivista Militare* 31, no. 4 (1975): 89–93, here 92.

[119] Tolloy, *Con l'Armata*, 205.

[120] Massignani, *Alpini e tedeschi*, 105ff.

the *Alpini* helped to prevent a complete envelopment of German (and Italian) forces. According to Massignani, their losses were higher due to deficiencies in radio equipment, aerial support and scarcity of self-propelled assault guns, sledges and half-tracks.[121] However, the *Alpini* Corps' levels of artillery and vehicles were not dramatically lower than those of the Italian II and XXXV Corps.[122]

Corni therefore (rightly) compared this abandonment narrative to the X Corps' story at El Alamein.[123] Yet, Corni and others have overlooked the self-styling of the *Alpini* as an elite unit, which prohibited any emphasis on victimhood alone. While the *Alpini* endorsed this 'wrong deployment' narrative, they tried to highlight their combat performance in order to uphold their claim to be an elite unit. One part of this narrative was to extol the deeds of the *Monte Cervino* Battalion, a highly trained formation on skis.[124] Again, the topos of few selected and especially trained soldiers emerged as a counter-narrative to that emphasising an alleged military incompetence.[125] In the official *Alpini* work, General Faldella accentuated the repulsion of partisan attacks during the retreat.[126] He thus nurtured a narrative that the *Alpini* were unbeaten in the field—even against treacherous enemies that attacked the Italians when they were weakest. He also cited a Soviet bulletin of 8 February 1943 that had allegedly stated: "the only corps that can claim to have remained unbeaten on Russian soil is the Italian *Alpini* Corps."[127] Yet, scholars have not found any evidence for the existence of this bulletin.[128] Thus, the 'wrong deployment' story was linked to a narrative of heroic conduct during retreat, but also the conviction that the Germans were the enemies, paving the way for a personal resurrection through involvement in the *Resistenza*.

Established mindsets and connections to the First World War helped to foster this narrative. The iconic image of the operations in Russia became the retreating columns, covered in snow, deprived of their

---

[121] Ibid., 129ff., 139ff.
[122] Which Faldella even listed, see Faldella, *Le truppe alpine*, 210–11.
[123] Corni, "Wüste bis zum Don."
[124] Faldella, *Le truppe alpine*, 194ff., 249ff., 343.
[125] *Monte Cervino* is today's honourary name of the elite 4th *Alpini* Parachute Regiment.
[126] Faldella, *Le truppe alpine*, 192.
[127] [Gen.] Emilio Faldella, "Nel centenario del Corpo degli Alpini," *Rivista Militare* 28, no. 5 (1972): 623–29, cited on 628. The same myth can be found in Petacco, *L'armata*, 153.
[128] Patricelli, *L'Italia delle sconfitte*, 236–37.

weapons—images that implied multiple angles of victimhood, and could easily be related to the First World War and depictions of the *Alpini*'s home mountains in Italy.[129] The Piave was either expressively or indirectly compared the Don.[130] Both imagined and real landscapes—snow, unhospitable terrain, rivers, retreats and suffering—were intertwined to build up a powerful narrative of victimhood and resurrection (and, in a sense, linked to a 'good war').[131] This time, these symbols were not linked to the Julian Alps, the Karst plateau, the Piave and the Isonzo, Caporetto and Vittorio Veneto, but to the Russian steppe, the Don, and ultimately northern Italy. The retreat thus became a prologue to the *Resistenza*,[132] which further fostered the myth of the *Alpini* as a likeable and 'good' military formation.

The link from the *Alpini* to the War of Liberation has to be understood in terms of the Army's attempts to find a place for itself in the liberation narrative. The partisans became heroes, while the Italian co-belligerent army—and veterans in general—received fewer acknowledgements in the new Republic.[133] Yet, for the Army it was important from early on to show the role they had played in the 'good cause' after 8 September 1943.[134] Therefore, minor skirmishes like Monte Lungo and Filottrano were reinterpreted as rites of redemption and the initiation of a newborn Italy. This narrative was, however, very much overshadowed by the *Resistenza* myth.[135] The *ritirata dal Don* narrative

[129] Folco Portinari, "Introduzione," in *I racconti di guerra*, ed. Mario Rigoni Stern (Turin: Einaudi, 2006), v–xxiii, here xvi, xviii.

[130] Vicentini, e.g. compared the front length and troop density on the Don to that on the Piave in 1918, ibid., *Noi soli vivi*, 190. On the Piave, see Fortunato Minniti, *Il Piave* (Bologna: Il Mulino, 2000), 123ff.

[131] Indeed, these were similar to *topoi* that had influenced the public memory in the case of Caporetto, Mario Isnenghi, *I vinti di Caporetto nella letteratura di guerra* (Padova: Marsilio, 1967).

[132] Tolloy, *Con l'Armata*, 207. The Italian partisans even adopted the Russian song *Katjuscia* in their repertoire (with different lyrics), Petacco, *L'armata*, 156.

[133] Mondini and Schwarz, *Dalla guerra*, 127ff.; Giusti, *La campagna*, 271.

[134] The history of the Italian Army's commemoration of the War of Liberation still needs to be written, for now, see Vallauri, *Soldati*. Many interesting points about the problems of this refound Italian people's war tradition can be found in Botti and Ilari, *Il pensiero*, 374–403.

[135] A rare exception was the praise coming from Giulio Andreotti: see "Il contributo delle forze armate nella guerra per la liberazione," *La Stampa*, 21 Apr. 1965, 9.

functioned in society, but was hardly beneficial to a future *esprit de corps*. Despite the public narrative, as described in the memoir literature, the *Alpini* themselves have always placed great emphasis on their battle performance—particularly at Nikolayevka.

Nikolayevka as 'Last Stand' Narrative and *lieu de mémoire*

Due to their late arrival in September 1942, most units of the *Alpini* Corps had few opportunities to distinguish themselves,[136] and the retreat in January 1943 was mainly marked by skirmishes. Amidst the chaos, stragglers of the *Alpini* units seized villages in order to protect themselves against the cold. The Soviets tried to block important escape routes to trap the remnants of the Axis forces, for example at Nikolayevka. This battle has become a symbol of military valour in Italy,[137] and a closer look reveals that many narratives could comfortably be brought together in its commemoration.

Nikolayevka was a small town halfway between Belgorod and Rossosh. The Italians had undertaken a swift reconnaissance jointly with three German self-propelled assault guns in the morning hours of 26 January 1943,[138] and decided to capture the village to defend a vital crossroads for retreat.[139] The Italian forces included the *Vestone* battalion of the 6th *Alpini* Regiment (the only fully combat-ready formation with an additional pioneer company), the *Verona* and *Val Chiese* battalions that were reduced to company strength, and mixed artillery units with four 75/13 pieces, and six 47/32.[140] The numbers of stragglers are, like the opposing Soviet force, hard to assess. Lieutenant-Colonel Chierici (GOC 6th *Alpini* Regiment) ordered the *Verona* Battalion to attack the village's left flank, pushing towards the station (which included a railway embankment that dominated much of the terrain) and then moving (uphill) to the other flank, joining rank with one of the *Vestone*'s company, which was meant to attack the right flank in order to envelope the

---

[136] Parts of the *Julia* had aided the II Corps in December, Hamilton, *Sacrifice*, 76ff.

[137] Scotoni, *L'Armata Rossa*, 17.

[138] BA-MA, RH 31-IX/35, Salazer—'Gefechtsbericht Rückmarsch *Alpini*', 23 Mar. 1943, fol.96.

[139] Detailed in Faldella, *Le truppe alpine*, 439ff. See also Caruso, *Tutti i vivi*; Hamilton, *Sacrifice*, 163ff.

[140] Faldella, *Le truppe alpine*, 441.

enemy. The *Val Chiese* (also in company strength) was destined to wage a frontal attack to conquer first the station, then the church, supported (in a second wave) by artillery and the German assault guns.[141] In short, the Italians attacked an entrenched and numerically superior enemy on higher ground over open snow-covered plains after several days of (fighting) retreat in wintertime Russia.

The onslaught began at 9.30 in the morning. Despite fierce resistance it looked as if the Italian plan would work out. Some objectives were reached (e.g. the station, but not the embankment), but a violent struggle over the town ensued. The Italians repelled counter-attacks and waited for ammunition to pursue their attack. Faldella has argued that the German forces, which were intended to support the central attacking column, retreated after losing one gun to strong anti-tank fire—and thus left the Italians in the lurch.[142] Italian reinforcements that reached Nikolayevka at noon could not tilt the balance, either.[143] General Giulio Martinat, Chief of Staff of the *Alpini* Corps, personally led a charge against the rail embankment in the afternoon and fell at the head of his troops.[144] As night-time approached, conquering the village became decisive in order to have shelter—not least for the "thousands of wounded."[145] When the *Edolo* Battalion of the 5th *Alpini* Regiment (*Tridentina*) arrived with other stragglers in the evening, General Luigi Reverberi gathered every man he could muster and personally spearheaded the attack with several officers.[146] This final charge overcame the enemy's resistance. After ten hours of combat the Italians had won the day and had inflicted high casualties on the Soviets, who lost hundreds of dead and wounded, several artillery batteries, and plenty of other materiels.[147]

[141] Ibid., 440–41.

[142] Ibid., 443.

[143] The *Tirano* Battalion (5th *Alpini*) consisted of only 150 men who had just overcome the severe fighting at Arnautovo, some five kilometres away. Nuto Revelli was part of the *Tirano*, which supported the *Vestone* on the right flank, Faldella, *Le truppe alpine*, 445.

[144] Ibid., 446. The *Alpini* later devoted a song to him, see Petacco, *L'armata*, 149–51.

[145] Faldella, *Le truppe alpine*, 447.

[146] Ibid., 448. Reverberi had allegedly yelled "*Avanti Tridentina*, Avanti!" from the top of a German assault gun, which became an iconic tale and featured in many depictions of the battle.

[147] Ibid., 448. The casualty numbers and total troops involved in these battles are difficult to assess—for both sides.

The generals became vital for the 'Nikolayevka myth': a victory against a vastly superior enemy through sheer willpower, desperate gestures (bayonets and hand grenades) and the personal example of the senior commanders.[148] Reverberi was captured and interned by the Wehrmacht after 1943, and dismissed during the *epurazione* due to accusations coming from the Communist senator Edoardo D'Onofrio. Still, the headquarters of today's *Tridentina* Brigade in Bressanone bear his name and he remains a celebrated figure in the *Alpini* journal.[149] General Gabriele Nasci joined the partisans after 1943, returned to the War Ministry in September 1945, and subsequently became the Chair of the Committee for the granting and revocation of Military Decorations of Valour (1946–1947).[150]

Mario Rigoni Stern, Nuto Revelli and Giulio Bedeschi took part in the battle and their writings increased its prominence[151]; even though they are nowhere to be found in Faldella's long eulogy concerning the heroic deeds at Nikolayevka.[152] Thus, for the *Alpini* this battle fulfils the same function that El Alamein did (and still does) for the paratroopers. It is branded as a heroic sacrifice and battle against all odds, in which courage and willpower alone overcame both enemy and inadequate materiel—if not to the point of victory, then at least to the point of a glorious defeat or at least a "glorious retreat."[153] The *Alpini* could only accept the master narrative about the Don by including this element. It upheld their military honour and the self-perception as an elite unit. Thus, Nikolayevka was initially glorified in the military sphere,[154] but

[148] Ibid., 444, 448. Faldella claimed that forty officers had died during the battle. Crimes against civilians that occurred right before the battle were unsurprisingly muted, Scotoni, *Il nemico fidato*, 275–77.

[149] Mariolina Cattaneo, "Luigi Reverberi raccontato dal figlio," *L'Alpino* 92, no. 1 (2013): 8–9.

[150] Faccini and Ferrari, "Nasci," 539ff.

[151] Revelli was part of the *Tirano* Battalion, Rigoni Stern a Sergeant in the *Vestone*. Bedeschi even devoted one of his edited volumes to Nikolayevka, see Giulio Bedeschi, *Nikolajewka: c'ero anch'io* (Milan: Mursia, 1972).

[152] Faldella, *Le truppe alpine*, 448ff.

[153] Alessandro Rossi, "Voci da Niko," *L'Alpino* 93, no. 2 (2014): 20–21, here 21. A history of the Italian memory of El Alamein remains to be written, for now, see Di Giovanni, *I paracadutisti italiani*, 158; Corni, "Wüste bis zum Don."

[154] [Lt. (*Alpini*)] Silvano Fincato, "Attraverso la sacca. Memorie di un alpino nella campagna di Russia," *Rivista Militare* 2, no. 1 (1946): 95–110, here 104ff.; L. Lollio, "Luigi Collo: '40 sotto zero a Nikolajewka," *Rivista Militare* 30, no. 3 (1974): 137. See also the

slowly transcended into the wider public, helped, as always, by popular journalistic accounts,[155] and sanctioned by President Ciampi in 2003.[156] The *Alpini* also strove to establish a physical connection to the battlefield. The *Alpini* Association (*Associazione Nazionale Alpini*, ANA) was from the beginning very active.[157] Subsequently, they also built a school for disabled children in Rossosh. It was meant to show the *Alpini*'s humanism (also as a sort of payback for the help received by civilians during the retreat) and as a reference to the brotherhood shown by the *Alpini* at Nikolayevka in 1943.[158] The ANA also promotes scholarly work on the Don operations together with the University in Voronezh (and in the Trentino region).[159] The end of the Cold War made frequent pilgrimages possible, during which soil from Nikolayevka was taken back to several minor monuments in Italy.[160] The desire to build a memorial in Nikolayevka speaks for the endeavour to create a place for commemoration in an area that had long been sealed off by the Iron Curtain.[161]

In conclusion, the memoir literature deriving from the campaign against Russia primarily attacked the Germans, the Italian military's performance and its senior leadership. Messe became the most visible opponent of operational criticism and denied any wrongdoings on Soviet territory. The analysis of the memoir literature has shown

---

positive review, E. Fasanotti, "Nikolajewka, c'ero anch'io. *Giulio Bedeschi*," *Rivista Militare* 29, no. 4 (1973): 575–76; [Gen.] Mario Gariboldi, "Nikolajewka. La battaglia che fu vinta dalla tenacia," *L'Alpino* 65, no. 3 (1984): 28–29; also Argentieri, *Messe*, 186.

[155] Caruso, *Tutti i vivi*.

[156] "Ciampi: 'Nikolajewka pagina di eroismo e umanità'," *L'Alpino* 82, no. 2 (2003): 17.

[157] Associazione Nazionale Alpini, "Il ricordo della campagna di Russia," in *La campagna di Russia. Nel 70° anniversario dell'inizio dell'intervento dello CSIR*, eds. Antonello Biagini and Antonio Zarcone (Rome: Nuova Cultura, 2013), 29–33.

[158] Fausto Lorenzi, "Nikolaewka. Il modo migliore per ricordare," *L'Alpino* 63, no. 11 (1982): 6–10.

[159] Giorgio Scotoni, "La memoria della guerra sul Don e l'esperienza italo-russa di cooperazione nella regione di Voronezh (1990–2010)," in *La campagna di Russia. Nel 70° anniversario dell'inizio dell'intervento dello CSIR*, eds. Antonello Biagini and Antonio Zarcone (Rome: Nuova Cultura, 2013), 251–63.

[160] "La terra di Nikolajewka," *L'Alpino* 83, no. 2 (2004): 5.

[161] This combination of desire for and physical exclusion from the site of memory was similar to Caporetto, which became part of Yugoslavia in 1947, Foot, *Italy's Divided Memory*, 34.

diverging emphases in the civilian and military sphere. Politically motivated memoirs established many myths that scholars have all too often taken as credible sources. In contrast to Tolloy's full-fledged attack, the *Alpini* myth was more acceptable after the war: it connected the victim narrative, memories of the First World War and the *Resistenza*. The new Italian Army—which also used the lineage from the 'War of Liberation' as a founding (and recreation) myth—could therefore find some useful overlaps with their own narrative. Indeed, sacrifice, humanism and volunteerism are still seen as defining elements of the *Alpini* today. The preceding chapters have investigated myths and memoirs and separated fact from fiction. After these topoi of victimhood, combat performance and crimes have been analysed, the following chapter will look at the public arena: How were the memories and narratives on the *campagna di Russia* negotiated after 1943? In fact, without taking into account the Italian domestic situation and the Cold War framework it is impossible to understand why these myths and memories could persist and why the Italian campaign on the Eastern Front was instrumentalised and its memories so vehemently contested.

CHAPTER 11

Contested Memories During the Cold War

The campaign on the Eastern Front has always been an important part of Italian collective memory[1] and therefore also an aspect of the troubled attempt to get to grips with the 'Fascist War'.[2] Some scholars have described a "relatively homogenous"[3] memory, yet especially the early debates show a different picture. In fact, the memory of the *campagna di Russia* became a sharp political battlefield during the Cold War: the myths and memories became embroiled in the interaction between foreign and domestic politics. Depending on one's political standpoint, the POW issue became a question of victimhood or justified reprisal, while the operations in Russia was either framed as an incompetent and criminal war of extermination or as an honourable fight. The Russian campaign became a battlefield between lobbies that fought over politics, the interpretation of history, and in this process 'negotiated' a narrative. On one side were the Christian Democrats under De Gasperi (including the Catholic Church with the fervent anti-communist Pope Pius XII), and the military sphere (often led by Messe) who defended the Army's operational skill, moral conduct, officer corps, and the POWs in Russia, while on the other side the Italian Communist Party (PCI) and the Italian Socialist Party (PSI) repeatedly accused the senior army leadership of

[1] Giusti, *La campagna*, 7.
[2] Mondini and Schwarz, *Dalla guerra*, 117ff.; Focardi, *Il cattivo tedesco*, 77ff.
[3] Osti Guerrazzi and Schlemmer, "I soldati italiani," 391.

having led the common soldier to the slaughter and worsened his fate through their military incompetence. Additionally, it is important to remember that the PCI wanted to extoll the partisans' deeds and brand them as 'true' liberators (and not the co-belligerent army). Thus, the Italian National Partisan Association (ANPI) functioned as close ally of the Left, not least in securing more than moral recognition for the partisans, i.e. financial compensation in form of pensions.[4] It is therefore vital to recognise the role of the PCI and the general framework of Italo-Soviet relations from 1943 to the conclusion of the Peace Treaty in late 1946, a period which was defined by the Italian quest for recognition and reintegration into the international system.[5] At the same time, the highly volatile domestic situation saw the abolition of the monarchy in the constitutional vote on 2 June 1946 and the stabilisation under De Gasperi's Christian Democrats in the national elections of 18 April 1948. The following will analyse the political instrumentalisation of these interconnected issues (combat performance, officers, war crimes, and POWs) in the political arena, the press, and in courtrooms to show their importance for the narrative about events in the Second World War.

Italo-Soviet Relations and the Return of POWs 1945/1946

Up to the point that Italy left the Axis camp in September 1943, the Soviets were not involved in the Anglo-American dealings with the Badoglio government. Their subsequent attitude was that Italy should be firmly held accountable to the armistice terms and not be treated as an ally.[6] Thereafter, their presence in the Allied Advisory Commission for Italy and the Allied Control Commission was more *pro forma*, as the real power rested in the hands of the British and Americans. Andrey Vyshinsky (1883–1954) was appointed as Soviet delegate to the Advisory Commission. He had become infamous for his role in the political trials of the 1930s and subsequently served as Deputy Foreign Minister

---

[4] Mondini and Schwarz, *Dalla guerra*, 134ff.

[5] Mario Isnenghi, *Dalla Resistenza alla desistenza. L'Italia del 'Ponte' (1945–1947)* (Bari: Laterza, 2007). On the interplay between domestic politics and the Soviet Union, see Agarossi and Zaslavsky, *Togliatti e Stalin*.

[6] TNA, FO 371/37356, Soviet attitude towards Italy, 28 Sept. 1943.

(1940–1949), before ultimately succeeding Molotov (up till 1953).[7] His tenure during this period was crucial: he combined a talent for diplomacy, drawing on his excellent French and bourgeois habitus, with his expertise in legal matters, which was much called-upon in a time of peace treaties and conventions.[8] After a long illness, he finally arrived in Brindisi on 3 December 1943—apparently paranoid about spies.[9] The Italians and British immediately noted that besides reaching out to Communists and Socialists he aimed to introduce "representatives of anti-Fascist groups into the government",[10] and to repatriate Italian exile communists.[11] He also tried to return the scattered Soviet prisoners of war. Vyshinsky took a hard line on this issue, demanding repatriations even without their consent (if necessary by force). This put him at odds with the Western allies and later the UN, which aimed to strengthen the rights of displaced persons. This stance of his is important for understanding his approach in regards to the Italian prisoners.[12]

Vyshinsky also offered guidance on the *epurazione* (purges) and criticised what he saw as a soft-touch approach *vis-à-vis* former Fascist officials.[13] Similarly, Badoglio's attempt to negotiate on an equal footing and his rejection of advice how to run Italy were unwelcome.[14] Indeed, the relations between the Badoglio government and the Soviets remained ambiguous: the Italians attempted to exploit Allied differences

---

[7] Arkadi Waksberg, *Gnadenlos. Andrei Wyschinski* (Bergisch Gladbach: Lübbe, 1991).
[8] Still, he had little to no expertise on Italian affairs, ibid., 337ff., 353.
[9] He even stuffed his hotel room's keyhole with paper, IWM, Doc.13329, 05/481, Maj. E.B. Howard—Diary, Part One, 6 Dec. 1943, fol.41.
[10] TNA, FO 371/37356, Clark Kerr (Moscow) to FO, 12 Nov. 1943.
[11] DDI, X:I, doc.102, Prunas to Badoglio, 20 Dec. 1943; Morozzo della Rocca, *Politica*, 21ff.
[12] Waksberg, *Wychinski*, 341–42.
[13] DDI, X:I, doc.109, Prunas to Badoglio, 30 Dec. 1943; and ibid., doc.118, Prunas to Badoglio, 12 Jan. 1944. The Italians declared repression to be one only way of removing former Fascists. On the short and incomplete process of de-fascistisation see Romano Canosa, *Storia dell'epurazione in Italia. Le sanzioni contro il fascismo 1943–1948* (Milan: Baldini & Castoldi, 1999); Hans Woller, *Die Abrechnung mit dem Faschismus in Italien 1943 bis 1948* (Munich: Oldenbourg, 1996); Roy Domenico, *Italian Fascists on Trial, 1943–1948* (Chapel Hill: University of North Carolina Press, 1991); Botti and Ilari, *Il pensiero*, 415ff.
[14] See the not so amicable exchange between the two in DDI, X:I, doc.115, 10 Jan. 1944.

to break out of their isolation and become more than a 'co-belligerent' power, while the Soviets tried to gain more influence outside Eastern Europe and remain on a equal footing with the Anglo-Americans—not least to strengthen Tito in Yugoslavia, the Italian Communists, and the partisans in northern Italy.[15] Vital turning points were the first official meetings on 8 and 10 January 1944 in Salerno between Vyshinsky and Renato Prunas (1892–1951), the Secretary-General in the Foreign Ministry.[16] On the first day, Prunas also enquired into the fate of Italian prisoners in Russia—asking for precise numbers, names, and conditions.[17] Prunas put forward several arguments for his approach to Badoglio: an official statement would undermine RSI propaganda, the Italian people had not been in favour of attacking Russia, the Army had behaved very humanely on Russian soil, and witnessing German barbarism had led to a split with their Axis partner.[18] Yet, Vyshinsky maintained "that some Italian units were guilty of atrocities against the population in the occupied Soviet territories, [but he] admitted that our [the Italian] conduct has been, in general, much more humane than the German one."[19] Thus, Prunas perceived Vyshinsky as "well disposed" toward Italy[20]—an impression that was shattered during the Peace Treaty talks over two years later.

After these meetings, Italy continued to regain leverage by exploiting internal rivalries among the Allies, while the Anglo-Americans looked with suspicion at their rapprochement with the Kremlin.[21] On 14 March

---

[15] Mario Toscano, *Designs in Diplomacy: Pages from European Diplomatic History in the Twentieth Century* (Baltimore: The Johns Hopkins Press, 1970), 260–69; Salvatore Sechi, "Die neutralistische Versuchung. Italien und die Sowjetunion 1943–1948," in *Italien und die Großmächte 1943–1949*, ed. Hans Woller (Munich: Oldenbourg, 1988), 95–129. This included claims on parts of the Italian navy, Toscano, *Designs*, 265f., 279ff.; and the desire to build a Soviet airforce base in southern Italy, much to the concern of the Allies and Badoglio's government, see TNA, FO 371/43830, Macmillan to FO, 12 Mar. 1944.

[16] Prunas was the de facto Foreign Minister, while Badoglio held the position on paper.

[17] The meeting is brilliantly retold in Toscano, *Designs*, 269ff.

[18] DDI, X:I, doc.118, Prunas to Badoglio, 12 Jan. 1944, Attachment.

[19] Ibid.

[20] Toscano, *Designs*, 273.

[21] Ibid., 299; James Edward Miller, *The United States and Italy, 1940–1950: The Politics and Diplomacy of Stabilization* (Chapel Hill: The University of North Carolina Press, 1986), 90ff. Indeed, the Soviets portrayed their early recognition as a benevolent gesture, whereas in fact it was mere power politics *vis-à-vis* the Western Allies. Yet, the Italians

1944, Italy reestablished diplomatic relations with the Soviets (who had not informed their western partners beforehand)[22] by sending Pietro Quaroni (1898–1971) as new envoy to Moscow. In their everyday dealings, the Soviets were willing to gloss over the past and the Italian representative remarked in September that he heard for the first time ever about a potential misbehaviour by Italian troops.[23] Still, Quaroni was not allowed to visit the Italian prisoners. Only the trade union leader Giuseppe Di Vittorio was invited to the Suzdal camp in August 1945. The site had been refurbished, and despite the fact that he had not been permitted to speak with any prisoners he wrote a positive report on his tour.[24] The Soviets did not grant any information on the Italian POWs until summer 1945 on the grounds that Italy had denied any information on Soviet citizens in their hands between 1941 and 1943, and, after all, they considered themselves too busy finishing a war that Italy initiated.[25] This can also be seen as revenge for the Italian refusal to supply lists with captured Soviet soldiers during the war (on the ground that the USSR had not signed the Geneva convention).[26] Nevertheless, Quaroni thought playing the Soviet card to be an ideal means of increasing Italy's power in the battle with the Western allies over the pending peace settlement.[27] Alcide De Gasperi (1881–1954) had become Foreign Minister on 12 December 1944, and he used this priviledged position to draw the Western Allies' attention to the constitutional referendum and the local elections in March and April 1946.[28] De Gasperi understood the vital nexus between easing the surrender terms and guaranteeing desireable electoral results.[29] His Christian Democrats

thought it also showed the Kremlin's willingness to forget the Italian participation in 'Hitler's war', DDI, X:III, doc.152, Carandini (London) to De Gasperi, 2 Feb. 1946.

[22] Much to their concern, see TNA, FO 371/43830, FO to Moscow, 12 Mar. 1944.

[23] DDI, X:I, doc.386, Quaroni to Bonomi, 2 Sept. 1944.

[24] Petacco, *L'armata*, 220.

[25] Morozzo della Rocca, *Politica*, 102–3.

[26] Tirone, "La politica," 198.

[27] Piero Craveri, *De Gasperi* (Bologna: Il Mulino, 2006), 183.

[28] He remained in this position until 18 October 1946, and became Prime Minister on 10 December 1945 (until 1953), guiding Italy through the constitutional referendum, the parliamentary elections, and assuring her admission to NATO; see ibid., 171ff.

[29] Ibid., 176.

(*Democrazia Cristiana*, DC) proved a vital partner for the Americans in checking Soviet pressure to revise the Italian-Yugoslav border: thus, the public outcry about the POWs has to be seen in the context of the peace settlement.[30]

On 25 August 1945, the Soviets announced that they would repatriate 19,648 Italian prisoners. This declaration was unexpected as the Soviets saw POWs as an economic asset and legitimate booty, following a harsh *vae victis* approach.[31] In Italy, this message caused a great shock and public outcry, as the number of prisoners had been estimated to be around 85,000.[32] Morozzo della Rocca has highlighted the Italian government's failure to adequately prepare public opinion—particularly right-wing and Catholic circles—which spurred the instrumentalisation of the prisoners' the fate.[33] Indeed, the press launched vicious attacks against the Soviets, who still showed no desire to provide accurate lists or, for example, death certificates. Conversely, Moscow perceived the Italian protests as and "unexpected reaction"[34] and countered with allegations of Italian war crimes.

The majority of prisoners had returned by January 1946, but additional repatriations took place in summer. At the end of July, the Soviets simply declared the returns completed. This was a renewed shock for the families and press who had still held out hopes that several tens of thousands would return. The result was renewed outcry in Italy and diplomatic requests for more detailed information: only 12,500 of the 21,193 repatriated men had been soldiers of the CSIR or ARMIR.[35] Based on the tales of the returning men, the Italian authorities could reconstruct the fate of the ARMIR prisoners, their retreat from the Don, the death marches, and the camp conditions.[36] The shattered illusion and the homecomers' horrendous stories fuelled

---

[30] On this issue see Miller, *United States*, 162–68.

[31] Agarossi and Zaslavsky, *Togliatti e Stalin*, 161.

[32] Even the Communist Radio Mosca and *L'Alba* had placed the number of POWs at 80,000 during the war, Morozzo della Rocca, *Politica*, 106.

[33] Ibid., 111, 114–15.

[34] Ibid., 105.

[35] The Red Army had captured Italians from German prison or labour camps.

[36] Morozzo della Rocca, *Politica*, 107.

the virulent anti-Communism.[37] To understand the contested memories and debates, one has to look at the role of the PCI and its leader Palmiro Togliatti.

TOGLIATTI AND THE PCI

Togliatti had been in Russian exile since 1926 (with spells in France and Spain). In 1941, he directed the radio propaganda section of the Comintern. In this new role, he drew on his journalistic talents to augment his standing and used his almost daily broadcasts to ferociously attack the Italian soldiers on Russian soil.[38] He even fabricated stories of war crimes for *L'Alba*,[39] and continued his outbursts against the Italian Army in his edited volume *Discorsi agli Italiani*.[40] He showed no pity for Italians in Soviet hands. In fact, when his comrades were concerned about high mortality rates, Togliatti argued against appealing to the Soviets to improve their conditions. His rationale was if "more people realise that the aggression against other countries spells out ruin and death for their own, spells out ruin and death for every individual citizen, the better it will be for the future of Italy."[41] Togliatti returned to Italy on 26 March 1944 and led the PCI into a government of unity after the so-called "Salerno turn" (1 April 1944) to uphold a common front against Mussolini's puppet regime in the north and postpone political decisions about Italy's future.[42] From 18 June 1944, the new government under Ivanoe Bonomi (1873–1951) became more powerful (with Allied help) in restricting Communist influence.[43] When the country was

---

[37] Ibid., 113.
[38] Aldo Agosti, *Palmiro Togliatti: A Biography* (London: Tauris, 2008), 140.
[39] Alessandro Frigerio, *Reduci alla sbarra. 1949: il processo D'Onofrio e il ruolo del PCI nei lager sovietici* (Milan: Mursia, 2006), 39. Some parts of this book should be read with caution, as many claims are made without sufficient supporting evidence.
[40] Published in 1945 by *L'Unità* under the pseudonym Mario Correnti.
[41] Quoted in Agosti, *Togliatti*, 141; Agarossi and Zaslavsky, *Togliatti e Stalin*, 165.
[42] Toscano has rightly noted that the Prunas-Vyshinsky talks in January 1944 and the reestablishment of relations had opened the door for the PCI's participation in the Badoglio government, Toscano, *Designs*, 304.
[43] Miller, *United States*, 102ff., 136–37. Also his successor since 19 June 1945, Ferruccio Parri (1890–1981), managed to contain the Communist and Socialist pressures that came from the former resistance movement, ibid., 157ff.

liberated, old divides broke out again, and the constitutional referendum (2 June 1946) and the first general elections (18 April 1948) led to renewed domestic tensions. Thus, the PCI was both opposition leader and government party: caught between revolutionary ideals, and domestic and international realities.[44]

In the immediate postwar period, the PCI built up an ideal-type of the Soviet Union as land of freedom, peace, and happiness to which Italy should aspire. The maltreatment of prisoners did not fit this image. The PCI and Togliatti were afraid that homecomers' stories would shatter this idyll and unveil the role of Italian Communists in the camps.[45] Thus, they first attempted to prevent repatriations; then to limit them. In November 1945, they appealed to the Soviets to alter the repatriations—about which Moscow kept them little-informed. The Italian Communists also demanded the return only of officers, who had taken part in their in-camp re-education programmes.[46] Yet, they did so to little avail. Rather, tensions between the large majority of royalist officers and the few who had turned Communists caused brawls on the train journey home, and the Soviets had to protect the latter.[47] The PCI then followed a tactic of strict denial, claiming that the stories of repatriated prisoners were mere echoes of Mussolini's propaganda voiced by reactionaries, Catholics, and other anti-communists.[48] The Left press also attacked the new *Esercito* and its officer corps. British observers noted that these "slanderous campaigns" were aimed at convincing the people "that whatever may happen in the army is due to the inefficiency of the officers."[49] At the same time, pay increases for workers and concessions to former partisans dampened the mood in the Army and created a "feeling of apathy and futility" among its officers.[50] For the subsequent debates about Italian war crimes, it is therefore essential to understand the PCI's (and more generally the political Left's) tendency to—and interest in—denigrating the POWs and discrediting the Italian combat

---

[44] Agarossi and Zaslavsky, *Togliatti e Stalin*, 75–129; Ennio Di Nolfo, *Von Mussolini bis De Gasperi* (Paderborn: Schöningh, 1993), 90, 142ff.

[45] Agarossi and Zaslavsky, *Togliatti e Stalin*, 168.

[46] Ibid., 170–71.

[47] TNA, WO 202/991, MMIA, Intelligence Summary, 31 July 1946, fol.3.

[48] Agarossi and Zaslavsky, *Togliatti e Stalin*, 170.

[49] TNA, WO 202/991, MMIA, Intelligence Summary, 31 Aug. 1946, fol.4.

[50] Ibid.

performance, not only for political reasons, but also to defend the myths of an almighty *Resistenza* and 'good Stalinism'.[51] Yet, the PCI's many assaults on the armed forces were not left unanswered.

The former commander of the CSIR, Giovanni Messe, became the advocate of the military. In several newspaper articles, he attempted to uphold the honour of the Italian soldier and to demonstrate their good conduct *vis-à-vis* the civilian population.[52] Messe saw Togliatti's activities as one of the chief reasons behind the demeaning reports on the Italian behaviour in Russia and for the POWs' fate.[53] The great instrumentalisation of this issue in the press and the involvement of the two 'returnees' (Messe and Togliatti) demonstrated that these heated debates were about much more than the POWs: they brought together domestic and international politics, as well as questions about war crimes and military performance.

Messe's Post-1943 Career

While the scholarship on Messe's wartime exploits has been dominated by rather hagiographic efforts, we know even less about his post-war career.[54] Messe had been captured in May 1943, when he was newly appointed *Maresciallo d'Italia* and commander of the First Italian Army in Tunisia. His nationalist, royalist and anti-communist stance is evident from secret bugging reports in British captivity.[55] Yet, this should not be surprising, given that he had been aide de camp to the King. Besides his monarchism, which was widespread in the *Royal* Italian Army, also his anti-communism was probably no more developed than that of any French or British officer at the time. Messe never openly rebelled against Fascism and certainly was a fellow traveller, but none of the available documents (of varying sources) show him as an ideological warrior. When he spoke about his experiences on the Eastern Front in captivity, he highlighted the hard fighting and atrocities on both the Soviet

[51] Di Nolfo, *Von Mussolini*, 60–65.

[52] AUSSME, Fondo Messe, b.D(7), c.39, Anno 1945—Inesattezze circa il comportamento dei combattenti italiani in Russia, fol.2.

[53] Ibid., fol.1.

[54] Most recently, Conti, *Uomini*, 137ff.; see also Argentieri, *Messe*, 257–308. On his activities during the War of Liberation see Longo, *Messe*, 391–478.

[55] Osti Guerrazzi, *Noi non sappiamo odiare*, 112ff.

and German sides[56]—while upholding the dictum that the Italians had allegedly only hated the Germans.[57] Messe praised the Red Army, arguing the common Russian was fighting bravely for his homeland and not for Bolshevism.[58] He also warned of the Soviet "menace" and saw Communism as a greater threat to Italy than Nazism.[59]

After declaring war against Germany on 13 October 1943, the Badoglio government was granted 'co-belligerent' status, which partly fulfilled its desire to play a greater part in the fight against the Germans and the RSI. Badoglio recalled Messe in October 1943. Messe became—with support of his predecessor Ambrosio[60]—Chief of the General Staff on 13 November 1943.[61] Messe constantly attempted to attain combat duties for the Italian forces, beyond auxiliary tasks—not least to increase the country's political leverage and to regain prestige at home and abroad.[62] The British welcomed Messe's return, praising him as a "man of action, vigorous and not too much bound by his caste,"[63] and described Messe as viewing "himself a man with a mission to revive the Italian Army and drive the Germans out of Italy."[64] His appointment was very unpopular with the Left in Italy, who saw him as the embodiment of elite continuity; yet, this did not prevent him from funnelling aid to less political resistance cells.[65] The Italian Communists tried to convince the Allies that they were betting on the wrong horse. By providing information about alleged statements by Messe (such as praise for the Germans and resentment about the Allies' treatment of the Italians) the Communist Luigi Moro tried to persuade authorities in Bari of

[56]TNA, WO 208/4185, S.R.I.G. no.16, 18 May 1943.
[57]TNA, WO 208/4185, S.R.I.G. no.125, 17 July 1943.
[58]TNA, WO 208/4185, S.R.I.G. no.58, 4 June 1943.
[59]TNA, WO 208/4186, S.R.I.G. no.139, 19 July 1943; TNA, WO 208/4187, S.R.I.G. no.319, 2 October 1943. Not least because he feared the exposed position of Trieste and Fiume (Rijeka), TNA, WO 208/4187, S.R.I.G. no.309, 19 Sept. 1943.
[60]Cecini, *I generali*, 157.
[61]Argentieri, *Messe*, 205–8. Messe filled key positions with his close aides, e.g. Paolo Berardi and Taddeo Orlando. Other generals from British captivity were soon to follow.
[62]Vallauri, *Soldati*, 294ff., 315ff.
[63]IWM, 05/481, Maj. E.B. Howard—Diary, Part One, 22 Nov. 1943, fol.25.
[64]TNA, FO 660/378, Macmillan to FO, 29 Nov. 1943.
[65]Argentieri, *Messe*, 216ff., 238ff.

Messe's unreliability—a smear campaign they readily noted.[66] Several newspaper articles demanded a *tabula rasa* among the generals and staff officers, arguing that men who had led the Army under Fascism could not lead the nation in her war of liberation.[67] In fact, Allied authorities were changing guard in the Italian Army, and tried to sideline men like Ambrosio and Roatta.[68] Messe was in a difficult position for another reason: the RSI propaganda also attacked him and Mussolini personally called him a traitor.[69] Nonetheless, he remained Chief of the General Staff until May 1945, when a new decree abolished the rank of Marshal and thereby necessitated his retirement.[70] The Italian government had already proposed his removal in early April 1945, and it appears that this was a welcome possibility to sideline him.[71] In any case, Messe retired from active service on 27 March 1947.

This did not pitch him into total inactivity. In May 1947, British intelligence was provided with a report on Messe's activities. He had gathered a group of distinguished officers—which the British labelled neo-fascist[72]—to lobby jointly against excluding senior officers in the purges (*epurazione*), preserving the memory of General Bellomo and maintaining his family,[73] and discussing "means of developing in the armed forces a 'proud reserve' towards the Allies, especially towards

[66] IWM, 05/481, Maj. E.B. Howard—Diary, Part One, 23 Dec. 1945, fos.74–75.

[67] AUSSME, Fondo Messe, b.B(3), c.12, see the handwritten notes to the article "Il problema dell'esercito," *La Voce Repubblicana*, 18 July 1944.

[68] See the correspondence in TNA, FO 660/375.

[69] Argentieri, *Messe*, 218ff.; Benito Mussolini, *Memoirs 1942–1943* (London: Weidenfeld & Nicolson, 1949), 10–21.

[70] TNA, WO 204/2420, Italian Appointments, 8 Apr. 1945. The British seemed little concerned over Messe's departure and wholeheartedly embraced Claudio Trezzani as his successor.

[71] TNA, WO 204/3, Maj.Gen. Langley Browning to Lt.Gen. W.D. Morgan, 10 Apr. 1945, fol.3.

[72] The anti-British tone was arguably a reason for this title and subsequent reports showed that the majority of these officers were in the monarchist, not the neo-fascist, camp. The officers present were Marshal Ettore Bastico, and generals Gariboldi, Marazzani, Antonio Sorice, Enrico Frattini, Giuseppe Mancinelli, Alessandro Albert, Roberto Bencivenga, and Arturo Scattini.

[73] General Nicola Bellomo (1881–1945) had saved Bari from German occupation on 9 September 1943. He was later tried for executing British POWs and shot by the British on 11 September 1945, causing bitter Italian reactions.

the British, and to oppose the technical and moral changes in the Army suggested by the Allies", and finally "to discuss how best to maintain an anti-Russian attitude in the armed forces and to help those officers who held prominent appointments under Fascism."[74] Already during the War of Liberation, Messe had opposed anti-militarist tendencies and political interference in army matters.[75] The meeting showed Messe's readiness to take on key roles personally; but the 'Neo-Fascist' label was misleading.

Messe had declared his readiness to "openly take over the leadership of the monarchist movement" to General Armando Pescatori (1884–1957)[76] in June 1947 and requested permission from the former King Umberto II.[77] The *Partito Nazionale Monarchico* had a military wing (formerly the *Commissione Monarchica Militare*) that consisted almost exclusively of former officers commanded by General Edoardo Scala.[78] They were meant to cooperate with Guglielmo Giannini's populist *L'Uomo Qualunque* (Common Man Front) movement, which had its power base in southern Italy and Rome,[79] and possibly the Liberal Party and the DC in case of a Communist uprising. Thus, its military wing hoarded arms under the command of ex-generals in order to prepare the means to suppress an armed uprising.[80] Yet, these fears were nothing exceptional at the time if one bears in mind the Communist take-overs in Eastern Europe. The right-wing resistance movement in Venezia Giulia (3rd Corpo Volontari della Libertà, or 3 CVL) numbered around 10,000 men (with 5000 effectively armed) and was supported by the local *Mantova* Division.[81] Other irregular forces were added to these

---

[74] TNA, KV 3/266, Meeting of Neo-Fascist Senior Officers, 19 June 1947.

[75] Longo, *Messe*, 470ff.

[76] A close friend of Messe, he had been captured as GOC of the 2nd Libyan Division in December 1940.

[77] TNA, KV 3/266, Italy. Right-Wing and Monarchist Activities, 2 June 1947.

[78] TNA, KV 3/266, Italian Right Wing Groups, 5 Aug. 1947. See also Angelo Michele Imbriani, *Vento del Sud. Moderati, reazionari, Qualunquisti (1943–1948)* (Bologna: Il Mulino, 1996), 35–41.

[79] Sandro Setta, *L'Uomo Qualunque: 1944–1948* (Bari: Laterza, 1975).

[80] TNA, KV 3/266, Italian Right Wing Groups, 5 Aug. 1947.

[81] TNA, KV 3/266, Italy. Right-Wing Para-Military Organisations, 24 July 1947. In command of General Montezemolo, before him, General Armellini had followed the same policy.

formations, which were sponsored by the War Ministry,[82] the military intelligence (SIM), and the Americans.[83] The fear of Communist subversion and a (Soviet-backed) Yugoslav invasion was very real, and given the climate of this period it is rather unsurprising that anti-Communist figures were also taking precautions. Indeed, Messe appears to have been a connecting element between South and North, irregular ex-Fascists, monarchists, and the Army.[84] On 13 August 1947, the British reported that "Marshal Messe has now taken over the military direction of the whole anti-Communist movement in North Italy."[85] Yet, it would be wrong to see these activities as reactionary desires of former generals to overthrow the new republic[86]—likewise, the Liberal Party and even the *Uomo Qualunque* were not neo-Fascists.[87] The groups in northern Italy received financial backing from powerful industrialists and discussed the unification of the northern monarchist groups with De Gasperi and the Liberals, while "the American authorities [were] completely informed of all developments affecting the anti-Communist movement."[88] The Cold War had come to Italy; an important context that historians should not forget when analysing accusations from the political Left against the military, or Messe personally.

Messe's active pen kept him in the spotlight. As early as 1945, he wrote countless articles (often in the conservative *Il Tempo*),[89] in which he

---

[82] In fact, the War Ministry supplied and administered these formations, while the SIM shunned away, fearing investigations by left-wing politicians, TNA, KV 3/266, Italy. The Italian Right-Wing Movement. American Assistance, 11 Aug. 1947.

[83] The force was meant to be ready to protect Venezia Giulia and 'stay behind' if regular forces were compelled to withdraw by Yugoslav attacks, TNA, KV 3/266, Italy. American-sponsored force in Venezia Giulia, 21 Nov. 1946.

[84] See also Conti, *Uomini*, 141ff., 156, for a detailed description of which other former military figures were involved in these monarchist groups; and on Messe's leadership position and anti-Communist stance. Yet, Conti tends to paint these organisations as reactive formations that stood ready in case of a Communist take-over, rather than themselves seeking to overthrow the new republic, ibid., 156.

[85] TNA, KV 3/266, Italy. The Right-Wing Movement, 13 Aug. 1947.

[86] However, besides Bencivenga, also General Caracciolo di Feroleto and other generals were involved in neo-fascist and right-wing movements, TNA, KV 3/266, Italy. Political Notes, 15 Jan. 1947.

[87] Craveri, *De Gasperi*, 204.

[88] TNA, KV 3/266, Italy. The Right-Wing Movement, 13 Aug. 1947.

[89] "Apoliticità dell'Esercito," *Il Tempo*, 7 June 1947.

defended the military's track record—particularly against Communist allegations of criminal behaviour and operational incompetence in Russia.[90] The Left interpreted this as an attempt to whitewash the Army's closeness to Fascism and mediocre battlefield performances.[91] In 1947, his memoirs on the Eastern Front included a lengthy discussion of the prisoners' fate in Russia, as well as the role of the PCI, and Communist propaganda on alleged Italian cruelties.[92] His book was therefore also an attempt to publish a lengthy defence against the domestic and foreign allegations—most notably in form of Vyshinsky's denigrations at the Paris Peace Conference in September 1946.

THE PEACE TREATY CONFERENCE, 1946

The conference was held briefly after the constitutional referendum on 2 June 1946. The monarchy was abolished, but by a lesser margin than expected.[93] The vote for the constituent assembly gave the Christian Democrats the edge and dampened the mood in the Communist and Socialist camp. Yet, Italian and US officials remained concerned about a possible forceful takeover.[94] As described above, the Soviets declared the end of prisoner repatriations two months later, which again stirred public outcry. Hence, domestic and foreign affairs remained closely interrelated in the chaotic period until the elections in April 1948. Also the peace settlement was entangled in the general imbroglio of the early Cold War.[95] Since the Potsdam Conference in July 1945, the US had been pushing for a rapid and just settlement. The confrontation over Venezia Giulia (including Trieste) with Tito's Yugoslavia and fears of Communist subversion had increased US benevolence towards Italy and the willingness

---

[90]AUSSME, Fondo Messe, b.D(7), c.39, Anno 1945—Inesattezze circa il comportamento dei combattenti italiani in Russia, fol.2. He also defended Italian generals against Yugoslavian accusations and countered demands to extradite them, Conti, *Criminali di guerra*, 241ff.

[91]AUSSME, Fondo Messe, b.B(3), c.12, "Le carte di Messe," *La Voce Repubblicana*, 23 Aug. 1946.

[92]Messe, *La guerra*, 301–69.

[93]Craveri, *De Gasperi*, 235–38.

[94]Miller, *United States*, 190ff.

[95]More detailed in Sara Lorenzini, *L'Italia e il trattato di pace del 1947* (Bologna: Il Mulino, 2007).

for a lenient peace to aid the young democracy. This in turn influenced the Soviets' stance. Their disappointment about Italy's half-hearted acknowledgments of defeat, the rapid end of the *epurazione*, its cold relations with Yugoslavia,[96] as well as the often-virulent anti-Communist press meant that Moscow was little supportive during the lengthy negotiations between July 1945 and 12 December 1946.[97] After the harsh press reactions over the POW issue, the Soviets had spread accusations about Italian war crimes to justify their internment and hinted at the Italian their role as aggressors in the recent war. In the context of the Peace Treaty, such allegations were also instrumentalised to justify claims for redistribution and reparations.[98] A bargaining game thus developed.

Vyshinsky asked if the Italian government was willing to cede territory and offered approval for Italy's entry into the UN.[99] The Italians had realised the likely Soviet support for Yugoslavia's territorial claims,[100] and the connection of their own fate to the negotiations with Bulgaria, Romania, and Hungary (which were in the Soviet orbit). Italy's key interests, on the other hand, were securing Trieste and the border regions, re-negotiating their prior renunciation of its colonial possessions, easing military limitations, and receiving financial help instead of paying hefty reparations.[101] The Italians placed their bets on the Americans who had already eased the armistice restrictions and helped Italy's economic recovery. Still, Rome also hoped for a benign Soviet stance,[102] while the settlement was expected to be harsher than public

---

[96] The British noted "indications that Tito will refuse or delay signing [the] Peace Treaty owing to loss of prestige involved", TNA, KV 3/266, AFHQ to War Office, 2 Feb. 1947, fol.6.

[97] Sechi, "Die neutralistische Versuchung," 101ff., 111.

[98] Morozzo della Rocca, *Politica*, 175ff., 392.

[99] DDI, X:II, doc.332, De Gasperi to Tarchiani (Washington), 13 July 1945. In fact, the Soviets vetoed Italian membership until 1955, when her satellites Bulgaria, Romania, and Hungary were also accepted. The US had proposed immediate Italian membership at Potsdam, Miller, *United States*, 172.

[100] DDI, X:II, doc.144, Quaroni to De Gasperi, 23 Apr. 1945; and ibid., doc.193, Quaroni to De Gasperi, 13 May 1945.

[101] U.S. Department of State, *Foreign Relations of the United States (FRUS), 1946, Paris Peace Conference: Proceedings*, Vol. 3 (Washington: U.S. Government Printing Office, 1970), doc.22, Byrnes-Nenni Conversation, 31 July 1946.

[102] DDI, X:II, doc.310, Quaroni to De Gasperi, 4 July 1945.

opinion was prepared for.[103] Already the publicised draft in late July 1946 had created open anger in Italy. It had horrified De Gasperi, who still placed all his hopes on the coming conference.[104] Yet, Italian officials realised what damage had been caused by the conservative press's attacks on the Soviets, which weakened their hand.[105]

In his speech at the Paris conference on 10 August 1946, De Gasperi highlighted the fate of the tens of thousands of Italians who had been forced to flee from the 'Yugoslav yoke'. He cited Italy's contribution as a 'co-belligerent' and rejected as outrageous claims to her navy as war booty.[106] De Gasperi did not mention any of the bitter disappointments over the POW issue, clearly aware as he was of the Soviets' hostile mood and the delicacy of the subject—shortly after the Soviet declaration that the repatriations were completed. Thereby, De Gasperi's diplomatic tenor—admitting Italy's defeat, while hinting at her democratic past, and peaceful ideas for future cooperation—scored important points on different fronts.[107]

As the USSR's delegate, Vyshinsky became a vital figure at the Paris conference. As outlined above, his first-hand experience with the Italians immediately after the traumatic events of September 1943 had hardly raised his esteem for the country and Washington's grooming of De Gasperi further antagonised him.[108] Despite the heated atmosphere at the conference and Vyshinsky's notorious outbursts at international meetings, his bearing in Paris came as a great surprise.[109] The Italians were particularly astonished, as they had perceived him as "the most diplomatic in form, but the hardest in substance" of all Soviet leaders.[110]

---

[103] DDI, X:II, doc.314, Quaroni to De Gasperi, 6 July 1945.

[104] De Gasperi busily tried to rally other European leaders to revise the treaty proposals, which, for instance, allowed for the accord with Austria over South Tyrol, Craveri, *De Gasperi*, 246ff.

[105] DDI, X:IV, doc.88, Quaroni to De Gasperi, 31 July 1946. De Gasperi tried to restrain some anti-Communist tendencies in the press as late as 1950, Craveri, *De Gasperi*, 177. One must not forget that this was the early Cold War, and in the US, too, this was a high time of vicious anti-Communism in the papers, Miller, *United States*, 175.

[106] FRUS, *1946, Paris Peace Conference: Proceedings*, Vol. 3, doc.49, 10 Aug. 1946.

[107] Craveri, *De Gasperi*, 250–52.

[108] He had left Italy already after two months in mid February 1944.

[109] Waksberg, *Wychinski*, 393–96.

[110] DDI, X:III, doc.174, Quaroni to De Gasperi, 9 Feb. 1946.

In his speech on 5 September 1946, he took more demanding positions than expected in regards to reparations, decolonisation,[111] and supported more Yugoslav claims than had been expected.[112] Besides great power rivalry, the Soviets were dissatisfied with the Peace Conference and feared a renewed revanchism supported by old Italian elites and the virulent anti-Communist press.[113] Vyshinsky ridiculed the claim presented by Foreign Minister Ivanoe Bonomi on 2 September that Italy had defeated the Austro-Hungarian Empire in the battle of Vittorio Veneto in 1918.[114] Bonomi's reference to the First World War intended to underline Italian claims on Venezia Giulia and South Tyrol—the two contested areas with Yugoslavia and Austria, respectively. Vyshinsky's reply painted 1915 as a classical example of Italian political opportunism and aggressive imperialism.[115] Adding insult to injury, he claimed the spoils of victory over Austria for the Russian Army, stating that "everyone knows that the Italians are better at running than fighting."[116] Further, he branded marshals De Bono, Graziani, and Messe as incapable commanders and likened an association between contemporary Italian soldiering and ancient Rome to a comparison between "donkeys and lions."[117] Thus, the demeaning statements about Italians as soldiers were linked to fundamental Italian interests. The Italian outrage was enormous: feelings of indignation mixed with a stubborn pride and outcry about the

---

[111] The Soviets altered their position on this issue in February 1948, when it seemed opportune to hurt British ambitions in Africa and support an Italian trusteeship over Somalia to counter tensions over Trieste.

[112] DDI, X:IV, doc.68, Quaroni to De Gasperi, 26 July 1946; and ibid., doc.315, Quaroni to De Gasperi, 16 Sept. 1946. The Soviets supported the Yugoslavian attack on Roatta. His trial had been a key project in Count Sforza's early designs for de-fascistication, but Roatta 'escaped' from internment in March 1945. The Yugoslavs wanted to trial him as war criminal, Conti, *Criminali di guerra*, 109, 119ff., 285ff.

[113] Sechi, "Die neutralistische Versuchung," 119.

[114] Morozzo della Rocca, *Politica*, 186.

[115] Argentieri, *Messe*, 259–60; Lorenzini, *L'Italia*, 86.

[116] "Russians Sneer at Italian Record in Wars," *The Sydney Morning Herald*, 6 Sept. 1946, 1. In fact, most of his outbursts were not even included in the official protocol, Morozzo della Rocca, *Politica*, 211.

[117] AUSSME, Fondo Messe, b.D(7), c.39, Anno 1945—Inesattezze circa il comportamento dei combattenti italiani in Russia, fol.3.

treaty, which was perceived a humiliating *diktat*.[118] Vyshinsky's accusations made the Soviets highly unpopular in large parts of society[119]—and unquestionably so within the Army.[120]

The delicate internal situation required capable and reliable soldiers (and *Carabinieri*) in case of a Communist coup. But the reality was bleaker. The Italian Army was still in a poor state during the chaotic reorganisation, dependent on British material, and far less popular than the partisans.[121] Indeed, the government and the police were embarrassed by a leaked report on an alleged Communist terrorist organisation in September 1946 and De Gasperi had to apologise to the Soviets[122]—a feat that hardly raised trust in the government, but showed the delicacy of relations with the PCI, the USSR, and their interplay with the Italian security apparatus. Vyshinsky's comments were, in a sense, even worse as they were direct propaganda for the PCI and Socialists, whose party newspapers used this as a pretext to continue their attacks on the Army.[123] While the Left's repeated slurs could be dismissed as an internal affair, the Soviet Foreign Minister's depiction of the Italians as militarily useless cowards was a different story altogether. Despite the Italian Communists' and Soviet attempts to qualify Vyshinsky's heated outbursts[124]—his allegations could not be left uncountered. After all, the signing of the armistice after the battle of Vittorio Veneto (4 November 1918) was—and still is—armed forces day.

It fell again to Messe to publicly defend what many deemed to be the nation's honour. Similarly to the outbursts against Montgomery's

---

[118] Morozzo della Rocca, *Politica*, 187. Even Italian workers called a strike during the signing ceremony in February 1947. On reactions in Italy see Lorenzini, *L'Italia*, 107–16.

[119] In an obituary almost one decade later, he was still described as hostile and disrespectful towards Italy, see Amedeo Giannini, "Andrea Viscinski," *Rivista di Studi Politici Internazionali* 22, no. 1 (1955): 110–12.

[120] TNA, WO 202/991, MMIA, Intelligence Summary, 30 Sept. 1946, fol.1.

[121] On the reorganisation see Nuti, *L'Esercito*; Effie Pedaliu, "Britain and the Reconstruction of the Post-Fascist Italian Armed Forces, 1943–1948," *Cold War History* 2, no. 1 (2001): 39–68.

[122] Miller, *United States*, 193.

[123] The Baistrocchi trial triggered renewed attacks, TNA, WO 202/991, MMIA, Intelligence Summary, 30 Sept. 1946, fol.3. Detailed in Botti and Ilari, *Il pensiero*, 428ff.

[124] Diplomatic circles and Moscow's official press organs both attempted to alter his comments and argued that his depictions concerned the Fascist war effort alone and did not hold true for democratic Italy, Morozzo della Rocca, *Politica*, 187.

memoirs in 1957,[125] large parts of the Italian public rallied around the flag—personified by Messe—to repulse allegations of cowardice and dishonourable behaviour. On 15 September 1946, he published an article entitled 'donkeys and lions' in the conservative *Il Tempo*; in which he deemed the attacks on the generals as unqualified, as they embodied the nation like the simple soldiers, and one could neither say all of them had been incompetent in their roles, nor speak of a "fleeing army" in general.[126] The *Regio Esercito* had not been fascist, Messe added, but merely followed its duty to obey orders from the political leadership. Hereafter, the left-wing press attacked Messe, juxtaposed him to Garibaldi,[127] and justified Vyshinsky's statements.[128] Messe's rebuke was even seen as attempt to disturb the peace and the neutralist leanings in many circles.[129] The Communist deputies Togliatti and Terracini wanted to see Messe in court for his responsibility in the Russian campaign as "Hitler's mercenary," leading tens of thousands of Italians to certain death with bad equipment—and even insulting today's Soviet Union and her peace-loving citizens.[130] The Communist Mario Palermo placed the blame for the half-hearted *epurazione* on the Marshal's shoulders— despite the fact that he himself had been Deputy War Minister during the War of Liberation.[131] Messe went on the offensive in February 1947.[132] He not only repudiated these assertions but demanded a thorough investigation of the POWs' fate during internment and the conditions of those men still held hostage in the USSR.[133] Thereby, he turned the tables and accused the PCI of collaboration with the enemy at the

[125] Montgomery had described 8 September 1943 as the "biggest double cross" in history and had few positive words to say about the Italian military, which led to fierce reactions and even an official Italian protest, see e.g. Paolo Monelli, "Il generale quindici a uno," *La Stampa*, 4 Nov. 1958, 4.

[126] AUSSME, Fondo Messe, b.B(3), c.17, *L'Unità* del 11 settembre.

[127] Argentieri, *Messe*, 260.

[128] Morozzo della Rocca, *Politica*, 187.

[129] AUSSME, Fondo Messe, b.B(3), c.12, "La guerra di domani," *La Voce Repubblicana*, 28 Sept. 1946. Indeed, Messe later argued against neutralist positions, Argentieri, *Messe*, 264.

[130] AUSSME, Fondo Messe, b.B(3), c.17, Appunto, fol.1.

[131] Argentieri, *Messe*, 262–63.

[132] AUSSME, Fondo Messe, b.D(7), c.39, Anno 1945—Inesattezze circa il comportamento dei combattenti italiani in Russia, fos.4–6.

[133] AUSSME, Fondo Messe, b.B(3), c.17, Appunto, fol.2.

cost of the Italian prisoners. Togliatti bluntly told Messe to "shut up."[134] But the outcry over Vyshinsky's statements was not the end of matters. The disputes gained intensity during the long lead-up to the election in April 1948, as the threat of a PCI victory hung in the air. The DC had taken a first critical step toward closer alignment with the Western allies.[135] The election was therefore a decision between East and West—and the legacy of Italy's involvement on the Eastern Front featured strongly in this heated campaign.

THE ELECTIONS OF APRIL 1948

Between 1946 and 1948, the POW question remained the subject of wide debate in regional, daily, and weekly newspapers, and became an important matter in electoral campaigns.[136] Yet, as Morozzo della Rocca has noted, there was a different context for the Italian public reaction in 1945–1946 as compared to 1947–1948. In the immediate aftermath of the war, the prisoners were still in the USSR. The fear and anxiety of family members had spread to the general public and caused a general feeling of the need to 'bring the boys home', which was also used to gloss over Italy's part in the war itself. In 1947, the doubtless tougher fate of the prisoners in Russia could be contrasted to those in Western hands.[137] By way of comparison, in 1947, only 10,000 of 1.5 million prisoners who had been in US, British, or French captivity had not been repatriated.[138] Throughout 1947 the Italian Left argued that it was not the time to investigate the fate of the POWs, but to admit Italian guilt and to realise the real cause of the prisoners' internment—a line of argument which family associations, a large part of the press, and public opinion refused to follow.[139] Thus, it would be misleading to assert that the political Right instrumentalised the prisoners' fate, as a large part of Italian society was appalled about the possible death of so many of their countrymen in Soviet hands.

---

[134] Palmiro Togliatti, "Stia zitto il Signor Messe," *L'Unità*, 26 Feb. 1947.
[135] Craveri, *De Gasperi*, 257.
[136] Agarossi and Zaslavsky, *Togliatti e Stalin*, 172.
[137] Morozzo della Rocca, *Politica*, 394.
[138] Ibid. The countries had also supplied detailed lists.
[139] Ibid., 385.

After the Peace Treaty was signed, the government could act more explicitly, instead of leaving the field to the press.[140] In the end, De Gasperi and the Americans had followed a simple logic: "better a bad treaty that could be amended than no treaty."[141] The international climate had increased Rome's diplomatic leverage. The Truman Doctrine, the Marshall Plan, and the initiation of NATO all played their parts. Additionally, the Soviet-Yugoslav split became ever more apparent, the situation in Greece and Turkey was going from bad to worse in spring and summer 1947, and the Truman administration became more closely tied to the DC and the Catholic Church in securing Italy's economic and political stabilisation.[142] De Gasperi's trip to the US in January 1947 had brought further commitments. The Italian Left fiercely opposed his pro-American course and mixed their fight against 'Fascists' with the battle against new Cold War enemies whose Atlanticist contours were now developing.[143]

On 30 May 1947, De Gasperi changed his cabinet. He now presided over a minority government without the Communists and Socialists, which further polarised the domestic situation.[144] This move was intended to give him more rapid US financial and political aid by showcasing himself as strong man.[145] Soviet criticism became more pronounced thereafter, while Moscow also caused Togliatti some headaches: the Soviets refused Marshall Aid in their sphere, and in September 1947 the newly founded Cominform (Communist Information Bureau) condemned the PCI's alleged national focus. Thus, both domestic

[140] After the final sessions in New York in November and December 1946, the Council of Foreign Ministers finally concluded the Italian peace settlement. It was signed in Paris on 10 February 1947, and ratified by the Italian constitutional assembly on 31 July 1947. It entered into force on 15 September 1947. Italy had to pay small reparations, lost all her colonies (including those acquired before the Fascist seizure of power in 1922), had to accept minor border adjustments with France (and major ones with Yugoslavia), the armed forces were limited to 300,000 men and the fleet went into Allied hands. Trieste became a Free Territory until a final settlement on the city's status was reached. Detailed in Lorenzini, *L'Italia*, 99ff., 116ff., 155ff.; Clementi, *L'alleato Stalin*, 191–235.

[141] Miller, *United States*, 223.

[142] Di Nolfo, *Von Mussolini*, 197ff.

[143] Craveri, *De Gasperi*, 273–79.

[144] In December, he brought the Liberals, the Republicans, and Social Democrats (which had split from the Socialist Party) back into his coalition, see ibid., 267ff., 278ff.

[145] Di Nolfo, *Von Mussolini*, 210–18.

and international pressure on the PCI fuelled a "return to class struggle methods, if not to those of the civil war,"[146] which led to strikes, demonstrations, and street violence to the point that the "threat of revolution hung heavily over Italy in late November 1947."[147] While the US only thought about military intervention in case of a Communist invasion or insurrection, the Italian peninsula had by late 1947 become the prime theatre of the Cold War.[148] Similarly, in the lead-up to the elections in 1948, the Italian government and its armed forces feared a repeat of the Communist take-over that had happened in Prague on 24 February 1948. Besides the danger from the extremist Left, the *Uomo Qualunque* movement's surge to two millions votes in the constitutional assembly election in 1946, and the birth of neo-Fascist groups such as the Italian Social Movement (*Movimento Sociale Italiano*, MSI) gave cause for concern.[149] All paramilitary groups were banned in February 1948 and Mario Scelba (1901–1991), the 'Iron Sicilian' Minister of the Interior, increased his efforts to improve the Army and the whole security apparatus.[150]

As shown above, Messe had signalled his readiness to take up political positions. Thus, the Marshal ran as independent candidate to become senator for Brindisi (Puglia), and was endorsed by the *Blocco Nazionale* formed of Liberals and *Uomo Qualunque*. In his speeches, he styled himself as a liberal, warned of the Communist menace to freedom and democracy, demanded the reintegration of RSI soldiers, and took a pronounced 'Atlanticist' stance.[151] A Marshal in politics? The Left was more than sceptical. Messe's claim that the Army had been apolitical and would remain apolitical in the new state was received with particular disbelief, and thought to be an expression of concealed monarchism.[152]

---

[146] Ibid., 223.

[147] Miller, *United States*, 240.

[148] Ibid., 237.

[149] Franco Ferraresi, *Threats to Democracy: The Radical Right in Italy After the War* (Princeton: Princeton University Press, 1996), 15ff., 51ff.; Parlato, *Fascisti senza Mussolini*, 171ff.

[150] Craveri, *De Gasperi*, 326–31; Gabriella Fanello Marcucci, *Scelba. Il ministro che si oppose al fascismo e al comunismo in nome della libertà* (Milan: Mondadori, 2006), 128ff.

[151] Argentieri, *Messe*, 264.

[152] AUSSME, Fondo Messe, b.B(3), c.12, "L'apoliticità di Messe," *La Voce Repubblicana*, 10 June 1947.

Given the climate of accusations, trials, and domestic tension prior to the election on 18 April 1948 it should be no surprise that the POW issue caused renewed friction. Many repatriated prisoners spoke at rallies about the grim reality of Stalin's alleged 'workers' paradise'.[153] The government fuelled press articles on the Italian POWs in Russia, which received great attention and added to anti-Communist opinion.[154] On 11 February 1948, Italy demanded the release of the soldiers held for alleged war crimes near Kiev and the former Salò diplomats held in Bucharest and Sofia—as well as precise numbers and death certificates for the large majority of unidentified dead POWs.[155] No longer faced with the barriers thrown up during the Peace Treaty negotiations, the government in Rome thus reopened a diplomatic front that the Soviets had deemed closed.[156] In May 1948, the USSR suggested that the prisoners in Kiev be exchanged for thirty Russians who had been interned in Italy for desertion and collaboration with the Germans. Foreign Minister Sforza declared that these Italians in Kiev were neither war criminals nor prisoners and should be immediately released.[157] Another proposal by Vyshinsky to swap the Salò diplomats for a group of around 30 Soviets in Italian hands (Cossacks, deserters etc.) was not welcomed by Count Sforza, who deemed the release of the soldiers in Kiev "more important."[158] The Soviets believed the Italian demands excessive and were annoyed by the constant press campaigns. *Pravda* hit back in July 1948. Several articles described both individual and collective Italian war crimes, and the Soviets announced the creation of a commission to document such atrocities against Soviet civilians and Soviet POWs.[159] Thus, the POW issue was now used by the Italians to counter allegations of war crimes, not as before during the peace negotiations, where the Soviets employed this issue to claim reparations and gain diplomatic leverage.[160]

---

[153] Di Nolfo, *Von Mussolini*, 150ff., 233.

[154] Morozzo della Rocca, *Politica*, 396.

[155] Detailed in Francesco Bigazzi and Evgenij Zhirnov, *Gli ultimi 28. La storia incredibile dei prigionieri di guerra italiani dimenticati in Russia* (Milan: Mondadori, 2002).

[156] Morozzo della Rocca, *Politica*, 116, 387.

[157] Sechi, "Die neutralistische Versuchung," 117.

[158] Sforza's reply to Brosio, cited in Morozzo della Rocca, *Politica*, 388.

[159] Ibid., 390–91.

[160] Ibid., 392.

The Left vs Messe

After a chaotic election campaign, the result on 18 April 1948 led to sighs of relief in ruling circles in Washington and Rome. The Christian Democrats received 48.5 per cent of the vote and secured an absolute majority in parliament. Yet, the heated arguments about POWs and the Russian campaign were continued, also being instrumentalised in the disputes about Italian NATO membership.[161] Tolloy became a central protagonist in this debate. As described above, his memoirs were a harsh attack on the military establishment and particularly the general staff. They were serialised in eight parts in the Socialist *Avanti!* starting in February 1946, and reprinted in September 1947. Other articles in June and July had attacked Messe as well.[162] In a parliamentary statement on 3 and 4 August 1948 (on the "Origins and responsibility of the shameful speculation about the missing soldiers in Russia"), Tolloy demanded an end to the accusations against the USSR and an acknowledgement that the real culprits for the ARMIR's disaster were Messe and other senior officers.[163] Tolloy also held that the Italian Army had tried to instil ideological fervour in the soldiers—that is, the same anti-Communism that pervaded among many of its representatives after the war. Unsurprisingly, Tolloy's statements resulted in vicious press reactions as many conservative circles branded him an Italian quisling.[164] Tolloy repelled allegations that he had denigrated the courage of simple soldiers and insisted that his criticism was directed at the senior army leadership.[165]

At the same time, at an assembly of CSIR and ARMIR veterans on 21 November 1948 in Florence, two Communist sympathisers (both junior officers) had proposed support for the Soviet positions regarding war crimes and the POW issue, and opposition to what they portrayed as Messe's defamations of the USSR.[166] The dispute continued over winter, and this small group of Communist veterans formed a committee

---

[161] Detailed in Ilari, *Storia militare*, 51ff.; Craveri, *De Gasperi*, 355ff., 368ff.
[162] Pagan, *Il prezzo*, 215–36.
[163] Printed in AUSSME, Fondo Messe, b.A(1), c.4.
[164] AUSSME, Fondo Messe, b.A(1), c.5. For which some were also dragged to court.
[165] "Tolloy risponde," *La Libertà d'Italia*, 31 Mar. 1949.
[166] "Contro i diffamatori dell'Unione Sovietica, contro l'indifferenza per i reduci dell'Armir," *L'Unità*, 12 Mar. 1949.

(*Comitato di Iniziativa Romano per l'Inchiesta sull'Armir*, CIRIA) that closely cooperated with the ANPI in attacking Messe, which the left-wing press celebrated as evident sign that Messe was wrong, as now even 'the veterans' united against him.[167] However, the veterans were far from united in their opinion and this small group was following a clearly political line. The CIRIA linked their accusations to the demand that Italy should abstain from joining NATO, supported other political goals of the PCI, and vice versa, received backing from the left-wing press.[168] Yet, there were different voices coming from (bigger) veterans' associations.

During the campaign for the April elections, the National Union of Veterans of the Russian Campaign (*Unione Nazionale Italiana Reduci di Russia*, or UNIRR) had published a book in which three veterans accused the exile Communist D'Onofrio and others of agitation and harsh interrogations in the prison camps.[169] D'Onofrio had been a staunch lobbyist in preventing a mass return of Italian POWs.[170] The *Democrazia Cristiana* used the UNIRR publication for political purposes by rallying the sentiments of waiting families, and two days before the election the Communist daily *L'Unità* declared that D'Onofrio would go to court. He had become an important member of the PCI and the party had to fight over such matters of historical interpretation in order to hold up its vote. The trial itself took place after the election, but still attracted great public attention over its three-month duration (16 May until 16 July 1949).[171] D'Onofrio quickly realised that things were going badly: particularly the testimony of Don Enelio Franzoni, a former army chaplain in the *Pasubio* who had been decorated with the Gold Medal for Military Valour, put him on the defensive.[172] Thus D'Onofrio appealed to the PCI and also to the Soviets to provide help. The Soviet

---

[167] AUSSME, Fondo Messe, b.D(7), c.54, PCI. Comitato Nazionale di Iniziativa per l'inchiesta sull'ARMIR, 24 Mar. 1949.

[168] AUSSME, Fondo Messe, b.D(7), c.54, Note, 8 Feb. 1949.

[169] Agarossi and Zaslavsky, *Togliatti e Stalin*, 173.

[170] Petacco, *L'armata*, 222.

[171] Morozzo della Rocca, *Politica*, 97.

[172] Franzoni had been imprisoned in Russia and became a moral authority; he also aided Messe as a witness in his case against *L'Unità* in 1955, AUSSME, Fondo Messe, b.D(7), c.56, Testimoni citati dalla parte civile. His memoirs were posthumously published, see Enelio Franzoni, *Memorie di prigionia: Russia. Un sacerdote dal fronte alla deportazione, 1941–1946* (Chiari: Nordpress, 2008).

Ambassador proposed the use of forged testimony, but D'Onofrio demanded incriminating material against Franzoni.[173] Yet, these attempts could not prevent defeat. D'Onofrio lost the case and all his claims about defamations were found to be unjustified. In court, D'Onofrio allegedly told Giorgio Mastino Del Rio (1899–1969), the UNIRR defence lawyer and member of parliament for the DC from 1948–1957, that they had made a mistake by winning the case, as this would worsen the fate of those still in Soviet captivity.[174] Indeed, Soviet sources show that D'Onofrio attempted to stall repatriations after the trial.[175] Yet, this did not end his career. D'Onofrio was elected to parliament in 1953 and even became the chamber's vicepresident, while the far-right continued calling for his resignation.[176] Tolloy, inter alia, defended him and argued that there was no proof of his activities in Soviet camps.[177]

The D'Onofrio trial had alarmed the Soviets who decided to increase their efforts to counter anti-communist propaganda. In February 1949 two functionaries at the Foreign Ministry informed Vyshinsky of their compilation of documents on Italian crimes in Russia and informed him about another study, which had allegedly shown that Italian atrocities were comparable to the Germans' own.[178] However, a closer look revealed the opposite: the Italians had freed Soviet citizens from German captivity, and their soldiers had repeatedly clashed with the Wehrmacht over such issues; therefore, the Soviets decided against publishing it,

---

[173] Agarossi and Zaslavsky, *Togliatti e Stalin*, 173–74. They attempted to show that another military chaplain, Giovanni Brevi, had been placed on the list of war criminals due to Franzoni's testimony, and not due to D'Onofrio's actions. Brevi was only released in 1953, see his memoirs, *Russia 1942–1953* (Milan: Garzanti, 1955).

[174] As claimed in Petacco, *L'armata*, 228; Daniele Cherubini, *I prigionieri italiani in Unione sovietica* (Rome: Prospettiva editrice, 2006), 148. Concurrently, the twenty-eight remaining prisoners of the ARMIR stood trial in Kiev. On the accusations and the diplomatic tug of war, see Bigazzi and Zhirnov, *Gli ultimi 28*; Agarossi and Zaslavsky, *Togliatti and Stalin*, 158. Sixteen were repatriated in 1950 (including the three *Alpini* generals), but subsequent attempts for the remaining eleven (one had died in 1947) failed in 1952, not least due to Vyshinsky who was still Foreign Minister, according to Cherubini, *I prigionieri*, 156.

[175] Agarossi and Zaslavsky, *Togliatti e Stalin*, 175–76.

[176] Argentieri, *Messe*, 277.

[177] Giusto Tolloy, "Una manovra fallita," *Avanti!*, 15 Jan. 1955.

[178] The Soviets had already told the Italian Ambassador in Moscow, Manlio Brosio, in July 1948 that they were compiling documents on Italian war crimes, not least to put political pressure on Rome, Agarossi and Zaslavsky, *Togliatti e Stalin*, 79.

due to the likely counterproductive effect of not being able to show the desired results.[179] These repeated accusations on the domestic and international level demonstrate that the focus was slowly changing: initially, the Italians had blamed the Wehrmacht for the 'abandonment' on the Don, and then the Army's leadership had been attacked for its alleged incompetence. Now, war crimes had become the primary issue.

DEFENDING THE ARMY, 1950–1964

Messe retained his roles as the Army's advocate and target for the Left. The combination of his wartime deeds, his active pen, and his political career assured him a highly exposed and important role. In 1952, the British observed that Messe still had "considerable influence in the country and particularly over the Army […he] failed in elections as 'national *bloc*' Senator in his home province in April 1948, but remains a figurehead for the extreme Right."[180] Messe was more successful with his second attempt. Supported by the Christian Democrats (on personal initiative of De Gasperi), he was elected as independent Senator for his home region, Apulia, in June 1953,[181] and acted as an expert on defence matters for two terms.[182] The Communist daily saw the "Fascist Marshal" even as a possible new Defence Minister.[183] In this context, it is not suprising that his political enemies linked contemporary quarrels to past disputes. On 6 July 1951, the official organ of the Social Democrats, *La Giustizia*, published a commentary entitled 'Messe—Marshal of defeat'. The article was intended as an intervention in parliamentary debates about NATO and attacked Messe's war record.

[179] Ibid., 175; Cherubini, *I prigionieri*, 146.

[180] TNA, FO 371/102077, Leading Personalities in Italy 1952, 20. Indeed, Messe influenced many appointments and lobbied for former comrades. For example, he pressured Mancinelli's appointment as Chief of the Defence Staff over the head of several more senior officers, TNA, FO 371/113120, WT 1192/1, Clarke to Eden, 26 Mar. 1954, fol.2. Likewise, the Italian President's military adviser in 1956, General Alberto Roda, had fought with Messe as commander of the XX Corps' artillery in North Africa. Messe had demanded his release from allied captivity so he could take part in the War of Liberation, TNA, FO 371/124186, Leading Personalities in Italy 1956, 32.

[181] Gianfranco Franci, "Morto Messe, comandante dell'Armir e delle truppe italiane in Tunisia," *La Stampa*, 19 Dec. 1968, 9.

[182] AUSSME, Fondo Messe, b.x27, c.AA, Andreotti to Messe, 21 Dec. 1962.

[183] "De Gasperi vuole Messe a ministro della Difesa," *L'Unità*, 18 June 1953.

According to the anonymous author, Messe had constantly abandoned his troops and was also an enemy of the new Republic. Messe brought the case to court for defamation and won on 22 March 1952. *La Giustizia*'s director, Vincenzo Vacirca, publicly declared that all the statements made were false and that Messe had always fought heroically with his men.[184]

Conversely, the acclaimed journalist Indro Montanelli published a very benevolent sketch on Messe in his *Meetings* series in 1954. Montanelli bluntly stated his great sympathy for him, as he embodied proper bearing and moral conduct in war; especially during the defeat in Tunisia where Messe had surrendered after the Germans (a widespread Italian postwar narrative about the end of the war in North Africa). Thus, for Montanelli, the former Marshal symbolised the fact that "one does not divide wars into those won and in those lost, but those that were fought gallantly from those that were fought badly."[185] Montanelli described how this can-do attitude and inner steadfastness helped Messe to become a politician and *troupier* who got things done and led his men personally.[186] In fact, Messe linked his military past and standing, with his present role.

In 1955, he formed the *Unione Combattenti Italiani*,[187] a new ex-servicemen's association "in the hopes of countering the Communist and MSI tendencies of the old ones."[188] Yet, many critical voices on the Left asked which values exactly Messe desired to uphold in the new *unione*.[189] Messe and the *Unione Combattenti* abstained from the celebrations marking the tenth anniversary of the Liberation of Italy on 25 April 1955, which sparked fresh uproar.[190] His argument for doing

[184] Argentieri, *Messe*, 269–70.

[185] AUSSME, Fondo Messe, b.X27, c.Profili, Indro Montanelli, "Incontri: Messe," *Corriere della Sera*, 18 Nov. 1954, 3.

[186] Ibid.

[187] The *Unione Combattenti* maintained an office in the Ministry of Defence.

[188] TNA, FO 371/124186, Leading Personalities in Italy 1956, 24. As mentioned above, the role of veterans and their associations needs further research; for now, see Bistarelli, *La storia del ritorno*; Mondini and Schwarz, *Dalla guerra*.

[189] AUSSME, Fondo Messe, b.B(3), c.15, Ferruccio Ferrini, "Equivoci e caso Messe," *Il Pensiero Nazionale*, 31 Mar. 1955.

[190] The *Unione* celebrated the 24 May, the date of Italy's entry into the First World War in 1915, Delio Mariotti, "Le celebrazioni del 24 maggio," *La Stampa (Sera)*, 24 May 1955.

so—protesting against the exclusion of veterans of the RSI and the Spanish Civil War—was later judged in court not to have derived from Fascist sentiments or hostility against the new Republic.[191] But unsurprisingly it ignited debates about democratic ideals in the contemporary armed forces and Messe's own relation to the new state.[192] Old RSI grandees, like General Emilio Canevari, praised and defended Messe's initiative to allow veterans of the Spanish Civil War and the RSI into his association, deeming this as step towards greater national pride, and worthy of the 'apolitical' traditions of the Italian Army. He also thought the *Unione Combattenti d'Italia* could function as a bulwark against Communism (and there was, of course, an inherent contradiction in these claims).[193] This dispute in print ultimately led to a much-publicised legal case against the leading Communist newspaper: *L'Unità*.

MESSE VS. *L'UNITÀ* 1955–1956

Since the end of the war, *L'Unità* had repeatedly attacked Messe,[194] stating that he had "without doubt" been a Fascist and that he was an inglorious turncoat.[195] Tolloy particularly remained a prime participant in the constant quarrels and was dragged into court in 1954 for "continuously insulting the armed forces"—a judicial move that was supported by the Defence Minister.[196] However, the Tolloy trial was not the only example showing how history was negotiated (also) in court. A fresh scandal erupted in March 1955. Messe had been in favour of the European Defence Community (EDC), which he considered as a step toward greater European integration.[197] Yet, he warned of a freeriding mentality

---

[191] Argentieri, *Messe*, 297.

[192] AUSSME, Fondo Messe, b.A(1), c.4, Tolloy—Democrazia e Forze Armate, Speech in Chamber, 19 June 1956.

[193] AUSSME, Fondo Messe, b.B(3), c.15, Canevari to Brazilian Newspaper *Tribuna Italiana*, 22 July 1955.

[194] An overview can be found in AUSSME, Fondo Messe, b.D(7), c.53.

[195] Maurizio Ferrara, "Profilo di un guerriero," *L'Unità*, 23 Feb. 1955.

[196] Pagan, *Il prezzo*, 316ff.

[197] Messe's old comrade Mancinelli was a vital figure in the EDC negotiations; see Daniele Caviglia and Alessandro Gionfrida, *Un occasione da perdere. Le Forze Armate italiane e la Comunità Europea di Difesa (1950–54)* (Rome: APES, 2009).

and flagged the need to sustain Italy's independent capabilities and maintain military service as school for the nation.[198]

The Left used the failure of the EDC—felled when the French National Assembly voted against it—as a pretext to demand the abandonment of all 'western imperialist' organisations, including NATO, and to prevent German rearmament. In a heated senate meeting on 5 March 1955, the PCI senator Emilio Sereni (1907–1977) portrayed Messe as "general of defeat" in a war of aggression against Russia that the Italian people never wanted, stating that he had run away before disaster struck on the Don.[199] Messe later joined the session and was allowed to defend himself. He cited Stalin's alleged views, based on Robert E. Sherwood's book, that after the Finns, the Italians had been the most competent German allies.[200] Further, Messe argued that a honourable soldier like himself could not take advice from a deserter like Sereni.[201] On 9 March, Sereni was allowed to speak again in a tumultuous session where accusations of 'traitor', 'fascist', and 'deserter' filled the gallery. He stepped up his insults by depicting Messe as runaway general in all theatres and lackey of Mussolini and Hitler.[202] The Communist senator Umberto Terracini (1895–1983) called Messe not only a flag bearer of the extreme right, but also a "Fascist senator."[203]

The papers were filled with articles about Sereni's past and alleged wrongdoings,[204] and the usual fault lines emerged. General Giacomo Carboni, former head of military intelligence, anonymously published a pamphlet ('Communism against Messe. The Sereni Case', 1955) in which he supported Messe and the Army.[205] The former RSI General

[198] Argentieri, *Messe*, 272–73.

[199] Ibid., 278.

[200] Ibid., 279.

[201] Sereni had worked against the Italians during their occupation of France, which he had declared in a letter to the *Carabinieri* in July 1945, which Messe read out in the aula.

[202] Argentieri, *Messe*, 282.

[203] AUSSME, Fondo Messe, b.X27, c.Note biografiche varie, "Un nuovo vivace incidente al Senato tra Messe e Terracini," *Roma*, 9 Mar. 1955.

[204] See the wide collection in AUSSME, Fondo Messe, b.A(1), c.6, Sereni—Stampa. Messe also collected old documents from tribunals on Sereni and information concerning his exile in France during which he had spread anti-Italian propaganda (i.e. anti-Mussolini propaganda), AUSSME, Fondo Messe, b.A(1), c.7.

[205] See Messe's handwritten note on the cover, in AUSSME, Fondo Messe, b.A(1), c.8.

Emilio Canevari also defended the valour of Italian soldiers, especially in the Russian campaign,[206] and praised Messe as an ideal leader.[207] On 8 March, Luigi Pintor published a front-page article in *L'Unità* in which he vehemently criticised Messe's political positions (promoting nuclear weapons, NATO, and German rearmament) and linked these to accusations about his past, describing him as a promoter of fascist ideas in the Army, a "Fascist relic" and "Mussolini's general."[208] Adding greater detail, he accused Messe of having requested that Mussolini promote him to Marshal when he was in Tunisia, at a difficult moment for his troops. Thus, Pintor claimed that he had been more concerned with his own fame than his soldiers' fate and surrendered 'like a chicken' to Montgomery immediately after he had achieved his goal of taking up this rank. Pintor also criticised Messe's departure in Russia; arguing that he had foreseen the looming disaster and abandoned his men without securing them sufficient supplies. Therefore, he argued, Messe's past made him untenable for any political role.

Messe sued Pintor and the vice-director of *L'Unità*, Andrea Pirandello, for libel. The trial began in Rome on 7 July 1955 and attracted enormous media attention. In Messe's private papers we find large swathes of newspaper articles, which demonstrate not only the importance he attached to this trial, but the general relevance of this case as it touched upon key questions of recent Italian history and was particularly important for the image of the Army.[209] In court, Messe stated that the order for honourable surrender in Tunisia had come from the *Comando Supremo* in Rome jointly with his own promotion to Marshal, which was intended as praise for the conduct of the whole First Army. As for Russia, he pointed out that he had been a last-minute substitute for General Zingales in 1941. Thus, he had not been responsible for the initial planning, but later tried to do what he could to improve matters. Messe claimed he had left on 1 November 1942 due to disagreements with Gariboldi and Mussolini, and not because defeat was

---

[206] AUSSME, Fondo Messe, b.B(3), c.15, Canevari Letter to Brazilian Newspaper *Tribuna Italiana*, 22 July 1955, fol.4.

[207] AUSSME, Fondo Messe, b.X27, c.Note biografiche varie, Emilio Canevari, "Chi è Messe," *Roma*, 9 Mar. 1955.

[208] Luigi Pintor, "Messe portabandiera dell'UEO," *L'Unità*, 8 Mar. 1955.

[209] AUSSME, Fondo Messe, b.E(8). The whole folder contains newspaper excerpts on the court sessions.

foreseeable[210]—after all, he remarked, he had also taken over command of a hopeless situation in Tunisia. He confirmed that Italian materiel had been poor and scarce on all fronts, but hinted at the political leadership, which bore the responsibility for these problems.[211] All his arguments were backed by a flood of (high and low ranking) testimonies and documents.[212] Messe could further refer to the court ruling from 1952, where he had successfully challenged the wording in a *La Giustizia* article, and the public prosecutor also strongly supported his positions. Pintor and Pirandello rallied witnesses but could not convince the judges.[213] On 27 March 1956, the court cleared Messe of all accusations, and found Pintor and Pirandello guilty of having falsified information in order to discredit him.[214] Messe had defended the Army's master narrative on the Second World War: a well-led apolitical force that had fought courageously with bad materiel, only to be defeated by an overwhelmingly strong enemy, bad political leadership, and inadequate pre-war preparations. Additionally, Messe could now present a legal ruling on this narrative.[215] This augmented his role as a guardian of Italian military honour.

However, even this court ruling did not preclude renewed attacks on Messe, on similar grounds.[216] Already during the trial, another article in *La voce repubblicana* described Messe as a former Fascist and culprit of the lost war, and painted his *Unione Combattenti* as a vehicle

---

[210] "Messe spiega perché si ritirò dal fronte sovietico e dalla Tunisia," *La Nuova Stampa*, 8 July 1955, 6.

[211] Argentieri, *Messe*, 294.

[212] The process is described more detailed in, Argentieri, *Messe*, 285ff. Messe's preparation and documents relating to the process can be found in AUSSME, Fondo Messe, b.D(7), c.40, c.41, c.42, c.43, and c.46. Even Mussolini's wartime memoirs—which included attacks on Messe—were cited as evidence of the latter's non-fascist stance.

[213] Messe had prepared dossiers on the witnesses, contained in AUSSME, Fondo Messe, b.D(7), c.43.

[214] The document can be found in AUSSME, Fondo Messe, b.E(8), c.Sentenza contro *L'Unità*. After their appeal, the initial verdict of eight months' confinement was changed into a high fine, Argentieri, *Messe*, 293–300.

[215] Even if we account for a possible bias of the judges and prosecutors, this marked an independent court ruling.

[216] Despite the fact that Messe widely published a declaration on the process in several newspapers, AUSSME, Fondo Messe, b.E(8), c.Testo remissione querela contro *L'Unità*, 27 Jan. 1958.

to disturb democratic life in Italy. The Marshal was juxtaposed with Eisenhower—i.e. a good soldier-politician—and attributed dangerous anti-constitutional leanings and Bonapartist traits.[217] Messe sent a letter to the newspaper's director, arguing that he had not opposed the DC, but merely preferred to run as an independent candidate. He insisted that the people of Brindisi were mature enough to choose their own candidate and provided a history lesson on generals in US politics. Messe reasoned that the obedience shown by Italian soldiers in these glorious but unfortunate campaigns (during the Second World War) had demonstrated their unquestionable allegiance to the legitimate government, which was a soldiers' only duty. He further stressed that soldiers' obedience was not to democracy itself—rather the only honour they had to uphold was that of the Italian nation.[218] Thus, Messe portrayed himself as loyal servant of the government and its institutions, in contrast to the author's depiction of him as a possible putschist.[219] Tolloy also continued his attacks on the Italian Army and Messe both in articles[220] and in parliament. He blamed Messe's political influence for the Armed Foces' allegedly general failure to appreciate the "spirit of the *Resistenza*" and the benefits of the Republic—an accusation against which Defence Minister Giulio Andreotti intervened personally.[221]

Messe continued to defend the Italian Army's operational performance and repelled allegations of war crimes, for example against the depictions provided in the 1964 movie *Italiani Brava Gente*. During a parliamentary debate Messe argued that none of the Italian soldiers (including the Blackshirts) had ever committed such crimes on Russian soil and named Nikita Khrushchev a key witness to this.[222] A movie on the Greek occupation had already resulted in a criminal case in 1953, on the grounds of publicly insulting the armed forces.[223] The Italian Army's

---

[217] AUSSME, Fondo Messe, b.B(3), c.12, Pantaleo Ingusci, "Maresciallismo e nazionalismo. Le baracche della retorica," *La Voce Repubblicana*, 4 Nov. 1955.

[218] AUSSME, Fondo Messe, b.B(3), c.12, Messe to Director of *La Voce Repubblicana*, 12 Nov. 1955, fol.5.

[219] Ibid.

[220] AUSSME, Fondo Messe, b.A(1), c.1956, Idea Italiana. Articoli su On. Tolloy.

[221] On 14 June 1960, AUSSME, Fondo Messe, b.A(1), c.4.

[222] Camera dei Deputati, Atti Parlamentari, IV Legislatura, Discussioni, 30 Sept. 1964, 10124.

[223] Agarossi and Giusti, *Una guerra*, 473.

ideal image of the Russian campaign was instead to be found in *Carica Eroica* (The Heroic Charge, 1952), which depicted the cavalry charge at Isbushensky.[224] This narrative of the *beau geste* and the allegories with old chivalrous cavalry battles spoke to the ideas of a noble war and courage in spite of bad material.[225] The fate of prisoners in the Soviet Union was captured in Vittorio De Sica's *Sunflower* (*I girasoli*, 1969), portraying a love story of characters played by Sophia Loren and Marcello Mastroianni.[226]

Messe always included the Blackshirts in his defence of the armed forces. In 1963, Brunello Vandano published parts of his *I disperati del Don* in *Epoca* magazine, in which he panned both the skill and the conduct of the Blackshirts. Messe argued that this criticism was unsubstantiated, as the *Tagliamento* had fought as well as the 3rd *Bersaglieri* Regiment.[227] In his opinion, this was just another smear campaign and he wrote a furious letter in which he described it as an "attempt to discriminate Italian soldiers based on the colour of their shirts. And this is truly outrageous. All soldiers, without exception, did their duty in the war, all loved their country equally, all obeyed to their obligations with equal passion and conviction. The political responsibility for the war does not rest on the soldiers. And I mean any soldier."[228] Thus, he not only emphasised the Blackshirts' professional skill, but included them in the apolitical narrative and granted them a *carte blanche* for their behaviour.

When Messe died in December 1968, the highest echelons of the Italian military paid tributes: President Saragat and Prime Minister

---

[224] See Lucio Lami, *Isbuscenskij. L'ultima carica* (Milan: Mursia, 1970).

[225] [Col.] Carlo De Virgilio, "Poloj. Ultima carica," *Rivista Militare* 39, no. 4 (1983): 135–41; Rodolfo Puletti, "G. Vitali: 'Trotto, galoppo…caricat! Storia del Raggruppamento truppe a cavallo—Russia 1942–1943," *Rivista Militare* 42, no. 6 (1986): 146–47; G. De Marco, "Giorgio Vitali: 'Sciabola nella steppa,'" *Rivista Militare* 32, no. 5 (1976): 137–38.

[226] The movie is rather unheroic as the character played by Mastroianni tries to evade military service. Generally, the Russians are depicted as generous and helpful, and the Italians as mere victims with iconic scenes of the retreat from the Don.

[227] AUSSME, Fondo Messe, b.X27, c.AA, Messe to Zigiotti, 9 Jan. 1963, fos.2–3. He also claimed that the *Giovani Fascisti* Division had behaved gallantly under his command in Tunisia.

[228] Ibid., fol.4.

Rumor also sent personal messages of condolence to his family.[229] In a way, his death marked the end of the first phase of political clashes between Left and Right in Italy. In 1963 the Socialists formed part of the government for the first time. This was not without hiccups—not least given the abortive coup in 1970—but the military had found its place in the new Republic and did not support any such attempts. In 2007, a journalist of the *Corriere della Sera* argued that "strangely not many remember him [Messe]" and that his name has been largely forgotten.[230] However, while Messe's place in the general collective memory may indeed have lost ground, the Army has arguably no greater twentieth-century role model (at the senior level). Messe therefore remains uncritically celebrated for his career and *defensio* of Italian valour—and his life is in dire need of an objective and scholarly biography.

In conclusion, the postwar period showed that the narrative on the *campagna di Russia* was fiercely contested—not least in the media, in courts, and even in parliament. Domestic and international politics influenced the debates on the prisoners in the USSR, operational performance, and war crimes. Messe, as the Army's most influential defender, glossed over some aspects of the campaign and refused to accept any wrongdoings. However, his depictions were closer to reality than most allegations coming from the Soviets and the Italian political Left. Indeed, the accusations against the senior leadership and charges of war crimes have never been analysed with the domestic and Cold War aspect in mind. And yet it is utterly vital to understand who raised them, when and why. Yet, given the dominant narrative in the memoir literature and the aforementioned weaknesses in the existing scholarship, it is unsurprising that these myths have been perpetuated for so long.

---

[229] Gianfranco Franci, "Morto Messe, comandante dell'Armir e delle truppe italiane in Tunisia," *La Stampa*, 19 Dec. 1968, 9.

[230] Marco Nese, "Il generale 'ardito' che disobbediva al Duce," *Corriere della Sera*, 17 Jan. 2007, 41.

CHAPTER 12

Conclusion

It is quite a challenge to cover a topic on which there exists so little academic literature. Much more research is needed, and the following conclusions are as indefinite and incomplete as those of any historical work—especially given the loss of many Italian primary sources. The main aim of this study has been to separate 'what really happened' from the myths and memories that so often blur the picture. It has thus attempted to link different historical subfields—military, diplomatic and cultural history—in order to provide a comprehensive and connected understanding of events, narratives and memories. The difficult access to Italian military files and underdeveloped scholarship has allowed the persistence of false assumptions based on distorted outside views, biased accounts and anecdotal evidence. Focusing on one theatre and its legacy has provided a means to draw more general conclusions about Italy in the Second World War and the contested legacy of the 1940–1943 period in the Cold War.

Seeking to understand Italy at war, the third chapter provided an overview of the country's development since the First World War and the state of its armed forces in 1940. Of all the major belligerents, Italy had by far the least developed economy and its industry could never have sustained a longer war effort. Earlier engagements in Abyssinia and the Spanish Civil War had already strained finances and materiel. This is not to say that the materiel was exclusively of bad quality—but it was mostly outdated and new developments came too little and too late.

This prevented the Italian Army from translating its fairly modern doctrines into reality. Likewise, the professional officers (and soldiers) were not as incompetent as is often stated. The scarcity of trained junior officers and NCOs, and the inadequate reserve officers constituted a chief weakness, when these latter should instead have functioned as the backbone of the Army. In sum, the *Regio Esercito* was not necessarily ready for war.

Then the campaigns during the so-called 'parallel war' in 1940–1941 were analysed. The operations against France, Greece and Britain in North Africa fostered a long-enduring image of cowardly Italian soldiers and inept commanders. While there is indeed much to be critical about in these operations, they are deserving of closer scrutiny. The chapter further examined the postwar memory and legacy of these campaigns in order to provide examples for comparison with the Eastern Front: North Africa remained an important lieu de mémoire (especially El Alamein), while the memories of the Balkans and the brief offensive against France descended into oblivion. Moreover, the chapter emphasised the need to look beyond the period of winter and spring 1940–1941 in order to attain a full understanding of Italy's war effort and the memories that resulted from it. The Army initiated a lessons-learned process and managed to enhance its combat efficiency in the North African desert despite material and structural deficiencies that grew stronger as the war progressed. Any coherent analysis of Italy in the Second World War must therefore include the period after spring 1941.

The ensuing chapters provided the first thorough, primary-source-based analysis of Italian operations on the Eastern Front. The first sketched out the CSIR's successful operational endeavours in 1941 and the constant adaptation to circumstances on the front in 1942. While noting the improvement in Italian performance, it also discussed both internal and external criticism. To be clear: the *Regio Esercito* was not a flawless fighting machine (if such a thing exists), but in no way was it as useless as frequently argued. Even if the material available reduced its effectiveness, the campaign in Russia stands for the Army's ability to make efficient use of it. The Italian demise on the Don in December 1942 and January 1943 can be rationally explained without referring to 'military culture' or any of the postwar myths: the ARMIR (and all invading forces) faced a formidable enemy that attacked with superior mass of numbers and materiel. The ARMIR expected the offensive, foresaw the problems, and did what it could to prepare and to defend its positions.

In order to support these claims, the next chapter looked at Soviet, and in more detail, at various German sources assessing the Italian divisions and officers in Russia. Against all expectations, these sources tell us that the Italian lines did not crack easily and rebut claims that incompetent senior officers botched operations or sacrificed their men. The easy claims about 'cowardly sheep led by donkeys' should thus finally be discarded. The German files did provide criticism at the tactical level—but not beyond normal. Hardly any army in history has been judged perfect, and it is thus necessary to compare these reports to similar evaluations within the Wehrmacht—or, indeed, any other army. Nonetheless, the positive tone of many of the German liaison staffs' remarks on the Italian divisions and officers—even during and after such a setback as the retreat from the Don—is surprising.

The study then analysed the three myths of Italian victimhood. First, it scrutinised the narrative, which portrays the Germans as a 'cruel ally who abandoned the Italians on the Don'. This tale of abandonment and sacrifice suited the (civilian) narrative that the seeds of contempt for Mussolini's regime and the Germans were sown on the Russian steppes, before this revolt then erupted in Italy itself in July and September 1943. When analysed in the proper context, one can identify similar Italian behaviour and General Ambrosio's desire to politicise the friction during the retreat can also be explained as a means of gathering 'political ammunition' against a looming enemy. Further, this was a helpful *fable convenue* against German narratives of Italian betrayal on 8 September 1943.

Secondly, the study demystified the allegations surrounding Italian war crimes—framing these as victimhood by defamation. Based on all the available evidence today, we can fairly claim that there was no Italian war of extermination on the Eastern Front. To be clear: the Italian Army did take part in the invasion of the Soviet Union and fought for the goals of a brutal regime, which brought death to millions of its citizens and her forces also killed innocents. Yet, criminal acts by Italian soldiers against civilians, regular soldiers and partisans were far fewer than those committed by German, Romanian or Hungarian troops. This is not an attempt to point the finger at others, to mute Italian crimes or to downplay atrocities. Exposing the *brava gente* cliché was a vital achievement, but we should not turn this on its head by suggesting that the Italian Army committed large-scale war crimes everywhere it went (which is often done without a sober look at sources). It would be absurd to think of good-hearted Italians behaving like a Samaritan army. Yet, the structural restraints—i.e. operating under the framework of cooperation with the Germans—as well as situational factors (first and foremost the absence of a strong partisan movement), differences in ideology (and the lack thereof) and plans for the conquered territories worked against any escalation of violence. Thus, attempts to associate Italian behaviour with a war of extermination not only lack credibility, but also run the risk of misrepresenting the findings of countless scholars who have studied the German war crimes in the Soviet Union and of those who worked with Russian sources.

The third victimhood narrative concerned the Italian prisoners in Soviet hands. Their treatment was instrumentalised from both sides of postwar Italian politics: the Right advanced exaggerated arguments about the Soviet treatment of the POWS while the Left downplayed the maltreatment so that it could preserve an idyllic view of Stalinist Russia. However, the (unexpectedly) small numbers of repatriations added to the memory that the Italians had been victims, and not invaders.

The following chapter examined the memoir literature, the Army's semi-public narrative and the myth of the *Alpini*. For too long, the memoirs have been uncritically accepted as honest or even "apolitical" (Rochat) accounts of the events on the Eastern Front. In short, the dominant narratives focused on sacrifice, the retreat and inept (senior) commanders. The most prominent writers (Tolloy, Rigoni Stern, and Revelli), in particular, had a clear political message and forged a tale of victimhood and revival that was often linked to the 'mental mindmaps' of the First World War. They advanced a story of redemption through the *Resistenza* thereby fitting into the Italian master narrative after the Second World War.

The memoir literature dominated civil-society narratives and memories, but the Army could not wholeheartedly accept attacks against its leadership, its professionalism or its 'honourable' conduct on Russian soil. The return of Italian prisoners from Soviet camps was the start of a long political struggle over the memory of the *campagna di Russia*. The Army, most prominently defended by Giovanni Messe, created its own narrative: loyal to its King, the (apolitical) *Regio Esercito* had bravely fought an unwanted war against all odds with poor materiel, alongside an unloved and cruel ally, albeit without itself becoming a heartless 'Teutonic barbarian' (thus brushing over own crimes). It is imperative to note these discrepancies between the civilian narrative and Army's view: even if some overlaps did exist, the Italian Army, as an institution that had to provide meaning and role models to its soldiers, could not embrace a narrative centred only on victimhood (particularly not during the Cold War). The *Alpini* were an example of how the positive connotation of the First World War, an elite unit's discourse about its 'heroic defeat'—especially the battle of Nikolayevka—and the victimhood-cum-resurrection in the *Resistenza* could be combined and transcended in the civilian sphere. Yet, as a look at the Army's internal discourse has shown, the battle of Nikolayevka and the commanding officers concerned were more important than the public might have realised. Similarly, while the Army's narrative was always upheld and defended, it could not contend with public memory (which should also not be seen as set in stone).

Finally, the last chapter analysed how these memories were instrumentalised and contested during the Cold War. The international political arena and Italy's domestic situation made it almost inevitable that the Russian campaign was much more debated than e.g. the war in North Africa. Disputes over the prisoners, Italian military performance, the officer corps and war crimes repeatedly returned to the front pages in tune with everyday political happenings, such as the Peace Treaty, Western alignment or German rearmament. Both the political Left and Right made use of these contentious issues that had stemmed from the still-recent war. These memories were contested in the press, in parliament and in court—which also gave the military sphere much more leverage in constructing an acceptable narrative, than for instance with its own bulky publications. Messe became the most important advocate for the Army. His role during the war, his staunch anti-Communism and his political career turned him into a prime target for the Left. Indeed, he is a good example of how Cold War politics still distort our perception of the Italian Army and its role in the Second World War—and another case of where further research is needed. A proper academic biography of Messe would be most desirable. Other fields to explore would be the role of veterans' associations, the Italian Army and its 'military culture' during the Cold War, or the influence of former generals on politics. This is particularly relevant given that the Army (and the vast security apparatus) retained an important function in the volatile domestic situation and has since 1982 become an active contributor to international peacekeeping missions, augmenting Italy's international standing and regaining lost prestige of the armed forces.[1]

In fact, looking at the findings of this study—which provide a more positive view of the Italians' combat performance, officer skill and relatively restrained behaviour on Russian soil—it becomes clear that it was not primarily the military and Messe who were forging myths in the postwar period, but rather the memoir literature, the political Left and the Kremlin. Their narratives were further from reality than Messe's or the Army's (all too positive) depictions, as they twisted facts in order to create enduring myths about dishonourable behaviour, inept officers and military incompetence. Alas, these latter were largely accepted by domestic and international academia and have distorted our understanding of Italy in the Second World War.

Likewise, while much has been written in recent years on the *brava gente* myth and the long neglect of Italian war crimes, there are many similarities with the Romanian and Hungarian cases. No army willingly accepted responsibility for defeat or openly spoke about atrocities on the Eastern Front. Indeed, even in the German case—where outside pressure started these debates—the myth of a chivalrous war and near-victory was long upheld. Setbacks were either attributed to 'General Winter' or to the Wehrmacht's allies. More comparative research is needed, regarding not only the combat performance of smaller nations on the Eastern Front, their views and cooperation with the Germans, but also the armies' and societies' memories and narratives deriving from the Eastern Front and the war in general.

The longevity of myths and memories in defining the contours of scholarship in Italy has hindered the correction of many false assumptions. Of course, memories are always a creation and not *what happened*. Yet, this becomes problematic when memory and memoirs create and cement myths, which are accepted as sound reconstructions of the past. The findings of this study will hopefully contribute to a sober analysis of further topics regarding the Italian military and the country's role in the war. Only multi-archival research and inter-disciplinary approaches will improve our knowledge on many events that have for too long remained only vaguely in sight. The study of military operations should

---

[1] On the vital role of the mission in Beirut, see Bastian Matteo Scianna, "A Blueprint for Successful Peacekeeping? The Italians in Beirut (Lebanon), 1982–1984," *The International History Review* 41, no. 3 (2019): 650–72.

not, therefore, be discarded as some antiquated field. Equally, it is necessary to understand how an institution like the military works and how its organisation culture evolves. An improved comprehension of the Italian Army will also aid an analysis of the German-led wartime coalition, of armies' organisational culture in conflict, and the effectiveness of different armies between 1939 and 1945.

The legacies of Fascism and the *Resistenza* have long obstructed many aspects of Italy's role in the Second World War. The Italian military have never had an easy relationship with the collective memory, which mainly amounted to the remembrance of its defeats. Adwa, Caporetto and the *8 settembre* were not only main features of Italian memory, but were in a sense a crescendo in scale: there followed the shattering of an expeditionary force, then a complete army in 1917, and ultimately the disintegration of the whole armed forces in 1943.[2] Yet, there was always something more to this: these events not only shattered the prestige of the Army, but were also extended to arguments about the rottenness of the country's ruling elites. The Army thus became a symbol for the decline (and dissolution) of a corrupt and inefficient state. In short, on several occasions discrediting the Army and the state went hand in hand. This makes the study of the Italian military and the discrediting of myths concerning its performance into a task fundamental to improving our understanding of wider currents of Italian history.

[2] Isenghi, *La tragedia necessaria*, 8, 60.

BIBLIOGRAPHY

Unpublished Archival Material

Archivio Centrale dello Stato (ACS)—The Italian National Archives in Rome
- Microfilm Collection T-821: Rolls 2, 9, 20, 22, 109, 113, 125, 127, 128, 130, 146, 200, 211, 230, 231, 247, 249, 252, 254, 255, 256, 257, 258, 259, 260, 344, 354, 355, 373, 383, 384, 456, 475, 482, 484, 494.
- Fondo Filippo Diamanti.

Archivio dell'Ufficio Storico dello Stato Maggiore del Esercito (AUSSME)—The Italian Military Archives in Rome
- Fondo Giovanni Messe (L-13).
- Fondo Gabriele Nasci.

Bundesarchiv Militärchiv (BA-MA)—The German Military Archives in Freiburg
- MSg 2/4388.
- N 64: Private Papers Fridolin von Senger und Etterlin.
- N 241: Private Papers Hans Meier-Welcker.
- N 422: Private Papers Hans Röttiger.
- N 433: Private Papers Enno von Rintelen.
- RH 2/1666.
- RH 2/1672.
- RH 2/1892.
- RH 2/2894.
- RH 2/2936.
- RH 20-17/766.

- RH 21-1/51.
- RH 31-IX/9.
- RH 31-IX/11.
- RH 31-IX/12.
- RH 31-IX/13.
- RH 31-IX/14.
- RH 31-IX/15.
- RH 31-IX/16.
- RH 31-IX/18.
- RH 31-IX/19.
- RH 31-IX/25.
- RH 31-IX/35.
- RH 31-IX/72.
- RH 31-IX/73.
- RH 31-IX/74.
- RH 31-X/9.
- RH 67/37.
- RM 11/60.
- RM 11/61.
- RW 5/v.424.
- ZA 1/1560.
- ZA 1/2028.

Imperial War Museum (IWM) Collections
- Doc.13329—Private Papers of Major E. B. Howard.
- EDS AL 2763/4—General Vittorio Ambrosio, Diary.

The National Archives and Records Administration (NARA)
- Microfilm Collection T-312, Roll 360.

The British National Archives (TNA)
- FO 371/37356.
- FO 371/43830.
- FO 371/96269.
- FO 371/102077.
- FO 371/113120.
- FO 371/124186.
- FO 660/375.
- FO 660/378.
- GFM 36/31.
- GFM 36/139.
- GFM 36/170.
- GFM 36/217.
- PREM 3/295/1.
- WO 106/3123.

- WO 106/6086.
- WO 202/991.
- WO 204/3.
- WO 204/2420.
- WO 208/4185.
- WO 208/4186.
- WO 208/4187.
- WO 208/4547.
- WO 208/4550.
- KV 3/266.

Printed Sources

Biagini, Antonello, and Fernando Frattolillo, eds. *Diario Storico del Comando Supremo, 9 vols.* Rome: USSME, 1986–1999.
Biagini, Antonello, and Fernando Frattolillo, eds. *Verbali delle riunioni tenute dal capo di S.M. generale, 4 vols.* Rome: USSME, 1982–1985.
Documenti Diplomatici Italiani (DDI), Series, Volume.
U.S. Department of State, *Foreign Relations of the United States, 1946, Paris Peace Conference: Proceedings, Vol. 3.* Washington: U.S. Government Printing Office, 1970.

Diaries and Memoirs

Amé, [Gen.] Cesare. *Guerra segreta in Italia, 1940–1943.* Milan: Bietti, 2011; first ed. 1954.
Battisti, [Gen.] Emilio, et al. *Italianzy kaputt? (Con l'Armir in Russia).* Rome: CEN, 1959.
Bedeschi, Giulio. *Fronte Russo: C'ero anch'io.* Milan: Mursia, 1982.
Bedeschi, Giulio. *Nikolajewka: c'ero anch'io.* Milan: Mursia, 1972.
Berardi, [Gen.] Paolo. *Memorie di un capo di stato maggiore dell'Esercito (1943–1945).* Bologna: ODCU, 1954.
Brevi, Giovanni. *Russia 1942–1953.* Milan: Garzanti, 1955.
Brucciante, Giuseppe, ed. *Ugo Cavallero: Diario 1940–1943.* Rome: Ciarrapico, 1984.
Carloni, [Gen.] Mario. *La campagna di Russia.* Genoa: Effepi, 2010.
Ciano, Galeazzo. *Diaries 1939–1943.* Garden City: Doubleday, 1946.
Corradi, Egisto. *La ritirata di Russia.* Milan: Longanesi, 1964.
Fortuna, Piero, and Raffaello Uboldi. *Il tragico Don. Cronache della campagna italiana in Russia (1941–1943).* Milan: Mondadori, 1980.

Franzoni, Enelio. *Memorie di prigionia: Russia. Un sacerdote dal fronte alla deportazione, 1941–1946.* Chiari: Nordpress, 2008.

Khrushchev, Sergei, ed. *Memoirs of Nikita Khrushchev, Vol. 1.* University Park: The Pennsylvania State University Press, 2005.

Lelyushenko, [Gen.] Dmitry D. *Moskva-Stalingrad-Berlin-Praga. Zapiski komandarma.* Moscow: Nauka, 1985; first ed. 1970.

Massa Gallucci, [Gen.] Alberto. *No! Dodici anni prigioniero in Russia.* Milan: Rizzoli, 1958.

Messe, [Marshal] Giovanni. *La guerra al fronte russo. Il corpo di spedizione italiano in Russia (CSIR).* Milan: Mursia, 2005; first ed. 1947.

Messe, [Marshal] Giovanni. *Lettere alla moglie. Dai fronti Greco-Albanese, Russo, Tunisino e dalla prigionia 1940–1944.* Milan: Mursia, 2018.

Moskalenko, [Marshal] Kiril S. *In der Südwestrichtung, Vol. 1.* Berlin: Militärverlag der DDR, 1975.

Mussolini, Benito. *Memoirs 1942–1943.* London: Weidenfeld & Nicolson, 1949.

Odasso, [Lt. Col.] Mario. *Col Corpo alpino italiano in Russia.* Cuneo: Panfilo, 1949.

Plehwe, [Lt. Col.] Friedrich-Karl von. *Blick durch viele Fenster. Erinnerungen 1919–1978.* Berlin: Frieling, 1998.

Plehwe, [Lt. Col.] Friedrich-Karl von. *Schicksalsstunden in Rom.* Berlin: Propyläen, 1967.

Provalov, [Gen.] Konstantin I. *V ogne peredovykh liny.* Moscow: Voenizdat, 1981.

Revelli, Nuto. *Il mondo dei vinti.* Turin: Einaudi, 2005.

Revelli, Nuto. *La guerra dei poveri.* Turin: Einaudi, 1962.

Revelli, Nuto. *La strada del davai.* Turin: Einaudi, 1966.

Revelli, Nuto. *Le due guerre: guerra fascista e guerra partigiana.* Turin: Einaudi, 2003.

Revelli, Nuto. *Mai tardi. Diario di un alpino in Russia.* Cuneo: Panfilo, 1947.

Rigoni Stern, Mario. *I racconti di guerra.* Turin: Einaudi, 2006.

Rintelen, [Gen.] Enno von. *Mussolini als Bundesgenosse. Erinnerungen des deutschen Militärattachés in Rom, 1936–1943.* Stuttgart: Wunderlich, 1951.

Roberts, Geoffrey, ed. *Marshal of Victory: The Autobiography of General Georgy Zhukov, 2 vols.* Barnsley: Pen & Sword, 2013.

Salvatores, [Gen.] Umberto. *Bersaglieri sul Don.* Bologna: Compositori, 1958.

Speidel, [Gen.] Hans. *Aus unserer Zeit. Erinnerungen.* Berlin: Propyläen, 1977.

Tolloy, [Maj.] Giusto. *Con l'Armata italiana in Russia.* Turin: De Silva, 1947.

Vicentini, Carlo. *Noi soli vivi. Quando settantamila italiani passarono il Don.* Milan: Mursia, 1997.

Wasilewski, [Marshal] Alexander. *Sache des ganzen Lebens.* Berlin: Militärverlag der DDR, 1977.

Newspapers and Journals

Articles in the *Rivista Militare* and other Italian periodicals will not be listed individually in the following due to concerns of space.

Avanti!
Corriere della Sera.
L'Alpino.
La Stampa.
L'Unità.
Rivista Militare.
Rivista di Fanteria.
Sydney Herald.

Secondary Literature (Incl. Journal Articles and Book Chapters)

Afanasyev, Nikolaj I. *Ot Volgi do Shpree*. Moscow: Voenizdat, 1982.
Agarossi, Elena. *A Nation Collapses: The Italian Surrender of September 1943*. Cambridge: Cambridge University Press, 2000.
Agarossi, Elena. *Cefalonia. La resistenza, l'eccidio, il mito*. Bologna: Il Mulino, 2016.
Agarossi, Elena, and Maria Teresa Giusti. *Una guerra a parte. I militari italiani nei Balcani 1940–1945*. Bologna: Il Mulino, 2011.
Agarossi, Elena, and Victor Zaslavsky. *Togliatti e Stalin. Il PCI e la politica estera staliniana negli archivi di Mosca*. Bologna: Il Mulino, 1997.
Agosti, Aldo. *Palmiro Togliatti. A Biography*. London: Tauris, 2008.
Anderson, Truman O. "A Hungarian *Vernichtungskrieg*? Hungarian Troops and the Soviet Partisan War in Ukraine, 1942." *Militärgeschichtliche Mitteilungen* 58, no. 2 (1999): 345–66.
Andreski, Stanislav. "Causes of the Low Morale of the Italian Armed Forces in the Two World Wars." *Journal of Strategic Studies* 5, no. 2 (1982): 248–56.
Antonelli, Quinto. "Fronte russo. Le forme della propaganda." In *Battaglie in Russia. Il Don e Stalingrado 75 anni dopo*, edited by Olga Dubrovina, 167–82. Milan: Ed. Unicopli, 2018.
Antonelli, Quinto, and Sergej I. Filonenko. *"Vincere! Vinceremo!" Cartoline sul fronte russo (1941–1942)*. Trento: Fondazione Museo storico del Trentino, 2011.
Argentieri, Luigi. *Messe. Soggetto di un'altra storia*. Bergam: Burgo, 1997.
Assmann, Aleida. "Re-framing Memory: Between Individual and Collective Forms of Constructing the Past." In *Performing the Past*, edited by Jay Winter, Karin Tilmans, and Frank Van Vree, 35–50. Amsterdam: Amsterdam University Press, 2010.

Avagliano, Mario, and Marco Palmieri. *Vincere e vinceremo! Gli italiani al fronte, 1940–1943*. Bologna: Il Mulino, 2014.

Axworthy, Mark. "Peasant Scapegoat to Industrial Slaughter: The Romanian Soldier at the Siege of Odessa." In *Time to Kill: The Soldier's Experience of War in the West*, edited by Paul Addison and Angus Calder, 221–32. London: Pimlico, 1997.

Axworthy, Mark. *Third Axis, Fourth Ally: Romanian Armed Forces in the European War, 1941–1945*. London: Arms and Armour, 1995.

Balestra, Gian Luca. *La formazione degli ufficiali nell'accademia militare di Modena (1895–1939)*. Rome: USSME, 2000.

Barkawi, Tarak. *Soldiers of Empire: Indian and British Armies of World War II*. Cambridge: Cambridge University Press, 2017.

Barker, [Col.] Arthur J. *Eritrea 1941*. London: Faber and Faber, 1966.

Bartov, Omer. *Hitler's Army. Soldiers, Nazis, and War in the Third Reich*. Oxford: Oxford University Press, 1992.

Bartov, Omer. *The Eastern Front, 1941–1945: German Troops and the Barbarisation of Warfare*. London: Routledge, 2001.

Basset, Stefano, and Filippo Cappellano. "L'esercito italiano e la guerra antipartigiana in Russia (1941–1943)." In *Battaglie in Russia. Il Don e Stalingrado 75 anni dopo*, edited by Olga Dubrovina, 119–43. Milan: Ed. Unicopli, 2018.

Battini, Michele. *The Missing Italian Nuremberg: Cultural Amnesia and Postwar Politics*. New York: Palgrave Macmillan, 2007.

Battistelli, Pier Paolo. "La 'guerra dell'Asse'. Condotta bellica e collaborazione militare Italo-Tedesca, 1939–1943." PhD diss., University of Padua, 2000.

Belardelli, Giovanni, et al., eds. *Miti e storia dell'Italia unita*. Bologna: Il Mulino, 1999.

Benadusi, Lorenzo. *Ufficiale e gentiluomo. Virtù civili e valori militari in Italia, 1896–1918*. Milan: Feltrinelli, 2015.

Bergdolt, Klaus. *Kriminell, korrupt, katholisch? Italiener im deutschen Vorurteil*. Stuttgart: Franz Steiner Verlag, 2018.

Berkhoff, Karel C. *Harvest of Despair: Life and Death in Ukraine Under Nazi Rule*. Cambridge: Harvard University Press, 2004.

Berkhoff, Karel C. *Motherland in Danger: Soviet Propaganda During World War II*. Cambridge: Harvard University Press, 2012.

Betts, Richard K. *Military Readiness: Concepts, Choices, Consequences*. Washington: Brookings, 1995.

Biagini, Antonello, and Antonio Zarcone, eds. *La campagna di Russia. Nel 70° anniversario dell'inizio dell'intervento dello CSIR*. Rome: Nuova Cultura, 2013.

Bialer, Seweryn. "Introduction." In *Stalin and His Generals: Soviet Military Memoirs of World War II*, edited by Seweryn Bialer, 15–44. New York: Pegasus, 1969.

Biddle, Stephen. *Military Power: Explaining Victory and Defeat in Modern Battle*. Princeton: Princeton University Press, 2004.
Bidussa, David. *Il mito del bravo italiano*. Milan: Il Saggiatore, 1994.
Bigazzi, Francesco, and Evgenij Zhirnov. *Gli ultimi 28. La storia incredibile dei prigionieri di guerra italiani dimenticati in Russia*. Milan: Mondadori, 2002.
Bistarelli, Agostino. *La storia del ritorno. I reduci italiani del secondo dopoguerra*. Turin: Bollati Boringhieri, 2007.
Bond, Brian. *Britain's Two World Wars Against Germany: Myth, Memory and the Distortions of Hindsight*. Cambridge: Cambridge University Press, 2014.
Bosworth, Richard J.B. "A Country Split in Two? Contemporary Italy and Its Usable and Unusable Pasts." *History Compass* 4, no. 6 (2006): 1089–101.
Bosworth, Richard J.B. *Mussolini*. London: Arnold, 2002.
Bosworth, Richard J.B. *Mussolini's Italy: Life Under the Dictatorship, 1915–1945*. London: Penguin, 2006.
Botti Ferruccio, and Virgilio Ilari. *Il pensiero militare italiano dal primo al secondo dopoguerra, 1919–1949*. Rome: USSME, 1985.
Bovio, [Gen.] Oreste. *In alto la bandiera. Storia del Regio Esercito*. Foggia: Bastogi, 1999.
Bovio, [Gen.] Oreste. *L'Ufficio Storico dell'Esercito*. Rome: USSME, 1987.
Brogini Künzi, Giulia. "Die Herrschaft der Gedanken. Italienische Militärzeitschriften und das Bild des Krieges." In *An der Schwelle zum totalen Krieg. Die militärische Debatte über den Krieg der Zukunft 1919–1939*, edited by Stig Förster, Bernhard R. Kroener, and Bernd Wegner, 37–111. Paderborn: Schöningh, 2002.
Buchanan, Andrew. "'Good Morning, Pupil!' American Representations of Italianness and the Occupation of Italy, 1943–1945." *Journal of Contemporary History* 43, no. 2 (2008): 217–40.
Burgwyn, James H. *Mussolini Warlord: Failed Dreams of Empire 1940–1943*. New York: Enigma, 2012.
Burgwyn, James H. "The Legacy of Italy's Participation in the German War Against the Soviet Union: 1941–1943." *Mondo Contemporaneo* 2 (2011): 161–81.
Buttar, Prit. *On a Knife's Edge: The Ukraine, November 1942–March 1943*. Oxford: Osprey, 2018.
Canosa, Romano. *Graziani. Il maresciallo d'Italia, dalla guerra d'Etiopia alla Repubblica di Salò*. Milan: Mondadori, 2004.
Canosa, Romano. *Storia dell'epurazione in Italia. Le sanzioni contro il fascismo 1943–1948*. Milan: Baldini & Castoldi, 1999.
Cappellano, Filippo, and Nicola Pignato. *Andare contro i carri armati: L'evoluzione della difesa controcarro nell'Esercito italiano dal 1918 al 1945*. Udine: Gaspari, 2007.

Cappellano, Filippo, and Pier Paolo Battistelli. *Italian Light Tanks 1919–1945*. Botley: Osprey, 2012.

Cappellano, Filippo, and Pier Paolo Battistelli. *Italian Medium Tanks 1939–1945*. Botley: Osprey, 2012.

Carrier, Richard. "Some Reflections on the Fighting Power of the Italian Army in North Africa, 1940–1943." *War in History* 22, no. 4 (2015): 503–28.

Carrier, Richard. "The Regio Esercito in Co-Belligerency, October 1943–April 1945." In *Italy and the Second World War: Alternative Perspectives*, edited by Emanuele Sica and Richard Carrier, 95–125. Leiden: Brill, 2018.

Caruso, Alfio. *Noi moriamo a Stalingrado*. Milan: Longanesi, 2006.

Caruso, Alfio. *Tutti i vivi all'assalto. L'epopea degli alpini dal Don a Nikolajevka*. Milan: Longanesi, 2003.

Cavallo, Pietro. *Italiani in guerra. Sentimenti e immagini dal 1940 al 1943*. Bologna: Il Mulino, 1997.

Cavallo, Pietro. *Viva l'Italia. Storia, Cinema e identità nazionale (1932–1962)*. Naples: Liguori, 2009.

Caviglia, Daniele, and Alessandro Gionfrida. *Un occasione da perdere. Le Forze Armate italiane e la Comunità Europea di Difesa (1950–54)*. Rome: APES, 2009.

Cecini, Giovanni. *I generali di Mussolini*. Rome: Newton Compton, 2016.

Cervone, Pier Paolo. *Enrico Caviglia, l'anti Badoglio*. Milan: Mursia, 1992.

Ceva, Lucio. *Africa Settentrionale 1940–1943. Negli studi e nella letteratura*. Rome: Bonacci, 1982.

Ceva, Lucio. "Fascismo e militari di professione." In *Ufficiali e società. Interpretazioni e modelli*, edited by Giuseppe Caforio and Piero Del Negro, 379–436. Milan: FrancoAngeli, 1988.

Ceva, Lucio. "La campagna di Russia nel quadro strategico della guerra fascista." In *Gli italiani sul fronte russo*, edited by Enzo Collotti, 163–93. Bari: De Donato, 1982.

Ceva, Lucio. *La condotta italiana della guerra. Cavallero e il Comando Supremo 1941/1942*. Milan: Feltrinelli, 1975.

Ceva, Lucio. *Le Forze armate*. Turin: UTET, 1981.

Ceva, Lucio. "Testimonianze sulla guerra di Grecia." *Risorgimento* 31, no. 1 (1979): 103–6.

Ceva, Lucio. "The North African Campaign 1940–43: A Reconsideration." *Journal of Strategic Studies* 13, no. 1 (1990): 84–104.

Ceva, Lucio, and Andrea Curami. *La meccanizzazione dell'Esercito italiano dalle originial 1943*, 2 vols. Rome: USSME, 1989.

Cherubini, Daniele. *I prigionieri italiani in Unione sovietica*. Rome: Prospettiva editrice, 2006.

Christoforow, Wassili S., Wladimir G. Makarow, and Matthias Uhl, eds. *Verhört. Die Befragungen deutscher Generale und Offiziere durch die sowjetischen Geheimdienste 1945–1952*. Berlin: De Gruyter Oldenbourg, 2015.

Cinelli, Gianluca. *Nuto Revelli*. Turin: Aragno, 2011.
Cohen, Eliot A., and John Gooch. *Military Misfortunes: The Anatomy of Failure in War*. New York: Free Press, 1990.
Conti, Davide. *Criminali di guerra. Accuse, processi e impunità nel secondo dopoguerra*. Rome: Odradek, 2011.
Conti, Davide. *Gli uomini di Mussolini*. Turin: Einaudi, 2017.
Conti, Flavio G. *I prigionieri di guerra italiani*. Bologna: Il Mulino, 1986.
Collotti, Enzo, ed. *Gli italiani sul fronte russo*. Bari: De Donato, 1982.
Cooke, Philip. *The Legacy of the Italian Resistance*. New York: Palgrave Macmillan, 2011.
Corner, Paul. *The Fascist Party and Popular Opinion in Mussolini's Italy*. Oxford: Oxford University Press, 2012.
Corni, Gustavo. "Briefe von der Ostfront. Ein Vergleich deutscher und italienischer Quellen." In *Die "Achse" im Krieg. Politik, Ideologie und Kriegführung 1939–1945*, edited by Lutz Klinkhammer, Amedeo Osti Guerrazzi, and Thomas Schlemmer, 398–432. Paderborn: Schöningh, 2010.
Corni, Gustavo. *Raccontare la guerra. La memoria organizzata*. Milan: Mondadori, 2012.
Corni, Gustavo. "Von der nordafrikanischen Wüste bis zum Don: Der Zweite Weltkrieg in der öffentlichen Erinnerung Italiens nach 1945." In *Krieg. Erinnerung. Geschichtswissenschaft*, edited by Siegfried Mattl et al., 87–110. Vienna: Böhlau, 2009.
Corum, James S. "The Spanish Civil War: Lessons Learned and Not Learned by the Great Powers." *The Journal of Military History* 62, no. 2 (1998): 313–34.
Corum, James S. *Wolfram von Richthofen: Master of the German Air War*. Lawrence: University Press of Kansas, 2008.
Coverdale, John F. *Italian Intervention in the Spanish Civil War*. Princeton: Princeton University Press, 1975.
Craveri, Piero. *De Gasperi*. Bologna: Il Mulino, 2006.
Crociani, Piero, and Pier Paolo Battistelli. *Italian Blackshirt, 1935–45*. Botley: Osprey, 2010.
Crociani, Piero, and Pier Paolo Battistelli. *Italian Soldier in North Africa 1941–1943*. Botley: Osprey, 2013.
Davies, Christie. "Itali Sunt Imbelles." *Journal of Strategic Studies* 5, no. 2 (1982): 266–69.
De Biase, Carlo. *L'Aquila d'oro. Storia dello Stato Maggiore Italiano (1861–1945)*. Milan: Borghese, 1970.
De Giorgi, Giulio. *Con la divisione Ravenna: tutte le sue vicende sino al rientro dalla Russia 1939–1943*. Milan: Longanesi, 1973.
De Felice, Renzo. *Mussolini l'alleato, 1940–1945. I. L'Italia in guerra 1940–1943. Tomo 1 – Dalla guerra 'breve' alla guerra lunga*. Turin: Einaudi, 1990.

De Felice, Renzo. *Mussolini l'alleato, 1940–1945. I. L'Italia in guerra 1940–1943. Tomo 2 – Crisi e agonia del regime.* Turin: Einaudi, 1990.
De Franceschi, Costantino, et al. *I servizi logistici delle Unità Italiane al fronte russo (1941–1943).* Rome: USSME, 1975.
Del Boca, Angelo. *Italiani, Brava Gente?* Vicenza: Neri Pozza, 2005.
De Leonardis, Massimo. *L'Italia e il suo Esercito. Una storia di soldati dal Risorgimento ad oggi.* Rome: Rai Eri, 2005.
Deletant, Dennis. "German-Romanian Relations, 1941–1944." In *Hitler and His Allies in World War II*, edited by Jonathan R. Adelman, 166–85. New York: Routledge, 2007.
Deletant, Dennis. *Hitler's Forgotten Ally: Ion Antonescu and His Regime, Romania 1940–1944.* Basingstoke: Palgrave Macmillan, 2006.
De Marco, Claudia. *Il mito degli Alpini, Vol. 1.* Udine: Gaspari, 2004.
De Ninno, Fabio. *Fascisti sul mare. La marina e gli ammiragli di Mussolini.* Bari: Laterza, 2017.
Dennis, Peter, and Jeffrey Grey, eds. *Victory or Defeat: Armies in the Aftermath of Conflict.* Newport: BigSky, 2010.
De Prospo, Mario. "Reconstructing the Army of a Collapsed Nation: The Kingdom of the South of Italy (September 1943–March 1944)." *Journal of Modern Italian Studies* 18, no. 1 (2013): 1–16.
Di Giovanni, Marco. "El Alamein: l'epica della sconfitta." In *Gli Italiani in guerra. Conflitti, identità, memorie dal Risorgimento ai nostri giorni, Vol. 4: Tomo 2*, edited by Mario Isnenghi and Giulia Albanese, 203–9. Turin: UTET, 2008.
Di Giovanni, Marco. *I paracadutisti italiani: Volontari, miti e memoria della seconda guerra mondiale.* Gorizia: Ed. Goriziana, 1991.
DiNardo, Richard L. *Germany and the Axis Powers: From Coalition to Collapse.* Lawrence: University Press of Kansas, 2005.
Di Nolfo, Ennio. *Von Mussolini bis De Gasperi.* Paderborn: Schöningh, 1993.
Doerr, Hans. "Verbindungsoffiziere." *Wehrwissenschaftliche Rundschau* 3, no. 6 (1953): 270–80.
Domenico, Roy. *Italian Fascists on Trial, 1943–1948.* Chapel Hill: University of North Carolina Press, 1991.
Dubrovina, Olga, ed. *Battaglie in Russia. Il Don e Stalingrado 75 anni dopo.* Milan: Ed. Unicopli, 2018.
Dubrovina, Olga. "Immagine del nemico. Meccanismo della costruzione." In *Battaglie in Russia. Il Don e Stalingrado 75 anni dopo*, edited by Olga Dubrovina, 159–65. Milan: Ed. Unicopli, 2018.
Duggan, Christopher. *Fascist Voices: An Intimate History of Mussolini's Italy.* Oxford: Oxford University Press, 2013.

Düsterberg, Rolf. *Soldat und Kriegserlebnis. Deutsche militärische Erinnerungsliteratur (1945–1961) zum Zweiten Weltkrieg*. Tübingen: Niemeyer, 2000.
Erickson, John. *The Road to Berlin*. London: Weidenfeld & Nicolson, 1983.
Faccini, W., and G. Ferrari. "Gabriele Nasci. Generale degli Alpini." In *Studi Storico Militari 1991*, 363–545. Rome: USSME, 1993.
Fanello Marcucci, Gabriella. *Scelba. Il ministro che si oppose al fascismo e al comunismo in nome della libertà*. Milan: Mondadori, 2006.
Falanga, Gianluca. *Mussolinis Vorposten in Hitlers Reich. Italiens Politik in Berlin 1933–1945*. Berlin: Ch. Links, 2008.
Faldella, [Gen.] Emilio. *L'Italia e la seconda guerra mondiale. Revisione di giudizi*. San Casciano: Cappelli, 1963.
Faldella, [Gen.] Emilio. *Storia delle truppe alpine, Vol. 3*. Milan: Cavallotti, 1972.
Favretto, Ilaria, and Oliviero Bergamini. "'Temperamentally Unwarlike': The Image of Italy in the Allies' War Propaganda." In *War and the Media Reportage and Propaganda 1900–2003*, edited by Mark Connelly and David Welch, 112–26. London: Tauris, 2005.
Ferraresi, Franco. *Threats to Democracy: The Radical Right in Italy After the War*. Princeton: Princeton University Press, 1996.
Filatov, Georgy S. *La campagna orientale di Mussolini*. Milan: Mursia, 1979.
Finaldi, Giuseppe Maria. *Italian National Identity in the Scramble for Africa: Italy's African Wars in the Era of Nation Building, 1870–1900*. Bern: Peter Lang, 2009.
Finazzer, Enrico, and Ralph A. Riccio. *Italian Artillery of WWII*. Sandomierz: Stratus, 2015.
Focardi, Filippo. *Il cattivo Tedesco e il bravo italiano: la rimozione delle colpe della seconda guerra mondiale*. Bari: Laterza, 2013.
Focardi, Filippo. *La guerra della memoria: la Resistenza nel dibattito politico italiano dal 1945 a oggi*. Bari: Laterza: 2005.
Focardi, Filippo, and Lutz Klinkhammer. "The Question of Fascist Italy's War Crimes: The Construction of a Self-Acquitting Myth (1943–1948)." *Journal of Modern Italian Studies* 9, no. 3 (2004): 330–48.
Fokin, Nikolai A., and Vladimir I. Sidorov. *Razgrom Italo-Nemetskikh voisk na Donu (Dekabr 1942 r.): Kratkii operativno-takticheskii ocherk*. Moscow: Voenizdat, 1945.
Fonzi, Paolo. "The Italian Occupation of Crete During the Second World War." In *Italy and the Second World War: Alternative Perspectives*, edited by Emanuele Sica and Richard Carrier, 51–75. Leiden: Brill, 2018.
Förster, Jürgen. "Die Wehrmacht und die Probleme der Koalitionskriegführung." In *Die "Achse" im Krieg. Politik, Ideologie und Kriegführung 1939–1945*, edited by Lutz Klinkhammer, Amedeo Osti Guerrazzi, and Thomas Schlemmer, 108–21. Paderborn: Schöningh, 2010.

Förster, Jürgen. "Il ruolo dell'8ª armata italiana dal punto di vista Tedesco." In *Gli Italiani sul fronte russo*, edited by Enzo Collotti, 229–59. Bari: De Donato 1982.
Förster, Jürgen. *Stalingrad. Risse im Bündnis 1942/43*. Freiburg: Rombach, 1975.
Förster, Stig. *The Battlefield: Towards a Modern History of War*. London: GHI, 2008.
Franke, Volker. *Preparing for Peace: Military Identity, Value Orientations, and Professional Military Education*. Westport: Praeger, 1999.
Franzosi, [Lt. Col.] Pier Giorgio. *I cento anni della Rivista Militare*. Rome: Tip. Reg., 1976.
Frieser, Karl-Heinz. *Blitzkrieg-Legende: Der Westfeldzug 1940*. Munich: Oldenbourg, 1995.
Frigerio, Alessandro. *Reduci alla sbarra. 1949: il processo D'Onofrio e il ruolo del PCI nei lager sovietici*. Milan: Mursia, 2006.
Galli della Loggia, Ernesto. *L'identità italiana*. Bologna: Il Mulino, 1998.
Galli della Loggia, Ernesto. *La morte della Patria*. Bari: Laterza, 2003.
Gariboldi, Mario. "L'Italia in Russia: L'ARMIR." In *L'Italia in guerra. Il terzo anno – 1942*, edited by Romain H. Rainero and Antonello Biagini, 297–307. Gaeta: Stabilimento Grafico Militare, 1993.
Garzia, Italo, Carmelo Pasimeni, and Domenico Urgesi, eds. *Il Maresciallo d'Italia Giovanni Messe. Guerra, forze armate e politca nell'Italia del Novecento. Atti del convegno di studi (Mesagne 27–28 ottobre 2000)*. Mesagne: Congedo, 2003.
Gentile, Gentile. "Alle spalle dell'ARMIR: documenti sulla repressione antipartigiana al fronte russo." *Il Presente e la Storia* 53 (1998): 159–81.
Germinario, Francesco. *L'altra memoria. L'Estrema destra, Salò e la Resistenza*. Turin: Bollatti, 1999.
Gianbartolomei, Aldo. "La campagna in Russia del CSIR e dei suoi veterani nell'ARMIR." In *L'Italia in guerra. Il terzo anno – 1942*, edited by Romain H. Rainero and Antonello Biagini, 273–96. Gaeta: Stabilimento Grafico Militare, 1993.
Gianuli, Aldo. *Le spie del Duce (1939–1943). Lettere e documenti segreti sulla campagna di Russia*. Sesto San Giovanni: Mimesis, 2018.
Goeschel, Christian. *Mussolini and Hitler: The Forging of the Fascist Alliance*. New Haven: Yale University Press, 2018.
Gooch, John. *Army, State and Society in Italy, 1870–1915*. London: Macmillan, 1989.
Gooch, John. "Italian Military Competence." *Journal of Strategic Studies* 5, no. 2 (1982): 257–65.
Gooch, John. *Mussolini and His Generals: The Armed Forces and Fascist Foreign Policy, 1922–1940*. Cambridge: Cambridge University Press, 2007.

Gooch, John. "Re-conquest and Suppression: Fascist Italy's Pacification of Libya and Ethiopia, 1922–39." *Journal of Strategic Studies* 28, no. 6 (2005): 1005–32.
Gosztony, Peter. *Hitler's Fremde Heere. Das Schicksal der nichtdeutschen Armeen im Ostfeldzug*. Düsseldorf: Econ, 1976.
Giusti, Maria Teresa. "Giovanni Messe. L'Uomo e il soldato." In *Lettere alla moglie. Dai fronti Greco- Albanese, Russo, Tunisino e dalla prigionia 1940–1944*, Giovanni Messe, 11–67. Milan: Mursia, 2018.
Giusti, Maria Teresa. *I prigionieri italiani in Russia*. Bologna: Il Mulino, 2003; rev. ed. 2014.
Giusti, Maria Teresa. *La campagna di Russia, 1941–1943*. Bologna: Il Mulino, 2016.
Giusti, Maria Teresa. "'Restare vivo è molto difficile…'. Gli italiani sul fronte orientale e l'immagine del nemico." In *Battaglie in Russia. Il Don e Stalingrado 75 anni dopo*, edited by Olga Dubrovina, 81–109. Milan: Ed. Unicopli, 2018.
Glantz, David M. *Barbarossa: Hitler's Invasion of Russia 1941*. Stroud: Tempus, 2001.
Glantz, David M. *From the Don to the Dnepr: Soviet Offensive Operations, December 1942–August 1943*. London: Cass, 1991.
Glantz, David M., and Jonathan M. House. *The Stalingrad Trilogy, Vol. 3: Endgame at Stalingrad. Book Two: December 1942–February 1943*. Lawrence: University Press of Kansas, 2014.
Glantz, David M., and Jonathan M. House. *When Titans Clashed: How the Red Army Stopped Hitler*. Lawrence: University Press of Kansas, 2015.
Greene, Jack. *Mare Nostrum: The War in the Mediterranean*. Watsonville: Typesetting, 1990.
Greene, Jack, and Alessandro Massignani. *Rommel's North Africa Campaign*. Conshohocken: Combined Books, 1999.
Greene, Jack, and Alessandro Massignani. *The Naval War in the Mediterranean 1940–1943*. London: Chatham, 1998.
Groß, Gerhard P. *Mythos und Wirklichkeit. Geschichte des operativen Denkens im deutschen Heer von Moltke d.Ä. bis Heusinger*. Paderborn: Schöningh, 2012.
Hamilton, Hope. *Sacrifice on the Steppe: The Italian Alpine Corps in the Stalingrad Campaign, 1942–1943*. Havertown: Casemate, 2011.
Hammermann, Gabriele. *Zwangsarbeit für den "Verbündeten": Die Arbeits- und Lebensbedingungen der italienischen Militärinternierten in Deutschland 1943–1945*. Tübingen: Niemeyer, 2002.
Hartmann, Christian. *Wehrmacht im Ostkrieg. Front und militärisches Hinterland 1941/42*. Munich: Oldenbourg, 2009.
Hartmann, Christian, Johannes Hürter, and Ulrike Jureit, eds. *Verbrechen der Wehrmacht. Bilanz einer Debatte*. Munich: Beck, 2005.

Harward, Grant T. "First Among Un-Equals: Challenging German Sterotypes of the Romanian Army During the Second World War." *The Journal of Slavic Military Studies* 24, no. 3 (2011): 439–80.

Hasenclever, Jörn. *Wehrmacht und Besatzungspolitik in der Sowjetunion. Die Befehlshaber der rückwärtigen Heeresgebiete 1941–1943*. Paderborn: Schöningh, 2010.

Hayward, Joel S.A. *Stopped at Stalingrad: The Luftwaffe and Hitler's Defeat in the East, 1942–1943*. Lawrence: University Press of Kansas, 1998.

Higham, Robin. *Diary of a Disaster: British Aid to Greece 1940–1941*. Lexington: Kentucky University Press, 1986.

Higham, Robin, ed. *Official Military Historical Offices and Sources, Vol. 1*. Westport: Greenwood, 2000.

Higham, Robin. "Introduction." In *The Writing of Official Military History*, edited by Robin Higham, vii–xii. Westport: Greenwood, 1999.

Hinkle, Wade P., et al. *Why Nations Differ in Military Skill*. Alexandria: Institute for Defence Analyses, 1999.

Hill, Alexander. *The Red Army and the Second World War*. Cambridge: Cambridge University Press, 2016.

Hogg, Ian. *Tank Killing: Anti-Tank Warfare by Men and Machines*. London: Sidgwick & Jackson, 1996.

Holmes, Richard. *Acts of War: The Behaviour of Men in Battle*. London: Cassell, 2004.

Howell, Esther-Julia. *Von den Besiegten lernen? Die kriegsgeschichtliche Kooperation der U.S. Armee und der ehemaligen Wehrmachtselite, 1945–1961*. Berlin: De Gruyter, 2016.

Hürter, Joahnnes. "Die Wehrmacht vor Leningrad. Krieg und Besatzungspolitik der 18. Armee im Herbst und Winter 1941/42." In *Der deutsche Krieg im Osten 1941–1944. Facetten einer Grenzüberschreitung*, edited by Christian Hartmann, Johannes Hürter, Peter Lieb and Dieter Pohl, 95–153. Munich: Oldenbourg, 2009.

Hürter, Johannes. *Hitler's Heerführer. Die deutschen Oberbefehlshaber im Krieg gegen die Sowjetunion 1941/42*. Munich: Oldenbourg, 2006.

Ilari, Virgilio. *Storia militare della prima repubblica 1943–1993*. Ancona: Nuove Ricerche, 1994.

Imbriani, Angelo Michele. *Vento del Sud. Moderati, reazionari, Qualunquisti (1943–1948)*. Bologna: Il Mulino, 1996.

Isnenghi, Mario. *Dalla Resistenza alla desistenza. L'Italia del 'Ponte' (1945–1947)*. Bari: Laterza, 2007.

Isnenghi, Mario. *I vinti di Caporetto nella letteratura di guerra*. Padova: Marsilio, 1967.

Isnenghi, Mario. *Le guerre degli italiani. Parole, immagini, ricordi 1848–1945*. Bologna: Il Mulino, 2005.

Jukes, Geoffrey. *Hitler's Stalingrad Decisions*. Berkeley: University of California Press, 1985.
Kahn, Martin. "'Russia Will Assuredly Be Defeated': Anglo-American Government Assessments of Soviet War Potential Before Operation Barbarossa." *The Journal of Slavic Military Studies* 25, no. 2 (2012): 220–40.
Kallis, Aristotle A. *Nazi Propaganda and the Second World War*. London: Palgrave Macmillan, 2005.
Kehrig, Manfred. *Stalingrad. Analyse und Dokumentation einer Schlacht*. Stuttgart: DVA, 1974.
Kehrig, Manfred. "Stalingrad im Spiegel der Memoiren deutscher Generale." In *Stalingrad. Mythos und Wirklichkeit einer Schlacht*, edited by Wolfram Wette and Gerd R. Ueberschär, 205–13. Frankfurt: Fischer, 2012.
Klinkhammer, Lutz. "Kriegserinnerung in Italien im Wechsel der Generationen. Ein Wandel der Perspektive?" In *Erinnerungskulturen. Deutschland, Italien und Japan seit 1945*, edited by Christoph Cornelißen, Lutz Klinkhammer, and Wolfgang Schwentker, 333–43. Frankfurt: Fischer, 2003.
Klinkhammer, Lutz, Amedeo Osti Guerrazzi, and Thomas Schlemmer, eds. *Die "Achse" im Krieg. Politik, Ideologie und Kriegführung 1939–1945*. Paderborn: Schöningh, 2010.
Knox, MacGregor. *Mussolini Unleashed, 1939–1941: Politics and Strategy in Fascist Italy's Last War*. Cambridge: Cambridge University Press, 1982.
Knox, MacGregor. "The Italian Armed Forces, 1940–3." In *Military Effectiveness, Vol. 3: The Second World War*, edited by Allan R. Millett and Williamson Murray, 136–79. Cambridge: Cambridge University Press, 2010.
Knox, MacGregor. "'Totality' and Disintegration: State, Party, and Armed Forces in National Socialist Germany and Fascist Italy." In *Die "Achse" im Krieg. Politik, Ideologie und Kriegführung 1939–1945*, edited by Lutz Klinkhammer, Amedeo Osti Guerrazzi, and Thomas Schlemmer, 80–107. Paderborn: Schöningh, 2010.
König, Malte. *Kooperation als Machtkampf. Das faschistische Achsenbündnis Berlin-Rom im Krieg 1940/41*. Cologne: SH-Verlag, 2007.
Korovin, Vladimir V. "Azioni militari dei partigiani sovietici contro gli eserciti tedeschi, italiani e ungheresi negli anni 1942–1943." In *Battaglie in Russia. Il Don e Stalingrado 75 anni dopo*, edited by Olga Dubrovina, 39–71. Milan: Ed. Unicopli, 2018.
Kotze, Hildegard von, ed. *Heeresadjutant bei Hitler 1938–1943. Die Aufzeichnungen des Majors Engel*. Stuttgart: DVA, 1974.
Krumeich, Gerd. "Schlachtenmythen in der Geschichte." In *Schlachtenmythen: Ereignis – Erzählung – Erinnerung*, edited by Gerd Krumeich and Susanne Brandt, 1–18. Cologne: Böhlau, 2003.
Labanca, Nicola, ed. *I Gruppi di combattimento. Studi, fonti, memorie (1944–1945)*. Rome: Carocci, 2005.

Labanca, Nicola. *La guerra d'Etiopia, 1935–1941*. Bologna: Il Mulino, 2015.
Lami, Lucio. *Isbuscenskij. L'ultima carica*. Milan: Mursia, 1970.
Lehnhardt, Jochen. *Die Waffen-SS: Geburt einer Legende. Himmlers Krieger in der NS-Propaganda*. Paderborn: Schöningh, 2017.
Loi, [Lt. Col.] Salvatore. *Le operazioni delle unità italiane in Jugoslavia (1941–1943)*. Rome: USSME, 1978.
Longo, Luigi Emilio. *Giovanni Messe. L'ultimo Maresciallo d'Italia*. Rome: USSME, 2006.
Longo, Luigi Emilio. *L'attività degli addetti militari italiani all'estero fra le due guerre mondiali (1919–1939)*. Rome: USSME, 1999.
Lopasic, Alexander. "Italian Military Performance in the Second World War: Some Considerations." *Journal of Strategic Studies* 5, no. 2 (1982): 270–75.
Lorenzini, Sara. *L'Italia e il trattato di pace del 1947*. Bologna: Il Mulino, 2007.
Luoni, Vittorio. *La "Pasubio" sul fronte russo*. Rome: Ateneo & Bizzarri, 1977.
Lynn, John A. "The Embattled Future of Academic Military History." *The Journal of Military History* 61, no. 4 (1997): 777–89.
Mack Smith, Denis. *Mussolini as a Military Leader*. Reading: Reading University Press, 1974.
Major, Patrick. "'Our Friend Rommel': The *Wehrmacht* as 'Worthy Enemy' in Postwar British Popular Culture." *German History* 26, no. 4 (2008): 530–45.
Mallett, Robert. *Mussolini and the Origins of the Second World War, 1933–1940*. Basingstoke: Palgrave, 2003.
Marsetic, Albino. *Dall'Adige al Don. Con il 79° reggimento fanteria in Russia*. Milan: Mursia, 2002.
Massignani, Alessandro. *Alpini e tedeschi sul Don*. Novale di Valdagno: Rossato, 1991.
Massignani, Alessandro. "Die italienischen Streitkräfte und der Krieg der 'Achse'." In *Die "Achse" im Krieg. Politik, Ideologie und Kriegführung 1939–1945*, edited by Lutz Klinkhammer, Amedeo Osti Guerrazzi, and Thomas Schlemmer, 122–46. Paderborn: Schöningh, 2010.
Mawdsley, Evan. "Sacrifice on the Steppe: The Italian Alpine Corps in the Stalingrad Campaign, 1942–1943: By Hope Hamilton." *War in History* 20, no. 1 (2013): 133–35.
Mawdsley, Evan. *Thunder in the East: The Nazi-Soviet War 1941–1945*. London: Hodder Arnold, 2007.
Mayda, Giuseppe, and Nicola Tranfaglia, eds. *Come ci hanno visti*. Rome: Della Volpe, 1965.
Megargee, Geoffrey P. *Inside Hitler's High Command*. Lawrence: University Press of Kansas, 2000.
Meier-Welcker, Hans. "Zur deutsch-italienischen Militärpolitik und Beurteilung der italienischen Wehrmacht vor dem Zweiten Weltkrieg." *Militärgeschichtliche Mitteilungen* 7, no. 1 (1970): 59–94.

Middeldorf, [Lt. Col.] Eike. *Taktik im Russlandfeldzug. Erfahrungen und Folgerungen*. Berlin: Mittler, 1956.
Miller, James Edward. *The United States and Italy, 1940–1950: The Politics and Diplomacy of Stabilization*. Chapel Hill: The University of North Carolina Press, 1986.
Millet, Allan R., Williamson Murray, and Kenneth H. Watman. "The Effectiveness of Military Organizations." In *Military Effectiveness, Vol. 1: The First World War*, edited by Allan R. Millett and Williamson Murray, 1–30. Cambridge: Cambridge University Press, 2010.
Minniti, Fortunato. *Il Piave*. Bologna: Il Mulino, 2000.
Mondini, Marco. *Alpini. Parole e immagini di un mito guerriero*. Bari: Laterza, 2008.
Mondini, Marco. "Between Subversion and Coup d'État: Military Power and Politics After the Great War (1919–1922)." *Journal of Modern Italian Studies* 11, no. 4 (2006): 445–64.
Mondini, Marco. "La festa mancata. I militari e la memoria della Grande Guerra, 1918–1923." *Contemporanea* 4 (2004): 555–78.
Mondini, Marco, and Guri Schwarz. *Dalla guerra alla pace. Retoriche e pratiche della smobilitazione nell'Italia del Novecento*. Verona: Cierre, 2007.
Montanari, [Gen.] Mario. *L'Esercito italiano allla vigilia della 2ª guerra mondiale*. Rome: USSME, 1982.
Montanari, [Gen.] Mario. *La campagna di Grecia, Vol. 1*. Rome: USSME, 1980.
Montanari, [Gen.] Mario. *Le operazioni in Africa Settentrionale, 4 vols.* Rome: USSME, 1993–2000.
Moore, Bob. "Enforced Diaspora: The Fate of Italian Prisoners of War During the Second World War." *War in History* 22, no. 2 (2015): 174–90.
Moore, Bob, and Kent Fedorowich. *The British Empire and Its Italian Prisoners of War, 1940–1947*. New York: Palgrave Macmillan, 2002.
Morina, Christina. *Legacies of Stalingrad: Remembering the Eastern Front in Germany Since 1945*. Cambridge: Cambridge University Press, 2011.
Morisi, Paolo. *The Italian Folgore Parachute Division: Operations in North Africa 1940–1943*. Solihull: Helion 2016.
Morozzo della Rocca, Roberto. *La Politica estera italiana e l'unione sovietica (1944–1948)*. Rome: La Goliardica, 1985.
Müller, Rolf-Dieter. *An der Seite der Wehrmacht. Hitlers ausländische Helfer beim 'Kreuzzug gegen den Bolschewismus' 1941–1945*. Berlin: Links, 2007.
Murray, Williamson. *Military Adaptation in War*. Cambridge: Cambridge University Press, 2011.
Murray, Williamson. "The German Response to Victory in Poland: A Case Study in Professionalism." *Armed Forces and Society* 7, no. 2 (1981): 285–98.

Murray, Williamson, and Richard Hart Sinnreich, eds. *The Past as Prologue: The Importance of History to the Military Profession.* Cambridge: Cambridge University Press, 2006.

Neitzel, Sönke. "Militärgeschichte ohne Krieg? Eine Standortbestimmung der deutschen Militärgeschichtsschreibung über das Zeitalter der Weltkriege." In *Geschichte der Politik. Alte und Neue Wege. Beiheft 44 der HZ,* edited by Hans-Christof Kraus and Thomas Nicklas, 287–308. Munich: Oldenbourg, 2007.

Neitzel, Sönke, and Harald Welzer. *Soldaten. On Fighting, Killing, and Dying: The Secret Second World War Tapes of German POWs.* London: Simon & Schuster, 2011.

Núñez Seixas, Xosé M. "Good Invaders? The Occupation Policy of the Spanish Blue Division in Northwestern Russia, 1941–1944." *War in History* 25, no. 3 (2018): 361–86.

Núñez Seixas, Xosé M. "Unable to Hate? Some Comparative Remarks on the War Experiences of Spaniards and Italians on the Eastern Front, 1941–1944." *Journal of Modern European History* 16, no. 2 (2018): 268–89.

Núñez Seixas, Xosé M. "Wishful Thinking in Wartime? Spanish Blue Division's Soldiers and Their Views of Nazi Germany, 1941–44." *Journal of War & Culture Studies* 11, no. 2 (2018): 99–116.

Nuti, Leopoldo. *L'Esercito italiano nel secondo dopoguerra 1945–1950.* Rome: USSME, 1989.

O'Brien, Phillips P. *How the War Was Won: Air-Sea Power and Allied Victory in World War II.* Cambridge: Cambridge University Press, 2010.

Oliva, Gianni. *Storia degli Alpini. Dal 1872 a oggi.* Milan: Mondadori, 2001.

Oliva, Gianni. *L'alibi della Resistenza, ovvero come abbiamo vinto la seconda guerra mondiale.* Milan: Mondadori, 2003.

Overmans, Rüdiger. *Soldaten hinter Stacheldraht. Deutsche Kriegsgefangene des Zweiten Weltkriegs.* Munich: Propyläen, 2000.

Osti Guerrazzi, Amedeo. "Italians at War: War and Experience in Fascist Italy." *Journal of Modern Italian Studies* 22, no. 5 (2017): 587–603.

Osti Guerrazzi, Amedeo. *Noi non sappiamo odiare. L'esercito italiano tra fascismo e democrazia.* Turin: UTET, 2010.

Osti Guerrazzi, Amedeo. *The Italian Army in Slovenia: Strategies of Antipartisan Repression, 1941–1943.* New York: Palgrave Macmillan, 2013.

Osti Guerrazzi, Amedeo, and Thomas Schlemmer. "I soldati italiani nella campagna di Russia. Propaganda, esperienza, memoria." In *Annali dell'Istituto storico italo-germanico in Trento XXXIII 2007,* 385–417. Bologna: Il Mulino, 2008.

Overy, Richard. *Russia's War.* New York: Penguin, 1998.

Overy, Richard. *Why the Allies Won.* London: Jonathan Cape, 1995.

Pagan, Roberto, ed. *Il prezzo della libertà. Giusto Tolloy.* Reggio Calabria: Città del Sole, 2015.

Paggi, Leonardo. *Il popolo dei morti. La repubblica italiana nata dalla guerra (1940–1946)*. Bologna: Il Mulino, 2009.
Pallotta, Pietro. *L'esercito italiano nella seconda guerra mondiale attraverso i guidizi dei comandanti avversari e alleati*. Rome: Tip. Madonna delle Grazie, 1955.
Paris, Michael. *Warrior Nation: Images of War in British Popular Culture, 1850–2000*. London: Reaktion, 2000.
Parlato, Giuseppe. *Fascisti senza Mussolini. Le origini del neofascismo in Italia, 1943–1948*. Bologna: Il Mulino, 2006.
Patriarca, Silvana. *Italianità. La costruzione del carattere nazionale*. Bari: Laterza, 2010.
Pavone, Claudio. *A Civil War: A History of the Italian Resistance*. London: Verso, 2013.
Patricelli, Marco. *L'Italia delle sconfitte: Da Custoza alla ritirata di Russia*. Bari: Laterza, 2016.
Pavone, Claudio. "Appunti sul problema dei reduci." In *L'altro dopoguerra. Roma e il sud, 1943–1945*, edited by Nicola Gallerano, 89–106. Milan: FrancoAngeli, 1985.
Pedaliu, Effie. "Britain and the Reconstruction of the Post-Fascist Italian Armed Forces, 1943–1948." *Cold War History* 2, no. 1 (2001): 39–68.
Pelagalli, [Gen.] Sergio. *Efisio Marras. Addetto militare a Berlino 1936–1943*. Rome: USSME, 1994.
Perrett, Bryan. *Last Stand! Famous Battles Against the Odds*. London: Cassell, 1991.
Petacco, Arrigo. *L'armata scomparsa. L'avventura degli italiani in Russia*. Milan: Mondadori, 1998.
Petracarro, Domenico. "The Italian Army in Africa 1940–1943: An Attempt at Historical Perspective." *War & Society* 9, no. 2 (1991): 103–27.
Pieri, Piero. "Jugements sur l'armée italienne et responsabilités." *Revue d'histoire de la Deuxième Guerre Mondiale* 26, no. 7 (1957): 112–14.
Pieri, Piero, and Giorgio Rochat. *Pietro Badoglio*. Turin: UTET, 1974.
Pignato, Nicola, and Antonio Rosati. "Gervasio Bitossi: Primo Comandante della cavalleria carrista." In *Studi Storico-Militari 2004*, 5–95. Rome: USSME, 2007.
Pipitone, Daniele. "Imported Memories: The Italian Audience and the Reception of American Movies About the Second World War." *Journal of Modern Italian Studies* 21, no. 4 (2016): 627–48.
Pohl, Dieter. *Die Herrschaft der Wehrmacht. Deutsche Militärbesatzung und einheimische Bevölkerung in der Sowjetunion 1941–1944*. Frankfurt: Fischer, 2011.

Ranzato, Gabriele. "La guerra di Spagna." In *I luoghi della memoria, Vol. 3: Strutture ed eventi dell'Italia unita*, edited by Mario Isenghi, 331–44. Bari: Laterza, 1997.

Rasero, Aldo. *Alpini della Julia. Storia della divisione miracolo*. Milan: Mursia, 1972.

Rasero, Aldo. *L'eroica "Cuneense". Storia della divisione alpina martire*. Milan: Mursia, 1985.

Rasero, Aldo. *Tridentina avanti! Storia di una divisione alpina*. Milan: Mursia, 1982.

Raspin, Angela. *The Italian War Economy, 1940–1943*. New York: Garland, 1986.

Rass, Christoph. *"Menschenmaterial": Deutsche Soldaten an der Ostfront. Innenansichten einer Infanteriedivision 1939–1945*. Paderborn: Schöningh, 2003.

Revelli, Nuto. "La ritirata di Russia." In *I luoghi della memoria, Vol. 3: Strutture ed eventi dell'Italia unita*, edited by Mario Isenghi, 365–80. Bari: Laterza, 1997.

Revelli, Nuto. *Il mondo dei vinti*. Turin: Einaudi, 2005.

Reynolds, David. *In Command of History: Churchill Fighting and Writing the Second World War*. New York: Random House, 2005.

Riall, Lucy. *Garibaldi: Invention of a Hero*. New Haven: Yale University Press, 2007.

Rochat, Giorgio. *L'Esercito italiano da Vittorio Veneto a Mussolini, 1919–1925*. Bari: Laterza, 2006; first ed. 1967.

Rochat, Giorgio. *L'Esercito italiano in pace e in guerra*. Milan: Rara, 1991.

Rochat, Giorgio. "La guerra di Grecia." In *I luoghi della memoria, Vol. 3: Strutture ed eventi dell'Italia unita*, edited by Mario Isenghi, 346–64. Bari: Laterza, 1997.

Rochat, Giorgio. "La prigionia di guerra." In *I luoghi della memoria, Vol. 3: Strutture ed eventi dell'Italia unita*, edited by Mario Isenghi, 381–402. Bari: Laterza, 1997.

Rochat, Giorgio. *Le guerre italiane, 1935–1943. Dall'impero d'Etiopia alla disfatta*. Turin: Einaudi, 2008.

Rochat, Giorgio. "Memorialistica e storiografia sulla campagna italiana di Russia 1941–1943." In *Gli Italiani sul fronte russo*, edited by Enzo Collotti, 465–82. Bari: De Donato 1982.

Rochat, Giorgio. "Qualche dato sugli uffciali di complemento dell'Esercito nel 1940." *Ricerche storiche* 18, no. 3 (1993): 607–35.

Rochat, Giorgio, and Giulio Massobrio. *Breve storia dell'Esercito italiano dal 1861 al 1943*. Turin: Einaudi, 1978.

Rodogno, Davide. *Fascism's European Empire: Italian Occupation During the Second World War*. Cambridge: Cambridge University Press, 2006.

Roggiani, Fermo. *Bersaglieri d'Italia. Dal ponte di Goito a Beirut.* Milan: Cavallotti, 1983.
Römer, Felix. *Der Kommissarbefehl: Wehrmacht und NS-Verbrechen an der Ostfront 1941/42.* Paderborn: Schöningh, 2008.
Rosen, Stephen P. "Military Effectiveness: Why Society Matters." *International Security* 19, no. 4 (1995): 5–31.
Rottmann, Gordon L. *World War II Infantry Fire Support Tactics.* Botley: Osprey, 2016.
Rotundo, Louis, ed. *Battle for Stalingrad: The 1943 Soviet General Staff Study.* Washington: Pergamon-Brassey's, 1989.
Rovighi, [Gen.] Alberto. *Le operazione in Africa Orientale (giugno 1940–novembre 1941), Vol. 1.* Rome: USSME, 1988.
Sadkovich, James J. "Anglo-American Bias and the Italo-Greek War of 1940–1941." *The Journal of Military History* 58, no. 4 (1994): 617–42.
Sadkovich, James J. "German Military Incompetence Through Italian Eyes." *War in History* 1, no. 1 (1994): 39–62.
Sadkovich, James J. "Italian Morale During the Italo-Greek War of 1940–1941." *War & Society* 12, no. 1 (1994): 97–121.
Sadkovich, James J. "Italian Service Histories and Fascist Italy's War Effort." In *The Writing of Official Military History*, edited by Robin Higham, 91–125. Westport: Greenwood, 1999.
Sadkovich, James J. "Of Myths and Men: Rommel and the Italians in North Africa, 1940–1942." *The International History Review* 13, no. 2 (1991): 284–313.
Sadkovich, James J. "Some Considerations Regarding Italian Armored Doctrine Prior to June 1940." *Global War Studies* 9, no. 1 (2012): 40–74.
Sadkovich, James J. "The Italo-Greek War in Context: Italian Priorities and Axis Diplomacy." *Journal of Contemporary History* 28, no. 3 (1993): 439–64.
Sadkovich, James J. "Understanding Defeat: Reappraising Italy's Role in World War II." *Journal of Contemporary History* 24, no. 1 (1989): 27–61.
Saini Fasanotti, Federica. *Etiopia 1936–1940. Le operazioni di polizia coloniale nelle fonti dell'Esercito italiano.* Rome: USSME, 2010.
Samsonov, Aleksandr M. *Stalingrado. Fronte russo.* Milan: Garzanti, 1961.
Santarelli, Lidia. "Muted Violence: Italian War Crimes in Occupied Greece." *Journal of Modern Italian Studies* 9, no. 3 (2004): 280–99.
Scarpellini, Emanuela. "Winston Churchill e la memoria della seconda guerra mondiale in Italia." In *La seconda guerra mondiale e la sua memoria*, edited by Piero Craveri and Gaetano Quagliariello, 223–33. Soveria Mannelli: Rubbettino, 2006.
Schäfer, Kristin A. *Werner von Blomberg. Hitlers erster Feldmarschall.* Paderborn: Schöningh, 2006.

Scheibert, Horst. *Panzer zwischen Don und Donez. Die Winterkämpfe 1942–1943*. Friedberg: Podzun-Pallas, 1979.
Schlemmer, Thomas. "Das königlich-italienische Heer im Vernichtungskrieg gegen die Sowjetunion. Kriegführung und Besatzungspraxis einer vergessenen Armee 1941–1943." In *Faschismus in Italien und Deutschland. Studien zu Transfer und Vergleich*, edited by Armin Nolzen and Sven Reichardt, 148–75. Göttingen: Wallstein, 2005.
Schlemmer, Thomas. "Die comandi tappa der 8. Italienischen Armee und die deutsche Besatzungsherrschaft im Süden der Sowjetunion. Momentaufnahmen aus dem Spätjahr 1942." *Quellen und Forschungen aus italienischen Archiven* 88 (2008): 512–46.
Schlemmer, Thomas. *Die Italiener an der Ostfront 1942/43. Dokumente zu Mussolinis Krieg gegen die Sowjetunion*. Munich: Oldenbourg, 2005.
Schlemmer, Thomas. "'Gefühlsmässige Verwandtschaft'? Zivilisten, Kriegsgefangene und das königlich-italienische Heer im Krieg gegen die Sowjetunion 1941 bis 1943." In *Die "Achse" im Krieg. Politik, Ideologie und Kriegführung 1939–1945*, edited by Lutz Klinkhammer, Amedeo Osti Guerrazzi, and Thomas Schlemmer, 368–97. Paderborn: Schöningh, 2010.
Schlemmer, Thomas. "Giovanni Messe. Ein italienischer General zwischen Koalitions- und Befreiungskrieg." In *Von Feldherren und Gefreiten. Zur biographischen Dimension des Zweiten Weltkriegs*, edited by Christian Hartmann, 33–44. Munich: Oldenbourg, 2008.
Schlemmer, Thomas. "Italy." In *Joining Hitler's Crusade: European Nations and the Invasion of the Soviet Union, 1941*, edited by David Stahel, 134–57. Cambridge: Cambridge University Press, 2017.
Schlemmer, Thomas. "'Tedeschi a piedi'. Der Rückzug deutscher und italienischer Truppen am Don im Winter 1942–1943 am Beispiel des Grenadierregiments 318." In *Annali dell'Istituto storico italo-germanico in Trento XXXII 2006*, 127–49. Bologna: Il Mulino, 2007.
Schlemmer, Schlemmer. "Zwischen Erfahrung und Erinnerung. Die Soldaten des italienischen Heeres im Krieg gegen die Sowjetunion." *Quellen und Forschungen aus italienischen Archiven und Bibliotheken* 85 (2005): 425–66.
Schreiber, Gerhard. "Italiens Teilnahme am Krieg gegen die Sowjetunion. Motive, Fakten und Folgen." In *Stalingrad. Ereignis – Wirkung – Symbol*, edited by Jürgen Förster, 250–92. Munich: Piper, 1993.
Schreiber, Gerhard. "Problemi generali dell'alleanza italo-tedesca 1933–1941." In *Gli Italiani sul fronte russo*, edited by Enzo Collotti, 63–117. Bari: De Donato 1982.
Schwarz, Guri. *Tu mi devi seppellir. Riti funebri e culto nazionale alle origini della Repubblica*. Turin: UTET, 2010.
Scianna, Bastian Matteo. "A Blueprint for Successful Peacekeeping? The Italians in Beirut (Lebanon), 1982–1984." *The International History Review* 41, no. 3 (2019): 650–72.

Scianna, Bastian Matteo. "A Prelude to Total War? The Abyssinian War (1935–36) in the Eyes of Foreign Military Observers." *The International Journal of Military History and Historiography* 38, no. 1 (2018): 5–33.

Scianna, Bastian Matteo. "Forging an Italian Hero? The Late Commemoration of Amedeo Guillet (1909–2010)." *European Review of History: Revue européenne d'histoire* 26, no. 3 (2019): 369–85.

Scianna, Bastian Matteo. "Rommel Almighty? Italian Assessments of the 'Desert Fox' During and After the Second World War." *The Journal of Military History* 82, no. 1 (2018): 125–46.

Sciolla, Loredana. *Italiani: Stereotipi di casa nostra*. Bologna: Il Mulino, 1997.

Scotoni, Giorgio. *Il nemico fidato. La guerra di sterminio in URSS e l'occupazione alpina sull'Alto Don*. Trento: Panorama, 2013.

Scotoni, Giorgio. *L'Armata Rossa e la disfatta italiana (1942–43)*. Trento: Panorama, 2007.

Scotoni, Giorgio. "La disfatta delle fanterie italiane sul Don nel dicembre 1942. 'Piccolo Saturno' e la battaglia di Arbuzovka." In *Battaglie in Russia. Il Don e Stalingrado 75 anni dopo*, edited by Olga Dubrovina, 221–33. Milan: Ed. Unicopli, 2018.

Scotoni, Giorgio, and Sergej I. Filonenko, eds. *Retroscena della disfatta italiana in Russia nei documenti inediti dell'8ª Armata*, 2 vols. Trento: Panorama, 2008.

Searle, Alaric. "A Very Special Relationship: Basil Liddell Hart, Wehrmacht Generals and the Debate on West German Rearmament, 1945–1953." *War in History* 5, no. 3 (1998): 327–57.

Sechi, Salvatore. "Die neutralistische Versuchung. Italien und die Sowjetunion 1943–1948." In *Italien und die Großmächte 1943–1949*, edited by Hans Woller, 95–129. Munich: Oldenbourg, 1988.

Setta, Sandro. *L'Uomo Qualunque: 1944–1948*. Bari: Laterza, 1975.

Shepherd, Ben H. *Hitler's Soldiers: The German Army in the Third Reich*. New Haven: Yale University Press, 2016.

Shepherd, Ben H. *War in the Wild East: The German Army and Soviet Partisans*. Cambridge: Harvard University Press, 2004.

Sica, Emanuele. "June 1940: The Italian Army and the Battle of the Alps." *Canadian Journal of History* 47, no. 2 (2016): 355–78.

Sica, Emanuele. *Mussolini's Army in the French Riviera: Italy's Occupation of France*. Chicago: University of Illinois Press, 2015.

Sica, Emanuele, and Richard Carrier, eds. *Italy and the Second World War: Alternative Perspectives*. Leiden: Brill, 2018.

Sigg, Marco. *Der Unterführer als Feldherr im Taschenformat. Theorie und Praxis der Auftragstaktik im deutschen Heer 1869 bis 1945*. Paderborn: Schöningh, 2014.

Smelser, Ronald, and Edward J. Davies II. *The Myth of the Eastern Front: The Nazi-Soviet War in American Popular Culture.* Cambridge: Cambridge University Press, 2008.
Smyth, Howard McGaw. *Secrets of the Fascist Era.* Carbondale: Southern Illinois University Press, 1975.
Stahel, David. *Kiev 1941. Hitler's Battle for Supremacy in the East.* Cambridge: Cambridge University Press, 2012.
Stahel, David, ed. *Joining Hitler's Crusade: European Nations and the Invasion of the Soviet Union, 1941.* Cambridge: Cambridge University Press, 2017.
Stahel, David. *Operation Barbarossa and Germany's Defeat in the East.* Cambridge: Cambridge University Press, 2010.
Stefani, Filippo. "L'8 settembre e le forze armate italiane." In *L'Italia in guerra. Il quarto anno – 1943,* edited by Romain H. Rainero and Antonello Biagini, 155–60. Gaeta: Stabilimento Grafico Militare, 1994.
Stefani, Filippo. *La storia della dottrina e degli ordinamenti dell'Esercito italiano, Vol. 2: Tomo 1.* Rome: USSME, 1985.
Stewart, Andrew. *The First Victory: The Second World War and the East Africa Campaign.* New Haven: Yale University Press, 2016.
Steinberg, Jonathan. *All or Northing? The Axis and the Holocaust 1941–1943.* London: Routledge, 1991.
Stramaccioni, Alberto. *Crimini gi guerra. Storia e memoria del caso italiano.* Bari: Laterza, 2016.
Strang, Bruce G. *On the Fiery March: Mussolini Prepares for War.* Westport: Praeger, 1995.
Sullivan, Brian R. "Fascist Italy's Military Involvement in the Spanish Civil War." *The Journal of Military History* 59, no. 4 (1995): 697–27.
Sullivan, Brian R. "The Downfall of the Regia Aeronautica, 1933–1943." In *Why Air Forces Fail: The Anatomy of Defeat,* edited by Robin Higham and Stephen J. Harris, 135–76. Lexington: University Press of Kentucky, 2006.
Sullivan, Brian R. "The Italian Soldier in Combat, June 1940–September 1943: Myths, Realities and Explanations." In *Time to Kill: The Soldier's Experience of War in the West,* edited by Paul Addison and Angus Calder, 177–205. London: Pimlico, 1997.
Sullivan, Brian R. "The Path Marked Out by History: The German-Italian Alliance, 1939–1943." In *Hitler and His Allies in World War II,* edited by Jonathan R. Adelman, 116–51. London: Routledge, 2007.
Sullivan, Brian R. "The Primacy of Politics: Civil–Military Relations and Italian Junior Officers, 1918–1940." In *Forging the Sword: Selecting, Educating, and Training Cadets and Junior Officers in the Modern World,* edited by Elliott V. Converse III, 65–81. Chicago: Imprint, 1998.
Sweet, John J.T. *Iron Arm: The Mechanization of Mussolini's Army, 1920–1940.* Westport: Greenwood, 1980.

Tirone, Emilio. "La politica italiana verso la popolazione civile e i prigionieri di guerra sul fronte russo." In *Battaglie in Russia. Il Don e Stalingrado 75 anni dopo*, edited by Olga Dubrovina, 189–212. Milan: Ed. Unicopli, 2018.

Töppel, Roman. "Das Ritterkreuz des Eisernen Kreuzes und der Kampfwert militärischer Verbände." *Zeitschrift für Heereskunde* 12 (2012): 180–90.

Toscano, Mario. *Designs in Diplomacy: Pages from European Diplomatic History in the Twentieth Century*. Baltimore: The Johns Hopkins Press, 1970.

Trani, Silvia, and Pier Paolo Battistelli. "The Italian Military Records of the Second World War." *War in History* 17, no. 3 (2010): 333–51.

Trigg, Jonathan. *Death on the Don: The Destruction of Germany's Allies on the Eastern Front, 1941–1944*. New York: The History Press, 2013.

USSME. *L'8ª Armata Italiana nella seconda battaglia difensiva del Don*. Rome: USSME, 1946.

USSME. *L'Italia nella relazione ufficiale sovietica sulla seconda guerra mondiale*. Rome: USSME, 1978.

USSME. *Le operazioni del C.S.I.R. e dell'ARMIR dal Giugno 1941 all'Ottobre 1942*. Rome: USSME, 1947.

USSME. *Le operazioni delle unità Italiane al fronte russo (1941–1943)*. Rome: USSME, 2000; first ed. 1977.

Ungváry, Krisztián. "Hungarian Occupation Forces in the Ukraine 1941–1942: The Historiographical Context." *The Journal of Slavic Military Studies* 20, no. 1 (2007): 81–120.

Ungváry, Krisztián. "The Hungarian Theatre of War." In *Germany and the Second World War, Vol. 8: The Eastern Front 1943–1944*, edited by Karl-Heinz Frieser et al., 846–959. Oxford: Oxford University Press, 2017.

Vallauri, Carlo. *Soldati. Le forze armate italiane dall'armistizio alla Liberazione*. Turin: UTET, 2003.

Valori, Aldo. *La campagna di Russia. CSIR-ARMIR: 1941–1943*. Rome: Grafica nazionale editrice, 1951.

Van Creveld, Martin. *Kampfkraft. Militärische Organisation und Leistung 1939–1945*. Freiburg: Rombach, 1989.

Van Creveld, Martin. *Supplying War: Logistics from Wallenstein to Patton*. Cambridge: Cambridge University Press, 1977.

Virtue, Nicolas G. "Fascist Italy and the Barbarisation of the Eastern Front, 1941–43." MA diss., University of Calgary, 2007.

Virtue, Nicolas G. "'We Istrians Do Very Well in Russia': Istrian Combatants, Fascist Propaganda, and Brutalization on the Eastern Front." In *Italy and the Second World War: Alternative Perspectives*, edited by Emanuele Sica and Richard Carrier, 266–98. Leiden: Brill, 2018.

Vitali, Giorgio. *Trotto, galoppo…caricat! Storia del Raggruppamento truppe a cavallo. Russia 1942–1943*. Milan: Mursia, 2010.

Waksberg, Arkadi. *Gnadenlos. Andrei Wyschinski.* Bergisch Gladbach: Lübbe, 1991.
Watts, Barry, and Williamson Murray. "Military Innovation in Peacetime." In *Military Innovation in the Interwar Period*, edited by Williamson Murray and Allan R. Millett, 369–415. Cambridge: Cambridge University Press, 1996.
Walker, Ian W. *Iron Hulls, Iron Hearts: Mussolin's Elite Armoured Divisions in North Africa.* Ramsbury: Crowood, 2012.
Wegner, Bernd. "Vom Lebensraum zum Todesraum. Deutschlands Kriegführung zwischen Moskau und Stalingrad." In *Stalingrad. Ereignis – Wirkung – Symbol*, edited by Jürgen Förster, 17–37. Munich: Piper, 1993.
Wegner, Bernd. "Erschriebene Siege. Franz Halder, die 'Historical Division' und die Rekonstruktion des Zweiten Weltkrieges im Geiste des deutschen Generalstabes." In *Politischer Wandel, organisierte Gewalt und nationale Sicherheit*, edited by Ernst Willi Hansen, Gerhard Schreiber, and Bernd Wegner, 287–302. Munich: Oldenbourg, 1995.
Wegner, Bernd. "The War against the Soviet Union 1942–1943." In *Germany and the Second World War, Vol. 6: The Global War*, edited by Horst Boog et al., 841–1215. Oxford: Oxford University Press, 2001.
Wimpffen, Hans. "Die Zweite Ungarische Armee im Feldzug gegen die Sowjetunion. Ein Beitrag zur Koalitionskriegführung im Zweiten Weltkrieg." PhD diss., University of Tübingen, 1968.
Wiskemann, Elisabeth. *The Rome-Berlin Axis.* London: Oxford University Press, 1949.
Wood, James A. "Captive Historians, Captive Audience: The German Military History Program, 1945–1961." *The Journal of Military History* 69, no. 1 (2005): 123–47.
Woller, Hans. *Die Abrechnung mit dem Faschismus in Italien 1943 bis 1948.* Munich: Oldenbourg, 1996.
Woller, Hans. *Mussolini. Der erste Faschist.* Munich: Beck, 2016.
Yeomans, Rory. "Croatia." In *Joining Hitler's Crusade: European Nations and the Invasion of the Soviet Union, 1941*, edited by David Stahel, 158–89. Cambridge: Cambridge University Press, 2017.
Zaloga, Steven J., and Leland S. Ness. *Red Army Handbook 1939–1945.* Stroud: Sutton, 2003.
Zamagni, Vera. "Italy: How to Lose the War and Win the Peace." In *The Economics of World War II*, edited by Mark Harrison, 177–223. Cambridge: Cambridge University Press, 2000.
Zarubinsky, Oleg. "Collaboration of the Population in Occupied Ukrainian Territory: Some Aspects of the Overall Picture." *The Journal of Slavic Military Studies* 10, no. 2 (1997): 138–52.

Index

A

Albania, 42, 69, 70, 73, 75, 82, 83, 91, 93

Alpini, 27, 28, 30, 36, 54, 64, 113, 121, 125, 128, 129, 131, 144–146, 154, 159, 169, 179–182, 185, 194, 195, 199, 200, 206–208, 210, 216, 217, 222, 223, 234, 237, 248, 250, 256, 257, 264, 267, 277, 278, 281, 283–292, 318, 332, 333

Ambrosio, Vittorio, 26, 182, 231–234, 274, 302, 303, 331

Armata Italiana in Russia (ARMIR), 28, 29, 90, 96, 110, 112, 113, 116, 125–127, 130, 132–134, 136, 138–143, 151–154, 168, 174, 179, 182, 189, 191, 193, 196, 197, 199, 206, 211, 222, 230, 245, 253, 256, 261, 270, 275, 279, 285, 298, 316–318, 330

B

Badoglio, Pietro, 9, 25, 53, 67, 70, 71, 75, 76, 82, 83, 231, 278, 281, 294–296, 299, 302

Bedeschi, Giulio, 268, 283, 290, 291

3rd *Bersaglieri* Regiment, 90, 91, 94, 111, 113, 140, 241, 326

C

Cavallero, Ugo, 18, 25, 44–46, 53, 71, 87, 88, 96, 100, 114, 125–127, 138, 139, 143, 171, 195, 197, 205, 219, 221, 230, 231, 285

Celere, 54, 81, 83, 88, 89, 91, 92, 94, 95, 104–107, 109, 110, 112, 116, 119, 127, 129, 132, 137, 138, 143, 145, 146, 154, 206, 209, 212, 217, 223, 232, 277

Corpo di Spedizione Italiano in Russia (CSIR), 28, 30, 88–91, 93, 95, 96, 99–110, 112–116, 119–123, 125, 127, 129, 145, 147, 154,

189, 195–197, 205, 209, 242, 243, 245–247, 249–252, 276, 279, 291, 298, 301, 316, 330
Cosseria, 128, 133, 151, 154, 159, 161, 166, 168, 169, 193, 215, 217
Cuneense, 27, 128, 142, 154, 180, 207, 223, 257

D
De Gasperi, Alcide, 293, 294, 297, 300, 305–310, 312–314, 316, 319

E
Eighth Army. *See* Armata Italiana in Russia (ARMIR)
El Alamein, 1, 19, 65, 78, 141, 151, 222, 230, 268, 286, 290, 330

G
Gariboldi, 28, 126, 132, 134, 138, 140, 142–144, 171, 180, 199, 200, 207, 210, 220, 221, 224, 230, 232, 234, 252, 254, 268, 285, 291, 303, 323
Giovannelli, Vittorio, 91, 107
Graziani, Rodolfo, 25, 75–77, 81, 83, 219, 309
Greece, 26, 65, 66, 69–73, 91, 93, 95, 270, 278, 284, 313, 330
Gyldenfeldt, Hans-Wessel von, 197–200, 245

I
II Corps, 128–133, 144, 154, 155, 159, 161, 164, 171, 176, 179, 182, 192, 207, 221, 224, 288

298th Infantry Division, 142, 146, 154, 160, 161, 166, 171, 175, 213, 215, 233, 272

J
Julia, 11, 27, 128, 148, 154, 179–181, 215, 217, 218, 223, 288

L
Lancieri di Novara, 90

M
Manstein, Erich von, 191, 204, 211, 281
Manzi, Luigi, 91, 94
Marazzani, Mario, 88, 91, 94, 106–108, 119, 143–147, 243, 303
Marras, Efisio, 16, 26, 67, 69, 79, 82, 96, 112, 115–117, 126, 141, 143, 156, 174, 182, 197–199, 210, 215, 217, 221, 225, 234–236, 238, 249, 285
Messe, Giovanni, 14, 17, 26, 47, 54, 67, 71, 74, 76, 88, 90, 91, 93, 94, 96, 97, 100–117, 119–127, 137, 138, 142, 145–147, 186, 195–197, 199, 220, 242–244, 246, 247, 249, 252, 253, 271, 273–275, 291, 293, 301–306, 309–312, 314, 316–327, 332–334
Mussolini, Benito, 1, 8, 9, 12, 13, 15, 16, 18, 20–22, 25, 26, 31–35, 41, 42, 45, 61, 63, 64, 66–73, 75–78, 81, 87, 93, 105, 114, 125–128, 137, 138, 148, 181, 183, 195, 210, 211, 216, 223, 230–232, 234, 236, 238, 239, 243, 247, 248, 257, 258, 261,

274, 279, 282, 285, 299–301,
303, 313–315, 322–324, 331

N
Nikolayevka, 216, 268, 288–290, 333

P
Pasubio, 27, 89, 91, 93, 95, 101–111,
113, 116, 120, 123, 126,
129, 133, 137–139, 142, 143,
145–147, 154, 160, 161, 169,
209, 212, 215, 216, 218, 243,
246, 252, 274, 275, 317
Prunas, Renato, 295, 296, 299

R
Ravenna, xi, 27, 128, 133, 136,
139, 142, 151, 154, 160, 161,
163–166, 168, 169, 171, 193,
213–216, 221, 257, 279, 280
Revelli, Nuto, 36, 46, 223, 241, 268,
269, 281–284, 289, 290, 332
Rigoni Stern, Mario, 268, 281, 282,
287, 290, 332
Rintelen, Enno von, 16, 17, 70, 72,
76, 197, 207, 219, 239

S
Savoia Cavalleria, 90, 137
Sforzesca, 128, 132, 133, 136–139,
144, 146, 148, 154, 174, 175,
209, 212, 215, 217, 222, 232,
236, 280

T
Tagliamento Blackshirts, 95, 105, 111,
136, 140, 326

Tippelskirch, Kurt von, 70, 93,
132, 138–141, 143–146, 194,
197–200, 206, 207, 209, 210,
215, 216, 220–222, 236, 239,
246, 247
Togliatti, Palmiro, 14, 261, 263, 265,
294, 298–301, 311–313, 317,
318
Tolloy, Giusto, 139, 216, 236, 250,
268–273, 278, 280, 282, 283,
285, 287, 292, 316, 318, 321,
325, 332
Torino, 89, 91, 94, 95, 102, 104–107,
109–111, 115, 120, 126, 133,
146, 154, 175, 212, 215–217,
233, 235, 241, 257
Tridentina, 27, 128, 142, 154, 179,
181, 182, 218, 223, 277, 289,
290

U
Utili, Umberto, 93, 120, 121, 137,
220, 251, 274

V
Vyshinsky, Andrey, 294–296, 299,
306–312, 315, 318

Z
Zingales, Francesco, 91, 93, 220, 233,
234, 242, 323

Printed by Printforce, the Netherlands